Abstracts Lancaster County, Virginia, Wills
1653-1800

ABSTRACTS
LANCASTER COUNTY,
VIRGINIA, WILLS
1653-1800

By

IDA J. LEE

CLEARFIELD COMPANY

Originally Published
Richmond, 1959

Reprinted
Genealogical Publishing Co., Inc.
Baltimore, 1973

Library of Congress Catalogue Card Number 73-13080
International Standard Book Number 0-8063-0582-7

Reprinted for
Clearfield Company, Inc. by
Genealogical Publishing Co., Inc.
Baltimore, Maryland
1995

Made in the United States of America

Preface

THESE abstracts were begun some years ago, when in collaboration with Mr. W. MacF. Jones, it was planned to publish a more comprehensive study of Lancaster County, including marriage bonds, land grants, the 1782 Census, names of county officials to 1850, etc. The size of the book as well as the cost was found to be prohibitive and publication was abandoned.

It is hoped that this volume of abstracts may be useful to those interested in the history of Lancaster County.

IDA JOHNSON LEE.

ABSTRACTS from WILL BOOKS of LANCASTER COUNTY, *VIRGINIA*

ABBEY, Will. Appraised by Geo. Finch, Jno. Miller, Jno. Mott and Jno. Mitchell. Recorded 22 Apl. 1709—in W.B. 10, p. 157.

ACRE, William. Will. 6 Mch. 1688, pro. 15 April 1688.
Mentions: Wife (name not shown); son William; dau. Katherine, loaned to Mrs. Ann Brown; dau. Elizabeth loaned to Walter Welch; Mary Southing; brother and Executor, Randolph Miller. Recorded W.B. 5, p. 117.

ADAMS, John. Inventory. Dated 8 Mch. 1698. Recorded 10 Mch. 1698. Presented by Will Chapman. W.B. 8, p. 177.

ADDONSON, John. Will. 20 Oct. 1663. Recorded 9 Nov. 1665.
To Mich. Maconnah, my mate, all that I have. Wits. Geo. Howell. (Among loose wills.)

ALDERSON, Richard. Will. 15 Sept. 1695. Recorded 14 Jan. 1698.
Mentions: Wife Margaret; sons John and Richard; Gr. Daus. Ann Alderson, Margaret Alderson, Mary Alderson. Other devisees: Geo. Clarke, Jno. Linham, son of Jno. Linham. Extrs. Mr. Thomas Chattin and Mr. Randolph Miller. Wits. Clement Thompson, Thos. Chattin. W.B. 8, p. 85.

ALEXANDER, Anguish. Will. 28 Feby. 1742. Rec. 8 Feb. 1743.
Mentions: Wife Mary; sons James, Jesse, John, Robert and William; dau. Hannah. Extrx. Wife. Wits. Jno. Rogers and Jas. Monro. W.B. 13, p. 321.

ANDERSON, John. Inventory. Rec. 11 Mch. 1718. Presented by Jane Bush, Admx. W.B. 10, p. 283.

ANDERSON, Thomas. Will. 11 Jany. 1740. Rec. 13 Mch. 1740.
Legatees: Eliz. and Margaret Simmons, Mary and James Simmons, Ann Smith, Saunders Power, John Simmons. Extr. Jno. Simmons. Wits. Alex. Power and Ann Smith. W.B. 13, p. 196.

ANDERSON, Robert. Inventory & Appraisal. 11 Sept. 1747. Rec. 13 Nov. 1747. Returned by Mary Anderson, Admx. W. B. 10, p. 283.

ANDERSON, Webster. Inventory. Rec. 16 May 1760. Returned by Henry Tapscott, Adm. W.B. 16, p. 86.

ANGELL, John. Will. "Of Parish of Christ Church." Sons: Uriah and Benoni Angel. Dau. Rebeckah. Extrs. Wife and son Uriah. Wits. Nicholas Martin, Daniel Carter, Jno. Angell. 5 Jul. 1743. Rec. 7. Mch. 1744. W.B. 14, p. 52.

W.B. 14, p. 133. Susannah Angel, widow of Jno. Angel of Parish of Christ Church will not accept any legacy left her by will of decd. husband. 2 March 1744.

W.B. 15, p. 293. 8 June 1751. John Angell's estate. Absalom Moughon possessed with Benoni Angell's part.

ANGEL, John. Rec. 21 Oct. 1765.

John Angel died without making a will. Mary Angel, widow appointed Admx.

ANGELL, John. Appraisement. 21 Oct. 1765. Rec. 17 May 1766. By Henry Currell, James Mason and Thomas Mason. W.B. 18, p. 56.

ANGEL, John. Settlement. 18 April 1771. Rec. 16 May 1771.

To George Edwards, who intermarried with Mary Angel, widow of sd. John Angel. W.B. 20, p. 44.

W. B. 20, p. 37—21 Nov. 1771. John Fleet appointed Guardian to children of John Angel.

ANGELL, Robert. Will. 23 Dec. 1726. Rec. 8 Feby. 1727. "Of Christ Church Parish."

Mentions: Wife Frances; sons Charles and Josias. Extrs. Wife and son Charles Angell. Wits. Wm. Dymer, Jno. Angell, Jno. Brooks. W.B. 10, p. 512.

ANGEL, Samuel. Will. 11 Jan. 1772. Rec. 21 Feb. 1772. "Of Christ Church Parish."

Mentions: Wife Elizabeth; sons William, Samuel' and Robert Angel. Extrs. Wife, Ozwald Newby and Richard Ball. Wits. Eliza x Richardson; Jesse x Robinson, and Benjamin Robertson. W. B. 20, p. 34.

ANGEL, Samuel. Settlement. 17 Aug. 1784. Rec. 19 Aug. 1784. Thos. Pollard, Admr., Jno. Berryman, Wm. Yerby, James Brent and Benj. George, Appraisers. W.B. 20, p. 44.

ANGELL, William. Will. 20 Oct. 1659. Rec. 30 Oct. 1659.

Mentions: Son Uriah Angell, Admx. Daus. Margaret and Aalse Angell. Wits. Hugh Brent and Abya Bonnison. W.B. 2, p. 65. (25 Jan. 1659. Hugh Brent and Abya Bonnison present estate.)

ANGELL, Uriah. Will. 25 Feby. 1712. Rec. 10 Oct. 1716.
Mentions: Wife Mary; sons Robert and John; dau. Mary Kelley. Wits. Jno. Grason, Eliza P. Haynes, Susanna Grason. Extrs. Wife and sons Robert and John. W.B. 10, p. 187.

APPLETON, Abraham. Will. 20 Oct. 1659. Rec. 1 March 1660.
Legatees: Mrs. Obert, Richd. Lewys, Tho. Williams, Jno. Welse. Wits. Will Pin, Jno. Hudds. W.B. 2, p. 66.

APPLETON, Abraham. Will. 20 Oct. 1659. Rec. 30 Nov. 1659.
Legatee: Wm. Nessum. Wits. Will Powes, and Jno. Hudds. (Loose Wills)

ARMES, Daniel. Will. 8 Dec. 1700. Rec. 4 May 1701.
Mentions: Wife Martha; to son Daniel, his now dwelling and plantation; Wits. Jno. Fairman, Alce Aspray, Jno. Brown. Extrs. Wife and brother Walter Armes. Daughter Martha. W.B. 8, p. 102.

ARMES, Walter. Will. 12 Feby. 1717.
Mentions: Son Walter, my plantation 200 acres where Darby Briant lives. Son Daniel, my plantation 200 acres, where Jas. Kirk lives. Dau. Hannah, my plantation, 80 acres, where Jno. Marshall lives. Proved by oath of Mary Armes, widow of Walter Armes. Wits. Danl. Burns, Robt. Neesum. W.B. 10, p. 250.

ARMES, Walter. Order. 17 June 1765.
Walter Armes died without making a will. William Armes appointed Administrator. W.B. 17, p. 130.

ARMES, Walter. Inventory. 11 July 1765. Rec. 16 July 1765.
By Merryman Payne, Jno. Merryman, Chattin Chowning. Returned by Wm. Armes. W.B. 18, p. 41.

ARMES, Walter. Division of Estate. Rec. 20 Apl. 1767.
To William Armes—To Capt. Merryman Payne Guardian to John Armes, Sarah Armes, Judy Armes, and Lucy Armes. W.B. 18, p. 78.

ARMS, John. Account. 15 June 1789. Rec. 21 Dec. 1789.
Allotment to Judith Arms, widow. By Jno. Carpenter and Jno. Christopher. W.B. 22, p. 235.
16 June 1789. Rec. 19 Sept. 1791. Appraisal of Estate by Sam Moore, Jno. Stephens, Wm. George. W.B. 22, p. 313.
17 Feb. 1795. Rec. 21 Apl. 1795. Appraisal by Wm. Biscoe, Ozwald Newby and Jesse Chilton. W.B. 22, p. 449.

ARNOLD, John. Will. 10 Dec. 1683. Rec. 15 March 1683/4.

Mentions: Wife Grace; daus. Ruth, Sarah, Ann and Mary Arnold. Wits. Nich. George, Thomas Parfit, and Will Therriott. W.B. 5, p. 93.

ASHFORD, John. Will. No date. Recorded 1716.

"Sent for Parson Holt to write his will, who declined to do so." Nathl. Hedgeman, Luke McDonald, Nicholas Reid together wrote the will. All left his wife, whose name is not goven. W.B. 10, p. 160.

ATCHISON, William. Appraisement. 20 July 1768. Rec. 18 August 1768.

By Merryman Payne, Edward Carter and Charles Rogers. W.B. 18, p. 124.

ATKINS, Mark. Inventory. 2 August 1720. Rec. 12 July 1721.

Richard Lee, Gent. Admr. W.B. 10, p. 326.

AUSTIN, Thomas. Appraisal. 14 April 1731. Rec. 9 June 1731.

Returned by Fortunatus Sydnor, Admr. W.B. 12, p. 204.

BAILEY, Joseph. Will. 12 May 1672. Rec. 27 March 1674.

Sons John, Joseph; Wife Hannah. Extrs. Jos. Ball and Wm. Therriott. Wits. Henry Clarke and Thom. Thompson. W.B. 5, p. 7.

BALEY, John. Will. 8 Feby. 1694/5. Rec. 17 March 1694.

Mentions: Sons: Joseph and Peter James Baley; Dau. Elizabeth Baley; brother, Wm. Baley; sons John and William Baley; sister, Hannah Lane; Wife Elizabeth, who is also Extrx. Wits. Wm. Ball, Randolph Miller, Edward Cox. W.B. 8, p. 47.

BAILEY, William. Will. 17 Feby. 1703/4.

Mentions: Nephew John Bailey; Richard Watts and Wm. Hunter. Extr. Richard Watts. Wits. Thos. Sampson, Wm. Mitchell, Margt. Mitchell. W.B. 8, p. 121.

BAILEY, William. Will. Rec. 12 March 1734.

Son: James; Dau. Margaret Bailey; William Bailey, son of Peter James Bailey. Extrs. Jos. Stephens and Jno. Mitchell. Wits. Ralph Rutherford, Matthew Machen, Sabra Rutherford. W.B. 12, p. 332.

BAILEY, William. Appraisal. 12 March 1734. Rec. 14 May 1735. Returned by Jno. Mitchell and Jos. Stephens, his Extrs. W.B. 12, p. 336.

BAILEY, John. Inventory. 8 Feb. 1739. Rec. 14 March 1739. Returned by Jno. Bailey, Admr. W.B. 12, p. 149.

BAILEY, James. Will. 24 Oct. 1747. Rec. 14 Apl. 1749.

Legatees: Joseph Wharton and his son Joseph. Thomas Flynt, son of John Flynt. Extr. friend John Flynt. Wits. John Flynt, Ruth Flynt. W.B. 14, p. 234.

BAILEY, Joseph. Inventory and Appraisement. Recd. 15 June 1759. Returned by Margaret Bailey, Admx. W.B. 16, p. 61.

BAILEY, John. Will. 13 Sept. 1761. Rec. 16 April 1762.

Mentions: Wife Eunice; son John (not 21) son Charles; Daus. Ellen, Eunice, Hannah Mary and Jean; child unborn. Extrs. Wife Eunice and friend Col. Jas. Ball. Wits. James Ball. W.B. 16, p. 206.

BAILEY, Eunice, widow. Will. 8 Apl. 1772. Rec. 16 Apl. 1772.

Mentions: Sons: John, Charles and Jesse Bailey; daus. Ellen, Eunice, Hannah, Molly and Jenny. Extrs. friends, James Ball and Richard Mitchell, Gents. Wits. James Ball and Susanna Shearman. W.B. 20, p. 39.

BAILEY, Mrs. Eunice. Division. 21 Jany. 1773. Rec. 18 Feb. 1773.

To Hannah, Molly and Jesse Bailey. Above orphans part of estate of their father, Capt. John Bailey. Mr. Chas. Rogers and Mr. Jno. Payne, Gdns. of orphans. W.B. 20, p. 54.

BAILEY, John. Estate. Rec. 21 Oct. 1779. John Bailey possessed with Jesse Bailey's estate, Orphan of John Bailey, decd. W.B. 20, p. 172.

BAILEY, Capt. John. Will. 3 Oct. 1783. Rec. 19 Feb. 1784.

Sons: John, Hugh, Charles, Jesse. Daus. Sally, Molly, Catherine. Wife (no name). Extrs. Wife, Wm. Sydnor, Col. Jas. Ball, Maj. Henry Towles. (No witnesses.) W.B. 22, pp. 10, 11.

Above estate appraised 15 July 1784. W.B. 22, pp. 17-19.

BAKER, Thomas. Inventory. Oct. 1698. Rec. 11 Nov. 1698. Presented by John Brown and Elizabeth his wife. W.B. 8, p. 83.

BALL, William. Will. 5 Oct. 1680. Rec. 11 Nov. 1680.

To son Wm. Ball, my plantation, 2 patents of 540 acres. Wife Hannah; son Joseph Ball Patent of 1600 acres in Rappa. Co., Dau. Hannah, wife of Capt. David Fox only 5 shillings sterling, which is an overpayment both of her portion and deserts. Extrs. Sons William and Joseph. Wits. Thos. Everest, Jno. Mottly. W.B. 5, p. 70.

BALL, Capt. William, of Parish St. Mary's White Chapel. 28 Sep. 1694. Rec. 16 Nov. 1694.

Wife (name not given), three eldest sons: William, Richard and James Ball; Sons: Joseph, George, David, Stretchly and Samuel Ball. Dau. Margaret Ball. Extrs. sons William and Richard, and brother Capt. David Fox, Mr. Geo. Haile. Wits. Abraham Taylor, George Finch, Edwin Conway. W.B. 8, p. 45.

BALL, Mrs. Hannah, widow Col. Wm. Ball. 25 June 1695. Rec. 12 Oct. 1695.

Dau. Mrs. Hannah Fox; Gr. sons, William Ball and James Ball. Extrs. dau. Hannah Fox, and gr. son Wm. Ball. Wits. Richard Sanderson and Hannah Ball. W.B. 8, p. 51.

BALL, Mrs. Hannah, widow and relict Col. Wm. Ball. 5 Dec. 1694. Rec. 12 Oct. 1695.

Son Joseph Ball's children. Dau. Hannah Fox now wife of Capt. David Fox. Grsons. Wm. Ball, Richard Ball and James Ball. Extrs. Son Joseph and grson Wm. Ball. Wits. Ann Finch, Thomas Godin. W.B. 8, p. 52.

BALL, Thomas. Inventory. 14 Oct. 1702. Returned by widow and recorded. W.B. 10, p. 227.

BALL, Margaret, widow. Will. 6 Feb. 1697. Rec. 9 Sept. 1702.

Sons: William, James, Joseph, George, Richard, David and Samuel Ball. Dau. Margaret; sister Mary Rosier. Extrs. Sons William and Richard. Wits. Edward Cox and Mary Green. W.B. 10, p. 53.

BALL, Joseph, Psh. St. Mary's White Chapel. Will. 25 June 1711. Rec. 11 July 1711.

Wife Mary; son Joseph; daus. Hannah Travers; Anne Conway; Esther Chinn; Elizabeth Cornegie; Mary Ball; Eliza Johnson (dau. of his wife), dau. Mary, 400 acres of land in Richmond county; grandson James Cornegie (not 21) acknowledges gift to son Joseph Ball, and daus. Hannah Travers, Anne Conway and Esther Chinn made 11 Feb. 1707; Overseer John Hagan; negroes formerly belonging to Jon. Cornegie, decd. Extr. Joseph Ball. Wits. Geo. Finch, Elizabeth Finch, Margaret Miller, Joseph Taylor. W.B. 10, p. 88.

BALL, Richard, of Par. St. Mary's White Chapel, May 1726. Rec. 8 Feb. 1726.

Wife Sarah; daus. Sarah Selden, my plantation whereon I now live; Margaret Ball, wife of Wm. Ball Jr., plantation at mouth of Corotoman River; Hannah and Ester Ball. W.B. 10, p. 510.

BALL, Capt. Richard. Inventory and Appraisement. 8 Feb. 1726. Rec. 5 Aug. 1727.

Presented by Mrs. Sarah Ball, widow, Admx. W.B. 12, p. 17.

BALL, David, of St. Mary's White Chapel, 13 Dec. 1732. Rec. 14 Mch. 1732.

Nephews: David, son of Geo. Ball; George, son of Geo. Ball; Joseph, son of Geo. Ball Sr.; Joseph, son of Joseph Ball; Wm. Ball, son of Wm. Ball, his nephew. Brothers Samuel, William and James Ball. Extrs. James and George Ball. Wits. George and Jesse Ball.

"I give to the Ch. (St. Mary's White Chapel) one large bible, one large common Prayer book and one good service book. I desire to be buried at the Chh. and to have a stone of ten pounds price." W.B. 12, p. 240.

BALL, Joseph, 12 May 1738. Rec. 12 April 1738. Deed Gift to only child Frances Ball, a negro slave. Wits. E. Chinn Jr., Geo. Rogers. W.B. 13, p. 91.

BALL, Sarah. Will. 6 Aug. 1742. Rec. 10 Sept. 1742.

Legatees: Daus. Easter Glascock, Margaret Ball, John Selden, Gr. son Wm. Montague, Gr. dau. Frances Lawry. Extr. Wm. Glasscock. Mention is made of a marriage betw. her gr. son Richard Selden and the dau. of James Ball. Wits. Margaret Williamson, Eliz. McTire and Wm. Ball. W.B. 13, p. 301.

BALL, Sarah. Inventory & Appraisement. Rec. 9 Otober 1742. Returned by Wm. Glasscock, Extr. W.B. 13, p. 290.

Division of Negroes held by Sarah Ball as dower of estate of her husband Richard Ball, decd. recorded 12 Nov. 1742.

Divided between Mrs. Margaret Ball, Mr. Wm. Glasscock, Mr. Richard Selden and Mr. William Montague. W.B. 13, p. 294.

BALL, Sarah, widow. Inventory, rec. 9 March 1743. Returned by Wm. Glasscock, Gent. Extr. W.B. 14, p. 10.

BALL, William. Inventory & Appraisement 9.9 Apl. 1741. Rec. 12 Nov. 1742, by Margaret Ball Admx. W,B. 13, p. 297.

BALL, Col. William. Will. 14 Aug. 1744. Rec. 8 Mch. 1744.

Grandsons: Wm. Ball, son of son Wm. Ball, decd., Benj. Ball, Richard Ball, John Ball, son of son Geo. Ball, Williamson Ball, son of son Geo. Ball, George Ball, Williamson Ball, son of son William, decd.

Son: George Ball, Daughters in law, Margaret Ball, widow;. Mrs. Judith Ball wife of son George Ball. Daughters: Sarah McCarty, Judith Glascock, Ellen Chichester, Hannah Ball. Niece, Sarah Opie. Extr. son George Ball. Wits. Jesse Ball; Wm. Downman; Michael Dillon. W.B. 14, p. 55.

BALL, Jesse. Appraisement. Rec. 11 March 1747. Returned by James Ball Jr. Gent, Admr. W.B. 14, p. 172.

BALL, Mrs. Mary Ann. Will. 12 Feby. 1749/50. Rec. 9 Mch. 1749. Daughters: Frances and Hannah. Wits. Dorothy Fountain; Elizabeth Ball; James Ball. W.B. 14, p. 273.

BALL, Mrs. Mary Ann. Inventory. 11 May 1750. Rec. and returned by Wm. Montague Jr. Adm. W.B. 14, p. 273.

BALL, Elizabeth. Inventory & Appraisement. 13 July 1750. Returned by Leanna Jones, Admx. W.B. 14, p. 291.

BALL, William. Division estate. 19 July 1751. Rec. 16 Aug. 1751. To Mrs. Margaret Ball, widow; Williamson Ball, Elizabeth Ball, Benjamin Ball, Richard Ball, and Mr. John Jones, who married Sarah, one of the daughters of the Decd. Wits. James Ball Jr., Richard Selden, Wm. Montague. W.B. 15, p. 54.

BALL, James. Will. 15 July 1754. Rec. 15 Nov. 1754.

To Gr. son Burgess Ball, land in King George, Spotsylvania and Stafford; son James Ball; Daus. Sinah, and four grandsons: Jesse Ball son of my dau. Frances, James Ewell and James Ewell son of Eve Ewell, and John Selden, land in Prince William County. Daughter Eve. Dau. Selden. Grandson John Taylor; Gr. son Jabey Downman; Gr. son James Downman. Extr. son James Ball. W.B. 15, p. 191.

(W.B. 15, p. 195—in division of negroes of James Ball, shows that Burges Ball was son of Jeduthan Ball.)

BALL, William. Orphans Acct. 18 Feby. 1765. Lettice Ball appointed Guardian of Mary Ball, orphan of William Ball. W.B. 17, p. 98.

BALL, Benjamin. Will. 20 Oct. 1760. Rec. 18 Feb. 1765.

To mother, Mrs. Margaret Ball. To Miss Mary Young, of Essex, a mourning ring to be procured from England. Extrx. mother, Mrs. Margaret Ball. Wits. Mungo Harvey, David Currie. W.B. 18, p. 30.

BALL, Williamson. 15 June 1765. He died without making will and Richard Ball and Mungo Harvey appointed by Court as Administrators. W.B. 17, p. 134.

BALL, Williamson. Inventory. 15 July 1765. Rec. 15 July 1765. Returned by Col. James Ball, Mr. Geo. Heale, Mr. John Chin, Gents. W.B. 18, p. 41.

BALL, Williamson. Inventory Estate in Westmoreland. 15 July 1765. Returned by Jno. Weedon, James Degge and Wm. Hilton. W.B. 18, p. 54.

BALL, Col. Spencer. Depositions concerning. 31 Aug. 1769. Rec. 18 May 1770.

(1) Deposition of Spencer Mottrom Ball, Gent, age 33 years. That sometime after the marriage between Winder Kenner and the desponent's sister Mary, daughter of the late Col. Spencer Ball, regarding her dower etc.

(Note: Order p. 65. Winder Kenner, Gent. appointed Gdn. to Mary and Elizabeth Kenner orphans of Brereton Kenner, dec.)

(2) Deposition of John Williams, age 36 years concerning fortune of Col. Spencer Ball, decd he intended to give his dau. Mary, who intermarried with Winder Kenner.

(3) Deposition of Richard Hull, gent, aged 52 years. Taken before Chas. Bell and John Williams, two of His Majesty's Justices for the county of Northumberland. States that after Winder Kenner intermarried with Mary Ball, dau. of the late Col. Spencer Ball, he asked Col. Ball what he intended to give Winder Kenner etc.

BALL, Jesse. Will. 6 Nov. 1775. Rec. 20 Aug. 1778.

Wife, Agatha Ball; Sons: James, Jesse Conway Ball, Jno. Smith Ball; Daus. Betty Lee Ball and Agatha Conway Ball. Extr. Brother James Ball and son James Ball and wife Agatha.

Codicil 16 Apl. 1778. "It is my will that my negroes be divided between my children, James, Jesse Conway, John Smith, Betty Lee, Nancy, and the child my wife is now with" Friend Peter Conway to be Extr. Wits. James Ball, James Newby, James Ball Jr. W.B. 20, p. 144.

BALL, Margaret, widow. Will. 20 June 1777. Rec. 16 Oct. 1783. Dau. Sarah Jones. Son Richard Ball, one of negroes given by last will of my father-in law William Ball; Gr.son, William Ball; Gr.Dau. Alice Ball, dau. of son William, dec. and Priscilla, his wife, dau. of Wm. Glasscock, now Priscilla Harvey, wife of Mungo Harvey. Gr. daus.: Margaret, Betty and Hannah Milner. To James Harvey, son of Mr. Mungo Harvey land in Lancaster devised me by my father; to John Harvey, son of Mr. Mungo Harvey: Margaret Ball. Late Husband William Ball. Extrs. Gr. son William Ball and Mr. Mungo Harvey. Wits. Ozwald Newby, Wm. Newby, Ozwald Newby Jr. W. B. 22, p. 3-4.

W.B. 22, pp. 47-49—Mrs. Margaret Ball's estate in Westmoreland County, appraised, and returns made by Wm. Monroe, Sr., Jno. Weedon and Chicott Edrington.

BALL, William. Will. 17 June 1785. Rec. 22 July 1785. Wife Catherine; Daus. Catherine and Florindor; Nephew William Ball. Mentions Mrs. Elizabeth Gilpin, of the town of Whitehaven, county of Cumberland, Eng. Extrs. Wife Catherine, Dr. Walter Jones, Wm. Steptoe, Philip L. Grymes, Wm. Chowning, and Col. Henry Towles. Wits. Geo. Carter, Ozwald Newby, Jr., Wm. Chilton Jr., and Thos. Chowning. W.B. 22, pp. 86-87.

W.B. 22, pp. 117-118. Appraised Estate of Dr. William Ball, by Jno. Chowning, Wm. Bristow and Joseph Stephens.

BALL, Mrs. Lettice. Will. 16 October 1788. Rec. 15 Dec. 1788. Son, Dr. William Ball, decd., Dau. Mary Graham (first married John Ball). Gr. Daus: Mary Bland Ball; Letty Ball; Cordelia and Florindor Ball daughters of son Dr. Wm. Ball, decd. Dau. in law Mrs. Catherine Ball; gr. son William Ball. Gr. gr. dau., a daughter of Judith Blackburn. Extrs. Col. James Ball Jr., and Richard Bland Lee, of Loudon Co. Wits. Mary Page Newby, Jno. Chowning, Ozwald Newby. W.B. 22, p. 193.

BALL, Col. Jesse. Orphans Acct. December 1780. Rec. 16 Feby. 1789. Orphans: Jesse Conway Ball, John Smith Ball, Ann Ball and

Wm. Ball—James Ball and James Ball Jr., former Guardians. Richard Selden Guardian. Returned by Wm. Warren, Wm. Brent and James B. Ball. W.B. 22, p. 206.

BALL, James. Will. 3 Sep. 1789. Rec. 21 Dec. 1789.

Gr. Dau. Mary Edwards, negroes purchased of her father, Mr. Thos. Glascock, and after the death of her husband Maj. Leroy Edwards, to be divided between James Ball McCarty and Mildred Smith McCarty her half brother and sister. Gr. sons: James Ball (500 a. land) Jesse Conway, John Smith and William Ball sons of son Jesse Ball. Son James Ball land purchased of Burges Smith, adjoining Jesse Conway and Capt. Richard Selden's mill, containing 150 acres. Daus. Mildred Selden, Sinah Beale, Judith Fauntleroy, Ann Ball, Frances Lee and Sarah Ball. Son James Ball, Extr. No witnesses. W.B. 22, p. 117.

BALL, Col. Jesse. Orphans Acct. 21 Dec. 1789. Rec. 18 Jan. 1790. John Smith Ball, the orphan. Capt. Richard Selden former Guardian, Jno. Gordon, present Guardian. Report by Wm. Warren and Richd. Cundiff. W.B. 22, p. 245.

BALL, James. Inventory. James Ball Extr. Rec. 21 Apl. 1794. W.B. 22, p. 412.

BALLENDINE, William. Will. 24 Dec. 1735. Rec. 11 August 1736. "Of Parish of St. Mary's White Chapel."

Mentions: Wife, Mary Ann; sons: (eldest) William and John; Daughters: Hannah and Frances Ballendine. Extrs. Wife and sons-in-law Charles and Bertrand Ewell. Wits. Wm. Bertrand and David Smith. W.B. 13, p. 15.

BALLY, George. Will. 24 Jany. 1676. Rec. 9 May 1677.

Wife, Elizabeth; dau. Mary Balley; John Pine; James Merritt; Edward White; James Clark; Anthony Thompson. Extr. Wife. Wits. Edward Carter, Anthony Thompson. W.B. 34, p. 28.

BANTON, Thomas. Inventory. 9 Sept. 1698. Rec. 11 Nov. 1698. Presented by Edw. Bainton. W.B. 8, p. 84.

BANTON, Edward. Inventory. 9 April 1701. Returned by Jacob Haines and recorded. W.B. 10, p. 204.

BANTON, Rebeckah. Will. 1 Oct. 1750. Rec. 15 Feb. 1754.

Legatees: Wm. Bond, Richard Edwards, Wm. Hinton, Henry Hinton, Robert Dudley's dau. Ann, and Mary Cox—living in

Westmoreland. Extrs. Thos. Edwards, Sr., Samuel Hinton and Wm. Bond. Wits. Wm. Bond, Jno. Bond. W.B. 15, p. 303.

BARKER, Thomas. Will. 10 Apl. 1703. Rec. 13 Sept. 1703.
Wife (not named); sons: Thomas, (my plantation where I now live) William. Daus.: Mary, Elizabeth, Catherine. Other devisees: William and Samuel Fox, who are Overseers. Extrs. Sons Thomas and William. Wits: Thos. Martin, Richd. Flint, John Barlow. W.B. 8, p. 132.

BARKER, Thomas. Will. 21 July 1709. Rec. 10 Aug. 1709.
Wife, Judith; daus. Katherine and Judith. Extrs. Wife and Wm. Davenport, brother-in-law. Wits. Jno. Paine, Will Paine and Elizabeth Martin. W.B. 10, p. 31.

BARKER, Thomas. Inventory. 10 Aug. 1709. Rec. 12 Oct. 1709. Presented by Judith Barker, widow. W.B. 10, p. 36.

BARKER, William. Nuncupative Will. 12 July 1709. Rec. May 10, 1710.
"My will is that Wosah be returned to Betty and all rest of my estate I give to my brother present when these words were spoke." W.B. 10, p. 43.
Inventory above estate returned 14 June 1710. W.B. 10, p. 93.

BATE, Jonathan. Will. 15 Oct. 1680. Rec. 12 Feb. 1681. No devisees. Benj. Doggett to be paid and made Extr. Wits. Robert Webb, Hen. Webb. W.B. 5, p. 73.

BEACH, George. Administration granted Ellinor Beach, his widow. 15 Apl. 1658. Mr. Montague, Sec. Mr. Booth, Mr. Vose, Mr. Montague and Wm. Noosham appraisers. W. B. 1, p. 367.
Appraisement above estate 24 June 1656. Rec. 23 Sept. 1656, by Peter Montague, William Nusham, Hump. Booth. W.B. 2, p. 39.
Acct. Sales, above estate by Eleanor Beach, widow of Geo. Beach, 4 Feb. 1656. W.B. 2, p. 39.

BEACHUM, John. Nuncupative Will. Rec. 14 May 1697. Patrick Mitchell, age 40 years, deposed that John "Beachy" left his estate to his child. Mary Davis, aged 34 yrs., makes the same deposition. W.B. 8, p. 62.

BEALE, John E. Inventory. 20 Nov. 1777. Rec. 19 March 1778. W.B. 20, p. 120.

BEALE, John Eustace. Settlement. Dec. 1789. Rec. 19 July 1790. Charles Lee Admr. Mentions widow and orphans (no names). Returned by Henry Lawson and Rawleigh Shearman. W.B. 22, p. 279.

BECK. Inventory. 13 Nov. 1717. Rec. 11' Dec. 1717. Proved by Ellinor Mills, late Ellinor Beck, Admx. W.B. 10, p. 248.

BECK, Ellinor. 9 May 1733. Rec. 13 June 1733. Returned by Joseph Burns, Adm. W.B. 12, p. 268.

BECKINGHAM, Robert. Will. 20 Jany. 1675. Rec. 1 April 1675. Wife Elizabeth; brothers-in-law: Jno. Burroughs and Jno, Cume. Sisters: Elizabeth Cume and Martha Burroughs; Father, Robert Beckingham; brother-in-law, Arthur Elmore; Uncle, Vincent Beckingham; kinsman, Gilbert Haman; Gyles Cole; Capt. Richd. Taylor and Elizabeth his wife; Capt. Wm. Francis and Rebecca his wife; Maj. Saml. Griffin and wife, Mr. Barton Wilkes, John Stretchley, Dr John Gilford. Extrs. Wife, Capt. Wm. Francis and Maj. Saml. Griffin. Wits: Jas. Barton, Jno. Gifford, Jno Stretchley, Isaac Robinson. W.B. 5, p. 19.

BELL, John. Will. Recorded 20 Jan. 1656. Devisees: Widow Bryant and her 2 children, Alex. Poeteous, Thomas, his mate, and Cyptyan, B.P. Wits. Jas. Bagnall, John Gregory. W.B. 2, p. 43.

BELL, Henry. Will. 29 Apl. 1695. Rec. 10 July 1695. Dau. Rebecca Bell; sons: William and Henry Bell; wife, Rebecca Bell; Katherine Bell, dau. of Thomas and Sarah Bell. Extrs. frind Mr. Andrew Jackson, Capt. Wm. Lister, Dr. James Innis, Mr. Nicholas Wren, Sr. Wits: Wm. Bousch, Elizabeth Wrenn, Thos. Bell. W.B. 8, p. 49.

BELL, Phillis. Inventory, recorded 11 Apl. 1733. Returned by Thos. Flint, Admr. W.B. 12, p. 258.

BELL, Rev. John. Will. 18 Feb. 1742. Rec. 10 June 1743. Wife Elizabeth, her dower in 2470 a. land in Pr. William county, and plantation in Lancaster; Sons: William, Thomas, James, John and Charles. Gr. son: Charles Jones son of dau. Ann, decd. Daus. Ann, Elizabeth, and Mary. Son-in-law, Shapleigh Neale and his wife, my dau. Margaret. Mentions land given dau. Margaret, wife of Shapleigh Neale by his brother, Dr. Alex. Bell, decd. Son John (not 21) 1770 a. land in Pr. William Co., also lot and house in town of Falmouth, King George County. Son

William, 300 a. in Pr. William Co., son Thomas, land in Pr. William Co., "given and bequeathed by Dr. Alexander Bell, my decd. brother." Son Charles, land in Lancaster. Extrs. Wife and son John. Wits. Thomas, James and John Leathead, Thos. Edwards. W.B. 13, p. 334.

BELL, Rev. John. Inventory in Lancaster and Pr. William counties. Returned by John Bell, one of his Extrs., and recorded 10 June 1743. W.B. 14, p. 46.

BELL, Elizabeth. Will. 5 May 1749. Rec. 11 May 1750.

Daughter Mary Bell; sons: Thomas, James and Charles Bell, Mr. John Bell. Extrs. son Thomas, and Dale Carter. Wits. Richd. Sheppens, Thos. Grassett. W. B. 14, p. 281.

BELL, Charles, Parish Christ Church. 1 Nov. 1780. Rec. 13 July 1781. WILL.

Wife, Elizabeth Bell; brothers James and Thomas Bell; Godson Richard Lee; my dear sister's children that she has by Col. Burnley. Extrs. Wife and brothers Thos. and James Bell, friend and relative Maj. Jno. Hull and friend Col. Gordon. Wits: Edwin Conway, James Bell, Sarah C. Conway. W. B. 20, p. 198.

BELL, Thomas, Christ Church Parish. Will. 15 Feb. 1786. Rec. 15 Feb. 1790.

Wife, Ann Bell; sons: John and Charles Bell. Dau. Sarah Bell. Lot Winnie Darkis, furniture and cattle in his possession. Extrs. Wife, and son Charles Bell. Wits. Johnson Riveer, Wm. Riveer, Thomas Riveer. W.B. 22, p. 250.

Appraisement above estate 16 Feb. 1790. Rec. 21 June 1790 by Johnson Riveer, Jesse Robinson and Peter Riveer. W.B. 22, p. 272.

BELVAIRD, Robert. Will. 18 Jany. 1783. Rec. 10 March 1784.

Legatees: friends, John Miller, Betty Miller, Ann Newby, wife of Wm. Newby and dau. of Peter Miller, James Sutton, Nancy Flint, dau. of Thos. Flint, Judith Miller and her dau. Betty Miller, Ann Miller, wife of John Miller, and Betty Miller. Extrs. Andrew Robertson, James Gordon, James Tapscott. Wits. Geo. Miller, John Bean, Leannah Bean. W.B. 22, p. 19.

Appraisement above estate 20 May 1784. W.B. 22, p. 28.

BENNETT, Robert. Will. 29 Jany. 1697. Rec. 10 Mch. 1697.

Legatees: Godson Robt. Bennoll, Nath. Hedgman, Sr., Nath. Hedgman, Jr., Peter Hedgman, Robt. Schofield Jr., Peter Kilgore.

Extrs. Robt. Schofield, Jr., Peter Kilgore. Wits. John Pledger, Ellinor Schofield, Natl. Hedgman. W.B. 8, p. 78.

BENNETT, John. Inventory & Appraisal. 13 Dec. 1710. Rec. 9 May 1711.

Presented by Wm. Payne. W.B. 10, p. 78.

BENNETT, Catherine. Will. 29 Feb. 1723. Rec. 8 Apl. 1724.

Legatees: Mary Marshall dau, Thomas and Mary Marshall. Extr. Thos. Marshall. Wits: Wm. Jones, Hannah Betts. W.B. 10, p. 450.

BENNETT, John. Inventory & Appraisement. 9 Feby. 1749.

Inventory and appraisement, returned by Merryman Payne, Adm. W.B. 14, p. 272.

BERRY, John. Will. 21 June 1690. Rec. 15 Jany. 1691.

Wife Gillian; Sarah, only daughter given plantation I now live on. Extrx. Wife. Wits: Thos. Parker, Peter James, Rote Gill. W.B. 8, p. 30.

Invty. & Appr. above estate 22 Jan. 1692. Rec. 19 Apl. 1693. Exhibited in court on Apl. 12 1693 by Mr. Peter Currell and Gillin his wife, relict of Mr. John Berry. W.B. 8, p. 40.

BERRYMAN, John. Will. 16 Feb. 1786. Rec. 16 April 1787.

Mentions: Wife; Sons: (not of age) Gilson, land in Lancaster— Richard and James the youngest son. Daughters: To Sarah Foote (her mother's wedding ring) Martha; Frances Bushrod— youngest daughter. Mentions half blood of children. Owned land in Prince William county. Mrs. Frances Mapwell to care for children if his wife dies. Extrs. James Brent, Gent, Wm. Meredith. Wits: Wm. Norris, Gilbert Currell, Thos. N. Lawson, Henry Lawson, Geo. Brent.

Codicil Mch. 31 1786. W.B. 22, p. 145.

16 July 1787. Appraisal above estate by Henry Lawson, Isaac Degge, Martin Shearman. W.B. 22, p. 153.

BERTRAND, John. Will. 8 Dec. 1700. Rec. 10 7thber 1701.

Wife, Charlotte; son William, his present plantation; dau. Mary-ann. Cousin Paul Bertrand. Wits. Jos. Jones, Jno. Mathews, Jno. Rankin. W.B. 8, p. 105.

Following entry follows: 10 Feb. 1701—

Charlotte Bertrand, To the Worshipful Court of Land. Last night I did intend by God's help to att. Court this day to have waited on ye Worships in order to have had my husband's will proved, but I am taken ill, but hoping that ye worships wont take it ill I have for that reason sent my dear Husbands will by Mr. Charles Dodson to be proved before ye worships. Therefore I humbly beg of ye worships to admitt it to be proved and I shall in duty bound ever pray for ye worship's well fare." Teste:

(Signed) Edward White, (Signed) Thomas Roberts).

W.B. 8, 105.

BERTRAND, William. Will. 26 Feb. 1759. Rec. 17 Apl. 1761.

Gr. Dau. Elizabeth Griffin; Gr. son William Griffin (not 21) Gr. son Thomas Bertrand Griffin. Extr. Thos. Bertrand Griffin. Wits. Ozwald Newby, Mary Ann Griffin. W.B. 16, p. 127.

BEVANS, Thomas. Appraisal. 22 Mch. 1786. Rec. 21 Sept. 1786. By James Newby, Johnson Riveer, Wm. Weblin. W.B. 22, p. 133.

BISCOE, Robert. Will. Rec. 11 March 1747. Wife Elizabeth; son, John Biscoe. Mentions his children (no names). Extrs. Wife and son. Proved by Wm. James.

BISCOE, Elizabeth, widow. Deed to children, vizt. John Biscoe, Mary Hunton, Elizabeth Biscoe, Robert Biscoe, Sally Biscoe, Nancy Biscoe, Wm. Biscoe. Wits. Rawl. Shearman, Wm. Dymer, Geo. Currell. 14 Apl. 1756. Rec. 16 Apl. 1756. W.B. 15, p. 244.

BISCOE, John "Of Christ Church Parish." 24 Feb. 1773. Rec. 20 May 1773.

Wife Betty. "All my children." Extrs. Wife Betty, friends Matthew Myars, William Armes, Richard Chilton, Wm. Chowning. Wits. Ja. Ewell, Jno. Payne, Jeremiah Doggett. W.B. 20, p. 59.

BISCOE, John. Division estate. Dec. 1791. Rec. 16 July 1792.

Heirs: William, Lawson, Elizabeth and George Biscoe. By Henry Towles, John Chowning, Wm. George. W.B. 22, p. 348.

BISCOE, George, decd. Appraisal. by Edw. Blakemore, Henry Street, James Robb. Rec. 18 May 1795. W.B. 22, p. 457.

BLACK, Joseph. Inventory. 9 May 1677. Rec. 12 May 1677. Returned by Andrew Herbert. W.B. 2, p. 29.

BLACKERLEY, Eliza. Division estate. 17 Mch. 1781. Rec. 19 Apl. 1781.

William Hill one of heirs. W.B. 20, p. 191.

Idem. November 1782. To orphans of Martin Hill, vizt: Thomas,

John Hill, and William Everitt. By Jno. Fleet; Jno. Berryman; Henry Lawson, Wm. Meredith. W.B. 20, p. 253.

BLACKMORE, Edward. Will. 27 March 1738. Rec. 12 May 1738.

Wife, Hannah; sons, Thomas, Edward, John and Joseph. Daus. Sarah and Hannah. Extrs. Thos. Blackmore and Raw. Chinn. Wits. Jno. Rogers and Jos. Ball. W.B. 13, p. 90.

BLAKEMORE, Edward. Division Estate. 13 March 1746/7.

Legatees Thomas Hines, part, who married widow. Edward Blakemore, Gdn. of Joseph Blakemore, son of Edw. Blakemore, decd., Thomas Blakemore, Edward Blakemore, Joseph Blakemore, John Blakemore, Sarah Blakemore, Hannah Blakemore. W.B. 14, p. 140.

BLAKEMORE, Edward, "Parish of Christ Church." 1 Dec. 1771. Rec. 17 Apl. 1777.

Children when they arrive at age of 21; wife Jemime; son Edward. Extrs. wife and Henry Towles. Wits. Richard Mitchell, Henry Towles, Rawl. Chinn, Jno. Chowning, Rawleigh Stott. W.B. 20, p. 108.

17 Apl. 1777. Division above estate by Edw. Blakemore and Jno. Payne. W.B. 20, p. 152.

BLAKEMORE, Edward. Division of Estate. 17 Dec. 1781. Rec. 21 Feb. 1782.

To Bridget Payne, Edward, William, Sarah and Nancy Blakemore. W.B. 20, p. 222.

BLACKMORE, Edward. Division Lot #2. 27 Apl. 1777. Rec. 15 June 1789.

To Ann Blackmore, Sally Newton Blackmore, William Biscoe, Edward Blakemore, George Johnson, Mrs. Jemima Bristow. W.B. 22, p. 214.

BLANCH, Thomas. Will. 8 April 1698. Rec. 12 August 1698.

Wife Mary; sons: Thomas, William and James. Daughters: Susanna, Elizabeth and Mary. Extrx. Wife. Wits. Chris. Kirk, David Muray, Thos. Hubard. W.B. 8, p. 83.

BLUMHERD, Will. Nuncupative Will. Rec. 1 October 1688.

Jo. Edwards Cooper, aged 30 years, swears that Will Blumherd did give his master Mr. Vincent, and his landlady and her child, his property. Abigail Duckett, age 21 years, makes same deposition. Wits. Jno. Potter, Mr. Ellyott. W.B. 2, p. 57.

BOAT, John E. Inventory & Appraisal. 19 March 1772. By Rawleigh Shearman, James Pollard and John James. W.B. 20, p. 120.

BOATMAN, Henry. Will. 25 October 1721. Rec. 11 April 1722.

Wife. (Name not given) sons: Richard, Henry, John and Robert Boatman; Gr. son Henry Boatman; daughter, Anne Pasquet. Extrs. Wife and son Richard. Wits. William Ellis, Winifrede Olifant. W.B. 10, p. 365.

9 May 1722. Invty. above estate returned by Elizabeth Boatman and Richard Boatman, Extrs. W.B. 10, p. 376.

BOATMAN, John. Appraisal. 14 Apl. 1738. Recd. 12 May 1738. Returned by Johanna Boatman, Admx. W.B. 13, p. 88.

BOATMAN, Henry, "Parish of Christ Church." 21 Nov. 1743. Rec. 13 Jany. 1743. Will.

Sons: John and Henry Boatman; daughters: Mary, Hannah and Anna Boatman. Wife, Margaret. Extr. son Edward. Wits. Henry Carter, Geo. Brent, William Walker. W.B. 14, p. 3.

13 July 1744. Division above estate.

Legacy left Mary Boatman by her grandmother Frances Edwards. Legacy left her by her father. Widow's part of estate. Legacy left Henry Boatman by grandmother Frances Edwards; Legacy left Hannah Boatman; Legacy left Ann Boatman. W.B. 14, p. 26.

BOATMAN, Mary. Inventory. 11 July 1746. Rec. 8 Aug. 1746. Returned by Richard Boatman, Adm. W.B. 14, p. 117.

BOATMAN, Edward. Inventory. 8 August 1746. Returned by Richd. Boatman, Adm. W.B. 14, p. 117.

BOATMAN, Robert. Will. 17 December 1749. Rec. 9 March 1749. Wife Apphia; sons: Richard, Waterman and Henry Boatman; Daughters: Elizabeth; Sarah Ann; and Nancy Boatman. Wits. Wm. Miller, Jno. Davis, Jos. Davis. W.B. 14, p. 273.

BOATMAN, Richard. Will. 1 December 1760. Rec. 21 May 1764. To William, son of brother John Boatman; Richard Boatman Junior, son of brother Robert Boatman, decd. Extrs. nephews Richard Boatman, Jr., and Wm. Boatman. Wits. James Hill, James Pinckard, Dale Carter. W.B. 18, p. 11.

BOATMAN, Apphia, widow. Will. 24 April 1771. Rec. 20 Jany. 1789. Sons Richard and Waterman Boatman; Daughters: Elizabeth, Joannah, Sarah Ann and Nancy Boatman. Gr.son, Henry Cundiff. Extrx. daughter Nancy Boatman. Wits. Dale Carter, James Carter. W.B. 22, p. 199.

BOND, John. Inventory. 13 Sept. 1699. Rec. 15 Sept. 1699. returned by John Edwards. W.B. 10, p. 186.

BOND, William. Inventory. Rec. 17 Sept. 1762. Returned by John Bond, Admr. W.B. 16, p. 235.

BOND, Sarah. Rec. 17 Sept. 1764.

"Sarah Bond, relict of John Bond, who departed this life without making a will, to have possession of her part of her late husband, Thomas Sharpe's negroes, and the remainder to be divided among the orphans, vizt: Elizabeth and Sarah Sharpe orphans of Thos. Sharpe, decd., by James Ball, their Guardian.

Idem., p. 606.

Thomasin Sharpe, orphan of Thos. Sharpe; Charles Rogers, her Guardian; Elias Edmonds Sharpe and Anne Sharpe, orphans of Thos. Sharpe, Sarah Bond appointed their Guardian.

17 Sept. 1764. Rec. 5 Oct. 1764. Appraisement above estate, returned by Mrs. Sarah Bond. She to be alloted part of her former Husband, Mr. Thomas Sharpe's estate. W.B. 18, p. 22.

October court 1779. Sarah Bond, widow of John Bond allotted land of her former husband, Thos. Sharpe, now in possession of Wm. Chowning. By Henry Towles and Matt. Myers. W.B. 20, p. 172.

21 Oct. 1779. Division John Bond's estate to widow Sarah, children, Mary Edmonds, Alice Bond, Catherine Bond, Frances Bond. W.B. 20, p. 154.

BONISON, Abbiah. Will. 21 March 1663.

Wife Honora Bonison; sons: John and Thomas; Friends, Hugh Brent and Thomas Makeshard, Extrs. Wits. Richard ————?, John Andrews. Loose Wills.

28 July 1670. Inventory above estate in possession of Honora Bonison, presented by Hugh Brent and recorded 9 Nov. 1670.

BONISON, Abia. Account of his father's estate Recorded by him 10 Sept. 1679. W.B. 5, p. 59.

BONISON, Thomas. Inventory. 12 Apl. 1684. Rec. 9 July 1684. Presented by Elizabeth Bonison relict. W.B. 5, p. 97.

BONISON, Abraham. Will. 4 Feby. 1685/6. Rec. 12 Feb. 1685.

Legatees: Abraham Correll, Cozen Carne, cozen Augustine Carne,

Father-in-law John Dickson. Wits. Jno. Kelley, Jno. Carne, Abraham Correll. W.B. 5, p. 104.

BOOTARIT, William. Nuncupative Will. Rec. 5 Oct. 1656. "Wm. Bootarit some short time before his death did say that at whose house he should die, to the same he would give his estate. Estate to Sam Perry, in whose house he died."

BOWMAN, William. Will. 11 June 1750. Rec. 10 Aug. 1750. Daughters Sarah, Mary and Betty Bowman. Son William Bowman; Gr.daughter Joannah. Extr. son. Wits. Wm. Bowman, Sarah Bowman. W.B. 14, p. 296.

BOYD, John. Will. 27 June 1781. Wife Mary; sons: William, Thomas, John and Robert. Daughters: Nancy and Winnefred, three youngest children and one now in utero. Extrs. John Leland, Thomas Garner. Wits. Richard Hall, Jno. Leland. W.B. 20, p. 199.
26 March 1786. Rec. 21 April 1785. Sd John Boyd's Orphans Acct.
Settlement of Thomas Potts Guardian Acct. Mary Boyd, present Guardian. W.B. 22, p. 24.

BOYS, Robert. Inventory. 9 Nov. 1692. Rec. 11 Nov. 1692. Returned by Edward Carter. W.B. 8, p. 76.

BOYER, Robert, "smith"—Inventory. 8 Nov. 1693. Rec. 18 Dec. 1693. Presented by Mr. Anthony Gerrard. W.B. 8, p. 42.

BRADLEY, John. Will. 12 Feby. 1709. Rec. 10 May 1710. To Mrs. Martha Howard his whole estate. Legacy to Margaret Coner; Owed Margaret Connor 2000 lbs. tobacco and Causnock 900 lbs. tobacco. Wits. Jno. Stott, Jno. Hall. W.B. 10, p. 33.

BRADSHAW, Edward. Will. 17 Jany. 1655. Rec. 17 June 1655. Legatees: Moore Fauntleroy; John Jones, son of Rice Jones; Winifrede Griffin, dau. of Thos. Griffin; Jane, dau-in-law of Rice Jones; Vincent Stanford. Wits: Reynold Johnson, Arthur Clarke, Anne Garrett, Vincent Stanford. W.B. 2, p. 33.
(Administration of this estate granted Thos. Griffin 6 Mch. 1655. W.B. 1, p. 257.)

BRADY, Elizabeth, Estate. Rec. 9 March 1726. James Cammell Jr., Admr. W.B. 10, p. 533.

BRADY, Elizabeth. Will. "Of Christ Church Parish." 28 Aug. 1777. Rec. 15 June 1778.

Daughter Elizabeth Brady my whole estate until gr.dau. Easter Longwith comes of age. Extrx. Dau. Elizabeth Brady. Wits. Wm. West, Mary Pollard, Betty x Clayton. W.B. 20, p. 134.

BRANAN, John. Will. 2 Jany. 1749/50. Rec. 11 May 1750.

Wife Margaret; sons: Thomas and John. Extrs. Wife and friend Mr. Wm. Sydnor. Wits: James Ball Jr. W.B. 14, p. 280.

BRANCH, Arthur. Inventory. 13 May 1674. Rec. 23 May 1674. by Walter Beach and Wm. Thatcher. W.B. 5, p. 2.

BRASH, William. Inventory, presented by relict and recorded 9 Aug. 1709. W.B. 10, p. 46.

BRAY, Richard. Nuncupative Will. 20 Sept. 1689. Recorded 9 April 1690.

Wife Mrs. Ann Bray, all estate and she to return to England and live like a gentle woman. Boy Ned to have something "because I brought him out of his native country." Richard Bray's noncupative will.

Sister that has two daughters is given nothing. Proved by oath of Will Shorter, Elizabeth Guy and Hannah Singleton. Will was made the day before he died, 20 Sept. 1689. W.B. 8, p. 1.

BRENT, Hough. Will. 8 Jany. 1671. Rec. 13 Mch. 1671.

Eldest daughter Joane, land that was cleared by Mr. Wade. Daughters, Elizabeth, Martha (Neck of land called by name of Thatchers Neck) and after her death and death of other daughter to go to son Hough. John Coan; Mr. Thomas Haines; Fortunatus Sydnor. "To my man" Howell a calf. Issue of John Hankins living in green land. Overseer: Friend Mr. Thomas Haines and Fortunatus Sydnor. Wits. John Andros, John Thomas. (In loose papers marked 1653-79.)

BRENT, Hugh. Inventory. 10 October 1716. Rec. 9 Jany. 1716. Presented by Hugh Brent, Admr. W.B. 10, p. 195.

BRENT, William. Will. 2 July 1740. Rec. 8 August 1740.

Wife Letitia; Sons: William and James; daughters: Sarah and Frances Brent and Elizabeth Hinton; friend Robert Biscoe. Extrs Brother Hugh Brent, Jas. Haynes, Capt. Wm. Steptoe, and cousin James Brent. Wits. Isaac Currell, Jane Heard, Robt. Biscoe. W.B. 13, p. 177.

BRENT, Letitia. Deed of gift to three children, John, Letitia and James Brent. rec. 9 Mch. 1744. W.B. 14, p. 53.

BRENT, George. Will. 6 July 1748. Rec. 18 August 1748.

Sons: George, Charles (not of age) and Thomas; daughters: Lucy Brent (not of age) Amy Haines, Judith King. Grandchildren: Wm. King, John King and Mary King, children of dau. Judith King. Extr. Thomas and Geo. Brent and Antho. Kirk. Wits. John Hubbard, John Norris, Dale Carter. W.B. 14, p. 206.

Division of above estate recorded 9 June 1749—among his 6 children vizt: Thomas, George and Charles Brent and Judith King, Amy Haynes and Lucy Brent. W.B. 14, p. 247.

Inventory and Appraisement returned by Thos. Brent, Extr. Rec. 27 Sep. 1748. W.B. 14, p. 222

BRENT, Hugh. Will. 14 June 1750. Rec. 8 March 1750.

Wife Catherine; daughters: Catherine, Sarah and Judith. Extrs. cousin Hugh Brent, and wife Catherine. Wits. Merryman Payne, Thos. Sharp. W.B. 15, p. 15.

BRENT, James. Will. 19 April 1750. Rec. 11 May 1750. Wife Katherine. Extrs. Wife, Stockley Towles and Maurice Brent. W.B. 14, p. 280.

Inventory this estate returned by widow Catherine, 8 Feb. 1750. W.B. 14, p. 325.

BRENT, Hugh. Will. 28 Oct. 1748. Rec. 11 May 1750.

Sons: James, Maurice, William, land purchased of Tobin Horton, Hugh. Gr. Daughter, Mary Brent, daughter of my deceased son William Brent. Wife Elizabeth, and her nine children, Ellinor, Nicholas, Maurice, Richard, George, Mary, William, Haynes and Ann. Friend Robert Edwards son of Mr. Thos. Edwards. Extrs. Wife and sons Nicholas and Maurice. Trustees: Thos. Edwards and Thos. Pinckard. Wits. Jno. Horton, Geo. Horton, Willoughby Allerton, Richard Edwards. W.B. 14, p. 280.

16 Aug. 1754 is recorded Acct. with Hugh Brent's Orphans: Betty, Katherine, Sarah, Judith and James Brent. W.B. 15, p. 174.

BRENT, Catherine. Will. 6 Sept. 1760. Rec. 20 February 1761.

Son Hugh. "I lent Mr. Anthony Kirk and my daughter Sarah my negro wench etc. in their possession" at their death to be divided among their children. "I lend to Mr. William Stamps and my daughter Elinor my negro fellow etc" After their death to their children. Daughter Beheathland. To Mr. John Curd and my daughter Lucy my negro girl etc. and after their death to their children begotten by each other. Sons: John, Willoughby and Stockley (last two not 21 years) Extr. Mr. Baldwin Smith and Stockley Towles. Wits. Antho. Kirk, Sto. Towles. W.B. 16, p. 123.

BRENT, Hugh. Guardian for orphan. 16 Sept. 1763.
Edward Carter appointed Guardian for Judith Brent, orphan of Hugh Brent. W.B. 17, p. 22.

BRENT, James, Dec. Guardian for orphan. 15 October 1764.
Hugh Brent appointed Guardian of Stockley Brent, orphan of James Brent. W.B. 17, p. 71.

BRENT, Judith. 17 Sept. 1764. Judith Brent, Orph. of Mr. Hugh Brent Decd. to Edward Carter her Guardian. Debt on account of cash paid to Mr. Charles Rogers for a negro allotted of sd. Rogers to make up her mother's dower. W.B. 18, p. 20.

BRENT, Stockley. Will. 20 Nov. 1764. Rec. 17 June 1765.
Nephew James Brent, son of brother John Brent; Nieces: Catherine Stamps and Mary Stamps, daus. of William & Elinor Stamps (not 18), nephew John Stamps, and nephew Newton Stamps, son of William & Elinor Stamps. Extr. Friend Hugh Brent. Wits. Chas. Rogers, Henry Towles, Wm. Chowning. W.B. 18, p. 35.

BRENT, Elizabeth of Christ Church Parish). Will. 24 Nov. 1762. Rec. 19 July 1770.
Daughter Anne Brent. Ext. Neighbor Hugh Brent. Wits. Ellinor Brent, Elizabeth Fox and Hugh Brent. W.B. 20, p. 3.

BRENT, Richard. Appraisement. 12 Apl. 1771. Rec. 16 May 1771.
By James Kirk, William Yerby and Elmore Doggett. W.B. 20, p. 12.

BRENT, Charles. Will. May 4, 1767. Rec. 19 March 1772.
Brother George Brent; Eliza King, daughter of my cousin Wm. King; cousin Ann Flower, dau. of my sister Judith Brent. Extrs. brother Geo. Brent, cousin Wm. King. Wits. Dale Carter, Jno. King, Wm. King. W.B. 20, p. 40.

BRENT, Stockley. Appraisement. 16 Jany. 1772. Rec. 22 Jany. 1778.
By Wm. Yerby, Jas. Kirk and Nicholas Brent. John Brent, Grd. of his son James Brent's part of Stockley Brent's Ext. W.B. 20, p. 37.

BRENT, Hugh Brent (Christ Church Parish). Will. 27 Jan. 1778. Rec. 19 Feby. 1778.

Sons: James, Newton and George Brent; daughters: Frances Maxwell and Sarah Berryman; Grand daughter Elizabeth Maxwell. Daughter Katherine Brent all the negroes that I got by marriage with her mother, Easther Brent. Wife Judith Brent land for support of herself and children, Charlotte, Priscilla, Hugh, Martin Brent and child unborn. Extrs. son James Brent and friends Edwin Conway and Jno. Berryman. Wits. Richard E. Lee, William Norris and John Flowers. W.B. 20, p. 118.

BRENT, George. Will. 5 March 1778. Rec. 19 March 1778.

Sons: George and Charles Brent; daughters: Judith Hubbard, Lucy Brent, Molly Brent, Margaret Brent and Sarah Ann Brent. Extrs. Friend Capt. Edwin Conway, brother Thomas Brent and Samuel Yopp. Wits. Edwin Conway, Thos. Brent, Thomas Brent Jr. W.B. 20, p. 119.

Division above estate, recorded 19 August 1779, names: Margaret Brent, widow; Charles, Margaret, Lucy, George, Judith, Mary Ann, and Sary Ann Brent. W.B. 20, p. 167.

BRENT, Thomas. Will. "Being in the 58th year of my age"— Recd. 21 Feby. 1782.

Wife, Ann Brent; Children: George, Thomas, Vincent, Ann Brent. Son William Brent and daughter Judith Sullivant. Proved by Thos. Pollard, Jno. Parrott, Jeduthan Brent. W.B. 20, p. 221.

BRENT, Richard. Division Estate. Recorded 21 Feb. 1782.

John Brent, eldest son of Richard Brent Dec., Ann Brent, Dec. right of her dower; Burges Longwith who married one of the daus. before death of sd Ann Brent; John Brent, and Elizabeth Brent. By James Brent, Jno. Sulavent, Thos. Pollard. W.B. 20, p. 224.

BRENT, Hugh. Last division estate. Rec. 10 April 1781.

Mrs. Judith Brent, which, on her death, will belong to Mr. Newton Brent. By Richd. Mitchell, James Gordon, Henry Lawson. W.B. 20, p. 192.

BRENT, Thomas. Extr. Estate of Geo. Brent. June 1782. Rec. 18 Oct. 1783. Thos. Brent, decd. was indebted to Orphans of Geo. Brent, for whom he was Extr. Settlement made. By Elias Edmonds, Jno. Yearby, Wm. Edwards. W.B. 22, p. 5.

BRENT, Margret. Will. 27 Jany. 1784. Rec. 19 Feby. 1784.
Sons: George and Charles Brent. Daughters: Margret and Sarah Brent; Son-in-law and Extr., Jeduthan Brent. Wits Chas. Hubbard, Molly Brent, Lucy Brent. W.B. 22, p. 10.
Above estate appraised on 20 April 1784. (W.B. 22, p. 70.)

BRENT, Thomas Brent, decd., Wm. Brent, Admr. rec. 20 May 1784.
Thomas Brent; Vincent Brent; Ann wife of Daniel Brent. By Edwin Conway, James Tapscott and Jno. Cundiff. W.B. 22, p. 29.

BRENT, Margaret. Appraisal. Jeduthan Brent, Extr. Guardian to Margaret, Sarah Ann, George and Charles Brent. By Edwin Conway, Saml. Yopp, Chas. Hubbard. Rec. 17 March 1785. W.B. 22, p. 70.

BRENT, Hugh. Settlement of estate. Feby. 1785. Rec. 18 March 1785. By Henry Lawson, James Tapscott, Wm. Gibson. W.B. 22, p. 18.
Appraisal and Division by above named Etrs. 15 Oct. 1787. Heirs: Joseph Stevens, Presellah Brent, Hugh Brent, Martin Brent, Kenner Brent. W.B. 22, p. 116.

BRENT, James. Will. 13 May 1791. rec. 17 Dec. 1792.
Wife Elizabeth Brent; sons: James and William; Daughters, Susannah, Sarah Nutt Brent, Mary and Elizabeth Brent and a child yet unborn. Extrx. wife. proved by Martin Shearman and George Brent. W.B. 22, p. 357.
18 Feby. 1793. Appraisal above estate by Henry Lawson, Wm. Eustace, Wm. Gibson. (W.B. 22, p. 365.)

BRENT, George. Will. August 1784. Rec. 21 Sept. 1786.
Thomas Hubbard Admr. Heirs: Margaret Brent, George Brent, Sarah Brent, alias Kirk, Charles Brent, estate of Mrs. Margaret Brent, dec. By Edwin Conway, Elias Edmonds, Stephen Locke, John Sullivant.

BREWER, Paul. Administration of Est. granted Wm. Johnson, 8 June 1655. W.B. 1, p. 197.

BRIAN, Robert. Inventory, presented by Jane Callahan, relict, recorded 10 Dec. 1680.

BRIDGEFORD, Thomas, Christ Church Parish. Will. 23 Feb. 1784. Rec. 18 Mch. 1784.
Wife Ann; brother William Bridgeford's son Thomas, and Thomas Currell, son of my sister Judith Currell; Benjamin James,

son of Sarah James; Ann Cox, dau. of my sister Lucy Cox. Extr. Capt. Isaac Diggs; Wits. Lawson Hathaway, Joshua Crowther. W.B. 22, p. 20.

BRIDGEFORT, Thomas. Estate appraised March 1784. Rec. 20 May 1784 by Isaac Degge, Thos. Carter and James Pollard. W.B. 22, p. 28.

BRIDGFORT, Thomas. Appraisement by Epa Lawson, Nathl. Lawson, Thos. James 8th June 1744. W.B. 14, p. 20.

BRIDGFORD, Ann. Estate Appraised, 20 Jan. 1785. Rec. 21 April 1785. By Henry Lawson, Lawson Hathaway, Wm. Lawson. W.B. 22, p. 74.

BRIES, Thomas. Will. 24 April 1657. Rec. 22 May 1657.

Wife Martha all estate real and personal in England and Virginia. Extrx. Wife. Wits. Davy Fox, Thos. Haslan, Edward Dale. W.B. 2, p. 53.

(NOTE: In Order Book 3, it is shown that Martha Bries, widow of Thomas Bries, married William White of Rappahannock.)

BRIGGS, Ralph. Inventory. 3 December 1689. Rec. 14 Jany. 1689. Presented by Lidia Briggs. W.B. 5, p. 135.

BRIGHTMAN, William. Will. 28 May 1703. Rec. No. date.

Legatees: God daughter Elizabeth Reeves, daughter of John Reeves; Godsons William and John Reeves sons of Jno. Reeves and his wife Elizabeth. Extr. Jno. Reeves Sr. Wits. William Fox and Jno. Bradley. W.B. 8, p. 121.

BRISTOW, William. Appraisal. Oct. 1789. Rec. 21 Dec. 1789 by Wm. Bristow, Wm. Chowning, Jno. Chowning. W.B. 22, p. 234. Sale of above estate was held 21 June 1790. Among purchasers were: James Healy, Josiah Bristow, Henry Kidd, Geo. Blackley, Martho. Bristow, Richard Bristow, Samuel Smith, Geo. Dam, Isaac Kidd, Robt. Murray, Thos. Roan, Jno. Quarles, Wm. Berry. W.B. 22, p. 271.

BROCAS, Capt. William. Inventory & Appraisal. 24 May 1655. Rec. 11 Jany. 1655. By Bartram Hobart, William x Leech; Edm. Kemp; Row. Burnham; ffra. x Coale. W.B. 1, p. 203.

BROOKS, Frances. Estate appraised. 13 July 1744. Invty. returned by Absalom Moughon, her son. W.B. 14, p. 27.

BROOKS, Samuel. Inventory and Appraisement. April 1772. Rec. 15 July 1773, by Dale Carter, Jno. Davis, James Hill. Presented by Jemima Brooks.

BROOKS, Jemima. Will. 25 June 1772. Rec. 20 Oct. 1774.

Daughters Sary Ann Chilton, Jemima Chilton and Mary George; Sons: Stephen Chilton and William Chilton. Gr. Daughters, Judith and Elizabeth, daus. of Geo. Chilton. Extrs. sons William and Stephen Chilton and dau. Sary Ann Chilton. Wits. Dale Carter and Wilmot x Brooks. W.B. 20, p. 76.

BROWNE, Edward. Will. 4 Feby. 1663. Rec. 13 May 1663.

Landlady Mary Harrison; Mother Jane Browne in Summerset-shire, all goods that are due me in the ship called Rappahannock Merchant, whereof Samuel Ponfax is commander. Wm. Neesum, Extr. Wits. Thomas Harryson, Michael Wellington. (Loose Papers.)

BROWN, Nathaniel. Will. 22 June 1691. Rec. 13 Sept. 1693.

Godson, Samuel Bromley son of Daniell Bromley. Wife Ann Brown;. nephew William Cole of Province of Maryland. Stephen Tomlyn; James Lyell. Wits. Wm. Boner, Jno. Giles (age 21 years) Francis Bristol. W.B. 8, p. 40.

BROWN, Richard. Will, recorded 8 May 1717. Presented by William Cary, the principal legatee, but proved by Richard Chichester and Mary Lawson. W.B. 10, p. 213.

BROWN, John. Will. 15 June 1723. Rec. 9 Sept. 1724.

Wife Elizabeth; Daughter Sarah's children Phebe and Mary; sons William, Edward, Joseph and John; Extrs. Wm. Ball and Wm. Payne. Wits. Geo. Light, James Galer, Eaton Reeves. W.B. 10, p. 453.

BROWN, Benjamin. Will. 2 May 1728. Rec. 10 July 1728.

Wife Elizabeth; sons Benjamin, land where I live on; John Brown; Daughters Rebeckah, Sonna, Ann and Elizabeth. Extrs. Wife and son Benjamin. Wits. Jos. Pope, Robt. Dredin, Lazarus Smith. W.B. 12, p. 59.

Appraisement above estate returned by Benj. Brown and Eliba-beth Brown Extrs. 14th August 1728. W.B. 12, p. 70.

BROWN, Joseph. Inventory returned by John Brown, Admr. 14th September 1750. W.B. 14, p. 307.

BROZIER, Joseph. Estate. Recorded 12 July 1727. Mary Brozier. Admx. W.B. 12, p. 11.

BRUMLEY, Samuel. Will. 7 October 1748. Rec. 14 October 1748. Wife Margaret, son Samuel. Son Extr. Wits. M. Shearman, Sarah Ann Pritchett, Henry Newby. W.B. 14, p. 217.

BRUMLEY, Samuel. Division Estate. 15 March 1781. Rec. 18 April 1782.

Elizabeth Brumley, widows part; William Brumley; Daniel Brumley; William Brent in right of his wife, Ellen, dau. of sd. Brumley; Children of Betty, one of daus. of Samuel Brumley, late wife of Jonathan Pullen. By James Ball, James Ball Jr. and Wm. Sydnor. W.B. 20, p. 232.

BRUMLEY, William. Will. 13 Feby. 1788. Rec. 21 Jany. 1793.

Wife Sarah; nephew: Hugh Brent, son of Wm. Brent and Ellen his wife; Sarah McCarty dau. of Col. Thad McCarty. Ex. Col. Jas. Ball Jr., Ozwald Newby Jr. Wits: James Ball, James Ball Jr., Fanny Ball. W.B. 22, p. 358.

BRUSH, Mr. Abell. Appraisement. Recorded 14 April 1731 by Mary Brush, Admx. W.B. 12, p. 195.

BRYAN, Mary, widow. Deed of Gift. Rec. 30 Sept. 1656. To Thomas, Robert and Eliza Bryan three cows and their increase. W.B. 1, p. 288.

BUCKAN, Catherine. Appraisal. 22 Oct. 1793. Rec. 16 June 1794.

Heirs: Nicholas Pope Buckan, Wm. Goodridge, David Buckan, Spencer Currell. By: Martin Shearman, Lawson Hathaway, Gilbert Currell. W.B. 22, p. 430.

BUCKLES, John, of Christ Church. Will. 15 Feby. 1734. Rec. 12 March 1734.

Daughters: Margaret, Lucy and Ann Buckles; Frances Robb, dau. of James Robb. Michael Ryan to be paid for teaching his children. Extrs. Son-in-law James Robb and Wm. Edwards. Wits. Henry Carter, Robt. Carter, Jno. Meredith. W.B. 12, p. 332.

BUCKLES, Ann, of Christ Church Parish. Will. 1 Aug. 1775. Rec. 19 Oct. 1775.

Legacies to Thomas and Agatha Rob, sister Frances Rob, Frances Denny, Margaret Rob and Sarah Carter. Wits. Elias Edmonds. W.B. 20, p. 88.

Division of above estate, 18 Jany. 1776. Rec. 21 Mch. 1776. To Mrs. Robb, Margaret Robb, Elias Edmonds, Job Carter, Agatha Robb. By Jno. Yerby, Edwin Conway, James Kirk Jr. W.B. 20, p. 96.

BUCKLY, Frances. Inventory. Rec. 27 August 1706. W.B. 8, p. 257.
"   "   Noncupative Will, Recorded 6 April 1703.
Frances Buckley, aged 52 years, says her husband Thomas Buckly left her his Extrx. in his will, and she leaves her brother Richard Stephens his Executor, and hopes he may give the children something. Wits. John Chilton Sr., Jno. Stott, Mary Chapell. W.B. 8, p. 256.

BUCKLEY, Thomas. Will. 22 Jany. 1702. Rec. (no date).
Wife Frances;. Grandsons: James and William Hill, children of Robert Hill; John Chilton. Overseers: Brother and Richard Stephens. Extrx. Wife. Richard Stephens and Hannah his wife to have the upbringing of his children, James, William and Frances Hill. Wits. Jno. Mullis, Richard Stephens, James Foster. W.B. 8, p. 128.

BUCKLEY, John. Inventory and Appraisal. 10 Oct. 1733. Rec. 9 Jany. 1733. Mary Buckley Admx. W.B. 12, p. 288.

BUNN, John. Will. 1 March 1675. Rec. 12 July 1676.
Oldest daughter Jane; wife Elizabeth; sister Ursula Vivian. John Wren. Wits: John Hutchingson, John Hutchins. W.B. 5, p. 24.

BURGESS, Charles, of St. Mary's White Chapell. Will. 4 Nov. 1732. Rec. 14 Mch. 1733.
Wife (name not given). Sisters, Margaret, Eliz., Jane and Ann (all in England). Extrs. Wife, James Ball, Edwin Conway. Wits. Thos. Thornton, Jno. Mitchell, Jos. Ball. W.B. 12, p. 239.

Note: W.B. 12, p. 335 appears: 12 Feby. 1734. Rec. 9 Apl. 1735: John Brewer and Mary his wife, late widow of John Vangover, decd. and Extrx. of Chas. Burgess, gent, dec'd., concerning divers legacies given by sd Vangover to ye sd Mary and of which Chas. Burges was Extr. Wm. Lowry, one of orphans of James Lowry, one of the legatees of sd Vangover.

Estate of sd Charles Burges. As recorded 10 Oct. 1740.
Jesse Ball guardian of Margaret, Frances and Eliza Burges, orphans of Charles Burges decd. W.B. 13, p. 187.

Division of Negroes, of Charles Burges estate. 12 Aug. 1743. Rec. 9 March 1743.

James Ball Jr., as Adm. of his wife, Mrs. Margaret Ball, decd., one of the daus. and co-heirs of Chas. Burges, dec. division of negroes from those belonging to Frances and Elizabeth Burges, surviving daughters of sd Chas. Burges, with consent of Jesse Ball, their guardian etc. Negroes belonging to Baldwin Mathews Smith, gent, in right of his wife, Frances, dau. and co-heir of Charles Burges dec. and those belonging to Elizabeth Burges. W.B. 14, p. 10.

Division of Chas. Burgess Estate. 10 Apl. 1751. Rec. 18 Apl. 1752.

Robert Armistead and Elizabeth his wife, dau. of Chas. Burgess; Burgess Smith, son of Baldwin Mathews Smith and grandson of Chas. Burgess. Wits. Peter Conway, Geo. Payne, Thos. Chinn. W.B. 15, p. 91.

BURGIN, Laughly. Will. 30 Nov. 1750. Rec. 14 Dec. 1750.

Legatees: Margaret Horton "who now lives with me" my wife's chest etc. James Harper. Extr. Capt James Gordon, Dale Carter. Wits. Wm. Bowman, Sarah Bowman. W.B. 14, p. 322.

BURNHAM, Rowland. Will. 12 Feby. 1655. Rec. 1 March 1656.

Wife Alice; daughter Eleanor Burnham; Sons: Thomas, John and Francis. All lands south of Rappa. River, where I now live, also three English servants, John Henley, David Wilkins and John Lewys. Brother Thos. Holmes and his wife Margery, my sister of York River. Francys Cole and wife Alice, of Rappa. River. Extrs. Francys Cole, Thos. Holmes. Wits. Francys Cole, Jno. Vause, Robert Taylor. W.B. 2, p. 46.

Record of Jany. 14 1656.

Rowland Burnham decd. did not appoint Executors. Alice Burnham, the relict is granted administration. W.B. 1, p. 309.

BURNS, John. Oral Will. 10 Jany. 1720/21. Rec. 10 May 1721.

Legatees: Wife (name not given), and Billy Taylor. Wits. Anne Burn and Ann Ball. W.B. 10, p. 311.

NOTE: Anne Bourne and Samuel Ball, Admr. of Estate of James Bourne, 10 May 1721 (p. 312). Inventory returned by Anne Burne, admr. 14 June 1721. (p. 320)

BURWELL, Nathaniel. Sale of Estate. 20 Oct. 1789. Rec. 15 Feby. 1790. By James Ball Jr., Sheriff. Mrs. Frances Burwell one of purchasers. W.B. 22, p. 253.

BUSH, Abraham. Will. 14 Feby. 1686. Rec. 10 Aug. 1687.

Wife Ann, plantation I now live on. After her death to youngest son Isak. Sons Thomas, George, Abraham, John. Daughters, Charity Eliz., Marsey. William Alexander, devisee. Wits. Walter Welsh, Wm. Rawly, Rich. Eaton. W.B. 5, p. 115.

BUSH, Ann. Will. 7 August 1689. Rec. 13 Feby. 1690.

Sons: Wm. Alexander and John Bush; daughters, Mary and Elizabeth Bush; sons Isaac Bush; Jacob Bush; Katheryn Taylor. Extrs. Wm. Alexander. Wits. Henry Puller, Thomas Christoffe, Margaret Younge. W.B. 8, p. 9.

BUSH, Isaac. Inventory. Recorded 11 May 1726. Hannah Bush and Saml. Brumley, Admrs. W.B. 10, p. 479.

BUSH, Hannah. Inventory and Appraisal. 12 Nov. 1736. Rec. 8 Apl. 1737. Returned by Wm. Sammon, Adm. W.B. 13, p. 31.

BUSH, John. Inventory. Rec. 15 May 1761. Returned by James Ball, Adm. W.B. 16, p. 143.

BUSH, James, of Christ Church Parish. Will. 16 Nov. 1765. Rec. 18 Aug. 1766.

Wife and children; son Peter Bush. Extrs. Wife, and son-in-law Peter Riveer. Wits. Jno. Hazard, Jno. Riveer, Joanna Riveer, Judith Hazard. W.B. 18, p. 67.

Above estate appraised, and recorded 15 Sept. 1766. Presented by widow, and proved by Jno. Hazard, Jno. Reveer and Joanna Reveer, wits. W.B. 17, p. 216.

Division of James Bush's estate 4 Jany. 1782. Rec. 21 Feby. 1782. W.B. 20, p. 224.

Margaret Bush, deceased. James Newby, Johnson Riveer, Jesse Robinson Jr. and Ozwald Newby have divided the same agreeable to last will and testament of James Bush, decd. to: James Bush, Peter Bush, Peter Riveer, Peggy Mason, Betty Bush and Nancy Bush.

BUTLER, Peter, of Christ Church Parish. Will. 25 Dec. 1716. Rec. 10 Jany. 1716.

Wife Mary; son Walter; daughters, Mary, Anne, Rebecca and

Judy. Extr. Jno. Grayson. Wits. Jno. Gibson, Tobias Roach, Wm. Rankin. W.B. 10, p. 189.

BUTLER, John. 16 Sept. 1765, John Butler, orphan of Wm. Butler bound to James Gibbs to learn trade of Ship-carpenter. W.B. 17, p. 168.

BUTLER, William. 16 March 1767. William Butler died without making a will. Certificate of administration granted to Wm. Griggs. W.B. 17, p. 237.

Division estate of Wm. Butler. 21 May 1767. Rec. 20 Aug. 1767. James Gibbs, who married with widow of Wm. Butler, one third; Wm. Griggs, Admr. for orphan two thirds. W.B. 18, p. 88.

BUXTON, John Jr. 11 August 1738. Robert McTire appointed guardian for Frances Buxton, orphan of John Buxton Jr., decd. W.B. 13, p. 110.

BUCKSTONE (Buxton), John, Jr. Appraisal Estate. May 12, 1738. Returned by Robert McTire, Admr. W.B. 13, p. 11.

BUXTON, Ann. Inventory. 11 July 1739. Rec. 13 July 1739.

(Her estate was from her daughter Frances.) Returned by Robert McTire.

* * * * *

BYERS, Alexander. Inventory. Recorded 14 June 1745. Returned by Geo. Ball, gent, Admr. W.B. 14, p. 81.

CALE, Nathaniel. Will. 25 Nov. 1690. Rec. 10 Dec. 1690.

Sisters: Mary Ives, Elizabeth King. Brother: Charles Cale; Uncle Raw. Travers. Requests he be buried at White Chapel Church by his grandfather-in-law. Wits. Jno. Mathews, Alex. Dane, Hen. Taft. W.B. 8, p. 8.

CALLAHAN, Darby. Will. 18 Jany. 1686. Rec. 10 June 1687.

Estate to be divided into four equal parts and to every one of my children I give one of these parts, only the estate of Eliza Brian, which I have disbursed for the estate of her father Robert Brian. Cozens, Geo. Philips, and James Philips. Brian Pullen, son of Henry Pullen, brother James Philips and Thos. Briant, Extrs. Wits. Peter James and Wm. Brasie. W.B. 5, p. 112.

CALLAHAHAN, John. Inventory and Appraisal. 10 Apl. 1741. Rec. 8 May 1741. Returned by Mary Callahan Admx. W.B. 13, p. 218.

CALLAHAN, Mary. Inventory. 8 Aug. 1761. Rec. 10 Dec. 1761. Returned by Chas. Rogers. W.B. 16, p. 180.

CAMPBELL, Alexander. Inventory and Appraisal. Returned by Rebecca Campbell, Admx. W.B. 13, p. 272.

CAMMELL, William. Will. Recorded 10 Feb. 1743.

Daughters: Betty and Sarah; Sons, James and Ezekiel Cambell. Not signed. Proved by oath of Chas. Coppedge. W.B. 14, p. 5.

Inventory of Wm. Cammell returned 13 Apl. 1744 by James Cammell. W.B. 14, p. 13.

Settlement of estate of James Cammell, 13 May 1752. Between James Cammell Adm. and Francis Timberlake, Gdn. of Ezekiel Cammell, orphan of sd William. W.B. 15, p. 95.

Settlement James Cammell's estate. 20 Aug. 1752. Rec. 21 Aug. 1752.

Sarah Cammell, orphan of Wm. Cammell, decd. her part of her decd. brother James Cammell's estate. By Thos. Edwards Jr., Wm. Haydon, Edney Tapscott. W.B. 15, p. 112.

CAMMELL, James. Deed of Gift. To daughter Jean, wife of John Norris—a female slave. Wits. Jno. Bailey, Geo. Davenport, Johnston Riveer. 15 Apl. 1757. Rec. 15 Apl. 1757. W.B. 15, p. 289.

CAMPBELL, Ezekiel. Will. 3 May 1757. Rec. 20 May 1757.

Aunt, Frances Kelley; Gr. father, Hugh Kelley; Mr. Nicholas Read; Mrs. Elizabeth Read; Gr. mother Mary Kelley, Uncles, Roger Kelley, Hugh Kelley, Winterbottom Kelley, and William Kelley. Extrs. Uncles, Roger and Hugh Kelley. Wits. Thos. Hunton, Nicholas Read, Wm. Kelley. W.B. 15, p. 292.

CAMMELL, James. Will. 11 Dec. 1761. Rec. 16 Sept. 1763.

Wife Hannah, from estate of her brother Geo. Shelton. Daughter, Maryanne Harris, daughter Jean Norris, daughter, Agnes Mitchell; son James Cammell. Friend Col. James Ball, who is to be Extr. Wits. Jno. Bond. W.B. 17, p. 21.

CAMMELL, James. 15 Dec. 1766. Sarah Cammell, widow, appointed Guardian to her child, Ann Conway. W.B. 17, p. 226.

Division of estate of above James Cammell. 16 Feby. 1767.

To widow; to dau. Ann Cammell, delivered to Sarah Cammell, Gdn.; George Cammell, delivered to Winifred Cammell, Gdn.; Ellin Cammell, delivered to Winifred Cammell, Gdn.; Hannah

Cammell, delivered to Winifred Cammell, Gdn.; Judith Cammell, delivered to Winifred Cammell, Gdn. W.B. 18, p. 76-77. Appraisement Estate 19 May 1766. Rec. 18 June 1766. W.B. 18, p. 62.

CAMPBELL, John. Will. 18 Jan. 1776. Rec. 21 March 1776.

Wife Lettice. At her death to be divided between her five children; Elizabeth, William, Rawley, Matthias and Sarah James. Niece Bessy Hunt. Extrs. Wife Lettice, Mr. Nicholas Campbell and Isaac Digges. Wits. Thos. Edwards, Chas. Lee, Thos. Carter. W.B. 20, p. 94.

CAMPBELL, Winifred. Will. 2 May 1781. Rec. 19 July 1781.

Son, George Campbell. Daughters: Ellen, Hannah and Judith Campbell. Extr. son George. Wits. Wm. Stonum, Betty Burn. W.B. 20, p. 200.

CAMPBELL, James. Jany. Ct. 1788. Rec. 18 Feby. 1788. James Brent and Sarah his wife, Gdns. to Ann Conway Campbell alias Elliott, orphan of James Conway, decd. By Edwin Conway, James Tapscott, Wm. Chowning. W.B. 22, p. 189.

CAMPIN, William. Will. 4 Dec. 1769. Rec. 15 Feby. 1770.

Wife (not named). Son William. Son-in-law, William. Extr. Jno. Robinson. Wits. Jno. Robinson, Reuben Doggett, Hannah Doggett. W.B. 18, p. 162.

CARNE, William. Will. 10 March 1656. Rec. 6 Aug. 1656.

Legatees: Jno. Watterman, Wm. Frissell. Wits. Jno. Ball, Jno. Needles. Loose papers.

CARNE, William. Will. 18 July 1656. Rec. 23 Sept. 1656.

To Jno. Watterman; Wm. Friele. Mentions debts from Thos. Barfoot, Francis Garner, Dunkyn Roy, Geo. Affeld, Jno. Colelo; Patrick Miller; James Bonner; Jno. Bell; Richd. Hacker; Lt. Col. Elliott; Andrew Certiff, Col. Gwinn. Wits. John Ball, Jno. Needles. W.B. 2, p. 38.

CARPENTER, Thomas. Inventory 11 March 1695. Rec. 10 Sept. 1695. Returned by Thos. Buckly. W.B. 8, p. 112.

CARPENTER, Nathaniel. Will. 4 Jany. 1725. Rec. 8 June 1726.

Wife (name not given). Son Nathaniel, my plantation. Daughters Hannah and Ellinor Carpenter. Wits. Thos. Chattin, Wm. Goodridge, Geo. Heale. W.B. 10, p. 480.

CARPENTER, Thomas, of Richmond county. Will. 19 Feby. 1718. Rec. 10 July 1728.

Wife Mary; Daniel Scurlock, 100 acres in Stafford County; Jno. Tarpley, the younger, Gr. son to Jno. Tarpley, Sr. Extrx. Wife. Wits. Jno. Tarpley, Susan Bryan, Hannah Kelley, Danl. Scurlock. W.B. 12, p. 60.

CARPENTER, Nathaniel. Will. Recorded 16 Dec. 1757.

Son, John Carpenter at death of his mother in law;. my dear and loving wife Frances Carpenter. Youngest daughter Rachel Carpenter. Daughter Ann Stott. W.B. 15, p. 312.

CARPENTER, John. Of Christ Church Parish. Will. 13 Jany. 1767. Rec. 20 Aug. 1767.

Wife, Ellen; sons: William and John; daughter Ann. Extrs. Wife and friends, Richard Miller, Thad. McCarty and Thos. Stott. Wits. Stephen Stott, Thos. George, Sarah Stoneham. W.B. 18, p. 84.

CARPENTER, Frances. Appraisement. 19 Jany. 1789. Rec. 18 March 1789. By Richard Goodridge, Jesse Robinson and James Norris. W.B. 18, p. 138.

CARROLL, William M. Inventory and Appraisal. Returned by Robt. Mitchell, gent. Admr. on 13 April 1744. W.B. 14, p. 22.

CARTER, John. Will. 10 Aug. 1689. Rec. 9 Nov. 1689.

God-daughter Frances Nash at age of 16; John Nash at age of 14; Thomas Nash at age of 14; Godson Elias Edmonds; Godson Damerson Parke; friend Wm. Nash, to be executor. Wits. Jno. Walker, Jno. Lomerford, Edw. Littlefield. W.B. 5, p. 133.

CARTER, John. Will. 15 September 1669. 6 January 1669.

Son, John Carter; son, Robert 1000 acres of land that was deserted by Col. Mathews and taken up by me, (vizt.) the neck of land that Wm. Thatcher and Wm. Hutchings has taken. Daughter, Elizabeth Utie. Wife, Elizabeth and her young son (whose name is intended to be Charles). Before marriage to present wife had made deed of gift to son John. Mr. Thomas Haynes, Mr. Thomas Maistard and Mr. David Miller to be appraisors of estate. Extr., son John. Codicil, 16 Sept. 1669. To cozen John Carter one hogshead of tobacco. Wits. David Mils, Edward Carter, Thos. Edmonds, Jos. Willis.

Bones of deceased wife and son George to be dug up and laid by me in the chancel of Christ Church Parish in Lancaster County, in a coffin. Loose wills.

CARTER, John. Will. 10 August 1687. Rec. 19 Nov. 1689.

Godson Elias Edmonds, god-daughter Frances Nash. Other devisees Thomas and John Nash. Wife, name not given. Extr. friend Wm. Nash. Wits. Jno. Walker, Jno. Lunsford, Edw. Litchfield. W.B. 5, p. 133.

CARTER, Col. John. Inventory. Jany. 27 1690/91. Rec. 10 July 1691.

Presented by Robert Carter, one of the overseers in the presence of Mr. Hancock Lee, Mr. Rowland Lawson, Dr. James Junio, Edward Herbert. Mentions things delivered to Madame Eliz. Wormley as part of legacy given her by will. W.B. 8, p. 20.

Note: On page 8, W.B. 8, is recorded that Col. John Carter, decd. did by his last will appoint Mrs. Elizabeth Carter, his daughter, Extrx., and her grandmother, his mother-in-law, his brother Robert and Mr. Morris, overseers.

* * * * *

CARTER, John. Will. 4 June 1690. Rec. 13 June 1690.

Wife, not named. Daughter, Elizabeth. Brothers, Robert and Charles Carter. Other devisees Mr. Jackson, Mr. Morris, Dr. Innis. Extrx. Dau. Elizabeth. Overseers daughter's grandmother, brother Robert and Mr. Morris. Wits. Jno. Morris, Jas. Innis. W.B. 8, p. 3.

CARTER, Col. Robert. Inventory. 13 March 1690/1. Rec. 15 March 1691.

Presented by Edwin Conway. W.B. 8, p. 31.

CARTER, Aaron. Inventory & Appraisal. 16 Apl. 1756. Rec. 21 May 1756. Returned by Martha Carter. W.B. 15, p. 249.

Division Aaron Carter's Estate. 19 Nov. 1772. Rec. 17 Dec. 1772.

Martha Carter 1/3, Katherine Carter 1/3, Molly Carter 1/3, Philip Brooks for his wife Elizabeth, one of daus. of Aaron Carter, 1/3; Mildred Carter 1/3, Aaron Carter 1/5, delivered to Martha Carter. By Richard Mitchell, Henry Tapscott, Wm. Sydnor. W.B. 20, p. 51.

CARTER, Catherine. Will. 3 May 1749. Rec. 14 July 1749.

Brothers Harry and Josiah Carter and Robert Carter. Sister, Ann Carter. Brother Harry's wife Lucretia. Extr. brother Henry Carter. Wits. Jno. Pullen, Jno. Carter, Dale Carter. W.B. 14, p. 248.

CARTER, Catherine. Will. 27 April 1788. 21 July 1788.

Sons, Edward (land) and Martin Carter. Daus. Catherine Bean and Hannah Hunton. Gr.daus. Mary and Catherine Kirk. Extrs. Edward Carter and Peter Bean. Wits. James Fleming, Wm. Garner, Peter Beane.

(22 July 1785. Mrs. Catherine Carter Gdn. orphans of James Kirk. W.B. 22, p. 95.)

CARTER, Charles. Letter to Richard Edwards, Clerk. Dated Corotoman Sept. 10, 1771.

Dear Sir: I have directed my Overseer, Isaac Pitman, to deliver to your care a little negro girl named Jenny, and I now declare by these few lines that I intend your son Thomas shall have an absolute property in together with her increase, as soon as he shall come to the age of 21 years, and in the meantime my will and intention that you take care of sd girl for the sd Thomas and that for so doing you have the use of her until your son Thomas comes of age, and no longer. Given under my hand and seal this 10th day of September in the year of our Lord seventeen hundred and seventy one.

Signed and sealed in presence of   Charles Carter (seal)
Isaac Pitman.   W.B. 20, p. 261.

CARTER, Dale. Will. 11 Dec. 1776. Rec. 19 Dec. 1776.

Wife Elizabeth Carter; sons, James, John, William, Augustine, Jeduthan, & Jesse. Daus. Ann Carter and Frankey Edwards. Extrs. Mr. James Gordon and James Carter. Wits. Spencer George, Geo. Carter, John Davis. W.B. 20, p. 100.

CARTER, Daniel. Division of Estate. Rec. 16 November 1759.

Elizabeth Carter 1/3; The rest divided in equal parts between children, vizt. Daniel Carter, John Carter, Francis Carter, William Kent, John Kent, John Kirk and Thomas Carter. W.B. 16, p. 75.

CARTER, Daniel. Appraisal. 20 Oct. 1794. Rec. 20 Jany. 1795. By Philip Warwick, Rawl. Davenport and John Dunaway. W.B. 22, p. 442.

CARTER, Edward, of Christ Church Parish. Will. 1 April 1783. Rec. 10 March 1784.

Wife Catherine. Sons Martin and Edward. Dau. Hannah Hunton wife of John Hunton. Grand daughters: Mary and Kath-

erine Kirk. Extrs. Wife Catherine, son Edward and Maj. Henry
Towles. Wits. James Gordon, Wm. Dunaway. W.B. 22, p. 17.

Appraisal of above estate 15 July 1784. W.B. 22, p. 32.

Division above estate Rec. 22 July 1785. by Wm. Warren, Wm.
Chowning, Jos. Shearman and Jno. Chowning. Heirs: Edward
and Martin Carter and Mrs. Carter. W.B. 22, p. 96.

Settlement with Martin Carter, 15 Sept. 1788. W.B. 22, p. 187.

CARTER, George. Appraised by James Brent, Martin Shearman and
Wm. Kirk. Rec. 16 Feby. 1789. W.B. 22, p. 202.

CARTER, George. Appraisal 17 Sept. 1792. Rec. 17 Dec. 1792. By
Lawson Hathaway, Nicholas Currell and Thomas Hunton. W.B.
22, p. 357.

CARTER, Geroge. Will. 4 Feby. 1791. Rec. 19 December 1791.

Wife Ellen Carter; son Joseph Carter, all my land. Daus. Jane
Berry and Ellen Phillips. Gr. Dau. Katy Chinn Carter. Extr.
son Joseph Carter. Wits. Matt. Myers, Ewell Webb. W.B. 22,
p. 322.

CARTER, Harry. Will 5 July 1775. Rec. 27 June 1784.

Wife Lucretia, son Thomas, daughters: Lucretia, Betty, Chloe,
Sinah. Extrx. Wife. Wits. Wm. Sanders, Joseph Locke, Milly
Miller. W.B. 22, p. 31.

Appraisal above estate rec. 15 July 1784. W.B. 22, p. 35.

CARTER, Henry. Will 21 March 1732. Rec. 10 Feby. 1743.

Sons, Gany, Harry, Robert (not 16) Josiah. Daughters: Kath-
erine, Ann and Elizabeth. Brother, Thomas Carter. Extr. cousin
Thomas, sons Gany, John and Harry. Wits. Thos. Carter, Thos.
Carter Jr., Edward Carter. W.B. 14, p. 6.

CARTER, John. Division estate. 18 Feb. 1777. Rec. 17 April 1777.

John Dogget possessed with 1/3 part of John Carter's estate having married Winifred Carter, one of the orphans of sd. John
Carter. Thomas Carter, Admr. W.B. 20, p. 109.

CARTER, John. Division estate. October Ct. 1782. Rec. 20 March
1783.

Widows dower; Spencer Carter's part of his father's estate, same
to Thomas Carter and Tapscott Oliver. By Henry Lawson, John
Bean, Benj. George, Presley Saunders. W.B. 20, p. 255.

CARTER, Joseph. Will. 12 Jany. 1764. Rec. 19 Aug. 1765.

Son Jermiah, land in Stafford and at death to his eldest son; son Joseph land in Stafford and Lancaster; son George land in Essex. Son Henry. To son Joseph. all negroes in Lancaster provided he gives his eldest sister's four children (by her first husband) 4000 lbs. tobacco, and 5000 lbs. tobacco to youngest sister Waters. Nephew Dale Carter. Extrs. son Joseph and nephew Dale Carter. Wits. Richd. Chichester, Edw. Carter, Gawin Lowry, Jno. Harris, Dale Carter. W.B. 18, p. 46.

CARTER, Joseph. Will. 1 July 1769. Rec. 18 July 1771.

Oldest daughter Maryan Bronaugh; wife Lettice Carter; children: Anthony, Alex., Sara hellen, Ann Pines, Joseph and Mary Page Carter. To Robt. Brent Esq. living in the county of Stafford 100 acres of land in that county where John Stark lives. Also owned land in Prince William county. Extrs. Wife Lettice, Thos. Myars, Matt. Myars and Dale Carter. Wits. Merryman Payne, Henry Carter, Wm. Boatman, Dale Carter. W.B. 20, p. 21.

Inventory above estate presented 17 Oct. 1771 by Lettice Carter, Matt. Myars and Dale Carter. W.B. 20, p. 29.

Division of Joseph Carters estate August Ct. 1778. Rec. 17 May 1781.

Mr. Rodham Lunsford who intermarried with the widow of sd. Jos. Carter. Samuel Haynie who intermarried with Ann P. Carter. W.B. 20, p. 192.

Settlement above estate. Rec. 16 September 1784.

Matt. Myers Extr. Mr. Rodham Lunsford in right of his wife Extrx. of Jos. Carter, James Ball, James Gordon, James Tapscott. W.B. 22, p. 51.

Division same. 22 July 1785. To Sarah Carter, heir. W.B. 22, p. 89.

CARTER, Josiah. Appraisal. recd. 15 July 1763. Returned by Betty Carter. W.B. 17, p. 11.

Division of Josiah Carters estate 20 Jany. 1768. Rec. 19 Jany. 1768.

Divided among widow and children Betty and Nancy Carter. W.B. 18, p. 107.

Record 25 Sept. 1782 of appointment of John Degge as Guardian for Nancy Carter, orphan of Josiah Carter. By Jno. Cundiff, Geo. Norris, Willm. Schofield. W.B. 20, p. 244.

CARTER, Martha. Inventory and Appraisement 29 Aug. 1782. Rec. 21 November 1782. By James Newby, Wm. Sydnor and Thos. Stott. W.B. 20, p. 244.

CARTER, Mary. Will. 10 Feby. 1792. Rec. 16 July 1793.

Sons Thomas Pollard and James Pollard. Daughter Mary James. Extrs. James Pollard and John James. Wits. Spencer Carter, Jno. Bean, Presley Saunders. W.B. 22, p. 349.

Note: Records of 18 June 1764 (W.B. 17, p. 50) show the appointment of John Carter and his wife Mary as Admrs. of Thomas Pollard.

CARTER, Moses. Will. 3 Jany. 1739. Rec. 11 Apl. 1740. Mother and two sisters. Brother Aaron Carter, sister Kettren Carter. Wits. Wm. Tyler and Ann Parrish. W.B. 13, p. 152.

Inventory this estate and appraisal, Recd. 7 May 1740. Returned by Robt. & Margaret Galbraith. W.B. 13, p. 161.

CARTER, Peter. Will. (Of St. Mary's White Chappell) 5 July 1721.

Wife Margaret, son Aaron, daughter Catherine. Wife's son Moses, plantation 1 now live on. Wife's daughter Margett. Extrs. Wife and his two brothers Thomas and Henry Carter. Wits. Edwd. Harris, Jos. Carter and Ann Carter. W.B. 10, p. 332. Record 11 Aug. 1738. John Pollard appointe Gdn. Aaron Carter, orphan of Peter Carter decd. W.B. 13, p. 106.

CARTER, Thomas. Will. 16 August 1700. Rec. 14, Nov. 1700.

Wife Katherine; sons: Edward, John, Henry, James and Thomas, to whom is given my now dwelling and plantation. Son Henry in England. Son-in-law, William George has recd. 1560 lbs. tobacco from estate of his gr.father in law, Edward Dale, given his wife. Extrs. Wife and Thomas Carter. Wits. Jno. Davis, Thos. White, Richd. Stephens. W.B. 8, p. 95.

CARTER, Thomas. Will. 24 Apl. 1728. Rec. 10 Oct. 1733.

Wife Arabella; sons: Thomas, land where I now live; Peter, land in King George Co., James, Dale, Charles, Edward, Joseph and Daniel. Gr.sons Jesse Carter and Thos. Carter. Extrs. Wife and son Peter. Wits. John Harry and Job Carter. W.B. 12, p. 279.

CARTER, Thomas. Will. (of Christ Church Parish. 17 Apl. 1735. Rec. 9 July 1735.

Wife Jane; sons Jesse and Thomas. Extrx. Wife. Wits. Henry, Harry, & Edw. Carter. W.B. 12, p. 342.

14 Apl. 1749. Thos. Carters Est. to Jesse Carter, orphan. W.B. 14, p. 236.

CARTER, Thomas. Will. 25 Sept. 1775. Rec. 19 Dec. 1776.

Sons: John, Edward, Thomas, Rawleigh, James and George Carter. Daughters: Judith Chilton, Millicent Cummings, Lucy Smither, Sarah McTire (a negro boy from estate of her 1st husband Robt. Henning Jr.) Alice Griggs. Dau. in law Ann Hunton. Gr.son Chas. Chilton, son of my dau. Mary, having already given his brother Thomas Chilton a like sum. Thomas Carter's son Edward Carter. Cousin, Dale Carter.

Extrs. Sons Edward and Rawleigh Carter. Wits. Dale Carter, Jeduthan James, Rich. Stephens and Wm. Stephens. W.B. 20, p. 98.

CARTER, Thomas. Will 20 Feb. 1781. Rec. 15 March 1781.

Wife Ann; brother Edward Carter. Extrs. Wife Ann and Thos. Towles. Wits. John Julian, Edward Carter and Thomas Towles. W.B. 20, p. 188.

CARTER, William. "Parish of Xt Church." Will 22 June 1728. Rec. 14 May 1735.

Mentions three children, but names only two, i.e. son Travis Carter and daughter Elizabeth Carter. Extrs. Daniel Carter and Isaac Currell. Wits. Solomon Horn. W.B. 12, p. 339.

CARTER, William. Inventory and Appraisal. Recorded 11 Apl. 1740. Returned by Winifred Carter. W.B. 13, p. 155.

CARTER, William. Appraisal by Wm. Dyman, Geo. Wale, Geo. Flower. Rec. 16 Dec. 1757. W.B. 15, p. 312.

Division estate of William Carter, recorded Mch 18, 1765.

Thomas Carter Guardian of William, George and Elizabeth Carter after widow's portion is set off. W.B. 18, p. 33. (Thos. Carters Apptmt. W.B. 17, p. 98.)

Further record of estate W.B. 18, p. 89, 17 Sept. 1767.

Division estate recorded 21 Jany. 1773. between George and Elizabeth Carter, by Harry Currell, Nicholas Currell, Thomas Lawson. W.B. 20, p. 52.

CARTER, William. Appraisal, rec. 16 Feb. 1790. By Jno. Miller, Henry Hinton, Jos. Kem. W.B. 22, p. 256.

CHAPLIN, James. Will. 18 Sept. 1682. Rec. 12 Jant. 1682/3.

All left to Rowland Lawson except a heifer to John Lawson.

Wits. Fortunatus Sydnor. Signed. Jo. Lawson, Ann. Bonison. W.B. 5, p. 83.

CHAPMAN, William. Will. 2 Sept. 1703. Rec. (no date).

Wife Grace, daughter Elizabeth. Extrs. Wife and Geo. Flower. Wits. Jno. Steeno, Thos. Simmons, Elizabeth Bell. W.B. 8, p. 137.

CHAMBERS, Robert. Will. 4 Feby. 1653. Rec. 10 April 1654.

Legatees: Jo. Weir; Francis Weir; Honner Place; Jow Hill an honest poor man living about Kent on Sevurne. Anthony Fullgham; Mrs. Taylor "in consideration of her charge and endeavor to cure me of my infirmities" Proceeds of sale of a shallop etc. to be distributed to the poor of God's children in Boston, in New England. Sale of Tobacco etc., to be divided equally between my mother-in-law, three aunts and sister Elizabeth. Extr. John Weir. Wits. Richard Coleman, Thomas Win. W.B. 2, p. 8.

CHAMBLETT, Randolph. Will. 15 Jany. 1658. Rec. 30 March 1659.

Legatees: God-son Randolph Segar, Danl. Johnson, Anne Thatchwell, child of Mary Bennett, George Marsh. Extrx. Anne Thatchwell. W.B. 2, p. 59.

CHAPMAN, William. Inventory recorded Feby. 9 1703/4. W.B. 10, p. 126.

CHARLES, Thomas. Will. Apl. 29 1743. Rec. 14 Oct. 1743.

Wife Elizabeth, son Chattin, daus. Betty, Susan, Sarah. Teste: Ste. Towles, Chattin Chowning. W.B. 14, p. 1.

CHATTWIN, Thomas. Will. 28 Feb. 1696/7. Rec. 14 Jany. 1698.

Wife, Elizabeth; sons: John, Thomas and Joseph; Daus. Jane, Ann, Hannah, Mary and Millicent. Extrx. Wife. Wits. Jno. Mott Jr., Jno. Stannen. W.B. 8, p. 86.

CHATWIN, Elizabeth. Will. 2 Aug. 1722. Rec. 10 Oct. 1722.

Brothers James and Stephen Wilkinson. Father-in-law John Wilkinson and mother. Extr. John Wilkason. Wits. Rich. Ball and Matthew Machen. W.B. 10, p. 404.

CHATTIN, Thomas. Will. 13 Nov. 1735. Rec. 12 May 1736.

Wife Margaret, land in Prince William County. Sons: Joseph, my dwelling and plantation; Thomas Chattin. Daughters: Ann, wife of Geo. Doggett; Margaret, Sarah, Frances and Mary Chattin. Extrs. Wife, Geo. Doggett and Joseph Chattin. Wits: Jno. Metcalf, Thos. Dallis, James Moss. W.B. 13, p. 5.

CHATTIN, Thomas:

Inventory estate returned 10 March 1748 by Sarah Chattin, Admnx. W.B. 14, p. 229.

Division estate, rec. 16 Jany. 1745/6. to Widow; Joseph and Thomas Chattin; Francis and Mary Chattin. W.B. 14, p. 102. Record 15 March 1753. Thomas Muse intermarried with Sarah, widow Thos. Chattin, decd. John Chattin, orphan of sd. Thos. Chattin. W.B. 15, p. 127.

CHATTIN, Margaret, widow. Will. 23 Aug. 1750. Rec. 21 April 1758.

Son. Joseph; daughter: Ann Doggett; daughter: Sarah Lumpkin; Gr.son John Chattin, son of my son Thomas Chattin, decd. Gr.dau. Mary Johnston dau. of my daughter Margaret Johnston, decd. Gr.dau. Sarah Johnston, dau. my dau. Margaret Johnston, decd. Daughters Frances Chatten and Mary Chattin. Extrs. Daus. Frances and Mary and Mr. Jos. Chinn. Wits. John Smith, Ann Smith, Hannah Flint. W.B. 16, p. 7.

Division above estate, 21 Apl. 1758: To Mr. Jesse Carter his part, to Mr. John Muse his part. W.B. 16, p. 15.

CHEATOM, John. Inventory Rec. 18 Apl. 1755. Returned by Mary Cheatom, Admx. W.B. 15, p. 202.

CHETWOOD, Thomas. Inventory, 10 Oct. 1678. Rec. 14 Nov. 1678. W.B. 5, p. 51.

CHETWOOD, Thomas, Inventory and Appraisal. Rec. 9 Apl. 1746. Returned by Turner E. Chetwood, Adm. W.B. 13, p. 269.

CHETWOOD, Elizabeth, widow of Turner Chitwood. Deed gift, Rec. 15 August 1760, of present dwelling and plantation to children Betty, George, William and Rachel Chitwood. Stokely Towles, Trustee. W.B. 16, p. 105.

CHITWOOD, William. Will. 27 Apl. 1788. Rec. 21 July 1788.

Three children (no names) Extrs. Geo. Chitwood, Matt. Myars, Jesse Chelton. Wits. Jos. Stephens, Wm. Garner, Wm. Warrick, Geo. Biscoe. W.B. 22, p. 183.

Appraisal above estate, rec. W.B. 22, p. 188.

CHICHESTER, John, gent. Estate, recorded 9 October 1728, with Richard Chichester, Adm. W.B. 12, p. 73.

CHICHESTER, Ann. Will. 9 Feby. 1725. Rec. 10 Dec. 1729.

Husband, Richard Chichester; Aunt, Dorathea, wife of Jeremiah Greenham of Richmond county; Niece, Ellen Heale; Nephew, Joseph Chinn son of my brother Raw. Chinn; Thomas Chinn; Chichester Chinn; Ann Chinn; Sarah Chinn, children of my brother. Nephew Raw. Chinn, son of brother Raw. Chinn; John Chinn. Capt. Geo. Heale; William Payne and wife, Wm. Heale, Geo. Heale Jr., Ann Heale and Catherine Heale; Elizabeth Heale; Catherine Lindsay; Catherine Kirk; Sarah Heale; James Atchison. Extr. Rawleigh Chinn. Wits. Edmund Currell, Eliz. Heale, Catherine Quirk. W.B. 12, p. 123.

Inventory above estate returned by Rawleigh Chinn, Extr. 13 May 1730. W.B. 12, p. 172.

CHICHESTER, Richard. Will 14 April 1734. Rec. 12 June 1734.

Nephew Chichester Chinn, son of Rawleigh Chinn; Priscilla Reeves, dau of Amie Palmer, decd. Cousin Thos. Ware, son of Thomas & Eleanor Ware, to youngest dau. of him if such be found. She is to be heard of at Silverton at Mr. Ware's house at Dunnex, Silverton Town, 5 miles out of the city of Exton or at Lilliston in the parish of North Curry 4 miles out of Tanton in Sumersetshire. W.B. 12, p. 310.

CHICHESTER: Deposition dated 8 Apl. 1743, Rec. 8 Apl. 1743. of Henry Carter, aged 67 years; that he is well acquainted with Richard Chichester of the county of Lancaster and knew his father Mr. John Chichester and his mother Mrs. Chichester, and was intimately acquainted with Richard Chichester Esq., father of sd John Chichester and grandfather of sd Richard Chichester, and that the sd. John Chichester came into this county to his father Richard Chichester Esqr. and that sometime after the foresd. Mrs. Chichester and her son Richard Chichester came in the ship Brimton, of Weymouth, Giles Russell, Master, and that the sd. Richard was then a child but what age he was he knows not; that he lived here some years with his father and mother, and then his mother and he returned to England and lived for some years there; and that after the death of his mother he came back to Virginia to his grandfather, Richard Chichester Esq., and the sd Mrs. Chichester, during her stay here had no other child or children. W.B. 13, p. 318.

Deposition of Joseph Carter (made and recorded same date as above) aged about 54 years:

That he was well acquainted with Richard Chichester, who was Collector of Rappahannock River for many years, and there came a certain gentleman to Virginia, named John Chichester, which the sd. Richard acknowledged as his son, and after the sd John had lived some time in Virginia a gentlewoman came to him from England named Elizabeth Chichester, whom the sd. John Chichester received and acknowledged to be his wife and the aforesaid Richard received & acknowledged to be his son's wife. Sd. Elizabeth brought with her a son, very young, about4 or 5 years of age, who was called Richard Chichester and who was acknowledged as Child of John Chichester and grandson of Richard. After some years the sd Elizabeth was desirous to go home to England and carried her son Richard. John became ill with gout and very weak and wrote his wife in England, directed to Mrs. Eliza Chichester, Dorset. John Chichester then died and according to his will his father Richard Chichester administered on the estate. Sd. Richard wrote a letter to his son's wife's friends in England to send her son to Virginia as soon as possible and the letter was directed to Mr. Chiliot Symes, brother of Mrs. Eliza. Chichester. Sd. Richard son of John returned to America and lived with his grandfather Richard Chichester until his death in May 1734. W.B. 13, p. 319.

CHICHESTER, Richard. Will. 16 May 1743. Rec. 10 Aug. 1744.
Wife Ellen; Sons: Richard and John; Daughters: Elizabeth, Ellen, Mary and Hannah. Mentions estate in England. Extrs. Wife Ellen, son John; friends: Jesse Ball, Robt. Mitchell and Jos. Carter, Amy Carter, Gawin Lowry, Michael Dillon. W.B. 14, p. 29.
Record 10 Mch. 1748 of settlement of estate. Mr. Wm. Downman's part in right of his wife Ellen, widow of sd. Richard. W.B. 14, p. 232.

CHICHESTER, John. Will. 14 Sept. 1753. Rec. 15 March 1754.
Wife Jean, plantation I now live on. Dau. Mary Chichester; brother Richard Chichester, four sisters, Elizabeth, Ellen, Mary and Hannah. Brother Rawleigh Downman; Miss Elizabeth Griffin. Extrs. James Ball, Jr., Richd. Chichester. No witnesses. W.B. 15, p. 168.

CHICHESTER, Richard. Division of Personal Estate. Rec. 15 June 1757.
To Miss Hannah Chichester, Mrs. Jean Chichester, Miss Ellen

Chichester, Mr. Richard Chichester, Miss Mary Chichester. Mrs. Jean Chichester Admr. of Mr. John Chichester and Richard, Ellen, Mary and Hannah, orphans of sd. Richard. W.B. 15, p. 294.

CHILTON, Thomas. Inventory 8 July 1699. Rec. 16 July 1699. Presented by Mich. Chilton, relict. W.B. 8, p. 91.

CHILTON, George. Will. 21 Mch. 1708. Rec. 13 Apl. 1709. Wife Elizabeth, brother William. Extrx. Wife. Wits. Thos. Barker, Jno. Pynes, Danl. Gaines. W.B. 10, p. 1.

CHILTON, Stephen. Will. 8 Oct. 1717. Rec. 13 Augt. 1718. Sons: William, Charles, George, Benoni & Andrew. Friend John Coppedge. Wife, Mary. Gr.son Thomas Chilton; daughter Margaret. Extrs. sons George and William. Wits. John Rhodes, Richard Curtis, Benj. Dogget. W.B. 10, p. 269.

CHILTON, George. Will. 17 Oct. 1726. Rec. 12 Feb. 1728. Wife Elizabeth. Legatees: Geo. Chilton, son of Benoni Chilton; brother Wm. Chilton; Stephen, son of Wm. Chilton; William son of Wm. Chilton; Godson, Geo. Purcell. Samuel, Benoni and George, sons of Benoni Chilton. Stephen & Will, sons of Will Chilton. Wife's daughter Elizabeth Purcell and wife's gr.dau. Judith Purcell and her son George. Extrx. Wife. Wits. Margaret & John Miller, Edwin Conway. W.B. 12, p. 82.

Appraisement & Inventory above estate returned 5 Mch. 1728 by Elizabeth Smith, late Elizabeth Chilton, Admx. W.B. 12, p. 51.

CHELTON, Henry (Christ Church Parish). Will. 6 Mch. 1723. Rec. 5 Apl. 1730. Wife Mary; Sons: William, John, James; Daughter: Winifred. Overseers: Jerome Pasquet, Geo. Brent. Wits. Wm. Parlor, Henry Pasquet.

CHILTON Benoni, (Christ Church Parish). Will. 29 April 1730. Rec. 14 March 1732. Wife Ann. Children: Jane and George, eldest; five youngest Judith, Stephen, John, Mary and Lazarus. Extrs. Wife, cousin Stephen Chilton, brothers Charles and Andrew Chilton. Wits. Wm. Miller, Geo. Connelly, Eliz. Connelly. W.B. 12, p. 246.

CHILTON, Thomas. Appraisal. Rec. 9 Mch. 1738. Returned by Winifred Chilton. W.B. 13, p. 127.

CHILTON, Charles. Will. 24 Aug. 1739. Rec. 12 Oct. 1739.

Son Edwin; Daus. Leannah and Hannah. Extr. son Edwin. Overseers Wm. Edmonds and Dale Carter. Wits. Henry Tapscott, Jno. George, Robt. Horton. W.B. 13, p. 143.

CHILTON, William. Will. 22 Sept. 1739. Rec. 8 May 1741.

Wife Rebecca; Sons: Stephen and William; Daus: Rebecca, Winifred, Judith, and Sarah Chilton. Grand daughter Mary. Extrs. Wife, son Stephen, son-in-law Stephen Mullis. Wits. Robt. Horton, Dale Carter, Henry Tapscott.

CHILTON, Thomas. 14 April 1749 Wm. Taylor, gent, appointed Guardian of Ezekiel Chilton, and Millicent Chilton, orphans of Thos. Chilton. W.B. 14, p. 234.

CHILTON, William. Will. November 1748. Rec. 11 Augt. 1749.

Brother, Stephen Chilton; Wife Mary Ann; sister Judy; Brother-in-law, Jno. Hobson. Godson, Wm. Chilton son of my brother Stephen Chilton. Extr. Dale Carter. Wits: George ————? W.B. 14, p. 253.

CHILTON, Ezekiel. Will. 9 Jany. 1754. Rec. 19 July 1754.

Sister Millicent Chilton. Brother-in-law John Gressett, son of "my mother." Extrs. Friend Dale Carter and Lee Griggs. Wits. Lee Griggs, Jno. Pasquet, Dale Carter. W.B. 15, p. 174.

CHILTON, William. Will. Recorded 21 Nov. 1755.

Son George Chilton; daughter Hannah Chilton. Extr. son George. Wits. Berryman Payne, Dale Carter. W.B. 15, p. 230.

Inventory above Wm. Chilton returned Jany. 14 1756 by Geo. Chilton, Extr. W.B. 15, p. 236.

CHILTON, George. Will. 10 July 1759. Rec. 17 Aug. 1759.

Brothers: William, Richard, Stephen, Thomas, and son of latter George. Sister Sarah Davis. To Judith Davis, dau. of John Davis. To Mr. James Cammell. Extr. Mr. James Cammell. Wits. Gawin Lawry, Margaret Connelly. W.B. 16, p. 67.

CHILTON, Stephen. Will. Sept. 19, 1761. Rec. 18 Dec. 1761.

Wife Jemima; brother William Chilton decd. and after the death of his widow, Maryann Chilton land left me by my father, and brother William. Two youngest sons William and Stephen. "All my children" (no other names). Extrs. Wife and Col. Wm. Tayloe and "my couin Wm. Chilton" and Dale Carter. Wits. Jno. Davis, Eliza Davis, Dale Carter. Codicil, 8 Nov. 1761,

"Youngest child Sarah Ann, (not 16). Wits. Stephen Chilton Jr., Winifred More, Dale Carter. W.B. 16, p. 180.

On 20 Augt. 1782 "I do hereby certify that Jemima Brooks, (late Chilton) made oath as to inventory of her deceased husband, Stephen Chilton's estate." W.B. 16, p. 180.

CHILTON, Judith. 19 Jany. 1767. Will proved by oath of Dale Carter and Moses Chilton.

Will of above Judith Chilton, 15 Dec. 1766. Rec. 19 Jany. 1766. Mother, Ann Chilton; brothers: Stephen and Moses Chilton; sister Mary; cousin Jemima Chilton. Extrs. Brothers Stephen and Moses Chilton & Dale Carter. Wits. Dale Carter, Thos. Chilton, James Carter. W.B. 18, p. 75.

CHILTON, Edwin. Will. 1 Jany. 1772. Rec. 21 March 1771.

To Wm. Davis, "my wife's brother." Sons William and Jesse. Wife Hannah. "All my children" (No names). Extrs. Wife Hannah, brother-in-law Wm. Davis, son Thomas and Dale Carter. Wits. Dale Carter. W.B. 20, p. 12.

18 April 1771. Will disputed by heirs at law. W.B. 20, p. 14.

16 Aug. 1771. Hannah Chilton, widow, her dower in estate of decd. husband Edwin Chilton. W.B. 20, p. 25.

CHILTON, Thomas. Appraisement. by Jas. Carter, Coleman Doggett, Spencer George. Rec. 20 Mch. 1777. W.B. 20, p. 104.

CHILTON, Charles. Appraisement by Spencer George, Stephen Chilton, Stephen Chilton Jr. Rec. 15 May 1777. W.B. 20, p. 112.

CHILTON, Moses. Will. 11 Feby. 1778. Rec. 19 March 1778.

Sister, Mary Chilton; Cozens: Judith Chilton, Betty Chilton. Extrs. Col. Jesse Ball and James Newby. Wits. James Newby, Eleazer Robinson. W.B. 20, p. 116.

Dec. 1778, Rec. 18 March 1779. Jonathan Pullen allotted certain articles and land for his wife's dower in estate of Moses Chilton. W.B. 20, p. 157.

CHILTON, Stephen. Inventory 20 Nov. 1777. Rec. 19 Feb. 1779 by Jas. Newby, Coleman Doggett, James Carter. W.B. 20, p. 124.

CHILTON, Ann. Inventory 20 Nov. 1777. Rec. 19 Feb. 1778 by Jas. Newby, Coleman Doggett and James Carter. W.B. 20, p. 125.

CHILTON, Charles. Settlement estate. 18 June 1778. Rec. 15 Oct. 1778. James Carter, Adm. Jemima Chilton, Guardian of her children.

CHILTON, Moses. 24 Dec. 1778. Rec. 24 Dec. 1778. James Newby Guardian of Newman Chilton orphan of Moses Chilton. W.B. 20, p. 169.

Jany. 1783. Elias Edmonds apponted Guardian. W.B. 20, p. 254.

CHILTON, William. Appraisement by Jno. Yerby, Jno. Miller & James Carter. Rec. 17 Sep. 1787. W.B. 22, p. 155.

CHILTON, Moses. Estate. By Wm. Sydnor & Ran'h. Tapscott 3 Nov. 1783. Rec. 15 Jany. 1784. W.B. 22, p. 9.

CHILTON, John. Division of Estate. Rec. 19 October 1786.

To Pheby Chilton, widow; Wm. Chilton, George Chilton, Mildred Robinson, Ellen Forrester and John Chilton. By Jas. W. Ball, Wm. Warren, Johnson Riveer and Ozwald Newby. W.B. 22, p. 138.

CHILTON, Edwin. Estate. 30 Jany. 1787. Rec. 19 Feb. 1787.

Sarah Chilton, daughter of Edwin Chilton and wife of Baker Angel. John Dye former guardian. By James Ball, Jr., and James Newby. W.B. 22, p. 142.

CHILTON, William. Will. 31 December 1790. Rec. 18 May 1791.

Sons: William & Richard Chilton; Daughter, Hannah Carter; Gr.sons: Merryman Chilton and William Chilton. Extrs. Sons William and Richard. Wits. Henry Towles, Wm. Chowning, Wm. Biscoe. W.B. 22, p. 305.

Appraisal above estate 21 Sep. 1791. Rec. 16 Apl. 1792 by Matt. Myers, Wm. Biscoe, Thos. Shelton, Joseph Carter. W.B. 22, p. 335.

CHELTON, William. Will. 6 October 1790. Rec. 18 July 1791.

Wife (no name); son: Mereman Chilton; Daus. Sally Carter, Lucy McTire, Milly Jones. Gr.dau. Judy Carter Chelton. Extrs. Machen Myers, Jos. Carter, Mereman Chilton. Wits. Geo. Carter, Wm. Warrick, Benj. Warrick. W.B. 22, p. 307.

CHINN, John. Will 15 Dec. 1691. Rec. 13 May 1692.

Wife, Alice; Sons: John and Rawleigh; Son John Trussell and my daughter Elizabeth his wife; Son, Thomas Chilton and my daughter Sarah Chilton his wife. Daughters: Ann and Kaatherine Chinn. Extrx. Wife Alice. Wits. Wm. Smith, Alex. Dun, Edw. Geffrey. W.B. 8, p. 34.

CHINN, Rawleigh. Will. July & August 1741. Rec. 12 March 1741/2.

Legatees: Sons; Joseph (land in Prince William County) Thomas; Chichester (land in Richmond and King George counties); Rawleigh; daughter Ann Shearman; Gr.son Rawleigh Shearman, (land in Prince William Co.) godson, Charles, son of Margaret Downman; Christopher and Elijah sons of sd Margaret Downman; Celia Nichols, daughter of Elizabeth Nichols; Joseph Durham, Dominick Newgent, Bryan Stott, Easter Chinn, and Wm. Glascock. Extr. Son Rayleigh Chinn. W.B. 13, p. 253.

CHINN, Easter. Will. 2 August 1749. Rec. 10 May 1751.

Sons: Joseph, Rawleigh and Thomas Chinn; Daughter Ann Shearman; Heirs of Chichester Chinn; Gr.son Rawleigh Shearman, son of Martin Shearman and Ann his wife; Gr.daughter Mary Shearman, dau. of Martin Shearman and Ann his wife. Gr.dau. Easter Shearman. Wits. Henry Tapscott, Margaret Tapscott. W.B. 15, p. 32.

CHINN, Easter. Inventory 10 May 1751. Rec. 14 June 1751. Returned by Easter Chinn, Extrx. W.B. 15, p. 41.

CHINN, Rawleigh. Appraisal and Division. Rec. 15 October 1756. Returned by Ann Chinn. Widow's part; Mr. Francis Christian's part; Miss Ann Chinn's part. W.B. 15, p. 267.

18 Feby. 1757. Division of land between Francis Humphrey Christian and Katherine his wife and Ann Chinn, daughter and coheir of sd Rawleigh Chinn. W.B. 15, p. 267.

CHINN, Thomas (of St. Mary's Parish). 8 Dec. 1767. Rec. 21 Jany. 1768.

Sons: Robert (plantation); Rawleigh; Thomas (land in Loudon Co.). Daughters: Easter and Susannah Chinn; Ann Elder, dau. of Sarah Elder; Three youngest children, Rawleigh, Easther and Susannah Chinn. Dominick Newgent. Extr. son Robert. Wits. Newgent, Ellen x Carpenter, Rawleigh Chinn. W.B. 18, p. 98.

Division above estate. 21 Jany. 1768. Rec. 18 Feby. 1768. to Rawleigh, Easther, Susanna and Robert Chinn. W.B. 18, p. 103.

CHINN, Joseph. Will. 1 June 1771. Rec. 19 May 1774.

Son: John Chinn; Daughter: Ann Edwards; daughter: Elizabeth Montague; Gr.daughters Jane Montague and Priscilla Chinn; Gr.sons Joseph Chinn and John Yates Chinn. Extr. son John.

Wits. Henry Tapscott, Will Pearcefull, James Warrick. W.B. 20, p. 71.

CHINN, Mrs. Ann, decd. Estate. 23 Feby. 1784. Rec. 18 Mch. 1784. Inventory. By Ran'h. W. Downman, Wm. Carpenter and Wm. Sydnor. W.B. 22, p. 22.

CHINN, Rawleigh. Division estate etc. Recorded 15 April 1784.

Among representatives of dau. Catherine, wife of Francis E. Christian and Ann, wife of Thaddeus McCarty. No. 1 to Mrs. Ann Lawson; No. 2 to Catherine; No. 3 to Mary; No. 4 to Mrs. Elizabeth Craine, No. 5 to Fanny; No. 6 to Frederick; Catherines representatives. No. 1 Mr. Rawleigh Christian; No. 2 Mr. John Christian, No. 3 Mr. Francis Christian, No. 4 to Mrs. Ann Carter. By Ran. W. Downman, Wm. Carpenter, Wm. Sydnor, Thos. Stott. W.B. 22, p. 23.

CHINN, Robert (Christ Church Parish). 16 June 1779. Rec. 18 March 1784.

Legacies to son Robert (not 21) plantation on which he lives). Dau. Sarah, Elizabeth, Susannah, Mary, and Ann Mitchell Chinn. Extrs. Richd. Mitchell, Thos. Belfield, Griffin Fauntleroy and Jno. Chinn. Wits. James Ewell, Martin Tapscott, Henry Rem, Wm. Tapscott. W.B. 22, p. 15.

Appraisal above estate 17 Nov. 1785. W.B. 22, p. 106.

Division of estate Rec. 16 March 1786. To Sarah, eldest daughter, wife of Wm. Fauntleroy Sydnor. Other children (no names) by James Ball, J. B. Downman, Richd. Mitchell. W.B. 22, p. 117.

Division, recd. 21 April 1788. To daughter Susannah, wife of Samuel Kercheval. By Jas. Ball, Raw. W. Downman, Wm. Sydnor, Wm. Carpenter. W.B. 22, p. 182.

Division Rec. 21 Dec. 1789. Mary Chinn, orphan, Saml. Kercheval, Gdn. Robert, Nancy and Elizabeth Chinn. W.B. 22, p. 241.

CHINN, John. Will (of Christ Church Parish). 10 Jan. 1791. Rec. 25 Feb. 1791.

Wife, Sarah; Sons: Joseph, John Yates (land in Richmond county) Bartholomew; William (not 21) and Rawleigh; Daughters: Sarah Yates; Elizabeth; Priscilla Downman and her daughter Fidelia Downman. Extrs. Joseph Chinn, Jno. Yates Chinn, Bartholomew Chinn. Wits. James Ball, Robt. Clerk, Raw. W. Downman, Wm. Hunt. W.B. 22, p. 292.

Appraisement estate recorded W.B. 22, p. 318.

Division of estate, Rec. 16 Feb. 1795. Heirs: Widow; Miss Eliz. Chinn; John Y.; Rawleigh; Joseph; William and Bartho. Chinn; Mrs. Sarah Y. Smith, Miss Fidelia Downman. By James Ball, Martin Shearman, Spencer Ball. W.B. 22, p. 443.

CHINN, Sarah. Division dower of late husband, John Chinn. 19 Jany. 1795. Rec. 17 Feb. 1795.

Heirs: Joseph Chinn; Dr. Jno. Y. Chinn; Bartho. Chinn; Jno. M. Smith (for wife's part) Eliz. Chinn; William Chinn, Raweligh Chinn. By Jas. Ball, J. B. Downman, Martin Shearman, Spencer Ball. W.B. 22, p. 446.

CHOWNING, Thomas. Will. 14 Jany. 1678. Rec. 16 Jan. 1688.

Wife Ann (also Extrx) Sister, Katherine Gregory; god-dau. Margaret Merriman; Cozen Thomas Chowning, Cozen Robert Chowning, Cozen Katherine Chowning. Wits. David Fox and Richard Flint. W.B. 5, p. 128.

CHOWNING, George. Will. 15 January 1718. Rec. 12 June 1717.

Son: Chatting; Daughter, Rachel. Extrs. Wife, (no name) and Wm. Payne. Wits. Henry Towles, John Chowning, Henry Johnson.

Proved by oath of Mary Chowning, one of Extrs. W.B. 10, p. 221.

CHOWNING, Chattin. Will. 11 December 1770. Rec. 16 Aug. 1771.

Wife, Elizabeth; Sons: William, John and Thomas; Daughters, Mary Dunaway, Margaret and Nancy Chowning; Gr.son Chattwin Chowning. Extrs. Wife, and son William. Wits: Thos. Towles, Stockley Towles, Nicholas Payne. W.B. 20, p. 57.

Inventory above estate presented by son Wm. Chowning 17 Oct. 1771. W.B. 20, p. 28.

CHOWNING, George. Appraisement 5 July 1773. Recd. same day. Presented by Hannah and William Chowning. By Gavin Lawry, Henry Carter, Matt Myars. W.B. 20, p. 61.

CHRISTIAN, Oliver. Will. 9 Sept. 1702. Rec. 14 October 1702.

Daughter, Ann Christian (not 18) (Richard Wood and his wife shall have nothing to do with my daughter). Extr. friend Bryan Phillips. Wits. John Stott, Thos. Chattin, Jon Mares. W.B. 8, p. 226.

CHRISTIAN, Chris. Appraisal, recorded 21 Jan. 1793 by Francis Rock, Peter Mason and Charles Dodson. W.B. 22, p. 208.

CHRISTOPHER, John. Appraisal, rec. 20 July 1795 by Henry Hinton, Thos. Ingram, Lawson Hathaway. W.B. 22, p. 460.

CLAPHAM, William. Rec. 6 October 1652. Wm. Clapham having married the relict of Epa. Lawson is granted administration of his estate. W.B. 1, p. 16.

CLAPHAM, William, Jr. Will. 16 Jany. 1659. Rec. 1 August 1660. Wife, Elizabeth; Son William, land on Hathaway's Creek in Fleet's Bay; Daughter Ann, and an unborn child. Extrs. Wife and brother-in-law Thos. Madestard. Wits. Thos. Hadestard, Will Lippett, T. Hunter. W.B. 2, p. 75.

CLAPHAM, William. Inventory. 8 Sept. 1675. Rec. 1 Oct. 1676. Returned by Jane Clapham. By Thos. Carter, Nicholas Wren, Jno. Carter, appraisers. W.B. 5, p. 34.

CLARKE, William. Inventory Rec. 12 Sept. 1688. Returned by Elizabeth Reeves (?) relict. W.B. 5, p. 125.

CLARKE, Nicolas. Will. 21 May 1709. Rec. 14 Jany. 1710. Wife Anne; brother James. Extrx. Wife. Wits. Mary Vose, Mel. Waters, Jos. Brossier. W.B. 10, p. 12.

CLARKE, Arthur. Will. 2 April 1718. Rec. 11 June 1718. Daughter Sarah; William Reeves brother. Father-in-law, Jno. Reeves and mother. To Wm. Reeves all lands in Accomac Co. Extrs. John and William Reeves. Wits. Eliz. Lyon, Wm. Lewis, Giles Lawrence. W.B. 10, p. 264.

CLARK, William. Will. Recorded 8 June 1750. Sons, Daniel, William, John and Benjamin Clark. Wife Winifred. Young children Oliver, Robert and Winifred. Extrs. Wife and friend Nicholas Martin. Wits. Anthony Garton, Hugh Kelly, Wm. Martin. W.B. 14, p. 288.

Appraisement Rec. 12 October 1750. returned by Winifrede Clark, Extrx. W.B. 14, p. 313.

CLARK, William. Appraisement. 20 Jany. 1764. Rec. 17 Feby. 1764. By Benjamin Kelly, Thomas Lawson, Epa. Lawson. W.B. 18, p. 1.

CLARK, William. Division of estate. December 1789. Rec. 19 April 1790. Heirs: Widow; Robert Clark; Baldwin Robinson, decd. (son of Elizabeth Clark the late wife of Eppa Robinson—the said Eppa heir at law to the said Baldwin) Joanna Clark, decd., (Robert

Clark heir at law). By Jas. Ball, Raw. W. Downman, Rawleigh Tapscott. W.B. 22, p. 258.

CLAYLAND, Allen. Inventory. 9 May 1688. Rec. 12 August 1688. Presented by Rebecca Corroll, relict. W.B. 5, p. 120.

CLEATON, Judith. Inventory. Rec. 10 May 1710. Presented by Darby Bryan. W.B. 10, p. 59.

CLAYTON, Charles. Inventory. 13 May 1748. Rec. 1748, June 10. Returned by Jas. Waugh, Extr. W.B. 14, p. 199.

CLAYTON, John. Will. 18 Feby. 1787. Rec. 18 June 1787.

Sons: William W. (land on which I now live); John E. Clayton. Daughters: Judah and Betty Clayton. Extrs. Wm. Kirk and Martin Shearman. Wits. Ezekiel Tapscott, Jno. Tapscott, Jno. Sullivant. W. B. 22, p. 151.

Appraisal of this estate Rec. 16 July 1787. W.B. 22, p. 153.

CLAYTON, William W. Appraisal. Rec. 15 September 1794. By Presley Sanders, Wm. Haydon and Thomas Haydon. W.B. 22, p. 438.

CLEMENS, William. Inventory recorded 10 Apl. 1689 by Ann Chowning. W.B. 5, p. 132.

CLEPHON, Charles. Will. 20 Sept. 1745. Rec. 18 May 1748.

Daughters: Betty, Ann, (furniture that was called her mothers); Son: John; Wife Eliza (should she die without lawful heir). Extrs. James Rob and James Waugh. Wits. Wm. Shelton, Benj. Shelton, Robt. Briscoe. W.B. 14, p. 195.

CLUTTON, Jesse. Appraisal 18 Apl. 1791. Rec. 20, Feb. 1792. By Hopkins Harding, Alexander Davis, Richard Nutt. W.B. 22, p. 325.

CLUTTON, John. Will 18 Oct. 1783. Rec. 10 March 1784.

Wife Phebe (plantation in Northumberland and Lancaster); Son John; Grand daughter Nancey Forrester. Extrs. wife, son John, Robt. Chinn. Wits. Thos. Mitchell, Richard Newby, Robt. Angell. W.B. 22, p. 10.

COATES, William. Inventory and appraisal, 8 June 1726. Rec. 13. July 1726. Presented by Mary Coates. W.B. 10, p. 501.

COATS, Thomas. Will 17 June 1748. Rec. 14 April 1749.

Son James; wife Martha; Daughters: Jane, Betty, Rachel and Sarah. Extrx. Wife. Wits. Daniel Magret, Anne Pratt. W.B. 14, p. 234.

COATS, John. Inventory, recorded 10 Feby. 1765. By Peter Miller, Saml. Brooks & Stephen ——? W.B. 18, p. 30.

COATS, George. Will. April 10 1769. Rec. 16 Nov. 1769.

Wife Susanna; daughter Fanny Coats; Children: Jesse Coats; Rawleigh Coats; Winney Mason; Ellin Runs; Betty Davis. Daughter Susannah Wells. Son John Coats. Extrs. Wife and James Newby. Wits. Thos. Pollard, James Newby. W.B. 18, p. 154.

CODD, St. Leger, of Cecil County, Md. Will. 9 July 1706. Rec 8 Sept. 1708.

Wife (no name) Sons: James (all lands in county of Kent); Berkely, (all lands in Corrotoman); St. Leger (land in Cecil Co. bought of Jno. Salisbury); Daughters: Beatrix, and Mary Paddison. Extrs. Sons Berkeley and St. Leger Codd and Thos. Smythe. Wits. Henry Anderson, Thos. Simson, Locklau Orchall and Rebecca Simson. W.B. 9, p. 264.

COCKRELL, Presley. Inventory. Rec. 19 Sept. 1763. By Robt. Walker, Spencer George, Moses George. W.B. 22, p. 2.

COFFEY, Hugh. Inventory. 12 June 1717. Rec. 10 July 1717. Returned by Francis Waddy, Adm. W.B. 10, p. 229.

COLE, Francis. Will. 1 July 1658. Rec. 1 October 1658.

Wife Alice (all plantation where I now live) Daughters Frances and Mary; Francis Brown, son of Francis Brown; Mr. Roger Radford. John Burroughs, servant. Extrs. Wife and daughter Frances. Wits: Roger Radford, Edward Dale. W.B. 2, p. 54.

COLEMAN, Richard. Inventory. 14 Oct. 1743. Rec. 11 Nov. 1743. Returned by Charity Coleman, Admx. W.B. 14, p. 2.

COLLINS, James. Inventory. 3 Aug. 1705. W.B. 10, p. 262.

CONE, John. Will. 6 Dec. 1697. Rec. 11 Feb. 1701.

Wife Elizabeth; Sons: George, John, Edward (the plantation where I now live) Daughters: Augustina, Mary Pursley, Margaret and Elizabeth Cone. Sons: Vertue. Extrx. Wife. Edward, Margaret and Elizabeth, children of wife Elizabeth. Wits. E. & Elizabeth Swan, Margaret Swann. W.B. 8, p. 107.

CONNELLY, Patrick. Appraisement 8 Sept. 1738. Rec. 13 Oct. 1738. Returned by Geo. Connelly, Adm. W.B. 13, p. 122.

CONNELLY, George. Inventory recorded 19 Jany. 1759. Returned by Frances Connelly. W.B. 18, p. 50.

CONNELLY, George. Will. 7 April 1770. Rec. 20 Feby. 1772.
Sons: Patrick, John, James (land in Richmond Co.) and William Connelly. Daughters Sarah James, and Mary Blincoe. Gr.Son: Richard Coleman, his mother Betty Coleman having received her part. Friend, Dale Carter. Daughter, Frankie who is not able to take care of herself or her estate being subject to fits, left in care of her brother-in-law John Blincoe. Gr.Children: Geo. Connelly Blincoe, Betty Blincoe and Ann Keene Blincoe. Gr.child, George Connely, son of my son Geo. Connelly, decd. Extrs. sons, John, James, William and Patrick Connelly and friend Dale Carter. Wits. Peter Miller, Saml. Brooks, Dale Carter. W.B. 20, p. 31.

CONNELLY, Patrick. Inventory 16 Oct. 1777. Recd. 19 Feb. 1778.
Commissioners: Henry Tapscott and Henry Towles, report he is not of sound mind.

CONNELLY, George. Will. 7 Feby. 1778. Rec. 22 July 1785.
Having enlisted on board the Tartar, frigate in service of the State of Virginia Mother, Frances Connelly; sisters, Rebecca Martin George, Frances George and Catherine George. Extr. Nicholas George. Wits. Matt Mters, Dan. George. W.B. 22, p. 87.
Appraisal above estate 21 Sept. 1786. By Henry Carter, Jno. Payne, Wm. Briscoe. W.B. 22, p. 131.

CONNELLE, William. Will. April 6 1683. Rec. 15 Sept. 1683.
Wife Joane; daughter: Christian plantation after decease of wife. Wm. Clark. Extrx. wife. Wits. Alex. Atkins, Sam Dickson, Robt. Gill. (Loose Wills)

CONNER, James. Will 8 Nev. 1728. Rec. 10 Dec. 1729.
Wife Judith sole legatee and Extrx. Wits. Wm. Rankin, Thos. Purcell, Wm. Townsend. W.B. 12, p. 149.
Inventory above estate returned 10 June 1730 by Judith Connor, Extrx. W. B. 12, p. 173.

CONNIERS, Dennis. Will. 3 Oct. 1656. Rec. 1 March 1656.
Lambert Moore godson; Land Mr. Miles Dixon and Cuthbert Potter, 100 acres of land formerly sold to Peter Dodson. Cozen Dennis Conniers. Lt. Col. Thos. Ludlow, overseer. Wits. Thos. Chetwood, Jno. Walker. (Loose Wills)

CONNER, William. Appraisal. 11 March 1747. Rec. 8 April 1748.
Returned by Isaac Conner, Adm. W.B. 14, p. 184.

CONWAY, Eleanor. Will 8 May 1718. Rec. 9 July 1718.

All her estate real and personal to her four children, Josias, Eliz., Winifred & Lazarus. Wits. Jno. Chilton, Brian and Ann Phillips. Extrs. brother Wm. Rogers, Edward Blakemore and Miles Walker. W.B. 10, p. 265.

CONWAY, Peter. Will 15 Dec. 1752. Rec. 16 Feb. 1753.

Mr. Henry Miller, decd., and his wife Elizabeth, now widow. Samuel Wornum. Wife Betty; son Peter (not 21). Daughter, Agatha. Extrs. James Ball, jr., Thos. Gaskins. Wits. Jno. Bond, Elizabeth Raives, Peter Miller, Wm. Rosson. W.B. 15, p. 120.

CONWAY, George. Will 3 Feby. 1754. Rec. 21 June 1754.

Wife Anne; Children (not named, but mentions a son). Wits. Isaac Taylor, Geo. Webb, Thos. Crowder, Jr. Extrs. Wife Anne and friend Mr. Walter Jameson. W.B. 15, p. 171.

Division above estate Rec. 21 July 1758. Mrs. Ann Conway, Gdn. of Edwin, George, Walker and Anne Conway, their part of their deceased father Geo. Conway's estate. W.B. 16, p. 29.

CONWAY, Edwin. Deed Gift to Grand daughter Sarah Ann McAdams, wife of Dr. Jos. McAdam of northumberland County Va. 3 negroes. 17 Jany. 1761. Recd. 20 Feby. 1761. Wits. Jno. Porter, Jas. Kirk, Jno. Degges. W.B. 16, p. 122.

CONWAY, Edwin. Will. 27 July 1763. Rec. 21 June 1764.

"Being in the 80th year of my age" to Peter Conway, grandson and my heir at law. Gr.son: George Conway, the two negroes that were alotted to his brother Peter Hack Conway, decd. out of the estate of his father, Geo. Conway. Gr. son, Walker Conway two negroes alotted to his brother Edwin out of his father's estate. Gr.son. Edwin Garlington; gr.son, Joseph Garlington; Gr. Dau. Agatha Conway; Gr. dau. Agatha Eustace; Gr.Dau. Ann Conway; Gr-Son. Edwin Conway; Mentions land in possession of Mr. Richard Boatman and land bought of Richard and William Porter; land bought of Jno. Taylor, Esq., decd., Friend Capt. Jas. Kirk; friend Saml. Hamilton. Rev. David Currie to read burial services. Extr. Gr.son Edwin Conway. Wits. Jas. Kirk, Harry Carter, Saml. Wornum, Lazarus Coppedge. Codicil: Gr.Gr. son Thomas Pinckard 20 £ current money. Mch. 1 1763. W.B. 17, p. 30.

CONWAY, George. Division of Estate. 20 Jany. 1764. Rec. 18 June 1764. Capt. Jno. Heath, Gdn. of Geo. Conway and brother

Walker Conway and sister Ann Conway. By Thos. Brent and Wm. Sanders. W.B. 18, p. 15.

21 Jan. 1768. Division to Nancy & Walker Conway. W.B. 18, p. 99.

CONWAY, George. Division of Estate. 20 Jany. 1764. Rec. 18 June 1764.

Capt. Jno. Heath Gdn. of Geo. Conway and his brother Walker Conway and sister Ann Conway. By Thos. Brent and Wm. Sanders. W.B. 18, p. 15.

21 Jany. 1768. Division to Nancy and Walker Conway. W. B. 18, p. 99.

CONWAY, Mrs. Betty. Division of Estate between her children, namely; Peter Conway; Jesse Ball in right of his wife Agatha. Appraissors Jas. Kirk; Edwin Conway, Dale Carter. Recd. 21 July 1758. W.B. 22, p. 117.

CONWAY, Walker. Appraisal. 19 Jany. 1789. Wm. Eustace, Admr. mentions land in Stafford Co. By Wm. Brown, Jno. Yerby, Geo. Morris. W.B. 22, p. 261.

CONREE, Dennis Jr. Inventory. 14 Apl. 1731. Rec. 12 May 1731. Returned by Dennis Conree Admr. W.B. 12, p. 196.

CONRY, Dennis, of Wicomoco. Parish. 1 Feb. 1734; Rec. 10 Dec. 1736. Will.

Wife Alce; sons: eldest John, (my plantation I now live on) Richard, Michael. Daughters: Eliz. and Alice. Extr. Son Richard. Wits. Thos. and Jno. Pitman. W.B. 12, p. 356.

CONYERS, Dennis. Will. 3 Oct. 1656. Rec. 1 March 1657.

Legatees: Lambert Moore; Myles Dixon; Cuthbert Potter; Cousin Dennis Conyers, servant to Col. Mathews., Col. Thos. Ludlowe, Mrs. Mary Potter. Extrs. Col. Thos. Ludlow, Cuthbert Potter. Wits. Thos. Chetwood, Jno. Walker. W.B. 2, p. 45.

COOKE, William. Inventory. Rec. 5 July 1680. Presented by Thos. Blanch and Susanna relict of Wm. Cooke, and wife of Thos. Blanch.

COOK, John. Appraisement. Rec. 1 Mch. 1725/26. Returned by Robt. Carter Esq. Amdr. W.B. 10, p. 503.

COOPER, Thomas. Inventory. 27 May 1658. Rec. 1 June 1658. by Thos. Powell. W.B. 2, p. 126.

COOPER, Thomas. Inventory. Recorded 13 Jany. 1713. W.B. 10, p. 161.

CORNELIUS, William. Will. 8 April 1720. Rec. 11 May 1720. Wife (name not mentioned) Son: Robert; Daughters: Mary and Martha. One other child (name not mentioned). Wits. Robt. Neasum, Jno. Cornelius, Elizabeth Spencer. Extr. son Robert. W.B. 10, p. 302.

CORNELIUS, Rowland. Inventory. Rec. 12 April 1727. By Martha Cornelius, Admx. W.B. 10, p. 544.

CORNELIUS, John. Inventory. 11 Mch. 1739. Rec. 11 Oct. 1740. Returned by Jno. Cornelius, Adm. W.B. 13, p. 154.

CORNELIUS, John. Appraisement. 13 Dec. 1774. Rec. 16 March 1775. By Jno. James, Jesse George, James Pollard. W.B. 20, p. 80.

CORNELIUS, William. Inventory. 28 May 1778. Rec. 18 June 1778. By Ozwald Newby, Thomas Flint, Jesse Robinson. W.B. 20, p. 135.

COTTEN, Thomas. Will. 2 Feby. 1709. Rec. 11 May 1710.

Wife Mary; son Richard. Legacies to Mrs. Bradly and John Maurice. Wits. Nathl. and Elizabeth Carpenter. W.B. 10, p. 10.

COTTON, Richard. Will. 27 Apl. 1718. Rec. 11 June 1718.

Legatees: Wm. Norris and his dau. Susanna, my god Dau., Rebecckah Brown, Chas. Lunsford, Plantation to Susanna Norris. Extr. Wm. Norris. Wits. Danl. Scurlock, Samson Finch. W.B. 10, p. 264.

Cox, Jo. Will. 23 Feb. 1655. Rec. 16 June 1655.

Cousin Nicholas White, 150 acres of land adjoinging land of Wm. Johnson. Edward Britton, Extr. Wits. Edward Britton, Fran. Overton. W.B. 2, p. 32.

Cox, John. Inventory. 19 Feb. 1693. Rec. 17 Mch. 1693. By Susannah Lawrence, relict. W.B. 8, p. 43.

Cox, John Sr. (Christ Ch. Parish) 23 Jan. 1735. Rec. 12 May 1736. Wife Ann. Sons: John Charles and William. Daughters, youngest Sarah, Frances, Mazey, Judith, Ann. Extrx. Wife. Wits. Robt. Biscoe and Jas. Flemins. W.B. 13, p. 7.

Cox, Thomas. Will. 15 Oct. 1752. Rec. 19 Oct. 1753.

Daus. Elizabeth Conner, Elizabeth Kelley, Judith Gorton, Mary

Cox, Christian Cox. Sons: Thomas, William and Edward Cox. Ex. Daughters Mary and Christian Cox. Wits. Abraham Currell, Jno. Kelley, Sarah Kelley. W.B. 15, p. 153.

Cox, Mary. Appraisal. Rec. 10 Mch. 1763. By Harry Currell & Simon Degge. W.B. 16, p. 253.

CRAGG, Dunkin. Inventory & Appraisal. 9 June 1707. Presented by Mary Cragg, widow. W.B. 2, p. 137.

CRAINE, James. Appraisal Jany. 1789. Rec. 21 April 1789. By James Newby, Richard Mitchell and William Mitchell. W.B. 22, p. 208.
16 April 1793. Sale above estate by James Tapscott, Admr. W.B. 22, p. 376.

CRASH, William. Inventory. Rec. 9 August 1709. W.B. 10, p. 46.

CRAWLEY, Hugh. Inventory. Rec. 9 July 1729 by Jas. McCarrol, Adm. W.B. 12, p. 108.

CREEL, Joseph. Will. 7 Jany. 1749. Rec. 11 May 1750.
Brothers: Absalom and Thomas Creel. Extr. brother Absalom. Wits. Rawleigh Downman, Thos. O. Hogan. W.B. 14, p. 281.

CROMARTY, Robert. Will. 17 April 1682. Rec. 12 May 1682.
Friends: Geo. Finch, James Strayton, David Mazey, Wm. Dey. Extr. Geo. Finch. Wits. William Abbey, John Abbey. W.B. 5, p. 79.

CROSTED, John. Inventory. Rec. 10 June 1718. Returned by Edw. Blackmore, Adm. W.B. 10, p. 262.

CROWTHER, Arenium. Appraisal. Rec. 19 Sep. 1771. By Wm. Yerby, Jas. Kirk, Jno. Yerby. W.B. 20, p. 25.

CRUMP, Adam. Will. 8 Sept. 1748. Rec. 16 March 1753.
Two sons by first wife, John and Thomas Crump, land in Fairfax Co. Two sons by last wife, Jno. Bushrod and James Crump, land in Maryland. Son John to be bound by his tutors to a physician, surgeon or apothycary. Son Thomas to be a Lawyer, or Clerk of Court. Wife Hannah Crump. Daughter by last wife, Hannah Bushrod Crump. Extrs. Peter Conway, James Gordon, Wm. Gordon, Harry Turner. Wits. Edwin Conway, John Heath, John Gordon. W.B. 15, p. 126.

CUNDIFF, John, (of Wicomico Parish). Will. 29 Jan. 1773. Rec. 16 Feb. 1775.

Sons: Benjamin, land I purchased of Elezemond Basye adjoining land my father gave me; John; Richard, land that Stephen Mullice gave by will to Jno. Cundiff Jr., and he made "sail" of sd. land to the sd. Richard Cundiff—in case he has no heirs to go to Milly Cundiff. Daughters: Millie Cundiff, Winifrit Pullen. Wife Ann Cundiff. Extrs. Sons Benjamin and Richard. Wits. Thos. Pitman, Geo. Hayes. W.B. 20, p. 79.

CUNDIFF, Richard (Wiccomica Parish). 3 Feby. 1776. Rec. 17 May 1781.

Wife Hannah Cundiff; daughters Judith Boatman and Elizabeth Pullen. Gr.Daughter Elizabeth Boatman. Extrs. Nathan Pullen and cozen Richard Cundiff. Wits. William x Edwards, John x Nichols, Joseph x Davis. W.B. 20, p. 196.

CORROLL, Teage. Gift to Sons. Recd. 1 June 1665.

Along with record of gifts is their ages etc. vizt.

Charles, son of Teage Corroll was borne January the 30, 1660. Abraham the son of Teage Corroll was borne September the 18, 1662; Isaac, the son of Teage Corroll was borne May the 4, 1664. W.B. 2, p. 320.

CORROLL, Teage. Will. 4 May 1666. Rec. 16 July 1666.

Children to have equal shares. Son Charles, son Abraham, son Isake. Friend Thomas Madeshard, Extr. Wits. Wm. Kelley, Wm. Smith. (Loose Wills)

CURROLL, John. Will. 2 Feby. 1694. Rec. 9 May 1695.

Daughter, Mary Curroll; wife Ann Curroll, Extrx. Wits: Jno. Moore, Michael Vergo, Bryan Grove. W.B. 8, p. 49.

CURRELL, Jacob. Will. 6 April, 1721. Rec. 12 July 1721.

Wife (name not given), Brother Isaac Currell. Two sons (names not given. Exors. Wife. William Martin, Abraham Currell. Wits: Henry Fleet, David Carter. W.B. 10, p. 325.

Inv. and appraisement of above estate by Mary Currell, Wm. Martin & Abraham Currell, exors. W.B. 10, p. 332.

CURRELL, Isaac. Will. 16 Jany. 1755. Rec. 17 Jany. 1755.

Son James. In case he died before my present wife Sarah. Son Jacob. W.B. 15, p. 200.

CURRELL, Abraham. Will. 13 Dec. 1753. Rec. 15 July, 1757.

Sons: Harry, Spencer and Nicholas Currell. Extrs. brother Nicholas Martin, son Harry Currell, son Nicholas Currell. Wits.: Nicholas Martin, Wm. Martin, Geo. Currell. W.B. 15, p. 296.

CURRELL, Isaac. Will. 12 March 1762. Rec. 18 April 1762.

Sons: Jacob and James Currell; daughters Rebeccah Currell and Sally Reaves, and Mary Armistead's children. Wife (not named) "the chest she had of Benj. Kelly." Extrs. Wm. Hathaway, Geo. Currell and sons Jacob & James Currell. Witss. George Currell, Wm. Hathaway. W.B. 16, p. 201.

Division above estate. Recorded 17 Sept. 1762. To Mrs. Leta. Currell, Jacob Currell, James Currell, Richard Blade, John Reaves, Jesse Robinson, Rebecca Currell. W.B. 16, p. 231.

CURRELL, Harry. Will. 4 Dec. 1782. Rec. 17 June 1785.

Son, Gilbert Currell; brother, Nicholas Currell; Gr.son; William Ford (not 21). Extrs. Gilbert & Nicholas Currell. Wits. Robt. Ferguson, Wm. James, Matthias James. W.B. 22, p. 77.

CURRELL, Nicholas, Jr. Appraisal. Rec. 16 July 1787. by Henry Lawson, Gilbert Currill, Lawson Hathaway and Wm. Lawson. W.B. 22, p. 152.

CURRELL, George. Will. 6 Feby. 1788. Rec. 21 July 1788.

Son Robert Currell, all my land; daughters: Eliz. Lightbourne; Lucy Garlington; Mary Harward Wiatt. Extr. son Robert. Wits. Jno. Lawson, Martin Shearman, Wm. Doggett. W.B. 22, p. 183.

Appraisal above estate Rec. 18 Jany. 1790 by Henry Lawson, Jno. Lawson & Jas. Currill. W.B. 22, p. 246.

CURRIE, David—Rector. Will. 5 July 1784. Rec. 21 March 1791.

Wife Elizabeth; Children: Armistead, Frances Hall, David, Ellyson. Gr.children: William Currie Beale; Ann Harwar Belfield; Ann Corbin Griffin. Brother Ellyson Armistead, of Northumberland. Mentions Rev. Samuel Smith McCroskey, of Hungars, Northumberland Co., Charles Carter of Shirley, Landon Carter, security. Extrx. Wife. Wits. Thomas Pinckard, Geo. Carter, John Gordon. W.B. 22, p. 300.

CURTIS, Richard. Will. 5 April 1688. Rec. 13 March 1688.

Wife, Mary. Her son Jno. Leathers. Mary Emanuel, daughter of Francis Emanuell, Henry Bell's wife Rebecca. Wits. Francis Emanuel, Henry Bell. W.B. 5, p. 124.

Inventory above estate, recd. 12 Sept. 1688. Presented by Mary *Boush*, relict. W.B. 5, p. 125.

CURTIS, Richard (Christ Church Parish). Will. 22 July 1743. Rec. 13 Apl. 1744.

Wife Elizabeth; son John Curtis; daughter Elizabeth Davis. Children of son George Curtis. Extr. son John. Wits. John Vass Jr., Henry Carter. W.B. 14, p. 12.

CURTICE, Thomas. Appraisal. Recd. 21 June 1790. Widow Elizabeth Curtice. By John Hill, John Doggett, Moses George. W.B. 22, p. 268.

DALE, Thomas. Inventory etc. Rec. 8 8bris 1654. Sara Dale, orphan. Inv. of estate given in by Richard Perrot, who married the widow. W.B. 2, p. 99.

6 May 1660. Recd. 20 May 1660. Acct. Estate Thomas Dale. 10 cows and heifer, ye youngest 2 yes old and 1 calfe given to my son Richard Perrot by his brother Thomas Dale, decd. W.B. 2, p. 129.

DALE, Edward. Will. 24 Aug. 1694. Rec. 17 March 1695.

Wife (name not given). Gr.children: Peter, Joseph and John Carter, Elizabeth and Katherine Carter. Daughter Elizabeth, wife of Wm. Rogers. Daughter, Catherine Carter. Extrs. Gr.son Edward Carter, dau. Elizabeth Carter, Gr.Dau. Elizabeth Carter (not 16). Wits. John Chilton, Thos. Carter, Henry Carter. W.B. 8, p. 56.

DAMERON, John. Will. 22 May 1782. Rec. 19 Dec. 1782.

Wife, Rachel Dameron; sons: Samuel and John Dameron. "It is my desire that all my debts due before marriage to my present wife shall be paid out of the estate I was formerly possessed of. Extrs. Isaac Hunt, Joseph Gaskins. Wits. John x Palmer, Lott Palmer. W.B. 20, p. 244.

DANIEL, Abraham. Apptmt. Guardian. Recd. 15 Dec. 1766. Leory Peachey appointed Guardian to Sarah Daniel, orphan of Abraham Daniel. W.B. 18, p. 226.

DANGERFIELD, John. Inventory. Recd. August Ct. 1710. "John Dangerfield ye son of Mary Ball, wife of James Ball as in hands of sd Jas. Ball, by inventory of estate of John Dangerfield's father John Dangerfield, decd." W.B. 10, p. 43.

DARE, William. Will. Recd. 14 June 1721.

Wife, name not given. Sons, Thomas and William. Extrs. Wife and James Ball. Wits. Thomazina Wale, Eliz. Thomas. (This will also mentioned mother and brother James.) W.B. 10, p. 316. Inventory above estate 14 June 1721. Rec. 12 July 1721, returned by Catherine Dare and James Ball, Extrs. W.B. 10, p. 327.

DARE, Thomas. Inventory. Rec. 11 March 1729 by Henry Horner. W.B. 12, p. 150.

DARE, William. Deposition of Mary Pinckard, widow, aged 66 years. That she was well acquainted with Wm. Dare, formerly Clerk of this Court, and Katherine his wife, daughter of Thomas Martin, and the deponent was at the wedding of sd William & Katherine and saw them joined together in the holy estate of matrimony by Rev. Andrew Jackson, clk. then minister of Christ Church Psh., about 36 years ago. Sd. William Dare died about a month since. They had several children but now only two are living, Elinor the wife of Peter Harley of Accomac county, and Elizabeth the wife of William Hammond, of Richmond county. Small estate of William Dare in Taunton, Gr. Britain left to his children. Recorded 8 April 1743. W.B. 13, p. 321.

DAVENPORT, John. Will. 14 Feby. 1683/4. Rec. 15 March 1683. Wife Margaret, Extrx. Sons George, John, William, Fortunatus, to whom is willed all the land found at the head of Morattico Creek. Wits. Brian P——?, Rowland Lawson, George Stott. W.B. 5, p. 92.

DAVENPORT, William (Of St. Mary's White Chapel). Will. 2 March 1710/11. Rec. 9 Jan. 1716.

Wife Rachel, and child unborn. Sons: John and William, all my land in Richmond county; youngest son Wood Davenport my now dwelling and plantation. Extrs. Wife, brothers George and Fortunatus. Wits. Wm. Payne, Jas. Wood, Rachel Wood. W.B. 10, p. 188.

Inventory & Appraisal above estate 10 Jan. 1716. Rec. 13 Mch. 1716. proved by Rachel and Geo. Davenport, Extrs. W.B. 10, p. 190.

DAVENPORT, George. Will. 12 Nov. 1759. Rec. 18 April 1760. Wife Mary; children (no names). Extr. father Wm. Davenport and Mr. Chattin Chowning. Wits. Geo. Scurlock, Saml. Neasum. W.B. 16, p. 85.

18 Feb. 1765 record of appointment of Wm. Davenport Jr. as Guardian of Nancy and John Davenport, orphans of Geo. Davenport, Decd. W.B. 17, p. 97.

18 Feb. 1765. Rec. 18 Mch. 1766. Wm. Davenport Jr. possessed estate of orphans of George Davenport, decd. and also William Dunaway (in right of his wife) with 1/3 part of sd. deceased estate. W.B. 18, p. 32.

DAVENPORT, Ann. Settlement of estate. Rec. 19 May 1774. In hands of Wm. Dunnaway. By Jesse Ball, James Selden. W.B. 20, p. 71.

DAVIS, Henry, the Elder, living in Corr. Will. 19 Nov. 1667. (No date of record.)

Son Henry, plantation I now live on. Youngest son, John Davis, plantation extending to Robt. Pritchard's. Son Richard Davis; Thomas Davis 100 acres part of land John Seaman lives on. Daughter Mary Davis. Wits. Samuel Gooch, Jno. Seaman, John Kennede. (Loose Wills)

DAVIS, Thomas. Will. 25 Oct. 1697. Rec. 12 March 1697/8.

Wife, Susanna; Sons: Samuel, the eldest, Thomas and John, to whom is given plantation I now live on. Daughters: Susanna, Martha and Elizabeth. Extrs. Wife, Timothy Stamps, cousin Richard Davis. Wits. Joseph Tayloe, Geo. Heale. W.B. 8, p. 77.

DAVIS, Caudry. Inventory. 10 July 1701. Rec. 2 Aug. 1701. W.B. 10, p. 212.

DAVIS, Henry. Will. 17 Nov. 1726. Rec. 8 Mch. 1726.

Wife Aleson and children (not named). Wits. Rich. Davis Sr. Rich Davis Jr. W.B. 10, p. 529.

DAVIS, John. Will. 30 March 1729. Rec. 11 June 1729.

Wife Geeles, Son: John Davis, Daughters: Hagar, wife of Saml. Rains; Hannah and Geeles Davis, and Margaret, wife of Samuel Northern. Extrx. Wife. Wits. Henry Carter, Chas. Chilton, Thos. Carter. W.B. 12, p. 97.

DAVIS, Richard (St. Mary's White Chapel). Will. 17 June 1736. Rec. 10 June 1737.

Wife (name not given) Sons: Richard, John and Henry. Daughters: Ann and Winnifret Davis and Thomazin Morgan. Property to be divided between Richard, John and Henry Davis, Eliz.

Wood, Susannah Cole, Ann Winifret Davis. Wits. James and Catherine Brent. W.B. 13, p. 50.

9 Sept. 1737 Appraisal recorded by Eliza. Davis, Admx. W.B. 13, p. 66.

DAVIS, Richard, Sr. (St. Mary's White Chapel Par.) Will. 17 June 1736. Rec. 10 June 1737.

Wife (name not given). Sons: Richard, John and Henry; Daughters: Ann, Winifret, Davis and Tomizinah Morgan. Property to be divided between Richard, John and Henry Davis, Elizabeth Wood, Susannah Cole, Winifret & Ann Davis. Wits. James & Catherine Brent. W.B. 13, p. 50.

Appraisal this estate returned 9 Sept. 1737 by Eliza. Davis. W.B. 13, p. 66.

DAVIS, Richard. Inventory returned 8 December 1749 by John Gollogher and Amos Davis, Admrs. W.B. 14, p. 266.

DAVIS, Ambrose. Inventory returned 11 May 1750 by Susannah Davis, Admx. W.B. 14, p. 283.

DAVIS, Moses. Will. 20 Feb. 1749. Rec. 13 Apl. 1750.

Wife Elizabeth; Children: Moses, Judith and William. Wits. Wm. Bond, Abraham Grigory, Elizabeth Smith. W.B. 14, p. 276.

DAVIS, Elizabeth. Inventory recorded 8 June 1750 by Samuel Sparks, Adm. W.B. 14, p. 288.

DAVIS, Susannah. Inventory. Recorded May 1 1751 by Amos Davis, Adm. W.B. 15, p. 34.

DAVIS, Joseph. Will 12 Feb. 1758. Rec. 21 Apl. 1758.

Wife Elizabeth; Son Joseph; Daughter Millicent Davis, son Robert. Extrs. Wife and Richard Boatman, Jr. Wits. Thos. Brent, Anna Boatman.

DAVIS, Thomas. Inventory. Rec. 20 Feb. 1761 by Mungo Harvey.

DAVIS, Henry. Inventory and Appraisal. Rec. 17 Dec. 1762 by Sarah Davis.

DAVIS, John. Will. 19 Feby. 1761. Rec. 19 Nov. 1764.

Wife Margaret; Daughters: Sarah, Winny; Judy to have 20 shillings the gift of her god-father Jos. Turner. Son, William. Extrs. Edward & Moses Chilton. Wits. Dale Carter, Sarah Carter. W.B. 18, p. 25.

16 Nov. 1769. Rec. 21 Dec. 1769—Division above estate. Mar-

garet Davis widow, and Wm. Davis, son and heir. W.B. 18, p. 158.

DAVIS, John. Will. 30 May 1768. Rec. 17 Nov. 1768.

Sons: John and Richard. Wife Elizabeth. Extrs. Wife and son John. Wits. Ann and Dale Carter. W.B. 18, p. 129.

DAVIS, William. Appraisement. Rec. 17 Sept. 1772 by Gavin Lawry, Edw. Carter, Henry Davis. W.B. 20, p. 47.

DAVIS, Moses. Division Estate. 28 Aug. 1777. Rec. 16 Oct. 1777. Ann Davis possessed of one third of estate of her deceased husband. W.B. 20, p. 116.

Appraisement above estate by Wm. Gibson, Martin George & Wm. Meredith. W.B. 20, p. 140.

DAVIS, Jeduthan. May Court 1781. Rec. 21 June 1781. Jesse Crowder Guardian of Jeduthan Davis' estate. W.B. 20, p. 198.

Order Ct. March 1784. Rec. 20 May 1784. Jesse Crowder, Adm. James Brent, Church Warden; Jno. Berryman, Isaac Degge, Wm. Meredith, Appraisors.

DAVIS, William. Division Estate. Feby. Ct. 1785. Rec. 19 August 1785. Division by Wm. Gibson, Adm. To wife who had married Joseph Kem; Children, Elizabeth, Richard and Judith Davis. By Jno. Yerby, Jas. Pinckard, Jno. Miller. W.B. 22, p. 104.

DAVIS, Ellenor. Will recorded 20 July 1789.

Sons: Manly and Burwell Davis. Daughter, Nancy Davis. Wits. Jesse C. Ball, Margaret Christon. W.B. 22, p. 221.

DAVIS, Leannah. Appraisal by Abner Palmer, Wm. Wiblin, Chas. Dodson. 21 June 1790. W.B. 22, p. 273.

DAVYS, Richard. Nuncupative will. Sept. Ct. 1678. Rec. Oct. 1678.

Hagar Martin, aged 50 years, states that her son Richard Davis, on his death bed gave to his brother John *Davis* all his estate. W.B. 5, p. 50.

DAY, Robinson. Inventory. 21 Feb. 1752. Rec. 21 Aug. 1752. Returned by Jno. Bond, Adm. W.B. 15, p. 107.

17 Nov. 1766. Rec. 18 June 1767. Division above estate. To Betty Day, orphan. W.B. 18, p. 82.

DEACON, William. Will. 20 June 1792. Rec. 19 Mch. 1792.

Wife, Ann, who is Extrx. Wits. Ezekiel Haydon, Jno. Simmonds. W.B. 22, p. 356.

DEGGES, Simon. Division estate. 30 Mch. 1780. Rec. 20 Apl. 1786. To Isaac Degges, Jno. Degges, Wm. Degges, Jno. Ross, and Christopher Gale. By Harry Currell, Thos. Carter and John Berryman. W.B. 20, p. 178.

DEGGES, Isaac. Will. 18 July 1792. Rec. 15 July 1793.
Relations: Mary Tunstall Degges and her sister Ann Degges; Simon son of brother Wm. Degges. Extrx. Wife Mary Degges, Mary Tunstall & Ann Degges. Wits. Jas. Maxwell, Gilbert Currell, Armistead Currie, Wm. Degges. W.B. 22, p. 385.

DEGGE, John. Appraisal. 20 Oct. 1794. Rec. 15 June 1795. By Wm. Davis, Jno. Doggett, James Carter. W.B. 22, p. 450.

DELANEY, William. Appraisal. 11 Aug. 1738. Rec. 8 Sept. 1738. Returned by Thos. Murphy, Adm. W.B. 13, p. 119.

DENNY, William. Inventory & Appraisal. 12 Feb. 1734. Rec. 12 March 1734. Returned by Margaret Denny, his sister. W.B. 12, p. 328.

DENNY, Edmond. Appraisal. 12 Nov. 1738. Rec. 11 Feby. 1735. Returned by Hannah Denny, Admx. W.B. 12, p. 360.

DENNY, Samuel. Indenture rec. 16 Sept. 1765. Samuel Denny, orphan of John Denny, bound to Mungo Harvey. W.B. 17, p. 168.

DENNY, Lucy. Mch. Ct. 1786. Rec. 20 Apl. 1786. Settlement of her Guardian Elias Edmonds. By James Brent, Isaac Degge, Lawson Hathaway. W.B. 22, p. 120.

DIE, John. Will. 22 May 1792. Rec. 18 June 1792.
Wife Sarah; son George; Daughters: Catherine Coats and Gene Die. Extrs. Jos. Chinn, Jos. Carter Jr. Wits. Rawleigh Davenport, Richard Flint. W.B. 22, p. 344.

DILLON, Michael. Inventory. Rec. 18 June 1752. by Merryman Payne, Adm. W.B. 15, p. 99.

DOBBS, Joseph. Appraisal. 23 Dec. 1789. Rec. 21 Feb. 1791. Elijah Perciful, Adm. By Geo. Norris, Jno. Yerby, Wm. Yerby. W.B. 22, p. 296.
Report of sale of estate, with Mary Dobbs among purchasers. W.B. 22, p. 297.

DOGGETT, Benjamin. Inventory. 1 Feb. 1681. Rec. 8 March 1681 Presented by Benj. Doggett. Wits. James Ridley, James Ellis. W.B. 4, p. 431.

Will of Benjamin Doggett, 14 March 1681. Rec. 12 June 1682.
Wife Jane; sons: Benjamin, Richard and William; daughters:
Jane and Anne. Eldest son Benjamin; daughter Jane in England.
Extrs. Mr. Thos. Martin, Mr. Jno. Mullin. Appraisors Mr.
Sheapheard, Mr. Furnifold, Mr. Wtkins, Mr. Wilkes. Wits. Jno.
Davis, Sthellian Kelly. W.B. 5, p. 81.

DOGGETT, William. Will. 20 Feb. 1716. Rec. 13 March 1716.
Wife (name not given) son William, daughter Jane. "All my
children" (no other names). Extrs. Edmond George, Edwin
Conway. Wits. Benj. Doggett, Rich. Doggett, John Bell. W.B.
10, p. 190.

DOGGETT, Richard. Will. 20 June 1721. Rec. 8 Nov. 1721.
Sons: Bushrod and George; Wife Elizabeth; daughter Ann. Other
children not named. Extrs. Wife, and son George. Wits. Hannah Stevens, Edwin Conway. W.B. 10, p. 337.
Inventory above estate rec. 11 July 1782 by Elizabeth Doggett,
widow. W.B. 10, p. 389.

DOGGETT, Benjamin. Will. 18 Sept. 1723. Rec. 12 Nov. 1723.
Wife Mary; Sons: John, William and Richard; grandson James
Doggett. Daughters: Elizabeth, wife of Philip Stroud, Hannah,
wife of Thos. Yerby; Ann, wife of Geo. Reves; Margaret and
Jane Doggett; youngest children, Thomas, Reuben, Mary and
Winifred Doggett. Extrs. Wife and son John. Wits. Elmore
George, Richd. Curtin, Harry Carter. W.B. 10, p. 446.

DOGGETT, Richard. Inventory. Rec. 14 June 1727 by Geo. Doggett,
Extr. W.B. 10, p. 559.

DOGGETT, William. 12 June 1728. Wm. Doggett appointed Guardian
of Benj. Doggett, orphan of Wm. Doggett, Senr. W.B. 12, p. 55.

DOGGETT, Mary, widow. Will. 24 June 1735. Rec. 10 Mch. 1737.
Legatees: Sons Wm. Thrailkill, Chris. Thrailkill; James Thrailkill; Thomas and Reuben Doggett; daughters Elizabeth, wife of
John Pinckard, and Winifret Doggett. Extrs. Thomas and Reuben Doggett. Wits. James and Charity Doggett. W.B. 13, p. 77.

DOGGETT, James. Will. 25 Jany. 1758. Rec. 19 May 1758.
Wife, Rebecca; Children: Jenny, Elizabeth, James, Spencer, Re-
becca and Lucy Doggett. Extrs. Wife and Richard Stephens.
Wits. Dale Carter, Wm. George Sr. W.B. 16, p. 18.
Division of estate rec. 18 July 1760. To widow Rebecca, and 6

children, Elizabeth, Rebecca, James, Spencer, Jane and Lucy. W.B. 16, p. 101.

DOGGETT, Benjamin. Inventory & Appraisal. 21 Aug. 1760. Rec. 19 Sept. 1760. Returned by Anne Doggett, Adm. W.B. 16, p. 110.

DOGGETT, Anne, widow. Will. 23 Nov. 1761. Rec. 18 Dec. 1761. Daughters, Betty, Mary Ann and Margaret Doggett; son, Emberson Doggett; daughter Leonora. Extrs. Son Emberson, Wm. Yerby, Jno. Nichols. Wits. Dale & Mary Yerby. W.B. 16, p. 177.

DOGGETT, Benjamin. Division of Estate. Rec. 19 Aug. 1763. Mary Doggett, orphan. W.B. 17, p. 19.

DOGGETT, James. Division of Estate. Rec. 17 Feb. 1764. Wm. Doggett, Guardian for James Donnelly wife's part; James Doggett, Spencer Dogget, Rebecca Dogget, Lucy Dogget. W.B. 18, pp. 2, 69.

DOGGETT, Benjamin. 15 Oct. 1764. Mary Ann Dogget, orphan of Benj. Doggett to Richard Hutchings, her Guardian. W.B. 18, p. 24.

DOGGETT, James. Rec. 18 April 1765. Rebecca George appointed Guardian of Rebecca and Lucy Doggett, orphans of James Doggett dec. Spencer Doggett bound to Geo. Phillips until 21 to learn trade of millwright. W.B. 17, p. 122.

15 Apl. 1765. Rec. Aug. 8, 1765. Rebecca & Lucy Doggett, orphans of James Doggett, decd. William Doggett their Gdn. W.B. 18, p. 52-53.

DOGGETT, Emberson. Division of Estate. Rec. 21 October 1765. To Betty Doggett, Richard Hutchings, Margaret Doggett, Maryan Doggett. W.B. 18, p. 53.

DOGGETT, Benjamin. Account of Estate by ——— Hutchings. Rec. 18 August 1766. Margaret & Marian Doggett, orphans of Benj. Doggett, decd. W.B. 18, p. 68. W.B. 18, p. 120.

DOGGETT, William. Will. 27 Dec. 1764. Rec. 16 April 1772. Sons: William and Coleman; Gr.son: John son of "my son" Coleman Doggett; five youngest daughters: the children of present wife: Sarah, Mildred, Joanna, Ann and Hannah. Wife Joanna; other daughters: Mary Ann, Betty and Lucy. Wits. Moses George, Dale Carter and Augustine Carter. W.B. 20, p. 39.

DOGGETT, Emberson. Division of Estate. Rec. 12 June 1767. and 19 August 1785. To Richard Hutchings, Bettie Doggett, Maryan Doggett, Margaret Doggett. W.B. 18, pp. 50 and 81.

DOGGETT, Reubin. Will. 13 March 1771. Rec. 16 July 1772.

Wife Hannah; sons Reubin and Jeremiah; daughters: Judith Doggett and Sarah Light. Extr. John Robinson. Wits. Geo. Chitwood, Wm. Chitwood, Jno. Robinson. W.B. 20, p. 44.

DOGGETT, John. Inventory 8 June 1780. Rec. 17 August 1780. By John Berryman, Thomas Carter, Wm. Gibson. Elmore Dogget appeared and would not suffer the widow to have her part of the land on which her late husband John Doggett lived, claiming the sd land during his life. W.B. 20, p. 182.

DOGGETT, Elmore. Will. 6 Feby. 1772. Rec. 17 May 1781.

Wife Lucy; sons: John, William and Elmore. Daughter: Elizabeth Curtis. Gr.son Elmore Doggett. Extrs. Son John, Richard Hutchings and Wm. Gibson. Wits. Wm. West, Nancy Doggett, Judith Scott, Wm. Gibson. Maryann Doggett, widow, entered her dissent. W.B. 20, p. 196.

Division above estate August Court 1781. Mary Doggett widow given her part and the rest divided according to the will of sd Elmore Doggett. W.B. 20, p. 208.

DOGGETT, Coleman. Will. 8 Feby. 1782. Rec. 21 Feby. 1782.

Sons: John, William and Dennis; daughters: Mary and Priscilla Doggett. Wife Mary. Extrs. son John, James Tapscott, Jno. Yerby, Elias Edmonds. Wits. Moses George, and James Gordon. W.B. 20, p. 223.

20 Feby. 1783. John Goodridge, guardian of Wm. Doggett, orphan of Coleman Doggett. By James Gordon, Jno. Yerby and Jno. Miller. W.B. 20, p. 254.

DOGGETT, John. 26 May 1783. Rec. 19 June 1783. Wm. Doggett, guardian of orphans and Thomas Mott who intermarried with Winifred, widow of sd. John Doggett. Maryan and George Doggett's part; William Doggett, Lucy Doggett and John Doggett. W.B. 20, p. 263.

19 June 1783. Wm. Doggett Guardian of John Doggett, decd., and Thomas Mott, who intermarried with Winifred, the widow of sd decd. The sd. orphans allotted their part of their father's negroes and divided the negroes left sd. orphans by their gr.father Elmour Doggett. Children: Maryan and George Doggett, William, Lucy and John Doggett. By John Berryman, Thos. Carter, James Brent. W.B. 20, p. 263.

DOGGETT, Coleman. 25 June 1783. Rec. 17 July 1783. Acct. Guardianship of Coleman Doggett with Lucy Mason, decd. with the Extr. of sd. Doggett. By Wm. Yerby, Jno. Yerby, Tho. Pollard. W.B. 20, p. 263.

DOGGETT, Mary, alias Mary McTyre, wife of John McTyre, guardian of her daughter Priscilla Doggett. Examination of account. Edwin Conway, James Tapscott. Rec. 22 July 1785. W.B. 22, p. 93.

DOGGETT, Mary, alias Mctire. Division Coleman Doggett's estate. Rec. 16 Feb. 1789.

Agreeable to will of Coleman Doggett, decd. To Mary Doggett, now Yopp, and John Doggett, guardian of William, Dennis and Priscilla Dogget, negroes of sd. Coleman. Money and negroes in hands of John McTire. By Jno. Degges, Jno. Yerby, John Miller. W.B. 22, p. 206.

DOGGETT, George. Will. 25 Nov. 1784. Rec. 17 Feby. 1785.

Sisters: Mary and Nancy Doggett; Godsons: John James and Thomas Pollard. Extr. James Pollard. Wits. Wm. Mason, Jno. Thrall, Jas. Pollard. W.B. 22, p. 58.

Appraisal above estate 17 Mc. 1785. By Henry Lawson, Jesse George, Jno. James. W.B. 22, p. 73.

DOGGETT, Coleman. Estate Settled. 2 June 1785. Rec. 19 August 1785. By James Gordon, James Pinckard, John Yerby. W.B. 22, p. 102.

DOGGETT, Thomas. Nov. 1785. 16 Feb. 1786. Division of estate and appraisal, according to will of his grandfather William Griggs. Heirs: William Doggett, Charlotte Connelly, Wm. G. Connoly, Patrick Connelly, Elmore Doggett. By Henry Lawson, James Brent, William Norris. W.B. 22, p. 113.

DOGGETT, Mary Ann. Will. 4 Jany. 1786. Rec. 16 Feb. 1786.

Daughter Betty Connelly Marsden whole estate during her life and at her death to be divided among her children. Wits. Elmour Doggett, Thos. Pollard. W.B. 22, p. 112.

DOGGETT, William. Orphans account. August Ct. 1785. Rec. 19 Oct. 1788.

John Goodridge, Gdn. of orphans of Coleman Doggett, decd. To Saml. Yopp Jr. due his wife Mary, for negroe. To Samuel Yopp Jr. Guardian of Priscilla Doggett for negroe. W.B. 22, p. 136.

DOGGETT, John. Orphans estate. Recd. 18 June 1787. Wm. Doggett Jr., Guardian of John Doggett, orphan of John Doggett decd. by James Brent, Jas. Ollard, Geo. W. Yerby. W.B. 22, p. 148.

21 Oct. 1788. Ezekiel Haydon possessed with his wife's part of estate of John Doggett decd., and also his wife's part of estate of Elmour Doggett in the hands of Wm. Doggett. By Jas. Brent, Jas. Pollard, Benj. George. W.B. 22, p. 189.

19 Jany. 1789. Maryan & George Doggett, orphans of John Doggett, decd. Thomas Mott, Guardian. Eppa Acres Percifull, Guardian. Settlement Guardians accounts. By James Robinson, Wm. Yerby. W.B. 22, p. 198.

20 July 1789. Maryann & George Doggett, orphans of John Doggett, decd. Eppa A. Percifull Guardian, Thomas Mott, Guardian. Accounts examined by Wm. Yerby & James Robinson. W.B. 22, p. 219.

DOGGETT, Reubin (Parish Christ Church). Will. 19 Aug. 1778. Rec. 21 Dec. 1789. To mother Hannah Wiblin; to Molly Thomas. Wits. Thos. Webb, Edward Carter. W.B. 22, p. 234.

Sept. Court 1777. Rec. 20 April 1790. Reuben Doggett, orphan of Reuben Doggett, decd. Wm. Wiblin, possessed with estate. Legacy left by Reuben Doggett's father which was paid by the late John Robinson to Wm. Wiblin.

DOGGETT, Wm. G. Inventory recd. 20 Jany. 1794. By Lawson Hathaway, Isaac Currell, John Haggoman, Martin Shearman. W.B. 22, p. 256.

DOGGETT, Mary. Will. 12 Jany. 1794. Rec. 21 Apl. 1794. Heirs: James Pollard and Ann Pollard. Wits. Jos. Locke and Jas. Pollard. W.B. 22, p. 415.

DONALDSON, Andrew. Verbal will. 2 April 1735. Rec. 13 Augt. 1735.

Wife Mary, and her children. The sd Andrew departed this life 7 Apl. 1735. Wits. Matthias James & Thos. Battany. W.B. 12, p. 346.

DONALDSON, Mary. Deed Gift to children. 16 Oct. 1751. Rec. 18 Oct. 1751. Estate "given me by my husband Andrew Donaldson, decd., by his will dated 7 April 1735." Son Andrew, son William, Daughters, Rozina Flemmon, ——— Collens. Gr.Children: Wm. Scrimsher, Andrew Scrimsher. W.B. 15, p. 70.

DOUGHTY, Enoch. Will. 27 Feb. 1675. Rec. 12 May 1677.

Francis Doughty & Jas. Phillips to sell all lands for his children. Wishes family to leave this country. Jno. Simpson, Jonathan Mate, Hugh Man. Wits. W.B. 5, pp. 27-28.

DOWNMAN, William. Inventory. 9 July 1654. Rec. 12 June 1655. By Dority Downman. W.B. 2, p. 13.

(Note, from W.B. 1, p. 145.) Whereas Wm. Downman died very poor, is not able to pay charges of administration, John Nichols, on ye behalf of his daughter, ye wife and relict of sd. Downman, the Court orders that the estate be appraised. 6 Jany. 1654.

DOWNMAN, Rawleigh. Will. 29 Dec. 1718. Rec. 11 March 1718.

Wife (name not given) and unborn child bequeathed plantation he now lives on. Son: William (plantation in Richmond Co. called Mt. Zion. Extrs. Wife, brother Wm. Downman, brother-in-law Richard Ball and Mr. James Hall. Wits. Thos. Chattin, Robt. Mitchell, Wm. Payne. W.B. 10, p. 282.

DOWNMAN, William. Orphans account. Rec. 11 May 1744. James Ball Jr., guardian to Jabez Downman, orphan of Wm. Downman; Jesse Ball guardian of Rawleigh Downman, orphan of William Downman. W.B. 14, pp. 17 and 205. (12 Aug. 1748.)

DOWNMAN, Rawleigh (Christ Church Parish). Will. 10 Mch. 1781. Rec. 19 Apl. 1781.

Wife Frances land in Richmond Co. bought of James Ball; Sons: Joseph Ball Downman, Rawleigh William Downman (plantation called Windsor Forest in Stafford Co.) also my silver coffee pot which I gave him in lieu of a two handled cup given him by his grandmother Frances Ball, decd. Plantation in Stafford and another in Fauquier to Joseph Ball Downman. Daughter Fanny Ball, wife of Major James Ball, all my Continental certificates." Extrs. John Chinn, Richard Mitchell, sons Jos. Ball and Rawleigh Wm. Downman. Wits. Thos. White, Elizabeth White, Wm. Sydnor, Robert Chinn. W.B. 20, p. 188.

DOZIER, John. Appraisement. 17 Feb. 1758. Rec. 21 July 1758. returned by Wm. Dozier. W.B. 16, p. 25.

DRAPER, John. Inventory. 9 May 1677. Rec. 13 May 1677 returned by Thos. Wilkes. W.B. 2, p. 32.

DRAPER, Thomas. Will. 13 Jany. 1687. Rec. 10 Octomer 1688. Wife Katherine; brothers, William and John Draper. Wits. Francis Bradly, John Winlock, Richd. Nutt. W.B. 5, p. 124.

Inventory above estate presented and recorded 13 June 1690. Returned by Katherine Draper, relict. W.B. 8, p. 5.

DRAPER, Josias. Will. 12 March 1712.

Wife Phebe, Sons: John, and Thomas; Daughters: Anne Steward. Extrx. Wife. Wits: Richd. Cooper, James Whaley, Wm. Jacobs, Will Walker. W.B. 10, p. 159.

DUN, Alex. Inventory recorded 8 Dec. 1701. W.B. 8, p. 217.

DUNAWAY, Darby (Parish St. Mary's White Chapel). 9 Dec. 1726. Rec. 14 May 1729.

Wife Mary; Sons: youngest Samuel, plantation I now live on, 2nd: William; eldest John; Daughters: eldest Catherine Delainey and Elizabeth Dunaway. Extrx. Wife. Wits. Thos. Chattin, Henry Stonum, John Gaines. W.B. 12, p. 95.

DUNAWAY, Samuel. Inventory. 8 Jany. 1747/8. Rec. 8 April 1748. returned by Frances Dunaway Admx. W.B. 14, p. 187.

DUNAWAY, William. Inventory rec. 21 April 1758. returned by Henry Tapscott. W.B. 16, p. 8.

DUNAWAY, Samuel. Will. 8 April 1789. Rec. 15 June 1789.

Wife Ann; Children, George Davenport Dunaway, Apey Dunaway, Molly Chowning Dunaway, Samuel Dunaway, John Dunaway, William Dunaway. Extrs. Wife and Joseph and George Davenport. Wits. Rawleigh Tapscott, Siller Flint, Rawleigh Davenport. W.B. 22, p. 210.

Appraisal of this estate recorded 20 July 1789. W.B. 22, p. 218.

Acct. Executor Jos. Davenport, rec. 21 Oct. 1794. W.B. 22, p. 441.

DUNCOMBE, Thomas (of Pianketank Parish). Will. 9 Sept. 1659. Rec. 1 March 1659.

Wife Mary, who is also Extrx. Wits. Robt. Smith, Saml. Heron. W.B. 2, p. 66.

DUNN, Arthur. Will. 16 Nov. 1655. Rec. 12 Apl. 1656.

God-son Christopher Robert, son of Bertrand Robert 300 acres land bought of Abraham Moon near head of Neamcock Creek. Richard and Mary, children of John Welch. Thomas Kidd, Bartram Robert, Anthony Harlow. Extrs. Bartram Robert. Thos. Kidd. Wits. Milton Ball, Thomas Kidd. W.B. 2, p. 22.

DYMAN, James. Noncupative will. Rec. 10 Oct. 1679. All estate to Elizabeth Balley, widow except his cattle which he gave to his child. Edward Carter age 53 years and Wm. Merriman, age 27 years, made deposition as to this will. W.B. 5, p. 65.

DYMORE, Nicholas. Will. 26 March 1697. rec. 2 July 1697.

Wife Elizabeth; son, William; daughters: Elizabeth and Sarah. Extrs. Wife and Capt. Wm. Jones. Wits. Robert Linnis, Robert Frame, Francis Ainge. W.B. 8, p. 68.

DYMER, William. Administration. Rec. 10 July 1728. James Haines and wife Sarah, Admx. of estate of Wm. Dymer. W.B. 12, p. 61.

DYMAN, Capt. William. Appraisement—rec. 20 June 1771 by Richard Edwards, James Kirk, Hugh Brent, Thomas Lawson. W.B. 20, p. 16.

Division of negroes belonging to above estate: Wm. Nutts part, Edwin Fieldings part certain negroes to remain in hands of Wm. Nutt, Admr. until Edwin Fielding gives security. W.B. 20, p. 30.

EATON, Mr. George. Inventory at request of Mr. Jno. Hunt, rec. 12 Oct. 1653. By Henry Fleet, David Fox, Richd. Ferman, Jo. Sharpe. W.B. 1, p. 6.

EDGAR, Dr. Alexander. Inventory. 13 Jan. 1730/31. Rec. 10 Feb. 1730. Returned by Wm. Martin, Adm. W.B. 12, p. 182.

EDMONDS, Elias. 24 June 1654. Rec. 10 Jany. 1654. John Meredith & Walter Heard, Admrs. Letter from Edwin Conway to Mr. Toby Smith, dated "from my house at the head of Corotoman Mch 27 1654"—states: that Mrs. Frances Edmonds made a noncupative will. Because he was a Papist it was thought he should not have the bringing up of children. Wants Meredith & Heard to give an account of Elias Edmonds estate. Calls himself "Overseer." W.B. 2, p. 6.

EDMONDS, Thomas. Nonsupative will. December Ct. 1677. Rec. 9 Jany. 1677. Elias Edmonds, son to William Edmonds. Extr. Wm. Edmonds. W.B. 5, p. 48.

EDMONDS, William. Will. 6 Apl. 1741. Rec. 8 May 1741.

Wife Catherine; children referred to (not named). Extrs. Wife and brother Robt. Edmonds. Wits. Henry Carter, Harry Carter, Thos. Brent. W.B. 13, p. 213.

EDMONDS, Robert. Will. 11 Nov. 1750. Rec. 10 May 1750.

Kinsmen: Elias, son of brother Elias Edmonds; John son of brother Wm. Edmonds, decd. William Edmonds, son of brother Elias Edmonds decd., Wife Ann; Robert Edmonds, son of brother

Elias Edmonds; Children of deceased brothers and sisters: Wm. Edmonds, Elias Edmonds and Ann Wharton; children of sister, Hanner Payne, sister Elizabeth Pinckard, and Sarah Sharpe. Extrs. wife, brother in law Geo. Payne and Thos. Sharpe. Wits. Hannah Edwards, Judith Miller, John Edwards. W.B. 15, p. 33.

Division above estate. Rec. 15 June 1753:

Children of Wm. Edmonds: Elias Edmonds, Frans. Bell, Joanna Hubbard, Wm. Edmonds, John Edmonds. Children of Frances Payne: Susanna Brent; Wm. Payne; Ann Payne; Geo. Payne; Frans. Payne; Catherine Payne; Margaret Payne; John Payne and Richard Payne. Children of Anna Wharton: Thos. Wharton; Jos. Wharton; Wm. Wharton; Lindsay Wharton; and Alice Wharton. Children of Elizabeth Pinckard: Robert, James, Charles and Richard Pinckard. Children of Sarah Sharpe: Elias Edmonds Sharpe, Tomazin, Betty, Sarah and Ann Sharpe. Children of Elias Edmonds: William, Elias and Robert Edmonds. W.B. 15, p. 132.

6 June 1763. Rec. 17 June 1763. John Starkey of Carteret County, N. C. and Alice his wife, daughter of Joseph Wharton, late of Craven Co., decd. appoints brother William Wharton attorney to recover from our uncle and guardian Mr. George Payne, of Lancaster county, Va., our part of the estate of Mr. Robert Edmonds of same place, our late uncle, decd. Wits. James Williams, Jno. Starkey. W.B. 17, p. 8.

Division of estate Robt. Edmonds. 17 June 1763. Rec. 14 Aug. 1763. Estate of W. Wharton and his sister Alice that his uncle Mr. Robert Edmonds did give them in the hands of Mrs. Frances Payne. W.B. 17, p. 19.

Rec. 20 Jany. 1764. Division Robt. Edmonds estate.

Estate in hands of Mrs. Frances Payne, widow, belonging to Lindsay, Joseph and Revel Wharton, orphans of Joseph Wharton, decd. from estate of Mr. Robt. Edmonds. W.B. 17, p. 30.

EDMONDS, Elias, the elder, decd. 8 Dec. 1749. Rec. 15 Nov. 1751. In his last will bearing date 24 Apl. 1745 gave to his grandsons William, orphan of Wm. Edmonds, decd., and Robert Edmonds, orphan of Elias Edmonds, the younger, decd. 452 acres land. W.B. 15, p. 81.

EDMONDS, Elias Jr. Division of estate. Rec. 17 July 1752. To Wm. Edmonds, Elias Edmonds, Robert Edmonds; deceased. Guardian of orphans of Elias Edmunds Jr. W.B. 15, p. 100.

EDMUNDS, William. Will. 26 Jany. 1697. Rec. 12 Feby. 1700.

Wife Jane; Sons: Elias and William, plantation whereon he now lives; Dau. Lucy. William Lawrence, writer of will. Wits. Margaret O'Connell, Wm. Lawrence.

EDMUNDS, Elias. Will. 24 Apl. 1745. Rec. 14 Feby. 1745.

Gr.son, Elias Edmunds, son of son William, and his mother-inlaw Mrs. Katherine Edmunds; gr.children: Elias; Francis; Johanna and William, children of son William; Son: Robert Edmunds. Gr.son Elias Edmunds, son of son Elias, decd. gr.sons Robert and William, sons of son Elias decd. Daughters: Frances Payne; Ann Wharton; Elizabeth Pinckard; Sarah Sharpe. Housekeeper: Ann Assey. Extrs. son Robert, son-in-law Joseph Wharton, gr. son Elias, son of Wm. Edmunds. Wits: F Edwards, Emanuel Walker, Ann Assey. W.B. 14, p. 129.

EDWARDS, John. Will. 3 Feby. 1667. Rec. 10 May 1667.

Wm. Ball to sell goods. Wife and three children (no names) left behind in England. Spencer Piggott, of Duke Place, London, Extr. Wits. Rich. Perrott, Wm. ————? and Henry Allen. (Loose Wills)

EDWARDS, Frances. Will.19 Jany. 1730; Rec. 10 Feb. 1730.

Grandsons: Henry, John and Edward Boatman and gr.daughter Mary Boatman, children of Henry Boatman. Gr.Sons John and William Edwards; gr.daughter Lucy Edwards; "4 children of daughter Mary, decd." daughter, Lucy Carter. Sons William and John Edwards. Extr. son William. Wits. Henry Carter, Chas. Chilton, Jno. Carter. W.B. 12, p. 187.

EDWARDS, William (of Christ Ch. Parish) will 18 Nov. 1736; Rec. 8 Apl. 1737.

Wife Elizabeth; Sons: John and William; daughters: Lucy and Frances—"seven children in all." Extrs. Wife and Thomas Yerby. Wits. Henry Carter, Thos. Pinckard, Mary Humphrey. W.B. 13, p. 26.

Division above estate 13 May 1737. Thos. Yerby Guardian to John Edwards, eldest son of Wm. Edwards, decd. W.B. 13, p. 34.

Orphans Estate—10 Oct. 1740. Thos. Yerby, Guardian of John Edwards. W.B. 13, p. 188.

8 May 1741. John Davis intermarried with the widow Edwards. John Griggs appointed Guardian of Thomas Edwards, orphan of Wm. Edwards, decd. W.B. 13, p. 221.

Appraisal & Inventory Wm. Edwards, decd. 8 Apl. 1737. Rec. 10 June 1737. Returned by Eliza. Edwards. W.B. 13, p. 52.

EDWARDS, Lucy. Appraisal. Rec. 21 June 1745. Returned by John Edwards, Admr. W.B. 14, p. 85.

EDWARDS, Thomas and wife Sarah. Deed gift, rec. 12 Nov. 1746. To son Thomas Edwards, land formerly belonging to John Ingram and wife Ann, father and mother of sd. Sarah. Wits. Saml. Hamilton, Robt. Edwards, Sarah Edwards Jr. W.B. 14, p. 131.

EDWARDS, Thomas. Will. 14 Nov. 1759. Rec. 15 Feby. 1760.

Wife (no name) Son Richard. Daughters Betty and Lucy, estate of my mother-in-law Mrs. Ann Ingram in Northumberland county; Sons: Thomas and Robert. Dau. Mary Fleet and release of her husband Maj. Fleet from my debt. Dau. Sarah Keene, and release of her husband Capt. Keene, from my debt. Niece Betty Whiting; Sister, Mrs. Dorothy Matthews; Daus.-in-law Mrs. Judith Fauntleroy and Mrs. Ann Haynie; Col. Landon Carter, Col. Armistead Churchill, Rev. Mr. Currie; Negro man Stephen which will belong to Mr. Swann's estate at wife's death; son Robert land known as Fleet's Point. Extrs. Sons Thomas and Richard Edwards. W.B. 16, p. 80.

Division of Negroes of Thomas and Lucy Edwards, decd. Rec. 21 Nov. 1760.

To Thos. Edwards, John Fleet, Newton Keene, Robert Edwards, Richard Edwards, and Elizabeth Edwards. W.B. 16, p. 116.

EDWARDS, Franky. Will 13 Oct. 1749. Codicil 2 Nov. 1750. Rec. 14 Dec. 1750.

Brother Thomas (not 21) Aunt Letty Schofield, widdow of Robt. Schofield; Aunt, Letty Griggs, wife of Wm. Griggs;. Aunt, Mary Griggs, wife of John Griggs; Aunt Eliza Griggs, wife of Lee Griggs; Letty Griggs' daughter Eliza.; Lee Griggs' eldest son Thomas. Thomas, son of Thomas Pinckard. Extr. Friend Thos. Pinckard. Wits. Betty Winter, Eliza Bentley, Benj. Kelly, Wm. Grigs. W.B. 14, p. 321.

EDWARDS, George. Deed Gift 19 Dec. 1759. Rec. 16 May 1760. To mother Elizabeth Davis, now wife of John Davis, and to Richard Davis her son, for love and affection, a negro which I had by division of my father's estate. W.B. 16, p. 89.

EDWARDS, Robert. Will. 30 July 1760. Rec. 17 April 1761.

Wife, Elizabeth; Sons: George, William, Jesse and Thomas.

Daughters: Elizabeth, Lucy, Mary and Judith Edwards. Extr. son George Edwards. Wits. Francis Timberlake, Joannah George. W.B. 16, p. 136.

EDWARDS, Sarah and her son Richard. Deed of Gift. Rec. 18 June 1761. Land in Lancaster containing 150 acres, which was vested in sd Sarah Edwards, as part of her dower in land from her former husband, John Swan, decd., But, whereas the sd. Sarah Edwards and her late husband, Thomas Edwards, decd. by deed conveyed the sd parcel of land to his son Richard Edwards, one of the parties to this deed, but sd deed not being legally proved and the sd Sarah becomes a party to this deed which sd parcel of land belongs to sd Ann Haynie in reversion as one of the daughters and coheirs of the aforesaid John Swan. W.B. 16, p. 132.

EDWARDS, John. Will. 10 Nov. 1761. Rec. 15 Jany. 1762.

Wife Hannah; sons: William, John, Thomas and Charles; Daus. Sally and Milly. Extrs. Wife Peter Miller and John Yerby, brother of my wife. Wits. Thos. Pinckard, Jno. Pinckard, and Dale Carter. W.B. 16, p. 183.

Division above estate 18 Feb. 1768. Rec. 19 May 1768.

To Mrs. Hannah Edwards; to William Edwards; to Thomas, John, Charles, Sally and Milly Edwards, orphans. W.B. 18, pp. 112-141.

Guardians to John Edwards Orphans. Rec. 17 Jan. 1771. Mr. Richard Ball Gdn. to Sally Edwards, Wm. Edwards, Gdn. to Milly Edwards. By Dale Carter, Thos. Brent, Jno. Yerby. W.B. 20, p. 10.

EDWARDS, Sarah (of Christ Ch. Parish) will 13 Dec. 1768. Rec. 21 March 1771.

Son Richard Edwards. who is also Extr. Wits. Hugh Brent, Nicholas Brent. W.B. 20, p. 26.

EDWARDS, Sarah, orphan of Jno. Edwards, decd. Appmt. of Richard Ball as her Guardian 10 June 1774. Rec. 21 July 1774. W.B. 20, p. 74.

EDWARDS, Thomas. Appraisement. 25 July 1778 by Edwin Conway and Jno. Cundiff. W.B. 20, p. 145.

Charles Bean intermarried with widow of sd. Thomas Edwards, decd., and on 18 April 1782, Geo. Norris apptd. Guardian of Agatha Edwards. W.B. 20, p. 231.

EDWARDS, George. Will. 4 Feby. 1783. Rec. 15 May 1783.
Wife Mary; daughters Elizabeth and Sally Edwards. Extrs.
Wife, Benj. George, Robt. Pinckard, Meredith Mahanes. Wits.
Edwin Conway, Craver Everitt, Jno. Clayton, Nicholas Lawson
George, Meredith Mahanes. W.B. 20, p. 261.

ELLETT, Thomas. Inventory. 17 Jan. 1784. Rec. 19 August 1784.
by Wm. Warren, Ozwald Newby, Rawl. Davenport. W.B. 22,
p. 41.

ELLIOTT, Anthony. Will. 12 August 1666. Pro. 9 Jany. 1666. Rec.
1 Feb. 1666.
Sons: William Elliott, third son Robert Elliott, second son Thomas
Elliott all land. Wife (name not shown) Brother John Armi-
stead, and son Wm. Elliott Extrs. Wits. Peter Conely, Anthony
Armistead. (Loose wills)

EMANUELL, Francis. Noncupative will. 9 Apl. 1690. Rec. 10, Apl.
1690.
Richard Edwards deposes (age 31) that Francis Emanuell did
say on his death bed that he would give his estate to his sister
Mary. Edward Berry, aged 22, makes same statement. W.B.
8, p. 1.

EMANUELL, Francis. Will. 13 Feb. 1669. Rec. 14 Apl. 1690.
Sons William and Francis; daughters: Honover, Avis, Katherine,
Margaret and Mary. Wife (name not shown). Wits. Jno. Brad-
ley, Wm. Boush. W.B. 8, p. 2.

EMBERSON, John. Will. 24 July 1721. Rec. 8 Nov. 1721.
Wife Margaret. Daughter Ann. God dau. Joan Kelley; Godson
James Kilgore. Extrs. Wife brother-in-law Jno. Kilgore. Wits.
Fortunatus Sydnor, Robt. Schofield, Jno. Davis. W.B. 10, p. 336.

EMBREE, William. Inventory. Rec. 11 Sept. 1685. By Sara Row-
buck, relict. W.B. 5, p. 101.

ENGLISH, Alexander. Will. 23 Jany. 1685. Rec. 10 March 1696.
Brother Will English. Other devisees: Jno. Kirby; Rawley Ball;
Wm. Ball, Jr.; Thomas Kirby, son of John Kirby; Wm. Ball Sr.
Extr. Wm. Ball. Wits. Jno. Bayle, Timothy Stamps. W.B. 8,
p. 70.

ENGLISH, Alexander. Will. 16 Dec. 1696. Rec. 16 April 1697.
Devisees: Jon. Paine, son of Wm. Paine. Mrs. Susanna Paine.

Wits. Richard Johnson, Richd. Heicknall, Gilbert Hornby. W.B. 8, p. 71.

Feby. 15 1696. Deposition of Richard Johnson, age 22, regarding will of Alexander English. W.B. 8, p. 62.

EUSTACE, Hancock. August 19 1763. Appoints John Mercer, gent., of Stafford county, attorney to receive money or other estate due him in right of his wife, from the Hon. John Blair, of Williamsburg, Va., Extr. of John Blair Jr., late of same place. W.B. 17, p. 14.

EVERIT, Thomas, of Northumberland County. Will. 26 July 1726. Rec. 13 Sept. 1727.

Wife Elizabeth; Sons: eldest John all land I have etc. Thomas, William, Rawleigh and Jesse. Daughters: Winifred Pullen; Eliz. Pullen; Mary, Sarah, Judith and Lucretia Everit. Extrs. Wife and son John. Wits. Chas. Craven, Matthew Garrett, Jno. Taylor. W.B. 12, p. 32.

EVERITT, Rawleigh. Will. 29 Dec. 1756. Rec. 20 May 1757.

Youngest child, Simmons (not 10 yes. old) Sons: Leroy, John and William Everitt. Wife Sarah, who with Harry Carter are named as Extrs. Wits. Wm. Sanders, Edward Sanders. W.B. 15, p. 290.

EVERITT, John. Will. 8 Nov. 1757. Rec. 21 July 1758.

Sons: Thomas Everitt (not 18 yrs. old) Craven Everitt, estate that his grandfather, Chas. Craven bequeathed to his daughter Betty, "mother of my son Craven Everitt." Thomas Everitt "part of his Aunt Lucy Shelton's part of her father's estate." Thomas Everitt at age of 21 to convey to his brother Craven Everitt an absolute fee simple estate in land bequeathed to his sd brother Craven. the right whereof accrued to sd son Thomas as it came by his mother. Extrs. Harry Carter, brother Thomas Everitt and Moses Pullen. Wits. Coleman Doggett, Jos. Davis, Thos. Brent. W.B. 16, p. 35.

EVERITT, Thomas. Estate appraised 16 Apl. 1772. Rec. 18 March 1773. By Ruth Everitt, Admx., Edwin Conway, James Gordon and Bridgar Haynie. W.B. 20, p. 55.

19 Dec. 1778. Wm. Griggs allotted negroes as dower to his wife, from estate of Thomas Everitt; Wm. Griggs also Guardian of Charles and John Denny Everitt, orphans of sd. Thomas Everitt. W.B. 20, p. 159.

21 August 1783. Mrs. Ruth Griggs allotted estate as Guardian of orphans Charles and John Denny Everitt, that was in the hands of Wm. Griggs, Admr., decd. W.B. 20, p. 266.

Feby. Court 1737. Rec. 16 April 1787. Thomas Everitt's orphans estate. Charles Everitt, orphan of Thomas Everitt, decd., Mrs. Ruth Griggs former Guardian. Said Ruth Griggs her dower in hands of sd Thomas Everitt. By James Ball Jr., Jas. W. Ball, Wm. Warren. W.B. 22, p. 147.

EWELL, Charles. Will. 13 Jany. 1721. Rec. 11 April 1722.
Wife (name not shown); sons: Charles, Bertrand & Solomon; Daus. Maryann & Charlotte; Brian Pullen's eldest son; Mentions land bought of Mathew Mews and land at Tollivers Mount purchased of Thos. Chittwood. Wits. Wm. & Hannah Ball, Brian Pullen, James Ball, Dan Macdonald, Susannah Bertrand. Extrs. Wm. Bertrand & Bryan Pullen. W.B. 10, p. 376.

Appraisement above estate. Recd. 9 May 1722 by Maryann Ewell one of Extrs. W.B. 10, p. 386.

12 Oct. 1734. Rec. 28 Feby. 1734. Darby Gallahew & Sharlott his wife vs. Wm. Ballendine & Mary Ann his wife, and Wm. Bertrand & Brian Pullen, Extrs. of Charles Ewell, decd., regarding legacy bequeathed sd. Charlotte in the last will of sd Chas. Ewell. W.B. 12, p. 334.

EWELL, Capt. Sol. Appraisement of estate 20 July 1768. Rec. 22 July 1768. By Chat. Chowning, John Taylor & Jesse Chilton. Inventory returned by Eve Ewell. W.B. 18, p. 118.

Division Estate rec. 19 Apl. 1770. Mr. James Ewell in right of his wife Mary, dau. of Solomon Ewell, 1/3 estate. W.B. 18, p. 167.

EYRE, Martha. Will. 8 December 1716. Rec. 14 April 1725.
Sole legatee and Executor, Arthur Clarke. Wits. Katherine Howard, Eliz. Smith and John Brown. W.B. 10, p. 466.

FAIRMAN, John (St. Mary's White Chapel Par). Will. 9 Jan. 1726. Rec. 8 Feb. 1726.
Estate to grandchildren my daughter had by John Marshall. Extr. Daniel Stephens. Wits. Wm. Semor, Jno. Flint. W.B. 10, p. 513.

Appraisement above estate recorded 8 March 1726. by Danl. Stephens, Extr. W.B. 10, p. 523.

FAUDRIE, Vachal. Appraisement recd. 25 June 1790. by Wm. George, Saml. Moore, Jos. Stephens. W.B. 22, p. 269.

FAULKNER, Mary. Appraisement. 25 Nov. 1775. Rec. 25 Dec. 1775 by Baillie George. W.B. 20, pp. 90-91.

FEAGINS, Daniel. Will. 29 Jany. 1722. Rec. 11 Nov. 1723.
Legatees: Mary, wife of Lazarus Sutton; Mary wife of Rich. Davis; Margaret Dauck; Lazarus Sutton; Elisha Waters. Wits. Aaron and William Taylor. W.B. 12, p. 178.

FENDLA, John. Will. 14 Dec. 1734. Rec. 12 Feb. 1734.
Extrs. Mr. Christopher Kirk and Geo. Thomas. Wife and children (no names); Eldest son John Fendla; eldest daughter Ellinor, "born a cripple." Wits. James Donallan, Jno. Mason. W.B. 12, p. 326.
Settlement above estate. 2 Oct. 1737. Rec. 14 Oct. 1737. George Flower, Extr. of John Fendly & Thomas Taff and Eliza his wife, late widow of sd. Fendly, set apart for Ellinor Fendly a negro boy. W.B. 13, p. 68.
John Fendla's orphans acct. Rec. 13 Nov. 1747. Gabriel Thatcher made guardian to George Fendla, orphan of John Fendla, decd. W.B. 14, p. 162.

FENDLA, John. Will. Rec. 21 May 1762.
Land to child wife, Judith Fendla, is now with. Daughter Susanna Fendla. Extrs. Anthony Kirk, George Fendla. Wits. Geo. Fendla, Geo. Flower. W.B. 16, p. 211.
15 October 1764. Judith Fendla, widow of John Fendla, decd. appointed Admr. of estate. W.B. 17, p. 71.
Division estate Jno. Fendla, decd. 19 Oct. 1769. Rec. 16 Nov. 1769. Widow Judith Fendla, two orphans, Susannah and Sarah Fendla. W.B. 18, p. 156.

FENDLA, George. Appraisal Estate 20 Dec. 1770. Rec. 21 March 1771. by Wm. Yerby, Jno. Yerby, James Kirk. W.B. 20, p. 11.
17 Nov. 1774. James Fendla, Admr. Geo. Fendla. James Kirk Gdn. to Betty Fendla. W.B. 20, p. 77.

FENDLA, John. Division of estate 15 Dec. 1774. Rec. 18 May 1775. To Thomas Dunaway, Sarah Fendla by James Selden, Johnson Riveer, Richd. Goodridge.

FERGUSSON, Robert. Appraisal 17 Dec. 1792. Rec. 16 June 1794. By Thomas Williams, William Palmer, Geo. Glasscock. W.B. 22, p. 426.

FERMAN, Nicholas. Appraisement. Rec. 14 Jany. 1656. By Rawleigh Travers & Thos. Griffin. W.B. 2, p. 43.

FINCH, George Jr. Inventory. 9Dec. 1743. Rec. 10 Feb. 1743. Returned by Geo. Finch. W.B. 14, p. 7.

FLEET, Henry. Will. 31 Jany. 1728. Rec. 9 May 1733.

Name wife not shown. Sons: Henry; William plantation I now live on; grandsons: Henry Currell, Major Brent, John Fleet; daughters Eliz. Currell, Judith Hobson, Mary Cox. Granddaughters: Ann Currell, Sarah Hobson, Judith Hobson, Eliz. Howson. Fleet Cox. Extrs. Son William, daus. Judith Hobson and Eliz. Currell. Wits. Edwin & Ann Conway, Edwin Conway, Jr. W.B. 12, p. 265.

Inventory above estate rec. by Abraham Currell. W.B. 12, p. 271.

FLEET, William. Inventory rec. 10 July 1734, by Henry Fleet. W.B. 12, p. 318.

FLEET, Henry (Christ Ch. Parish) will 26 Nov. 1735. Rec. 11 Feby. 1735.

Mother Eliz. Fleet, Saml. Hinton, Rebecca Banton, (my dwelling plantations) Thomas Edwards, David Pugh, Wm. Mugg, nephews George & John Fleet; Godson Rich. Edwards. Extrs. John Carter, Thos. Edwards, Sam Hinton. Wits. Thos. Edwards, David Pugh, Wm. Mugg. W.B. 12, p. 358.

FLEET, Henry. Will. 20 Dec. 1785. Rec. 15 Oct. 1787.

Brother John Fleet; sister Ann Hinton; Vincent Brent, Admr. Wits. Thos. N. Lawton, Wm. Cornelius, Thomas Ingram. W.B. 22, p. 157.

FLEET, John. Will. 12 July 1792. Rec. 17 June 1793.

Wife Mary; son John and his heirs "land I had from my uncle Henry Fleet" Daughters, Elizabeth Christian, Dolly Fleet, Judy Fleet. To John, Mary, Lucy, Richard, Ann & Benjamin Ingram, four negroes. Extrs. Wife, Jno. Fleet & Jno. Christian. Wits. Charles Ingram and Robt. Hill. W.B. 22, p. 385.

FLEMMINGS, Walter. Will. 24 Nov. 1655. Rec. 23 Sept. 1656.

Legatees: Robt. Burwell, Hugh Brent, tobacco and bill from Will Wilkinson at Corotoman. Wits. Isaac Walker, Eleanor Walker. Deposition Isaac Weaver(?) age 47 years regarding corn not mentioned in will.

Deposition Eleanor Walker, age 34 years, regarding same. W.B. 2, p. 40.

FLEMING, James. Inventory. 11 Sep. 1717. Rec. 9 Oct. 1717. presented by Martha Fleming, Admx. W.B. 10, p. 245.

FLEMING, Charles. Inventory. 21 Dec. 1772. Rec. 20 May 1773. By Jesse Ball, Jas. Ewell, Jas. Newby. W.B. 20, p. 58.

FLINT, Richard. Will. 18 April 1715. Rec. 11 Jany. 1720.

Wife Martha; Sons: Richard, John, Thomas, David, Alexander. Daughters: Phillis Nichols, Rebekah Chilton. Wits. Nathan Carpenter, Richd. Haynes. Overseers Wm. Payne & Wm. Dare. W.B. 10, p. 306.

FLINT, David. Will. 31 July 1743. Rec. 10 Feby. 1743.

Brother Thomas Flint; daughter Martha Sibly, wife of John Sibly; wife Martha Flint; Gr.son William Sibly. Extrs. Wife and brother Thomas. Wits. Henry Horne, Thos. Mason, Stephen Mackrift Thompson. W.B. 14, p. 6.

Inventory above estate recd. 19 April 1744 by Martha V. Flint, one of Extrs. W.B. 14, p. 16.

FLINT, Thomas (Christ Ch. Par). Will. 11 Jany. 1754. Rec. 17 Feb. 1764.

Daughter Mary Rogers; Gr. Dau. Margaret Rogers; daughter Sarah Hammonds, daughter Betty Norris, daughter Mary Flint; son Thomas Flint; Sons-in-law Jno. Rogers & Charles Hammonds wife Hannah Flint; Son-in-law, Jos. Norris. Extrs. Jno. Rogers & Jos. Norris. Wits. M. Shearman, Ann Shearman, Easter Shearman. W.B. 18, p. 2.

21 Feby. 1764. Rec. 16 July 1764. Deed of gift. Thomas Flint, father of Thomas Flint and grandfather of Betty Hammonds, dau. of Charles Hammonds did give the aforesaid Betty one negro girl. W.B. 18, p. 16.

FLINT, Thomas. Will. 17 March 1783. Rec. 17 April 1783.

Daughter, Molly (not 14) Wife Priscilla; Sons: Richard, Thomas and John Flint. Extrs. Wm. Sydnor, Col. James Ball, Col. James Ball Jr., Mr. James Wallace Ball. Wits. James Ball, Thos. Mitchell, Sally x Mitchell. W.B. 20, p. 257.

Appraisal above estate 23 Apl. 1783. Rec. 18 Dec. 1783 by Johnson Riveer, Jno. Clutton, Ozwald Newby. W.B. 22, p. 6.

Division estate 16 Apl. 1793. Rec. 16 June 1794. James Ball,

Extr. Heirs: Mary, Richard, Winney, John, Thomas & Nancy Flint. By Jos. Chinn, Bartho. Chinn, Rawleigh Tapscott, Jno. Carpenter. W.B. 22, p. 420.

FLOURANE, Thomas. Inventory. 13 June 1740. Rec. 11 July 1740. By Margt. Flourane, Admx. W.B. 13, p. 172.

FLOWER, George. Will. 7 October 1682. Rec. 12 Jany. 1682.

Son George, land; wife Marie; sister's son John Taylor; sister Mary Taylor; Morris Jones, son of Mr. Robert Jones, decd. Extrx. Wife. Overseers Jno. Pinckard, Wm. Jones. Wits. Thos. Lawrence, Tobias Horton, John Nickson. W.B. 5, p. 82.

FLOWER, John. Will. 18 Sept. 1693.

Son John to be with Richard Stevens until 21; daughter Mary to be with Katherine Carter wife of Thomas Carter until 16. Extrs. Thomas Carter, Rich. Stevens. Wits. William George, Henry Carter, John Cooke. W.B. 8, p. 83.

Inventory. 18 Dec. 1698. Rec. 14 June 1698/9. In Thos. Carter's hands for Jno. Flower's dau. Mary, and if she dies before she is of age then to his son John Flowers. W.B. 8, p. 90.

FLOWERS, John. Inventory. 19 November 1717. Rec. 11 Dec. 1717. Presented by Elinor Mills, late Ellinor Flowers, Admx. W.B. 10, p. 247.

FLOWER, George. Will. 17 Feby. 1720. Rec. 10 May 1721.

Wife Sary; Sons: Lee, George, Ransford; daughters: Elizabeth & Mary. Extrs. son Lee and John Sharpe. Wits. Jno. Wale, Hugh Rouland. W.B. 10, p. 310.

FLOWER, Lee. Inventory. Rec. 8 Nov. 1721. Returned by Geo. Flower, Admr. W.B. 10, p. 337.

FLOWER, George. Will. 27 Oct. 1749. Rec. 9 Feby. 1749.

Wife Elizabeth, son George; daughters: Elizabeth Davis; Ann Stephens; Leanna Thatcher; Mary and Judith Flower. Gr. Dau. Elizabeth Davis. Extrs. Francis Timberlake, Wm. Dymer, Geo. Flower. Wits. Ransford Flower, Geo. Flower Jr. W.B. 14, p. 269.

FLOWER, George. Will. 14 June 1762. Rec. 7 Dec. 1762.

Wife Lucy; sons: George and John; daughters: Betty and Nancy Flower. Extrs. Richd. Edwards, Hugh Brent. Wits. Thos. Shearman, Wm. Brent, Wm. Pitman. W.B. 16, p. 244.

Division above estate. Rec. 18 Feb. 1765.

Maurice Brent who intermarried with Lucy Flower, widow of

Geo. Flower, possessed with 1/3 estate. Thomas Brent, Guardian of orphans, Elizabeth, John and Ann Flower, possessed of remaining part. W.B. 17, p. 102.

18 Feb. 1765. Rec. Mch. 18 1765. Maurice Brent possessed with part of Geo. Flower's estate to which he is entitled by his intermarriage with widow. W.B. 18, p. 32.

May 19, 1774. Rec. 20 Apl. 1775. Division Geo. Flower estate. William Lawson, guardian of John Flower, Robert Robuck, husband of Elizabeth Flower, George Flower his part of his fathers estate in hands of Geo. Yerby, his guardian; Nancy Flower's part in hands of Geo. Yerby. W.B. 20, p. 81.

16 Augt. 1780. Widow's dower allotted her. W.B. 20, p. 181.

16 June 1768. John Flower, orphan of George Flower, decd. bound by his guardian, to Wm. Lawson to learn him to read and write and the trade of shop joiner and provide him good sufficient dyet, lodging & apparell & pay him when free as is appointed by Law to servants by Indenture or Custom. W.B. 18, p. 56 (back of book).

FLOYD, Edward. 27 Xber 1690. Rec. 13 March 1690.
Father Mr. Richard Floyd; mother (name not shown) sister, Ann Floyd; William Fox, Saml. Fox and Hannah Fox Jr., Mrs. Hannah Fox, "my mistris" Thomas Cooper, Ex. Wm. Fox. Wits. Thos. Cooper, Nathaniel Phipps. W.B. 8, p. 10.

6 December 1690. Rec. 10 June 1691. Edward Floyd being dangerously sick records debts due him. Wits. Thomas Cooper, Nathaniel Phipps. W.B. 8, p. 19.

FLOYNE, Teague. Inventory. 30 Nov. 1659. Rec. 1 March 1659. Presented by Eliz. Sulleband. W.B. 2, p. 67.

FONTAINE, Mrs. Dorothy. Appraisement. 19 Nov. 1762. Rec. 17 Dec. 1762. Returned by Martha Miller, Admx. W.B. 16, p. 242.

FOOTE, Wm. 10 Jany. 1652. Administration granted to Wm. Clapham. Edward Grimes & Wm. Noosham, Apprs. W.B. 1, p. 23.

FOTHERGILL, William. Inventory recorded 8 May 1717. W.B. 10, p. 210.

FOUCHEE, James. Will. 4 Sept. 1729. Rec. 11 Feb. 1729.
Wife (name not shown. Probably Ruth. See her will); son John; daughters: Charlotte, Susanna Bertrand. Extr. Son John. Wits. Edward Blakemore, David Smith. W.B. 12, p. 144.

FOUSHEE, Ruth. Will. 11 Jany. 1731. Rec. 9 Feby. 1731. (Of St. Mary's White Chappell).

Legatees: Margaret Everit, Wm. Mitchell, John Mitchell, Wm. Bertrand & his wife; Mrs. Ballendine; Daniel Tebbs; Margret Tebbs; Agnes Williams; Sarah Baily; Ruth Ston, Lucretia Wallis, Matthew Mauchaun's wife, Ann Williams, John Mott's wife, Peter Bailey's wife, John Mitchell, sister Mary Hart, Wm. Abby, Ellinor Back, Susanna Bertrand, Ann Williams, Margaret Baily & Sarah Baily, Charles Fleming. Extr. William Bertrand. Wits. Henry Newby, William Mills. W.B. 12, p. 214.

Fox, David. Will. 4 November 1669. Rec. 18 Jany. 1669. probated 11 April 1722.

Wife Anne. Sons David and Will; daughters: Hannah; Rebekah wife of Robt. Tomlin; Elizabeth. St. Mary's White Chapel parish twenty pounds for glazing and further use of sd Church. Extr. David Fox. Overseers: Will Hall and Edward Dale. Wits. Wm. Hall, Edw. Dale, Jno. M. Lemand, Geo. Cooper. W.B. 10, p. 366.

Fox, David. Will. 22 June 1702. Rec. 10 Oct. 1702.

Wife Hannah; sons: Sam, land bought of Mrs. Anna Pritchard wife of Mr. Ruben Pritchard; William, plantation I now live on. Daughter, Hannah, wife of Rodham Kenner. Extrs. Sons. Wits. Thos. Martin, Wm. Hodgkinson, Jas. Paul. W.B. 8, p. 111.

Fox, Samuel. Inventory. 14 June 1712. Rec. 8 July 1713. Returned by Col. Geo. Flete. W.B. 10, p. 162.

Fox, William (of St. Mary's White Chapel Par.) will 22 Mch. 1717. Rec. 12 Nov. 1718.

Wife Anne; daughter Mary; sisters: Hannah Spellman, Anne Fox & Catherine Heale. Nieces Frances Spellman and Frances Fox. Nephews: David Fox and Richard Kenner; Elizabeth Vaulx, Hannah Harris, Elizabeth, Sarah & Ellen Heale, daughters of Geo. Heale; Wm. Dare; Jas. Reeves; Wm. Attchison; Thos. Frazer; Mr. Geo. Heale; Maj. Wm. Ball; James Ball, Wm. Payne. Extrs. Wife Anne and Mr. Wm. Payne. Wits. Nicho. George, Geo. Wale, Eliz. Diggles. W.B. 10, p. 275.

Inventory above estate rec. 13 Feby. 1718. Proved by Anne Chichester, late Anne Fox, and Wm. Payne, Extrs. W.B. 10, p. 301.

Note: Will reads as follows: To St. Marys White Chapel Chh. a font which came in 1717.

"My wife to send for ye Lord's Prayer and ye Creed well drawn in gold letters and my name under each of them, sett in two black frames which I likewise give to ye said church."

Fox, Ann. Will. 13 March 1722. Rec. 1 June 1723.

Legatees: Brother Wm. Daingerfield; sister, Frances Thacker; cousin, Ann Thacker; Edwin Daingerfield, and his wife Elizabeth; Rev. Bartholomew Yeats and his wife Sarah; Vivian Ann Burgess; my daughter Frances Burgess wife of Chas. Burgess. Extrs. Charles Burgess and Frances his wife. Wits. Jane Williams, Rose Kaugh. W.B. 10, p. 435.

Fox, Capt. William. Inventory. Rec. 11 Feb. 1729. Returned by Chas. Burges, Adm. W.B. 12, p. 140.

FRISSELL, William, will 13 August 1675. Rec. 18 Sept. 1676.

Wife Ann. also Extrx. Son Francis; daughters: Ann, Margaret and one other child (not named). Wits. Robt. Cromartie, Jno. Harvey. W.B. 5, p. 26.

FRIZELL, Francisco. (of St. Mary's White Chapel Psh). will 23 Jany. 1732. Rec. 14 March 1732.

Daughters: Mary, Elizabeth; Margaret and Anne. Gr.daughter Beersheba Frizell. Extrs. daughters Mary and Elizabeth. Overseers Jas. Ball, Jno. Selden, Jno. Rains. Wits. John Curlet, Jas. Harding, Jos. Bottom. W.B. 12, p. 249.

Rec. of Court of 9th Nov. 1750.

Francis Frizell late of Lancaster Co. did by his last will devise all that land on which he lived to his daughters, Mary, Margaret and Elizabeth. Thomas Taff intermarried with Mary one of the daughters, left no heir and sd land descends to Elizabeth wife of Robert Martin. 30 acres of the land sold to Robt. McTire. W.B. 14, p. 316.

GALBREATH, Robert. Will. 10 Oct. 1749. Rec. 9 March 1749.

Cousin, Richard Weir; Ezekiel Morris; Margaret Carter. Extr. Cousin Richard Weir. Wits; Isaac White, Michael Dillon. W.B. 14, p. 274.

Inventory of above, returned by Isaac White, admr. 11 May 1750. W.B. 14, p. 285.

Suit: Isaac White, Pltf. vs Katherine Jones, Defd. Robert Galbreath had made a gift to his daughter-in-law Katherine Carter, since intermarried with Humphrey Jones. Dated 29 Sept. 1752. Rec. 18 June 1753. W.B. 15, p. 139.

GOLLOGHER, John. 25 Jan. 1750. Rec. 8 Mch. 1750.

Wife Sarah to have equal share with his children for what they had of their grandfather Richard Davis's estate "which is now in me hands." Boys not 21 and girl not 18. Ex. Wife. Wits: John Walters, John Bailey. W.B. 15, p. 15.

GALLAGHER, John. Appraisement. 8 March 1750. Rec. 8 Apr. 1750.

Sarah Gallagher, Administrator. W.B. 15, p. 25.

GALLOWAY, William, of Parish of Wiccomoco. 10 March 1781. Rec. 19 Oct. 1789.

Wife: Judith. Sons: George, William, Everitt, John & James Galloway & Dau: Lucy & youngest children. Exors: James Wallace & Elijah Percifull. Wits: Jesse Webb, James Wallace, Thos. Brent, Thos. Webb. W.B. 22, p. 226.

Appraisal. James Galloway, Adm. 21 June 1790. W.B. 22, p. 264.

GARETT, William. Will. 23 Feb. ——. Rec. 20 Nov. 1669.

Wife: Ann. Wits: Robert Walker. W.B. Bundle of loose papers, 1653-79, p. —.

GARLAND, Joseph. Nuncupative will. Rec. 11 Dec. 1712.

To David Ball, Sen. Proved by oath of John Bayley & John Murphy. W.B. 10, p. 161.

GARNER, Hannah. Appraisement. She formerly lived at the house of Gawin Lowry. Will, 19 March 1778. Rec. 17 Feb. 1780.

By Geo. Carter, John Harris, Rodham Lunsford. W.B. 20, p. 176.

GARNER, William, of Christ Church Parish. 8 Aug. 1790. Rec. 19 Apr. 1791.

Wife: Ellen Garner. Mentions children but not names. Extrx: Wife, Ellen Garner. Wits: Martin Norris, William George. W.B. 22, p. 305.

GARRET, Anthony. Appraisement & Inv. Rec. 13 Nov. 1678.

Presented by John Davenport. W.B. 5, p. 52.

GARTON, Tobias. Inv. Rec. 12 Oct. 1688.

Presented by Martha Garton. W.B. 5, p. 126.

92   ABSTRACTS LANCASTER COUNTY, VIRGINIA, WILLS—1653-1800

GARTON, Will, of Parish of Christ Church. 12 Dec. 1709. Rec. 8 Feb. 1709.

Sons, James, Anthony and Uriah, Daus: Katherine and Margaret. Exors: Sons and daus. Wits: Murter Noulin, Wm. Battery, Katherine Noulin, Elizabeth Bibelow. Son-in-law: Wm. Butler. W.B. 10, p. 63.

GARTON, Anthony. 12 Nov. 1763. Rec. 20 Jan. 1764.

Sons: Benjamin Garton, Anthony Garton. Daus: Elizabeth Cox, Elinor Kilpatrick. Gr.son: Benjamin Garton. Sons-in-law: George Jackson, Wm. Cox. Exors. Sons Benjamin and Anthony Garton. Wits: Harry Currill, Elizabeth Kelly, Peter Garton. W.B. 17, p. 27.

GARTON, Anthony. Appraisement. 20 Jan. 1764. Rec. 17 Feb. 1764.

By Harry Currill, William Martin, Simon Diggs. Division of estate between Benjamin Garton, Anthony Garton, Thomas Cox and Elinor Kilpatrick. Dated Feb. 26, 1764. Rec. 16 March 1764. W.B. 18, p. 1; W.B. 18, p. 5.

GARTON, Benjamin. 22 Sept. 1793. Rec. 21 Oct. 1793.

Son: Benjamin. Dau: Judith Clemons, Wife of John Clemmons. Dau-in-law: Mary Garton. Gradau: Sarah Cornelius Wife of William Cornelius and their sone John John B. Cornelius. Leviney Lawson. Ann Hill, Betty Hill and Judith Hill, daus of Rachel Crowther. Extrs: Lawson Hathaway, Benjamin Garton. Wits: Mathew James; Jno. King and Lawson Hathaway. W.B. 22, p. 397.

GARTON, Letice, Widow. 15 Feb. 1795. Rec. 15 June 1795.

Renounces benefits of will of Anthony Garton her late husband. W.B. 22, p. 458.

GASKINS, Phillip. 9 Apr. 1755. Rec. 18 Apr. 1755.

Son: John Gaskins (not of age). Wife: Mary Gaskins. "Mr. Joseph Chinn and his wife to have the care of my dau. Ann until she comes to age of 18." Wife to have care of 2 daus. Lucy & Hannah. 6 children: Lucy, Hannah, Ann, Judy, Mary and John. Exors: Son John and Thomas Myars. Wits: John Harris, James Richardson. W.B. 15, p. 203.

GASKINS, Thomas. Appraisal. 18 Feb. 1783. Rec. 15 Apr. 1793.

Edwin Gaskins, Adm. By Jno. Degges, Thos. Mott, Thos. Carter. W.B. 22, p. 373.

GEORGE, Nicholas. Prob. 20 May 1661. Rec. 1 June 1661.

Son: Nicholas. Dau: Grace George land adjoining John Edwards. Wife and 2 Daus cattle, etc. Wits: John Sharp, Henry Davis. W.B. Loose Wills.

GEORGE, Margaret. 8 Feb. 1668. Rec. 11 June 1670.

Dau: Sarah Marshall. Ex. Abraham Davis. Wits: Tho. Daniell, George Healee, Nicholas Healee & Richard Mereman. W.B. Loose Wills.

GEORGE, Richard. Inv. 20 Oct. 1675. Rec. 10 Nov. 1675. W.B. 5, p. 15.

GEORGE, John. 1 March 1692. Rec. 19 Apr. 1693.

Devisees: John Richard, John Brown, of northumberland, Wm. Abby, Richard Abby, Thomas Sampson (exor.), Landlady, Margaret Mitchell, Wm. Mitchell & wife Margaret. Wits: John Sampson, Ann Arnold. W.B. 8, p. 39.

GEORGE, Nicholas. 9 Mar. 1699. Rec. 12 July 1700.

Wife, Eliza Ann. Sons, Benjamin, Nicholas, Elmer, William. Dau. Ruth. Exors, Wife and Benj. George. Wits: James Ball, Wm. Baley. 3 sons-in-law. W.B. 8, p. 94.

GEORGE, William. 6 Feb. 1709. Rec. 10 May 1710.

All his estate to his wife to bring up her children. Wits: Ben Doggitt, Elinour George. W.B. 10, p. 17.

GEORGE, Will. Inv. & Ap. Rec. June 14, 1710.

Presented by Elizabeth George, widow and relict. W.B. 10, p. 56.

GEORGE, William. Inv. Rec. 11 Sept. 1717.

Presented by Robert. Marshall & Elizabeth his wife, adms. of Wm. George. W. B. 10, p. 242.

GEORGE, Nicholas, of Parish of Christ Church. 3 July 1733. Rec. 3 Aug. 1733.

Wife not named. Sons: Wm. Plantation he now lives on; David, plantation I now live on; Sam'l, Isaac, Nicholas and Benjamin. Daus., Lettice, wife of Abraham Harper. Exor. Son David. Wits: Henry Carter, Jno. George, Elmour Doggett. Exor. Benjamin George, Brother. W.B. 12, p. 275.

GEORGE, William. 23 Oct. 1749. Rec. 4 May 1749.

Daus: Mary Ann George and Judy George. Son: Isaac, Mentions others but not named. Wife: Mary. Exors: Wife Mary and son Isaac. Wits: Dale Carter, John Wright. W.B. 14, p. 244.

GEORGE, Elmore. 28 Jan. 1747/8. Rec. 12 May 1749.

Son: Moses George, the plantation I now live on; John George and his wife Eliza. Gr.son: Thomas George, son of Moses. Brother: Benjamin George. Gr.son: Elmore George, son of Moses. Dau: Jemima Chilton. Ex. Son Moses. Wits: Wm. George, Jr., James Doggett, Dale Carter. W.B. 14, p. 244.

GEORGE, Thomas. Adm. account. Rec. 14 July 1749.

Returned by Rebeckah George, adm. W.B. 14, p. 251. 13 May 1748. Rec. 18 June 1748.

Inv. returned by Rebeckah George, admx. W.B. 14, p. 196.

GEORGE, Benjamin. 29 Dec. 1746. Rec. 8 Feb. 1750.

Sons: Lazarus, Benjamin and Nehemiah George. Daus: Eliza Edwards, Judy Mason, Ruth Mitchell. Wife: Eliza George. Exors: Sons Benjamin & Lazarus. Wits: Geo. Connelly, John Wright, Geo. Connelly, Jr., Dale Carter. Codicil (30 Oct. 1750). Dau. Ruth Mitchell Now dead, her interest divided among her 4 children Ruth, Eliza, Grissel & Hannah. W.B. 15, p. 4.

GEORGE, Joseph. Inv. 8 Feb. 1750. Rec. 19 July 1751.

Returned by Wm. Chelton, Jun., Adm. W.B. 15, p. 46.

GEORGE, John. Inv. & Ap. 30 May 1758. Rec. 21 July 1758.

Returned by Eliza George. W.B. 16, p. 31.

GEORGE, William. 10 March. 1760. Rec. 16 May 1760.

Dau: Rebecca Connolly. Fr.son: Spencer Doggett and his two sisters Rebecca Doggett & Lucy Doggett. Dau: Lucy George. Wife: Rebecca George. Children: Martin, Betty, William, Henry, Spencer, Nicholas, Bayley & Jesse George. Exors: Wife and sons Martin & Wm. George. Wits: Judith Tucker, Dale Carter, Moses George. W.B. 16, p. 86.

GOERGE, William. Rec. June 5, 1760.

Returned by Rebecca George. Division of estate. To Wm. Payne, husband to the Widow of Wm. George, dec. W.B. 16, pp. 93, 255.

GEORGE, William. Inv. Rec. July 1, 1762.

Returned by Lucia Payne. W.B. 16, p. 348.

GEORGE, Benjamin G. Rec. 14 July 1760.

Sons: Benjamin & Enoch Land Lately purchased of Mr. John Eustace. Wife: name not given. Exors: Son Benjamin and friend Thos. Edwards. Wits: Anne George, Enoch George. W.B. 16, p. 103.

GEORGE, Elizabeth. 7 Dec. 1760. Rec. 20 Feb. 1761.

Sister: Winnifred More & Judy Davis, Mary Davis, wife of Moses Davis & Sarah Davis. Wm. Chilton, son of my sister Rebecca Brooks and also Juduthan Chilton her son. Ex. Friend Edwin Chilton. Wits: Dale Carter, Edwin Chilton. W.B. 16, p. 122.

GEORGE, William. Inv. 11 July 1762. Rec. 16 Dec. 1762.

Returned by Lucia Payne, late widow of Wm. George, dec. W.B. 17, p. 248.

Wm. Payne, the husband of the widow of Wm. George, dec., allotted ⅓ part of negroes. 17 Dec. 1762. W.B. 17, p. 249.

18 Feb. 1765. Wm. Payne appointed guardian of Ellinor & Daniel George, orphans of Wm. George. W.B. 17, p. 102.

GEORGE's orphans by Payne. Rec. 18 Aug. 1766.

Daniel, Ellen And William George, three orphans of Wm. George, dec., under guardianship of William Payne. W.B. 18, p. 67.

GEORGE, Moses, 9 Dec. 1771. Rec. 16 Apr. 1772.

Wife; Rebecca. Sons: Moses and Thomas. Daus: Mary Ann, Beckah, Jemima and Sarah. Exors: Wife and son Moses. Wits: Dale Carter, Samuel X. Brooks, William Chilton. W.B. 20, p. 40.

Inv. returned by Rebecca George. W.B. 20, p. 43.

GEORGE, Wm. Inv. & Division. Rec. 25 Oct. 1775.

To Daniel George, Ellen George, William Geroge. By Edward Blackmore, Wm. Chowning, Henry Towles. W.B. 20, p. 89.

GEORGE, Daniel, who intermarried with Elizabeth Read, Nicholas George his Attorney, Epaphroditus Timberlake, adm. of Nicholas Read, dec. Signed in Fauquier Co. Dated: 19 Nov. 1777. Rec. 19 Feb. 1778. W.B. 20, p. 126.

GEORGE, George. Appraisement. Rec. 17 Oct. 1782.

By Wm. Meredith, James Pollard, Wm. Mason, John James. W.B. 20, p. 249.

GEORGE, Lazarus. 3 July 1783. Rec. 16 Oct. 1783.

Wife: Judith. Sons: John—minor, Benjamin plantation descended to me by my father; William Robert. Daus: Elizabeth, Lucy, Judith. Ex. Robert Walker, Moses George, Benjamin George—son. Wit: Sarah Ann Walker, Winfred Walker, James Gordon. W.B. 22, pp. 5-6.

GEORGE, Thomas. 29 May 1782. Rec. 15 Apr. 1784.

Wife: Frankey. Sons: Martin, Nicholas. Daus: Frankey, Ann, Mary. Ex: Thomas Dunaway, Nicholas George, William Arms. Wits: John Merryman, Ann Merryman. W.B. 22, pp. 2-6.

GEORGE, Nicholas. 28 Sept. 1781. Rec. 22 July 1785.

Sons: William, Thomas, not 14 yrs. of age); Nicholas, not 21 yrs. of age); Gilbert. Daus: Catherine, Frances. Brother: Bailey George. Youngest son Thomas not 14. To son Gilbert land purchased of Nicholas Payne. To son Nicholas land purchased from Mrs. Betty Payne. Ex. Wife, Brother, Bailey George, Jesse George, Friend Matt. Myers. Wit. Matt. Myers, Spencer George, Jesse George. Will presented by Frances George, widow & Estrx. W.B. 22, p. 87.

17 Nov. 1785. Frances George renounces rights under will of her late husband, Nicholas George. W.B. 22, p. 109.

21 Sept. 1786. Appraisal. By Henry Carter, John Payne, William Briscoe. W.B. 22, p. 132.

GEORGE, Bailey. Appraisal. Oct. 1782. Rec. 15 June 1786.

By William Gibson, Lawson Hathaway, James Pollard. W.B. 22, p. 122.

GEORGE, Martin. Apprais. & Division of est. June 1787. Rec. 17 Dec. 1787.

Heirs: Widow her ⅓, Harrison George, William George, Joseph Hubbard, John Thrall, Rawleigh George, Zamouth George, Tarpley George. Division by: Henry Lawson; Isaac Degge, Lawson Hathaway & Henry Hinton. W.B. 22, p. 161.

19 July 1790. Map of lands and division. Heirs: Widow, William George, Harrison George, Joseph Hubbard, Rawleigh George, Zamoth George, John Thrall, Tarpley George. By Henry Lawson, Isaac Degge, Lawson Hathaway, Henry Hinton. W.B. 22, p. 288.

GEORGE, Juduthan. 12 May 1784. Rec. 21 Jan. 1788.

Wife: Darcus George. Dau: Betsy Waters B. George. Ex: Col. Edwin Conway & Capt. John Degge. Wits: Ezekiel Tapscott, Betty Tapscott, Mary Tapscott, John Tapscott. W.B. 22, p. 164.

GEORGE, Capt. Jesse. Appraisal. Rec. 17 Sept. 1702.

By Martin Shearman, Henry Lawson, James Pollard. W.B. 22, p. 350.

GEORGE, Anthony. Appraisal. 21 Dec. 1789. Rec. 18 Feb. 1793.

By Wm. Meredith, Geo. W. Yerby, William Doggett, jr. W.B. 22, p. 364.

GEORGE, Benjamin. Apprais. & Division of est. 20 Dec. 1791. Rec. 18 Feb. 1793.

Heirs: Catherine George, widow, Nicholas L., Fortunatus, and Martin George, Benjamin Warrick, Catherine George, Sarah George, Richard Yerby, Anney George, Enoch George. W.B. 22, p. 368.

GEORGE, Catherine. 4 Dec. 1793. Rec. 20 Jan. 1794.

Sons: Fortunatus and Enoch George. Daus: Sarah and Ann Edney George. Wits: George P. Oliver, Martain George, Sarah George. W.B. 22, p. 402.

16 Dec. 1793. Rec. 22 Apr. 1794.

Division of Estate. W.B. 22, p. 418. To Nicholas and Fortunatus George, Judith Yerby, Martin George, Catherine Schofield, Sharlot Warrick, Sally George, Enock George, Ann E. George.

GEORGE, Daniel. Appraisal. Rec. 15 June 1795.

By Henry Towles, William Biscoe & William George. W.B. 22, p. 456.

GIBBS, James. Appraisement. 15 Aug. 1771. Rec. 18 Sept. 1771.

By Michael Wilder, Jonathan Wilder, Bailie George, Thos. Pollard. W.B. 20, p. 26.

GIBSON, John. 21 Dec. 1697. Rec. 12 Aug. 1698.

Wife: Dorothy. Son: John. Other children but not named Extrx: Wife. Wits: Alex. Swan, Margaret Swan, Jno. Hughs. W.B. 8, p. 82.

GIBSON, Edward. Inv. & Ap. Rec. 12 June 1717.

Proved by oath of Robert Carter, Esq., adm. W.B. 10, p. 226.

GIBSON, Rebecca. 26 Mar. 1717. Rec. 12 Feb. 1717.

Sons: Wm. Martin, Isaac Currell, Abraham Currell, Jacob Currell, Nicho. Martin. Granddau: Elizabeth. Dau.-in-law: Elizabeth Martin. Dau: Elizabeth Cook. Wits: Elia. Fleet, Eliz. Martin, Jno. Angell. Grandson: John Cook. W.B. 10, p. 248.

GIBSON, Ruth. 7 Feb. 1709. Rec. 11 May 1739.

Legatees: Son, Robert Griggs Gibson, land given me by my father lying up Bay, also land in Essex; daus., Winifred and Elizabeth

Gibson; husband, Robert Gibson. Extrs.: Husband, Henry Lawson and Edward Newgent. W.B. 13, p. 132.

GIBSON, Robert. 9 Jan. 1739. Rec. 8 Aug. 1740.

Grandchildren: Ezek'l, Morice, Wm. and Eliz. Gilbert, who are children of my dau. Winifred Gilbert. Son: William Gibson. William and George Gibson sons of my brother, John Gibson. Friend: Nicholas Martin. Exor.: Son, William. Wits: Nicholas Martin, John Gibson, Thomas Edwards, the last a trustee. W.B. 13, p. 171.

GIBSON, William. 6 Mar. 1752. Rec. 15 May 1752.

Wife: Judith Meredith. Brothers-in-law: John Meredith & James Meredith. Sons: John and William Gibson. Daus: Sally and Judith Gibson. Exors: Wife, Judith and father-in-law John Meredith and his 2 sons John & Jas. Meredith. Wits: James Meredith, Harry Currell, Jonathan Wilder. W.B. 15, p. 95.

GIBSON, William. 15 May 1752. Rec. 17 July 1752. Inv. & Ap.

Returned by John Meredith & Judith Gibson, Exors. W.B. 15, p. 104.

GIBSON, William. Division of estate. 17 Sept. 1762. Rec. 15 Apr. 1763.

Mr. Rawleigh Shearman (by Judith Gibson's part of her father's estate. George Yerby, Jr. (wife's part of her father's estate) Mrs. John Yerby (by Wm. Gibson's part of his father's estate) Administrators, James Kirk, Wm. Yerby. W.B. 16, p. 255.

GILBERT, Ezekiel. 12 Apr. 1744. Rec. 8 June 1744.

Exors: Sons Ezekiel & Morris. Wits: Wm. Gibson, George Heuphryes, Nicho. Lawson. Wife: Elizabeth Gilbert. Children: Ezekiel, Morris and Elizabeth Gilbert. W.B. 14, p. 19.

14 Oct. 1748. Thos. Edwards guardian of Eliza Gilbert, orphan of Ezekiel Gilbert. W.B. 14, p. 217.

GILBERT, Ezekiel. Mar. 26, 1752. Rec. 17 July 1752.

Wife: Elizabeth Gilbert. Dau: Anna Stepto Gilbert. Brother: Maurice Gilbert "and his first son names after my name." Sister: Elizabeth Gilbert. Brother-in-law: Epaphroditus Lawson. Exors: Wife, Elizabeth and Major Conway and Maurice Gilbert. Wits: Will Dymer, Nicholas Brent. W.B. 15, p. 102.

GILBERT, Elizabeth, widow of Ezekiel Gilbert, Deceased. 8 Apr. 1758. To brother-in-law, Maurice Gilbert. W.B. 16, p. 198.

GILBERT, Maurice. 24 Apr. 1758. Rec. 20 Oct. 1758.

Sisters: Elizabeth Shearman, Ann Steptoe Gilbert, Mr. Thos. Pinchard, gent. and "cloth out of Edward Ker's store for his son Thomas." Robert and Richard Edwards, Rawleigh Shearman, Maj. Richard Selden, Mr. Francis Pinckard, Charlott Taylor and Thos. Pinckard, Jr. John Selden, Jr. Exors: Coll. Wm. Ball and Rawleigh Shearman. Wits: Richard Selden, Barbee Davis, Laz, Coppedge. W.B. 16, p. 42.

GILLETT, John. Inv. Rec. 12 Jan. 1652.

By andrew Gilson, George GT Taylor. W.B. 1, p. 36.

GILLS, Michael, Apprais. Rec. 10 July 1728.

Returned by David Smith. W.B. 12, p. 63.

GILMOUR, Robert. 23 May 1782. Rec. 18 July 1782.

Son: Joh, all that part of my estate in North Britain left me by my grandfather, Vizt: The Farms of Borland & Broombree, the parts of Hungary, low Neatherton & Yards in Neatherton and House at the end of Bridge in Kilmarnock. Son: Robert land in Frederick Co, right and title to my father's estate in North Britain. Wife: Mentions his cash account at the store kept by Wm. Lawson at Falmouth. Exors: Col. James Ball, Dr. Wm. Ball, David Galloway, Jr. John Deans, Mungo Harvey. Wits: Mungo Harvey, Judith Galloway, J. Dean, John Richardson. W.B. 20, p. 239.

GLAVE, Jos, of Worron hundred in ye County of Cheshire, England. 27 Jan. 1799. Rec. 8 May 1700.

All given to his mother Mary Hill. Wits: Chas and Elias King and Jno. Harris. W.B. 8, p. 111.

GOOCH, Samuel, of Lancaster sells land which Thomas Attowell gave by will to his eldest daughter Mary, "My Wife," deceased. Plantation called Cheeseman Creek in York County. 26 Oct. 1657. W.B. 2, p. 142.

GOODRIDGE, Wm. Jr. Inv. & Ap. Rec. 19 May 1758.

Returned by Richard Goodridge, adm. W.B. 16, p. 19.

GOODRIDGE, William, of Wiccomico Parish. 10 Mar. 1769. Rec. 21 Mar. 1771.

Son: John to have the sum of ten pounds in Household Goods or Stock to equal other children that are married. Dau: Susanna to have same to make her equal to other children who are married. Sons: Richard and George Goodridge. Dau: Betty Hunton. Dau; Mary Stoneham's children. She being decease. Wife; Elizabeth. George Stoneham security for Mary Stoneham's children. Exors: Sons, Richard, George & John Goodridge. Wits: Richard Mitchell, Thomas Pitman, Ambrose Pitman. W.B. 20, p. 11.

Division: Alexander Hunton's part, Richard Cundiff's part, George Stoneham, John Goodridege, George Goodridge. 14 June 1771. Rec. 20 June 1771. W.B. 20, p. 17.

GOODSELL, John. 14 Jan. 1675. Rec. 1 Apr. 1675.

Wife: Mary. Dau. Joane of Ireland. Exors: Peter Stevens, John Day. Wits: Thos. Sherwood, Sarah Sherwood, John Lee. W.B. 5, p. 14.

GORDON, James. Inv. Rec. 8 Feb. 1744. W.B. 14, p. 44.

GORDON, James. 6 Jan. 1767. Rec. 18 Feb. 1768.

Son: James Gordon (460 A. of land bought of Col. Edwin Conway and Mr. John Bell) Not 21) Wife: Mary. Daus: Mary Gordon Land bought of Mr. Chas. Bell; Elizabeth at age of 21. Sons: Nathaniel land bought of Mr. John Belfield and John Griggs at age of 21; John. Gr.dau: Milicent Chichester at age of 21. Friend Rev. Mr. James Waddle. Brothers: John Gordon's children. Brother: John Gordon all right to my land in the Kingdom of Ireland which was devised to me by the last will and testament of my Father" Cousins: George Gordon, Samuel Henning. And Robet. Henning. Friend: Bridgar Haynie. Exors: Wife and son James. Proved by Oaths of David Boyd and Bridger Haynie. W.B. 18, p. 105.

Inv. returned by Mary Gordon and James Gordon. W.B. 18, p. 127.

GORDON, Coll. James. Division. 19 Dec. 1771. Rec. 20 Aug. 1772.

To Elizabeth Gordon, Nathaniel Gordon, John Gordon, James Gordon, Rev. Mr. James Waddell in right of his wife. By Dale Carter, Henry Tapscott, Edwin Conway. W.B. 20, p. 45.

GRAHAM, John. Inv. Rec. 14 Sept. 1717.

Returned by Rebecca Graham. W.B. 10, p. 240.

GREENE, John. Rec. 1 Mar. 1654.

Wife: Mary Greene. Son: John Greene 200 acres of land and desires Andrew Gilson to keep the child. Wits: Andrew Gilson, John Smith. W.B. 2, p. 6.

GREGORY, Joseph. Inv. Rec. 14 June 1727.

Presented by Sarah Gregory, admx. W.B. 10, p. 556.

GREGORY, Abraham. Inv. & Ap. Rec. 8 June 1750.

Returned by Anna Gregory, admx. W.B. 14, p. 289.

GRIFFIN, Thomas B. 3 Feb. 1778. Rec. 21 May 1778.

Wife: Judith Griffin, dec. A marble Slab to be placed on the vault with following inscription: "here lies deposited the dear, sacred Remains of Judith Griffin, Daughter of Carter Burwell, Esq., born the 11 of April 1755, married to Thomas B. Griffin November 8, 1766, and snatched away by a violent sudden illness the 20 November 1769. She was the most affectionate, dutiful wife that ever blessed the married state, as pious and devout a soul as ever was received into Christianity and performed every Call and Duty in Life with the greates Pleasure and Sweetness. The best of Women and the Best of Wives. She had a son called LeRoy and a daughter named Lucy who both died soon after they were born and lye entombed with her."

Nieces: Nancy Corbin, Elizabeth and Judith Griffin, daus. of my brother LeRoy Griffin, dec. Sister: Elizabeth Adams and Mr. Richard Adams her husband. Brothers: Corbin Griffin, Wm., Samuel, Cyrus and John Taylor Griffin. Niece Mary Griffin, dau of my brother Cyrus. Neices: Nancy, Elizabeth and Judith Griffin, daus of my dec. brother, LeRoy Griffin.

Ex. Brother, Wm. Griffin. Wits: Samuel Brumly, Wm. Brent, Eapeannea Vernon. James Ball, jr. W.B. 20, p. 129.

6 Nov. 1778. Division of Negroes. Heirs: Corbin, John, William, Samuel & Cyrus Griffen. W.B. 20, p. 191.

GRIGGS, Robert. 22 Jan. 1683. Rec. 30 Jan. 1683.

Son: Michaell. Dau: Ruth Mottrom (her husband being deceased) Wm. Carter, Elizabeth Russell, Elizabeth Carter, Dau of Col. Jno. Carter. Ex.: Son Michael & dau. Ruth Mottrom. Wits: Robert Carter, Elizabeth Russell, Richard Grimes, Wm. Pritchard, Jno. ———. W.B. 5, p. 91.

GRIGGS, Michaell. 22 Mar. 1687/8. Rec. 15 Dec. 1692.

Wife: Ann Griggs. Brother-in-law: Robert Schofield. Sister-in-law: Elizabeth Schofield. Wits: Charles Lee, Elizabeth Lee, John Corking. Exors: Wife and brother-in-law, Robert Schofield. W.B. 8, p. 39.

GRIGGS, Thos. 20 Mar. 1725/26. Rec. 13 July 1726.

Wife: Frances. Sons: Robt. Thos., John, Lee, William. Daus.
Mary, Elizabeth, Letitia. Wits: Thos., Lee and Abraham Currell.
Extrx: Wife Frances. W.B. 10, p. 531.

GRIGGS, Lee. Appraisement. Rec. 19 Nov. 1773.

By Edwin Conway, John Bean, Henry Martin Horne. W.B. 20,
p. 67.

GRIGGS, William, of Parish of Christ Church. 10 Aug. 1780. Rec.
21 Feb. 1782.

Gr.sons: Wm. and Thomas Doggett. Dau: Elizabeth Carter.
Gr.children: Patrick Connolly, Charlotte Connolly and Wm.
Griggs Connolly. Exors: Henry Lawson, Thomas Lee, James
Pollard and Rev. Shearman. Wits: Henry Lawson, Nicholas
Currell, Jr., Thomas Lawson.

GRIGGS, Wm. Appraisement. Rec. 17 Oct. 1782.

By Bailie George, Lawson Hathaway, John Parrott. W.B. 20,
pp. 247, 260.

Elias Edmonds & John Goodridge, allotted part of estate. Ruth
Griggs, widow allotted her dower ⅓ of land. W.B. 20, pp. 247,
260.

GRIGGS, William. Division of Estate. Rec. 18 Feb. 1793.

Heirs: Wiliam Griggs Connerly, George James & Charlotte his
wife. By John Degges, John Miller & Jas. Tapscott. W.B. 22,
p. 367.

Account of estate. Elias Edmonds, Adm. 23 Aug 1786. W.B.
22, p. 129.

GROVES, John. Rec. 14 Apr. 1749.

Wife: Lucy Groves. Son: John Groves. Test. Ambrose Grayson,
Jeals Davis. W.B. 14, p. 234.

GRIMES, Edward. 7 Aug. 1653. Rec. 10 Feb. 1653.

Wife: Margaret. To William Wraton, Ann White and Mary
Gooch. Daughter-in-law: ffra: Attawell land in Rappahannock
Co. Ex.: Wife Mar: Grimes. Wits: Davey Fox, John Philips.
W.B. 1, p. 124.

GRYMES, Margaret, widow. 18 Feb. 1658. Rec. 1 Apr. 1658.

Sons: Wm Raughton and Wraughton. Son-in-law: Will White.
Dau: Anne White, Frances Roots. Thos. Raughton, son of Will

Raughton, Will White the younger. Wits: Nich. George, Thos. Marshall. W.B. 2, p. 61.

GUNTER, Chas. 28 Oct. 1750. Rec. 9 Nov. 1750.

Wife: Judith. 4 children: William, John, Jane and Charles. Ex: Wife Judith and son Wm. Wits: James Ball, Jr., Charles Flemming. W.B. 14, p. 316.

14 Dec. 1750. Ap. returned by Judith Gunter. W.B. 14, p. 320.

HACKETT, Thos. Inv. 11 Feb. 1656. Rec. 27 Jan. 1657.

Mary Hackett, Widow. W.B. 2, p. 125.

HALL, Mary. Inv. Rec. 9 Apr. 1718. W.B. 10, p. 259.

HALL, Caleb. 10 Nov. 1730. Rec. 11 Nov. 1730.

Nicholas Martin certifies that Richard Jackson and Ann his wife made oath before him that Kaleb Hall was 16 yrs. of age sometime last July. W.B. 12, p. 178.

HAMBLETON, John. 11 Nov. 1699. Rec. 13 Dec. 1699.

No devisees. Only provisions for payments of Debts. Exor: Philip Rogers. Wits: Mark Johannis, Jas Kelley, John Pyne. W.B. 8, p. 102.

HAMILTON, Samuel, of Christ Church Parish. 21 Dec. 1773. Rec. 17 Feb. 1774.

Wife: Ann Hamilton whole estate. Wits: William Meredith, Isaac Pitman. W.B. 20, p. 69.

HAMILTON, Ann. 23 Nov. 1774. Rec. 16 Jan. 1777.

Dau: Ann Meredith. Wits: William Meredith, William Yerby, John Meredith. W.B. 20, p. 101.

HAMON, Chas. 9 Oct. 1735. Rec. 12 Nov. 1735.

Wife: Darkis. Sons: Charles, Plantation I now live on; four others not named, left in care of Mr. Wm. Eustace until 21 yrs; of age. Exors: Wife and son Chas. Wits: Wm. Thomas, Jno. Hart, Clem Lattimer. W.B. 12, p. 355.

10 Mar. 1735. Apprais. returned by Darcus Thomas, Extrx. W.B. 12, p. 362.

Executors report of administration of Wm. Thomas & Darcus his wife, Extrx. of Chas. Hammon, dec. W.B. 13, p. 25.

HAMMONDS, James. Ap. 12 June 1741. Rec. 14 Aug. 1741.

Returned by George Duke, one of the Adms. W.B. 13, p. 237.

HAMMONDS, Charles. Orphans estate. Rec. 13 Sept. 1743.

James, Amos & Anne Hammonds, orphans of Charles Hammonds. W.B. 13, p. 342.

HAMMOND, Thomas. Inv. 12 Apr. 1745. Rec. 10 May 1745.

Returned by Charles Clephon & Elizabeth His wife, admx. W.B. 14, p. 75.

HAMMOND, Charles. Division of Estate. 14 Apr. 1749. Rec. 12 May 1749.

To orphans of Charles Hammond: Charles Hammond, James Hammond, Ann Hammond. W.B. 14, p. 238.

HAMMOND's, James, estate sold. 21 Dec. 1753. W.B. 16, p. 163.

HAMMOND, Charles. 13 Jan. 1767. Rec. 19 Nov. 1767.

Wife: Sarah. Sons: Thomas and Charles Hammond. Exors: Wife and son Thomas. Wits: Charles Hammond, Jr. Ezekiel Haydon, Eliza X. Hammond. W.B. 18, p. 94.

HANSFORD, Stephen. Rec. 8 July 1743.

Deposition of Stephen Hansford, of town of Abbotsbury in Co. of Dorset now of the Co. of King George in the Colony of Va., 44 Yrs. of age. States that he was well acquainted with Mr. John Chichester of the Co. of Devon, son of Richard Chichester of Rappahannock River in Va., and the sd. John Chichester intermarried with one Mrs. Elizabeth Sims, dau of Mr. Thomas Sims & Mary his wife of Goresol in the Co. of Dorset and sister of Chiliot Sims, Esq., of Exeter in the Co. of Devon. Sd. John Chichester a few yrs. after his marriage shipt himself to Va. leaving his wife & 2 sons behind and that sometime after his departure Mrs. Chichester and her youngest son Richard Chichester took their passage to Va. from Weymouth in the ship Brimton, Capt. Giles Russell, Commander. She arrived safely in Va. and lived there several years with her sd. husband John Chichester and about the year 1736 the sd. Elizabeth & her son Richard went back to england where in the year 1728 the sd. Elizabeth apparently died and Richard Chichester, her son, returned to Va. the summer after the death of his mother and found on his arrival that his father, John Chichester, was also dead. W.B. 13, p. 320.

HARDIN, Thos. Inv. 12 Jan. 1698/9. Rec. 14 Jan. 1698/9.

Returned by David Mazey. W.B. 10, p. 169.

HARPER, Robert. Rec. 10 Aug. 1750.

Wife: Ellin Harper. Child Unborn. Exors: Wife and Stokley Towles. Wits: Stokley Towles, Geo. Light. W.B. 14, p. 299.

Ap. returned by Walter Armes, one of the ex. mentions articles in Glouster Co. W.B. 14, p. 311.

HARRELL, Gilbert. 28 July 1753. Rec. 17 Aug. 1753.

Heirs: Wm. Taite (Also Extr.), Samuel Burn. Brother: James Harrell. Moss Watson. Wits: Wm. Montague, Ozwald Newby. W.B. 15, p. 146.

HARRIS, John. 21 Dec. 1661. Rec. Prob. 12 March 1661.

John Richons, his wife & children 400 acres of land, Ellenar Owns 500 a. of land, Humphrey Owens 200 a. of land, Nicholas Cocke and his son Morris Cocke 200 a. of land. Exors: Friends Humphrey Owen & Nich. Cocke. Wits: John Edwards, Thos. Foster. W.B. Loose Wills.

HARRIS, John. 9 Oct. 1683. Rec. 11 Dec. 1685.

Wife: Katherine, who is also Extrx. Dau. Katherine. Wits: Walter Wallis, Eliz. Wallis, Jas Ellis. W.B. 5, p. 103.

HARRIS, Katherine. Rec. 9 Mar. 1686.

Verbal will of Catherine Harris, proved by John Copens and Thos. Evans. Devisees: Thos Evans and her dau. Catherine, who was left in the care of George Page. W.B. 5, p. 110.

HARRIS, Gerry. 14 Apr. 1693.

Dau: Ann Harris, who is also Extrx. Mother-in-law: Mrs. Ann Chowning. Brother: Alexander Harris. Wits: Richd. Merriman, James Lowrie, Robert Cross, Jone Terrill. W.B. 8, p. 42.

HARRIS, Edward. Appraisement, & Inv. Rec. 11 May 1726.

Returned by Mary Harris, adm. W.B. 10, p. 488.

HARRIS, Josiah. Inv. 16 Jan. 1777. Rec. 20 March 1777.

By Elias Edmonds, James Pinckard, Jr., James Kirke. W.B. 20, p. 103.

HARRIS, Josiah. Division of estate. 4 Apr. 1781. Rec. 17 May 1781.

Job Carter who married the widow of sd. Harris, dec., possessed with his part of sd. estate. Sd. Carter guardian to Charlotte Harris, orphan of sd. Josiah Harris, pursuant to an order of Lancaster Ct. dated Sept. 1778. W.B. 20, p. 192.

HARRIS, John. 4 Mar. 1786. Rec. 16 Mar. 1786.

Son: James Harris plantation in Middlesex Co. Dau: Jane Davenport. Gr.daus: Jane Oliver Stott, Julianne Stott, Charlotte Harris. Exors: James Harris & George Davenport. Wits: Matt. Myers, Henry Carter, Joseph Carter. W.B. 22, p. 115.
20 July 1786. Appraisal & Division. Heirs: Charlotte Harris, Oliver Stott, James Harris, George Davenport. W.B. 22, p. 125.
20 Feb. 1790. George Davenport, Exor's account. W.B. 22, p. 263.

HARRIS, James. 23 Nov. 1786. Rec. 19 Feb. 1787.

Wife: Elizabeth. Sons: John (plantation, not 23), William Yerby Harris land in Middlesex, Josiah (youngest son). Daus: Fanny & Molly Harris. Exors: Wife, Matt. Myers & Cap. William Chowning. Wits: Matt. Myers, John Carter, Frederick Carter. W.B. 22, p. 142.

HARRISON, Daniel. Inv. 3 Oct. 1677. Rec. 12 Dec. 1677.

Presented by Mary Harrison. W.B. 5, p. 44.

HARRISON, Joseph. 23 Dec. 1699. Rec. 8 May 1700.

Wife: Frances. Son: Daniel, dwelling and plantation where I now live. Dau: Mary. Exors: Wife, Thos. Stapleton and Wm. Paine. Wits: Jno. Brown, Thos. Harway, Thos Chitwood. W.B. 8, p. 95.

HARROWER, Alex. Inv. 9 May 1740. Rec. 11 July 1740.

Returned by Martha Harrower, Admx. W.B. 13, p. 174.

HART, John. 8 Jan. 1708. Rec. 9 May 1711.

Wife: Elizabeth. Eldest son, John, my plantation I now live on, Thomas. Daus; Elizabeth, Mary, deceased. Exors: Robert Carter, Daniel McCarty of Westmoreland Co. and son, John. Wits: Peter Wood, Hugh Coffie and Thomas Hooper. W.B. 10, p. 81.

HART, John. Inv. 13 Apr. 1717. Rec. 1 May 1717. W.B. 10, p. 205.

HARTLAND, William. 26 Oct. 1696. Rec. 27 Aug. 1697.

Wife's not given. Daus: Elizabeth, Mary. To Elizabeth is given his plantation. Extrx: Elizabeth. Wits: Jas. Haines, Ann Currell. W.B. 8, p. 69.

HARVEY, Richard. Inv. 10 Nov. 1675. Rec. 1 Dec. 1675.

Presented by Mary Harvey. W.B. 2, p. 115.

HARVEY, Onesephorus, of Parish of St. Mary's White Chappel. 14 May 1732. Rec. 13 Sept. 1732.

Brother: Wm. and Thos. Harvey. Sister: Rebecca Harvey. Onesiphorus Dameron, Jr. Exor: Wm. Harvey. Wits: Jno. Selden and Wm. Chilton. W.B. 12, p. 224.

HARWOOD, George. 5 Jan. 1703. Rec. no date.

Legatees: Wife, Mary; Epaph. Lawson, my wife's eldest son; wife's son John Lawson and her children; Elizabeth Harwood, Catherine Lawson, Frances and Mary Harwood; Sister, Horn. Extrs.: Wife, Mary, and William Lister. Wits.: Geo. Horn, Lettisa Horn, Jno. Coleman. W.B. 8, p. 121.

HARWOOD, Mary, widow of George Harwood. Rec. 13 Oct. 1731.

Deed to her grandchildren, George & Wm. Currel, sons of Jacob Currel, dec. W.B. 12, p. 207.

HARWOOD, Mary. 5 Oct. 1737. Rec. 9 Dec. 1737.

Legatees: Catherine James, Mary James; Son, Jno. Lawson. Grandson: Epaph. Lawson, Geo. and Wm. Currol. Exors, Matthias James, and her two grandchildren. Wits: Walter James and Robert Biscoe, Eliza James. W.B. 13, p. 71.

13 Jan 1737. Ap. returned by Wm. Currell, adm. W.B. 13, p. 74.

HARWOOD, Ann. Inv. 11 Feb. 1742. Rec. 11 Mar. 1742.

Returned by Wm. Parrot, adm. W.B. 13, p. 316.

HART, John, Sr. Inv. Rec. 9 May 1711.

Returned by John Hart, Jr. W.B. 10, p. 83.

HATHAWAY, Francis. Inv. 10 June 1719. Rec. 8 July 1719.

Proved by oath of Robert Gibson, adm. W.B. 10, p. 296.

HATHAWAY, Wm. 16 Nov. 1771. Rec. 16 Jan. 1772.

Wife: Sarah. Sons: Lawson, James, Thomas and William Hathaway. Daus: Dolly and Mary Hathaway. Gr.son: John James. Gr.dau: Nancy James. Wits: Isaac Currell, James Pollard, William Lawson. W.B. 20, p. 31.

Division of estate: Sarah Hathaway, relict, 1/3, John, James, Thomas, Mary and Lawson Hathaway 1/6, Isaac Currell 1/6. 20 Feb. 1772. W.B. 20, p. 33.

HAVERNON, Symon. Inv. Rec. 8 Nov. 1721.

Presented by Margt. Havernon, Thomas Marshall and Wm. Jones. adm. W.B. 10, p. 341.

HAWKINS, John.   19 Feb. 1686.   Rec. 11 Mar. 1686.

Devisees: Sam'l Branch, Jno. Wells' son, Thos. Chattwin, Nathaniel Brown, Thos. Goostey, Alex. Atkins, Thos. Chowning. Exors: Thos. Chowning. Wits: Stephen Tomlin, Nathaniel Brown, Tho. Chattwin. W.B. 5, p. 110.

HAYDON, Wm., Jr.   Inv.   Rec. 21 June 1754.

Returned by Wm. Haydon. W.B. 15, p. 171.

HAYDON, William, of Wiccomoco Parish.   4 Mar. 1765.   Rec. 15 Apr. 1765.

Sons: John and Thomas Haydon and Ezekiel Haydon. Sons-in-law: Ambrose Jones, John Barret. Gr.dau: Tabitha Oldham. Gr.son: William Oldham. Dau-in-law: Lucy Haydon (provided she remains unmarried) Judith Haydon and Elizabeth Haydon, daus of My son William Haydon. John Haydon son of Lucy Haydon. Exors: Sons Thomas and Ezekiel. Wits: Thomas Edwards, Richard X Locke, William Oldham. W.B. 18, p. 34.

21 Oct. 1765.   Rec. 20 Apr. 1767.

Division of estate.   To John, Thomas & Ezekiel Haydon, Ambrose Jones, John Barret, Wm. Oldham's part of his grandfather's estate and Tabitha Oldham. W.B. 18, p. 78.

HAYDON, John, of Parish of Wiccomoco.   27 Mar. 1773.   Rec. 19 Aug. 1773.

Wife: Mary. Sons: Joh, William & Ezekiel Haydon. Daus. not named. Wit: Wm. Pasquet, John Haydon, Jr. W.B. 20, p. 64.

HAYDON, William, estate appraised.   Rec. 17 June 1765.   W.B. 17, p. 251.

Last Will and testament presented by Thomas Haydon & Ezekiel Haydon, Executors.   18 Apr. 1765. W.B. 17, p. 119.

HAYDON, Wm., Jr.   Division of estate.   21 May 1767.   Rec. 16 June 1767.

Elmore Dogget with his wife's part. John Dogget with his part. Betty Haydon's part in the hands of her father-in-law. W.B. 18, p. 81.

HAYDON, John, of Parish of Wiccomoco.   27 Mar. 1773.   Rec. 19 Aug. 1773.

Wife: Mary Haydon. Sons: John, William & Ezekeil Haydon. Daus: not named. Exors: Thomas Haydon and Ezekiel Haydon & wife. Wites: Benjamin George, William X. Pasquet, John Haydon, Jr. W.B. 20, p. 64.

HAYDON, Mary. 4 July 1787. Rec. 17 Sept. 1787.

Son: William Haydon ¼ part of my father's stock. Ezekiel Haydon. Daus: Tabitha Haydon & Elizabeth Muse. Gr.daus: Jane Muse, Lucy Haydon & Sally Haydon. Exors: William & Ezekiel Haydon. Wits: Ezekiel Haydon, James MuTt. W.B. 22, p. 155. Appraisal. W.B. 22, p. 173.

John Haydon & Mary Haydon. Division of estate. 21 Apr. 1788. Heirs: William Haydon, Ezekiel Haydon, orphans of John Haydon, dec., Tabitha Haydon, John Haydon, John Muse. By Benj. George, John Bean & Thos. Haydon, Jr. W.B. 22, p. 174.

HAYDON, Wm. Inv. Rec. 19 Jan. 1754.

Returned by Wm. Haydon one of the admors. W.B. 15, p. 163.

HAYNES, Thos. 15 Feb. 1678. Rec. 24 May 1679.

Son: James Haynes my plantation. Daus: Elizabeth Haynes. Margarett Haynes land bought in partnership with Mr. Robt. Griggs upon a creek called Slaughters creek. Marah & Martha Haynes. My "nevie" Thomas Reave 5000 lbs. of tabacco. "Nevie" James Haynes who is also now in Va. Brothers James Haynes & his son. Wm. Haynes and his son Thos. Haynes all my estate in England after death of my sister Joan to whom I do give it for her life time, which came to me by my father's will. Exors: Wife and children. Wits: John Molyne, Thos. Burroughs. W.B. 5, p. 54.

HAYNES, James, Jr. 22 Jan. 1747/8. Rec. 13 May 1748.

Wife: Amy Haynes. 2 daus;. Eliza Weather Haynes and Judith Haynes. Father and mother James and Sarah Haynes. Friend Wm. Dymer & Thos. Pinckard guardian of children. Ex. Father, James Haynes. Test. Thos. Pinckard, James Brent, Ann Flower. W.B. 14, p. 194.

HAYNES, James. 20 Aug. 1748. Rec. 11 May 1750.

Dau-in-law: Amy Haynes, wife of son James Haynes, Jr.,deceased. Wife: Sarah. 2 Grandchildren: Elizabeth Weathers Haynes and Judith Haynes. Dau: Frances Dymer, wife of Wm Dymer. Nephew: Thomas Haynes, son of brother Erasmus. Haynes. Exors: Wife, son-in-law Wm. Dymer, kinsman Thos. Pinckard. W.B. 14, p. 281.

HAYNES, James. Inv. Rec. 15 June 1753.

Returned by Thos. Pinckard, Ex. W.B. 15, p. 130.

HAYNES, Sarah. Inv. Rec. 15 June 1753.

Returned by Will Dymer, adm. W.B. 15, p. 129.

HAYNE, James. 1 Jan. 1711.

Wife: Elizabeth. Grandsons: Jas. Brent, Hayne Brent. Dau. Mary Hayne, Ellinor. Extrx: Wife. Wits: Edwd. Nugent, Dan'l Mackorty. W.B. 10, p. 175.

HAZARD, Joseph. Inv. 14 Oct. 1743. Rec. 9 Dec. 1743.

Returned by Jesse Ball, Gent., adm. W.B. 18, p. 3.

HAZARD, Joseph. Inv. 14 Oct. 1743. Rec. 9 Dec. 1743.

Returned by Jesse Ball, Gent., Admr. W.B. 14, p. 3.

HAZARD, John. 24 Feb. 1750/1. Rec. 8 Mar. 1750.

Son: Roughly Hazzard. If he dies to my next son. Wife and children. Wits: Henry Hazard, Wm. Stott. W.B. 15, p. 18.

HEAGINS, Daniel, of Northumberland Co. 29 Jan. 1722/3. Rec. 11 Nov. 1730.

Daniel Heagins, of Northumberland Co. in the psh. of Great Wiccocomoco. Ex. Friend Lazarus Sutton. Legatees: Mary Sutton, wife of Lazarus Sutton, Mary Davis wife of Richard Davis Dec., Margrett Duack, Elisha Warton. Wits: Aron Taylor, Wm. Taylor. W.B. 12, p. 178.

HEALE, Geo. 30 Dec. 1697. Rec. 2 Feb. 1698.

Sons: George all lands and plantation, Joseph, John, Nicholas. Daus: Sarah, Elizabeth, Ellen. Exor: Geo. Heale. Overseers: Robt. Carter and my son-in-law William Ball. Wits: Joseph Ball, Jas. Innis, Wm. Ball. W.B. 8, p. 74.

HEALE, George. Inv. & Division. 11 Mar. 1702.

Inv. returned by Madam Heale. Division: Mrs. Heale, Mr. George Heale, Mr. John Heale, Mr. Joseph Heale. W.B. 10, p. 228.

HEALE, Ellen, of St. Mary's White Chappell, widow. 15 Oct. 1710. 13 Dec. 1710 Rec.

Sons: Will, Joseph, George, Nicholas & John. Son Will to have land bought of Mr. Thos. Taylor & Elizabeth his wife, lying upon the braches of Capt. Richard Ball's mill Swamp. Daus: Ellen, Elizabeth, Sarah, Mrs. Hannah Ball wife of Capt. Wm. Ball. Exors: Sons Joseph, John & William Heale. Wits: Joseph Ball, James Stevenson, Joseph Taylor. W.B. 10, p. 43.

HEALE, George. Inv. Rec. 14 Feb. 1710.

Estate delivered to Mrs. Ellen Opie, Elizabeth Heale, Sarah Heale, John and Joseph Heale for the use of Wm. Heale as their part of the estate. W.B. 10, p. 71.

Estate of Mrs. Ellen Heale, dec., divided in 4 parts and delivered to Mrs. Ellen Opie, Mrs. Eliz. Heale, Mrs. Sarah Heale, Mr. John Heale and Jos. Heale for the use of Mr. Will Heale. 5 Jan. 1710. W.B. 10, p. 78.

HEALE, Wm. 6 Feb. 1731/2. Rec. 12 July 1732.

Wife: Priscilla. Son: George. Dau: Betty. Brother: Joseph Heale to have certain negroes made over to him and his former wife Elizabeth 25 Nov. 1725. Brothers: George & John Heale. Mrs. Pinckard, My wife's sister. Exors: John Heale, Wm. Downman and cousin Wm. Ball. Wits: Thos. Pinckard, Isaac Cundiff, Edwin Conway. W.B. 12, p. 357.

5 Aug. 1732. Inv. & Ap. returned by John Heale, his Exor. W.B. 12, p. 231.

HEALE, Geo. & Judith. Bond between Geo. Heale & Judith Heale, widow. Rec. 12 Nov. 1736.

William Heale, Jr., decd., only son of George Heale did sometime before his death intermarry with Judith Heale, daughter & co-heir of John Swan, of Parish of Christ Church, dec. W.B. 13, p. 24.

HEALE, William. Ap. & Division. 8 July 1737. Rec. 3 Sept. 1737.

Joseph Chinn, Gent. & Priscilla His wife for her part of her late husband, Mr. Wm. Heale's estate. W.B. 13, p. 62.

HEALE, George. 3 Sept. 1736. Rec. 13 May 1737.

Name of wife not given. Sons: None mentioned. Daus: Elizabeth Davenport, Sarah Heale land in Northumberland in Cherry Point; Catherine Heale, plantation on which I now live. Son-in-law: Lindsey Opie. Brothers: Joseph, and John Heal. Other legatee, Christopher Dominick Jackson, Surgeon in Westmoreland Co. to be paid for his attendance on me. Benjamin Neale. Exors: Brothers, John and James. Wits: Chris. D. Jackson, Wm. Mitchell and Benjamin Neal. W.B. 13, p. 45.

HEALE, John. 27 Nov. 1737. Rec. 13 Jan. 1738.

Legatees: Sister, Mrs. Hanah Ball and her children. Brother, Capt. George Heale's children; brother, William Heale's daughter, Betty. Cousins: Roadham Kenner and his sister. Nephew:

George Heale, son of my brother, William Heale, dec'd. Brother: Joseph Heale. Others—Henry Jenkins, Joseph Carter, John Rogers, William Stamps. Exors: George Heale, and John Rogers. Wits: William Ball Jr., James Bailey, Joseph Carter and Gavin Lawry. W.B. 13, p. 74.

HEALE, Joseph. 1 July 1740. Rec. 9 Oct. 1741.

Wife: Hannah. Nephew: George Heale. Niece: Betty Heale. Cousins: Jno. Rogers, Hannah Blackmore, Jos. Rogers, Edwd. Rogers, Jos Chinn. To be buried in graveyard where brothers Geo. & John are buried. Exors: Wife, Geo. Heale, Jos. Chinn and Jno. Rogers. Wits: Giles and Wm. Robinson and Jos. Ball. W.B. 13, p. 239.

HEARD, Walter. 20 Apr. 1676. Rec. 12 May 1677.

Wife: Elizabeth. Sons: Henry, land on Eastern branch Corrotoman. William, 300 A. on which I now live. Daus: Jane, Frances. Gr.dau. Elizabeth Parkquet. Other devisees: Thos. Edmonds; brother, Wm. Edmonds to see that his will was carried out. Exors: Wife, son, Henry. Wits: Dan'l Garrison & Thos. Edmonds. Appraisers named: Jeremiah Parkquet, Wm. Edmonds, Jno. Walker, Wm. Nash. W.B. 5, p. 28.

HEARD, Will. 19 Jan. 1709.

Wife: Not mentioned. Sons: eldest, Walter, Henry and John. Exors: Sons, Walter and Henry. Wits: Thos. Lee, Jane Wren, Lawrence Molde. W.B. 10, p. 112.

HEARD, Henry. Inv. Rec. 8 June 1726.

Returned by Jane Heard. W.B. 10, p. 489.

HEARD, Walter. 11 July 1677. Rec. 10 Sept. 1677.

Inv. returned by Elizabeth Heard. W.B. 2, p. 41.

HEARD, Walter. Inv. Rec. 12 Apr. 1727.

By Sarah Heard, adm. W.B. 10, p. 545.

HEARD, Walter. Inv. 13 Sept. 1727.

Returned by Sarah Heard, admx. W.B. 12, p. 36.

HEARD, William. 5 Dec. 1744. Rec. 4 Dec. 1744.

Sister: Elizabeth Heard. Uncle: William Cook. Friend: Nicholas Martin, Ex. Wits: Clemt. Bayly & Robt. Biscoe. W.B. 14, p. 35.

HEARD, Jane. 16 Dec. 1750. Rec. 8 Feb. 1750.

Dau: Lucy Kelly and her son George Kelley. Gr.dau.: Eliza

Oliver (not of age). Gr.son: George Kelley. Ex.: Son-in-law, Benj. Kelley and George Kelley. Wits: Jno. Steptoe, Ezekiel Gilbert, Isaac Currell. W.B. 15, p. 6.

HEARD, Henry. 25 Aug. 1750. Rec. 12 Oct. 1750.

Mother: Jean Heard "hole estate." Also ex. Wits: Isaac Currell & George Currell. W.B. 14, p. 315.

HENING, Robert, Jr. 27 Feb. 1771. Rec. 20 Feb. 1772.

Wife: Sarah Hening. Dau: Milly. Son: Lewis. Exors: Wife Sarah and friends Mr. Edwin Conway and Mr. Bridger Haynie. Wits: Dale Carter, Samuel X. Brooks, Jesse Garland. W.B. 20, p. 32.

Jan. 1783. "We have possessed Mr. Chas. Lee in right of his wife Milly with 4 negroes. James Gordon Guardian of Lewis Hening. 30 Jan. 1793. W.B. 20, p. 254.

HERBERT, Edward, of Parish of Christ Church. 8 Aug. 1692. Rec. 10 Nov. 1692.

Devisees: Mrs. Hannah Ball. Alex. English, Capt. Wm. Ball, Mr. Robt. Carter & his lady 40 shillings to buy them rings, friend Tobias Parsley, Mr. Edward Lemon agent in London. Exor: Tobias Parsley. Wits: John P——, Edmund Roads, Jno. Hart, Alex. English. W.B. 8, p. 38.

HERNE, Benjamin. 5 Mar. 1708. Rec. 13 Apr. 1709.

Devisees: Walter Armes, Walter Armes, Jr.; Landlady, Mrs. Mary Armes; Capt. Wm. Ball and "his 3 Mades," Thomas Hopper, Miles Armes; Landlord, Walter Armes. Ex. Friend, Walter Armes. Wits: Rachel Adn (?), Sarah Heale, William Ball. W.B. 8, p. 138.

HERNE, George. Inv. 11 May 1720. Rec. 8 June 1720.

Presented by Henry Herne, adm. W.B. 10, p. 304.

HEWSON, Wm. Inv. 10 Oct. 1688. Rec. 13 Oct. 1688.

Returned by Wm. Edmonds. W.B. 2, p. 127.

HILL, Robert. Inv. 11 Aug. 1698. Rec. 16 Sept. 1698.

Returned by Thos. Buckly. Mentions a silver spoon given to Jas. Hill, son of Robert Hill, dec. by his grandfather James and a small gold ring and a cradle given by his grandfather Thos. Buckly. Also a silver bodkin given to Mary Hill by her mother Mary Hill, dec. W.B. 8, p. 162.

114   ABSTRACTS LANCASTER COUNTY, VIRGINIA, WILLS—1653-1800

HILL, Job, no dates. Rec. 1709.

Wife: Susanna. Devisees: Wm. Ackers, Susanna Braxton, Dau. of Jno. Braxton. She to have the tract he now lives on. Wits: Wm. Mann, Will Campbell, Abraham Bush. W.B. 8, p. 125.

HILL, Thomas. Est. Rec. 12 June 1728.

Thomas Coleson, adm. W.B. 12, p. 58.

HILL, James. Inv. & Ap. 10 May 1748. Rec. 10 June 1748.

Returned by Elizabeth Hill, Adms. W.B. 14, p. 196.

HILL, Henry. 6 Feb. 1748/9. Rec. 15 Apr. 1749.

Brother: William Hill. James Ball, Jr., Jeduthan Ball. Wit. & Exor. James Ball, Jr. W.B., p. 237.

HILL, Robert. 20 Nov. 1761. Rec. Jan. 1762.

Children: James Hill and Mary Ann Hill be left to John Pasquet and wife. Dau: Judith Hill to "my brother" Wm. Hill. Wits: George Flower, James Kirk, George Fendla. W.B. 16, p. 184.

HILL, William. Inv. Rec. 21 May 1762.

Returned by Betty Hill, admx. W.B. 16, p. 209.

HILL, Elizabeth. Rec. 17 June 1765.

Died without making a will, James Hill Appointed administrator. W.B. 17, p. 132.

HILL, Elizabeth. Inv. 9 July 1765. Rec. 15 July 1765.

By Wm. Yerby, John Davis, Dale Carter. Returned by James Hill. W.B. 18, p. 40.

HILL, William. Division of estate. Rec. 13 Dec. 1766.

John Connally married the widow. Mentions 3 children but not names. W.B. 18, p. 74.

HILL, John, estate. Division recorded. 15 Dec. 1766. W.B. 17, p. 225.

HILL, Robert. 13 Oct. 1772. Rec. 15 Oct. 1772.

John Schon, guardian of Judith Hill, orphan of Robert Hill. W.B. 20, p. 48.

HILL, James. Appraisement & Inv. 17 June 1773. Rec. 15 July 1773.

By Dale Carter, James Pinckard, Jr., John Miller, Eliza Hill. Inv. returned by Eliza Hill. W.B. 20, pp. 63, 223.

Jan. 1782. Rec. 21 Feb. 1782. Fanny Hill Allotted her portion of the estate of James Hill, deceased, her father and possessed Thos. Hubbard her guardian with same. By James Gordon, Thad. McCarty, John Miller. W.B. 20, p. 223.

HILL, Wm. Division of Estate. Rec. 21 July 1774.

John Connolly Possessed with Widow's dower. John Hill with that part of estate due John Hill orphan of William Hill. James Kirk with Betty's part and John Connolly with that part belonging to Sally Hill. By Dale Carter, John Yerby, Will Yerby. W.B. 20, p. 74.

HILL, Nicholas. Inv. Mar. 1777. Rec. 18 Apr. 1777.

Jesse Denny, Admor. Appraised by Charles Coppedge, Thomas Yerby, William Pitman. W.B. 20, p. 110.

HILL, John. Appraisal. Sept. 1789. Rec. 19 Oct. 1789.

By James Carter, Jeduthan James, James Hill. W.B. 22, p. 227.

HILL, George. Rec. 16 July 1792.

Brother: William Hill. Mother: Syner Roberson. Wits: John Meredith. W.B. 22, p. 349.

HILMAN, Elizabeth. 23 Feb. 1744. Rec. 9 Mar. 1744.

Son: Thos. Hilman, Mary Cox, wife of Edward Cox, Lucy Hilman, Judith Hilman. Test. Wm. Clerk, Cornelius Mullen. W.B. 14, p. 53.

HINEAGE, Thomas. Est. 13 Nov. 1728. Rec. 13 Nov. 1728.

Margaret Hineage, admx. W.B. 12, p. 80.

HINTON, Timothy. 13 Nov. 1730. Rec. 12 May 1731.

Son: Samuel. Dau: Eliz. Pugh. Dau. of Sarah Pugh. Jno. Gill son of Eliz. Gill and Sarah Pugh. Exos: Henry Fleet, Sr. & Jr. Wits: Joanna George, Frances Kelly. W.B. 12, p. 200.

HINTON, Samuel, of Parish of Christ Church. 3 Apr. 1771. Rec. 21 June 1771.

Sons: Richard (given 1 shilling), William, Spencer, Henry (⅓ land in Dinwiddie Co. which I bought of Thomas William) Samuel and Fleet Hinton (to each ⅓ land in Dinwiddie.) Wife: Elizabeth to have ½ of negroes that will amount to the lands she received by will of Capt. Henry Fleet, dec. Exors: Five Sons, Wm. Henry, Spencer, Samuel and Fleet Hinton. Wits: John Fleet, Martin Hill, William Currell, Nicholas Pope. W.B. 20, p. 20.

HINTON, Fleet. Inv. 21 May 1778. Rec. 20 Aug. 1778.

By Thomas Lawson, Thomas Hunton, Thomas Ingram. W.B. 20, p. 142.

HINTON, Richard. Appraisement. Nov. 1779. Rec. 20 Jan. 1780.

By Thomas Lawson, Henry Lawson, Thomas Hunton. W.B. 20, pp. 175, 184.

Division: Widow's Dower. Children's part: Wm., Sarah, Elizabeth, Mary, Judith, Ann, Richard and Robert Hinton. 15 Feb. 1781. W.B. 20, p. 184.

HINTON, Fleet. Appraisal. 21 May 1778. Rec. 15 June 1789.

By Thomas Lawson, Thomas Hunton & Thomas Ingram. W.B. 22, p. 215.

15 Feb. 1790. Division. Lucy Hinton Chaharine Hinton's part. Henry Hinton, adm. 13 Oct. 1789. James W. Ball & Hancock Lee, Exams. W.B. 22, p. 254.

HINTON, William. 2 Mar. 1790. Rec. 17 Jan. 1791.

Son: Richard Brent Hinton, also other children. Exors: Brother, Spencer Hinton, & William Bromley. Wits; Martin Shearman, Ezikiel G. Shearman. Elizabeth G. Shearman. W.B. 22, p. 286. Appraisal. W.B. 22, p. 314.

HINTON, Judith. Appraisal. 16 Dec. 1793. Rec. 20 July 1795.

By Martin Shearman, Charles Edwards, James Pollard. W.B. 22, p. 463.

HOARD, William. Nuncupative. Rec. 10 May 1710.

Estate divided between his father and all his brothers and sisters. Wits: Walter Pasquet, Thomas Loe, John Lawson. W.B. 10, p. 18.

HODGKIN, Christopher. Inv. 10 June 1719. Rec. 14 Sept. 1720.

Presented by Mr. John Turbeville & Mrs. Jane Lawson. W.B. 10, p. 306.

HOGAN, George. Apprais. Rec. 20 Aug. 1762.

By Robt. McTire, Jno. Carpenter & Thos. James. W.B. 16, p. 228.

HOLLAND, Richard, of Wigan in Co. Of Lancaster. 15 Nov. 1733. Rec. 10 Apr. 1734.

Richard Holland, of Wigan in Co. of Lancaster, Taylor age 55 yrs. and upwards, appeared before Wm. Pole, Esq., Mayor of Corporation of Liverpool in the Co. of Lancaster, and made oath that he was Cousin German or Brothers' son to Lewis Holland, late factor at Wmsburg in Va. and who died there in or about the beginning of the month of Aug. in the year 1731, and the sd. Lewis Holland had at his death 3 sisters all yet living, that is to say, Elizabeth now widow of Richard Culshaw late of up-holland in the Co. of Lancaster, Shoemaker, decd; Esther now wife of James Frith of up-holland aforesd, husbandman, and Bridget now wife of Wm. Pryor of Orrell in the sd. Co., Gardiner. Wits: Jno. Breakshell, Thos. Darbyshire, Joseph Seddon, Richard Slater. W.B. 12, p. 242.

HOLLOWAY, Samuel. 31 Mar. 1721. Rec. 8 Nov. 1721.
Brother John Holloway's children, and sister's children; none named. Wits: Isaac Currell, Wm. Carter. W.B. 10, p. 338.

HOLLOWAY, Samuel. Inv. Rec. 14 Mar. 1721.
Returned by Robert Gibson. W.B. 10, p. 364.

HOLSEY, Wm. Nuncupative. Rec. Dec. 14, 1687.
Brother: Robert Holsey of Rapp. Co. Exor. Devisees: Mrs. Elizabeth Wilks, Mr. Rawleigh Travers. and Mr. Giles Travers and Mr. Downman. W.B. 5, p. 116.

HOPKINS, Robert. Inv. Rec. 10 Nov. 1718.
Returned by Hannah Hopkins, adm. W.B. 10, p. 279.

HORNE, Henry. Rec. 14 July 1749.
Wife: (no name given). Son: Henry. Exors.: Stockley Towles, Merryman Payne, Son Henry. Wits: Thos. Towles, Henry Martin Horne. W.B. 14, p. 249.
Inv. returned by Henry Martin Horne. 11 Aug. 1749. W.B. 14, p. 254.

HORNE, Rowland. 1 Apr. 1727. Rec. 12 Apr. 1727.
Legatees: Henry Horne and Robt. Biscoe, who also Exor. Wits: Sam'l Ball and Henry Lawson. W.B. 10, p. 547.

HORN, Henry M. Dec'd. Order Apr. 1784. Return 15 July 1784.
Inventory. John Cundiff, John Bean, Thomas Garner. W.B. 22, p. 36.

HORTON, Tobias. 8 June 1668 (sic). Rec. 14 June 1669 (sic).
Legatees: Wife, Elizabeth. Wife Elizabeth; Sons Tobias and Robert Horton; Dau. Rebecka; son-in-law, Richard Taylor. Extrs. Geo. Wale and Hugh Brent. Wits: Fortunatus Sydnor. Note: At Lancaster Court 13 Mar. 1740, on prayer of Tobias Horton

this will together with certificate of proof thereof was admitted to record. W.B. 13, p. 196.

HORTON, Ralph, intending for England. 5 June 1667. Rec. 1 May 1673.

Legatees: Hagar Davys and her sons, Henry Davys, Richard Davys and Thomas Davys. To John Davys, Mary Davys and Martha Davys. W.B. 4, p. 112.

HORTON, Tobias. Inv. 10 Oct. 1688. Rec. 13 Oct. 1688.

Returned by Martha Hutchings(?). W.B. 2, p. 126.

HORTON, Robt. 30 July 1706. Rec. 9 Br. 1706.

Wife: Sarah. Sons: Wm. Robt. John, Benj. Daus: Mary, Sarah, Frances, Elizabeth. Extrx. Wife. Wits: Jeffery Marbog, Pat Marbog, Geo. Flower. W.B. 8, p. 136.

HORTON, Tobias. 13 June 1748. Rec. 12 Aug. 1748.

Son: George Horton, land on which I now live. Son: John Horton and his wife Ellinor Horton. Ex.: son George. Wits: Thos. Pinckard, Hugh Brent, Sr., Isaac Taylor, John Wale. W.B. 14, p. 206.

HORTON, Tobias, Jr. Inv. Rec. 13 Dec. 1745.

Returned by George Horton. W.B. 14, p. 101.

HORTON, George, of Fleetsbay. 26 Apr. 1753. Rec. 15 June 1753.

Wife: Judith; children, George and John. Exors: Wife and Mr. Thomas Edwards. Wits: T. Edwards, Elizabeth Floyd, Maurice Brent. W.B. 15, p. 136.

HORTON, George. Estate settled. To Betty Horton and George Horton. W.B. 18, p. 57.

Rec. 18 June 1766.

HORTON, George. Division of estate. 7 Nov. 1768. Rec. 16 Mar. 1769.

Richard Huthings guardian to George Horton, orphan of George Horton, dec. In the hands of Nicholas Brent his former guardian and due from the estate of Betty Horton, dec. By James Kirk, Jno. Yerby, Wm. Yerby. W.B. 18, p. 135.

HORTON, George. Appraisement. By William Yerby, John Yerby, William Gibson. Dated 16 Apr. 1772. Rec. 21 May 1772. W.B. 20, p. 42.

HORTON, Ellinor, of Christ Church Parish. 18 Sept. 1776. Rec. 21 May 1778.

Son: John Hutchings. Gr.dau: Nancy Hutchings. Dau: Judith Norris. Gr.son: George Horton Norris. Ex. Son John Hutchings. Wits: Hugh Brent, James Brent. W.B. 20, p. 130.

18 June 1778. Appraisal. By Jas. Brent, John Parrott, Thos. Rouant. W.B. 20, p. 134.

HOWARD, Martha. 15 Mar. 1716/17. Rec. 10 Apr. 1717.

Daus. Catherine, Mary, Martha. Son: Thomas. Grandchild: Martha Flint, Sarah McCraidy. Exors: Wm. Dare and David Flint. Wits: Arthur Clark, Griffith Pritchard, Darby Bryan. W.B. 10, p. 191.

HOWELL, Thos. 23 Jan. 1727. Rec. 12 Feb. 1728.

Wife: Sarah. Sons: Jno., eldest, and Thos. Daus. Sarah and Modlin. Extrx. Wife. Wits: Jno. Davis and Walter James. W.B. 12, p. 81.

Dated 8 Mar. 1731. Rec. 10 May 1732.

Division of Estate. To Sarah Howell, widow. Extrx. Estate of sd. Sarah, now dec'd. To John and Thos. Howell, orphans of Thos. Howell. W.B. 12, p. 216.

Henry Fleet, guardian's account of estate. 10 May, 1732. W.B. 12, p. 219.

Estate of Sarah Howell, dec. To Maudlin, Sarah & Deborah Howell, orphans of Thos. Howell, dec. 9 May 1733, by Ezekiel Gilbert, their guardian. W.B. 12, p. 264.

HOWELL, Sarah. 27 Oct. 1730. Rec. 12 May 1731.

Sons: Jno. and Thos. Daus. Sarah, Maudlin and Deborah Howell. Wits: Jno. and Thos. Howell. W.B. 12, p. 199.

HUBBARD, Thos. of Christ Church Parish. 24 Jan. 1716. Rec. 10 Apr. 1717.

Wife: not named. Sons: Thos. and John. Daus: Elizabeth and Mary. Exors: son Thomas. Wits: John Nash, Cary Keble. W.B. 10, p. 192.

HUBBARD, Thos. 8 June 1745. Rec. 12 July 1745.

Dau: Betty Saunders & her children. Sons: Joseph and Ephraim Hubbard. Wife: Mary Hubbard. Exors: Wife Mary and Sons Joseph & Ephraim. Wits: Thomas Hubbard, Dale Carter, John Hubbard. W.B. 14, p. 84.

HUBBARD, John. 19 Jan. 1756. Rec. 19 June 1761.

Wife: Sarah Hubbard. Son: Thomas Hubbard and his son John. Dau: Judith Hubbard. Sons: William Hubbard, Joshua Hubbard. Exors: Wife Sarah and sons Wm. & Joshua. Wits: Wm. Rossin, John Norris, Joseph Hubbard, Dale Carter. W.B. 16, p. 149.

HUBBARD, Joseph. 30 Oct. 1764. Rec. 17 Nov. 1766.

Wife: Betty. Sons: Thomas, Joseph, James and William. Two youngest sons: John and Jesse. Dau: Hannah. Exors: Friends, William Yerby & William Sanders. Wits: John Yerby, William x Stamp. W.B. 18, p. 71.

Codicil 14 Oct. 1765. Child wife is "now big with" to share in estate. W.B. 14,

HUBBARD, Joseph, Dec. Rec. 20 Apr. 1767.

Widow renounces all benefits from his estate. W.B. 17, p. 252.

HUBBARD, Joseph. Division. 17 May 1770. Rec. 20 June 1770.

To Thomas, Joseph, James, Hannah & Wm. Hubbard. By Dale Carter, John Meredith, James Kirk. W.B. 20, p. 1.

HUBBARD, Wm. orphan of Joseph Hubbard, dec. 17 Nov. 1773. Rec. Nov. 18 1773.

John Yerby late guardian. Settlement by Dale Carter, Wm. Yerby, John Yerby. W.B. 20, p. 66.

HUBBARD, Joshua. Division of estate. Rec. Apr. 1783.

Division of estate among children: Charles, William, George, Ephraim and Amy Hubbard. By James Pinckard, Jeduthun Pinckard, George Norris. W.B. 20, p. 263.

HUBBARD, Wm. 16 Feb. 1780. Rec. 18 Sept. 1783.

Lower Precinct of Parish of Christ Church. Wife: Elizabeth. Sons: William, and Bushrod all my land and Betty Hubbard. Exec: Wife, Wm. Boatman. Wits: Joshua Hubbard, Charles Hubbard. W.B. 22, p. 1.

18 Sept. 1783. Estate appraised. W.B. 22, p. 22.

HUBBARD, William, dec, 13 Sept. 1792. Rec. 17 Sept. 1792.

Orphan of Joshua Hubbard. Appraisal. Thos. Gaskins, William Hubbard, George Brent. W.B. 22, p. 351.

HUBBARD, Joseph. Division. Apr. 1783. Rec. 21 Apr. 1788.

Heirs: John, Jesse & Amos. Hubbard. Betty Mott their mother

and former guardian. By Edwin Conway, Samuel Yopp, Wm. Edwards. W.B. 22, p. 172.

16 Dec. 1793. 20 July 1795. Joseph Hubbard's appraisal. By James Tapscott, Job Carter & Henry Hinton. W.B. 22, p. 461.

HUGHES, Ruth. Inv. 10 Apr. 1741. Rec. 8 May 1741.
Returned by Mary Callahan, admx. W.B. 13, p. 219.

HUMPHREYS, Geo. Inv. 8 Aug. 1746.
Returned by John Steptoe, adm. W.B. 14, p. 113.

HUMPHRIES, Joseph. Ap. Rec. 10 Mar. 1748.
Returned by Wm. Taylor, Gent., adm. W.B. 14, p. 230.

HUNT, Mary. Appraisal. June 1785. Rec. 19 Aug. 1785.
By Eppa. Lawson, Ia. Currell, Michael Wilder. W.B. 22, p. 103.

HUNTER, John. Division of estate. Rec. 23 Apr. 1742.
To Joshua Hunter's widow and her young son Fendly. George Duke in right of his wife. Robert Hunter, William Short, Nancy Hunter, Joshua Hunter, Jr. W.B. 13, p. 272.

HUNTON, Thomas. 22 June 1746. Rec. 11 July 1746.
Wife: Ann Hunton. 4 Sons: Thomas, Alexander, William and John. 4 Daus: Anna, Elizabeth, Mary Ann, Ann. Wits: Hugh Kelley, Walter James, Robt. Briscoe. W.B. 14, p. 123.

HUNTON, Thomas, of Christ Church Parish—8 Jan. 1794. Rec. 17 Feb. 1794.
Sons: Thomas Hunton Dec., (late of Middlesex) children, John Wren Hunton. Daus: Mary Richards, Elizabeth Newby, Ann Towell, Sarah Smock wife of James Smock, Lucy Richards. Gr. children: Eliz. Newby, Jean Pollard Newby, John Newby. Ex. John W. Hunton, Mark Towell, son-in-law, James Pollard, Lawson Hathaway. Wits: John James, Jr., Wm. Pollard, James Pollard. W.B. 22, p. 410.

HURST, Toby, Dec. Rec. 16 June 1656.
Adm. Granted Ja. Williamson. W.B. 1, p. 228.

HUTCHINGS, Jno. 3 Sept. 1723. Rec. 13 Dec. 1727.
Wife: Francis. Sons: Wm. H. GR.son: Jno. Hutchings. Daus: Frances, Ellinor, Judith. Extrx: Wife. Wits: Chris Kirk, Sarah Cox and Thos. Carter. W.B. 12, p. 41.
Bond Wm. Hutchings apt. guardian of Ellinor Hutchings orphan of John Hutchings. 14 Feb. 1727. W.B. 12, p. 46.

HUTCHINS, Frances, widow, of Christ Church. 7 Feb. 1733. Rec. 13 Mar. 1733.

Parish. Sons: William & John Cox. Daus: Ann Tarkelson, Elizabeth Cox & Judith Hutchins. Exors: Sons Wm. & John Cox. Proved by John Yerby. W.B. 12, p. 290.

Inv. of Frances Hutchins, *widow* & relict of John Hutchings, lately dec. W.B. 12, p. 293.

HUTCHINGS, William. Division of estate. Rec. 20 June 1760.

To William Hutchings, Richard Hutchings and Betty Hutchings their part of their father's estate. To John Yerby his part. W.B. 16, p. 95.

HUTCHINGS, John, Estate. Rec. 17 Sept. 1764.

John Hutchings, orphan of John Hutchings, dec. account given by David Morgan. Elizabeth Hutchings orphan. W.B. 17, p. 21.

HUTCHINGS, John. Appraisement. To John Hutchings, orphan of John Hutchings, dec., being part of his grandfather's estate. James Kirk his guardian. W.B. 18, p. 130.

HUTCHINGS, William. 18 Apr. 1770. Rec. 17 May 1770.

Sister: Mary Yerby. Cousin: William Hutchings. Exors: Friends Richard Hutchings and Wm. Yerby. Wits: Wm. Yerby, John Mason. W.B. 18, p. 169.

HUTCHINGS, Wm. Appraisement. By Wm. Yerby, James Hill, John Yerby, Sam'l. Yopp. Dated. 17 May 1770. Rec. 19 July 1770. W.B. 20, p. 1.

HUTCHINGS, Richard. 19 Nov. 1772. Rec. 20 May 1773.

Richard Hutchings, guardian of John Hutchings, orphan of John Hutchings, dec. possessed with his part of his grandfather's estate. By William Yerby, John Yerby, John Meredith. W.B. 20, p. 60.

HUTCHINGS, Richard. Inv. 17 Apr. 1777. Rec. 15 May 1777.

By John Berryman, William Gibson, Elmour Dogget. W.B. 20, p. 111.

HUTCHINGS, John, of Christ Church parish. 28 Nov. 1784. Rec. 20 Jan. 1785.

Wife: Sarah. Daus: Fanny E. Hutchings. Mentions William Yerby, son of Wm. Yerby & Fanny Meredith, dau of Wm. Meredith. Ex: Col. James Gordon & James Miller. Wits: Joseph Kem, Thomas Webb, John Miller. W.B. 22, p. 56.

20 Jan. 1785. Rec. 17 Mar. 1785. Appraisal. W.B. 22, p. 71.

21 Apr. 1789. Division. To Nathan Sprigs and his wife Sarah, also Fanny Everitt Hutchings. By Jas. Tapscott & Geo. W. Yerby. W.B. 22, p. 210.

HUTCHINGS, Richard. Feb. 1788. Rec. 21 Apr. 1788.

Wits: James Brent, Isaac Degge, James Pollard.

Wife: Leannah. Son: William Hutchings, estate of his uncle William Hutchings. W.B. 22, p. 182.

12 Nov. 1788. Division. Heirs: Widow, John Hutchings, William Hutchings, Richard, Thomas & Mary Ann Hutchings. W.B. 22, p. 194.

HUXFORD, Henry. 5 Jan. 1687. Rec. 4 Apr. 1688.

Wife: Joan, also Extrx. Five children not named. Wits: John Luke, Wm. Shankwood. Friend: Wm. Kenton and John Harris, overseers. W.B. 5, p. 118.

IRIS, John. 18 Apr. 1659. Rec. 1 July 1659.

Inv. taken by Will Ball, John Sharpe & Thos. Powell. W.B. 2, p. 63.

IRELAND, Wm. Rec. 6 June 1655. Inv.

Taken by Thos. Pettett & Clemnell Thrush and deposition made before Andrew Jellson. W.B. 2, p. 102.

JACKSON, Gilbert. Rec. 20 Nov. 1660.

Gilbert, the son of John & Amey Jackson was baptized November 6, 1660 and dyed the same night. W.B. 2, p. 390.

JACKSON, John. Aug. 5, 1661. Rec. 1 Oct. 1661.

Wife Ann and "child she now goes with." Wits: Richard Price, Lambart Moore. Loose Wills.

JACKSON, Andrew. 29 July 1710. Rec. 10 Oct. 1710.

Wife's name not given (deceased) Son: Loster. Brothers: Nathaniel & James Jackson. Sister: Mrs. Sarah McBurnie. Christ Church all my books for use of ye incumbent Elizabeth Butler & her mother Elizabeth Wallkinson my quondam servt. Brother James Jackson living on potter hill near belfast in ye Kingdom of Ireland. Sell to Richard Chichester land in White Chappell parish. Land to James Jackson that was bequeathed by my son Loster to his mother and by me and my wife conveyed to Mr. Thos. Carter and by him conveyed to me. W.B. 10, p. 41.

Codicil: 29 July 1710. To Elizabeth Wulkinson my Quandom servt and her Dau Elizabeth Butler her Mrs. harp & side saddle & wedding ring. To John Grason. Exors: James Jackson, Robt. Carter, Richard Chichester, John Tuberville, Henry Fleet, John Grason. Wits: Will Waugh, John Kelley, Will Woods. W.B. 10, p. 41.

JAMES, Porter. 2 Sept. 1692. Rec. 10 Nov. 1692.

Devisees: James Ball, Ann Therriot the land which was given to me by her father, Mr. Wm. Therriot, Porter James Baley, son of John Baley. Margaret Ball, Dau. of Capt. Wm. Ball. Exor: Capt. Wm. Ball. Wits: Wm. B——, George Smith. W.B. 8, p. 37.

JAMES, Elizabeth. 2 June 1697. Rec. 16, 7 Br. 1697.

Sole Legatee, Jane Bembridge, wife of Christopher B. Exor. Same. Wits: Ellinor Holland, Abraham Taylor, Thos. Loe. W.B. 8, p. 79.

JAMES, Walter. Jan. 1722. Rec. 8 May 1723.

Wife: Mary. Sons: Thos, Mathias, Walter. Daus: Rebekah, Mary Ann, Eliza. Others Jno. Angell and his Wife Susanna. Wits: Thos. Howell and Daniel Carter. W.B. 10, p. 423.

JAMES, Mathias. 6 Dec. 1729. Rec. 9 May 1740.

Wife: Catherine. Sons: Wm. J., Mathias, and Walter. Daus: Joanna and Ann. Exors: Wife and brother Walter James. Wits: Robt. Biscoe and Andrew Donnoldson. W.B. 13, p. 159.

JAMES, Appraisement. Rec. 12 Aug. 1748.

Returned by Joseph McAdam, Gent., adm. W.B. 14, p. 205.

JAMES, Matthias. Ap. & Settlement. 11 Mar. 1747/8. Rec. 13 May 1748.

Returned by Walter James, Ex. Estate lately in the possession of Catherine James, dec. Divided same according to will to Ann James, Walter James, Matthias James and Wm. James. W.B. 14, p. 189.

JAMES, Thomas, of Parish of Christ Church. 13 Jan. 1753. Rec. 18 Feb. 1765.

Wife: Joan James. Eldest Son: Thomas James. Second son: Hugh James. Youngest son: John James. Youngest dau: Margaret James. Daus: Elizabeth, Sarah and Mary James. Exors: Wife Joan James, James Kirk and Anthony Sydnor. Wits: Thos. Carter, Benoni Angell, John Spratt. W.B. 18, p. 29.

JAMES, Thomas. Rec. 18 Feb. 1765.
Will presented by Joan James, Extrx. W.B. 17, p. 98.

JAMES, Thomas. Appraisement. 18 Feb. 1765. Rec. 18 Mar. 1765.
By Wm. Dymer, Rawleigh Shearman, Wm. Hathaway, Thomas
Mason. W.B. 18, p. 31.

JAMES, William, Dec. Rec. 21 May 1767.
Estate appraised. W.B. 17, p. 267.

JAMES, Wm. Inv. & Ap. 20 Apr. 1767. Rec. 21 May 1767.
By Harry Currel, Walter James, Roger Kelley. W.B. 18, p. 80.

JAMES, William. 18 Oct. 1770. Rec. 20 Dec. 1770.
Lettice Campbell, wife of John Campbell, allotted her part of her
former husband, William James' estate. W.B. 20, p. 8.

JAMES, Bartley. 21 March 1771. Rec. May 1771.
Bartley James possessed with his wife's part of estate of Wm.
Waugh, dec. W.B. 20, pp. 43, 145.
19 Mar. 1778. Rec. 15 Oct. 1778.
Bartley James. Division. Elizabeth James, guardian of her 3
children: Bartlet, Mary and Elizabeth James. Spencer George,
guardian for John James, orphan. Lawson Hathaway, guardian
of Ann James, orphan. By Harry Currell, John Fleet, Thomas
Hunton, Nicholas Currell. W.B. 20, p. 145.

JAMES, William. Division of estate. 21 June 1771. Rec. 18 July 1771.
To Letty, Elizabeth, William, Matthias and Sarah James & Isaac
James. John Campbell, guardian of sd orphans, possessed with
the estate. By John Fleet, Nicholas Currell, Henry Currell,
Thomas Hunton, Isaac James. W.B. 20, p. 24.

JAMES, Thomas. Appraisement. May 1773.
Widow's dower. W.B. 20, p. 64.
15 Dec. 1773.
Wm. Gibson, guardian of Thomas James; John James, guardian
of Frances James. W.B. 20, p. 69.
Nov. 27, 1775. Rec. May 1776.
Division: Thomas James, Hugh James, John James, Bushrod
Riveer, Jonathan Wilder, James Mitchell. W.B. 20, p. 96.
15 Sept. 1774. Rec. 16 Feb. 1775.
John James as guardian of Frances James possessed with estate

of George & Thomas James, orphans of Thomas James, deceased, in the hands of Wm. Gibson & George Dogget. W.B. 20, p. 80.

JAMES, Benjamin. Estate appraised. 19 May 1774. Rec. 16 June 1774.

By Thomas Hunton, Will. Lawson, James Currell, Lawson Hathaway. W.B. 20, p. 73.

JAMES, Joan. Appraisement. 16 Mar. 1775. Rec. 16 Nov. 1775.

By Martin George, William Griggs, Henry Lawson. W.B. 20, p. 89.

JAMES, Walter. 29 July 1774. Rec. 18 Feb. 1779.

Wife: Elizabeth. Son: Bartlet James and his wife Elizabeth. Gr.son: John James, son of my son Bartlet. Dau-in-law: Sarah James during her widowhood or until my gr.son Charles James is arrived at age 21 yrs. Plantation called Copes. Gr. children: Elizabeth, Charles, Mary & Benjamin James. Daus: Barbary Hinton, Elizabeth George, Mary Pitman. Son: Benjamin James. Exors: Wife, Elizabeth and son Bartlet. Wits: Thomas Shearman, John Campbell, Lawson Hathaway, Thos. Carter. W.B. 20, p. 156.

JAMES, Sarah. Division of estate. 17 Sept. 1778. Rec. 18 Mar. 1779.

Heirs: James Hudnel, George Brent, Zachariah Barr. John Wale and Lawson Wale, orphans, by William Griggs their guardian. W.B. 20, p. 158.

JAMES, John, orphan of Bartlet James, dec. 5 Jan. 1783. Rec. 20 Feb. 1783.

Spencer George, guardian's account. Lawson Hathaway his present guardian. W.B. 20, p. 80.

JAMES, Isaac, dec'd. Mar. 1784. Rec. 15 Apr. 1784.

Inventory. Thomas Hunton, Thomas Carter, William Martin. W.B. 22, p. 25.

JAMES, Frances. Rec. 19 Feb. 1784.

Account John James adm. of Frances James estate. John Fleet, John Berryman, Thomas Carter, William Lawson. W.B. 22, p. 12.

JAMES, Isaac. Settlement of adm. acct. 15 Oct. 1787. Rec. 21 Apr. 1788.

Son: Robert James. Lawson Hathaway former guardian, Judith James present guardian. By Thomas Carter & Thomas Hunton. W.B. 22, p. 181.

JAMES, John, Jr. 27 June 1788. Rec. 19 Jan. 1789.

Sister: Ann James, Mother-in-law: Elizabeth James ⅓ part of my father's estate. Wits: William James & Robert Day. W.B. 22, p. 199.

JARROT, Thos. Division of estate between widow and child. Rec. 18 July 1782.

Presented by Fanny Jarrot. W.B. 20, p. 241.

JAUNCEY, William. 10 June 1678. Rec. 14 Apr. 1697.

William Jauncey, of Co. of Nothumberland, having a resolution to go out of ye country. To: Wm. Eustace, My grandchild, natural son of John Eustace and my daughter Sarah his wife. Other children of sd John Eustace and his wife. Godchild: Wm. Clapham. Overseer of will: Thos. Haynes, attorney Wm. Hancock, Robert Skelton and Mr. Francis Lee, of London, merchant. Brother: Mr. John Jauncey, living in Stradford, In Buckinghamshire at Pharington. Joseph Darby "now with me in this Country." Sister: Mary Belcher. Extrx: Dau. Sarah Eustace. Wits: Robert Shoull, Francis Wallis. W.B. 8, p. 63.

Deposition of Anthony Stepto, age 44 years. John Cosens, of Co. of Northumberland, came out of England in same ship with him and often spoke of his mother and sister. Sd. John Cosens died in 1674. His estate claimed by Wm. Jauncey in right of his wife Elizabeth, sister of sd Cosons. Sd estate left to Sarah and John Eustace. Sarah died in 1682, leaving 2 sons, Wm. ye eldest. Apr. 12, 1697. W.B. 8, p. 64.

Deposition of Elizabeth Swan, age 50 yrs. John Cosens died about the year 1674 or 1676 and his reputed sister Mrs. Elizabeth Jauncey with her reputed husband Wm. Jauncey and their dau. Sarah and her reputed husband, Mr. John Eustace, came all together to Va. and touched the Barbadoes on their way. The sd. Sarah was delivered of a son called William soon after their arrival and 2 yrs. later another son called John. 12 Apr. 1697. W.B. 8, p. 64.

Elizabeth Pinkard, age 50 yrs. Deposition. She was acquainted with John Cosens and heard him speak of his mother and sister and his brother-in-law, Wm. Jauncey. W.B. 8, p. 64.

George Harward. Age 38 yrs. Same deposition.

Patience Stepto, age 54 yrs. Same deposition and adds that they came in a ship called ye Isaac & Benjamin, Mr. John Plover, Commander, and she came in same ship with same Cosens. Elizabeth Harrod, age 34 yrs, makes same deposition.

JEFFERSON, Joseph. 8 Oct. 1692. Rec. 10 Nov. 1692.

To Edward Wayman. Wits: Denis Currell, James Longhman, David Conner. W.B. 8, p. 37.

JESSOX, Isaack. Inv. 6 July 1696. Rec. 14 Sept. 1696. W.B. 8, p. 124.

JENKINS, Henry. Inv. 8 Jan. 1747/8. Rec. 13 May 1748.

Have set apart that part of Mr. John Heale's estate whiich was in sd Henry Jinkins possession. Inv. returned by George Heale. W.B. 14, p. 193.

JOHNSON, Jo., dec. Rec. 6 Feb. 1655.

Adm. formerly granted Robt. Bushon(?) now granted George Johnson, brother of the deceased. W.B. 1, p. 256.

JOHNSON, John, Sen. Inventory. 4 Feb. 1656. Rec. 1 Mar. 1656. W.B. 2, p. 50.

George Johnson of York County Authorizes friend Thomas Willys attorney to recover any part of "my brother John Johnson's estate." 1 Dec. 1656. W.B. 2, p. 119.

JOHNSON, Edward. 29 Jan. 1686/7. Rec. 2 Mar. 1686/7.

Edward Johnson of parish of Farnham, Co. of Rappahannock. To William Macanico 3 cows being upon the plantation of Ennis Macanico, when he comes of age of 16. Ex: John Dodson. Wits: Daniell Edwards, Alex. Duke, Peter Ellmore. W.B. Loose wills.

JOHNSON, Henry. Est. Rec. 11 May 1722.

Eliza Johnson, Sill Johnson and Robert Neasum, adm. W.B. 10, p. 397.

JOHNSON, Simon. 20 Dec. 1728. Rec. Feb. 12, 1728.

Legatees: Mary Reves, Jas. Reves. Wits: Alex. Matson, Jno. Johnson. W.B. 12, p. 84.

Presented by Jas. Reves admx. 12 Mar. 1728. W.B. 12, p. 48.

JOHNSON, Jane. Inv. & Ap. 9 Apr. 1740. Rec. 13 June 1740.

Returned by Wm. Goodridge, adm. W.B. 13, p. 165.

JOHNSON, Neil. 13 Jan. 1767. Rec. 16 June 1768.

Wife: Rebecca Johnson, Neil Johnson Swanson, son of John Swanson and to Hannah Swanson, dau of John Swanson. Daus:

Barbara Lunsford and Maryan Johnson. Exors: Friends Anthony Sydnor and Hugh Brent. Wits: John Yerby, William Gibson, Judith Yerby. W.B. 18, p. 115.

JOHNSON, Archibald, of Christ Church Parish. 5 Aug. 1768. Rec. 16 Mar. 1769.

Housekeeper: Elizabeth Windsor. Friends: Mr. George Heale, Mr. Richard Mitchell. Exors: Mr. Geo. Heale and Richard Mitchell. Wits: Robert, John Pullen, Robert Chinn. W.B. 18, p. 137.

JONES, John. 8 Oct. 1683. Rec. 20 Nov. 1683.

Heir: John Burkston, son of Susanna Buxton. Wits: Henry Pullen, Edward Johnson, Wm. Arms. W.B. 5, p. 91.

JONES, John. Inv.—— 1683. Rec. 9 July 1684.

Presented by Susana Buxton. W.B. 5, p. 96.

JONES, Henry. Adm. account. Rec. 14 Mar. 1732.

Presented by Robert Mitchell. W.B. 12, p. 238.

JONES, Elizabeth. Inv. Rec. 19 July 1751.

Returned by Gavin Lowry, adm. W.B. 15, p. 46.

JONES, Sarah, widow. 19 Oct. 1783. Rec. 10 Mar. 1784.

Nephew: Dr. William Ball. Niece: Mary Graham. Cousins: Mrs. Prixcilla Harvey, James Harvey, John Harvey, Anne Harvey, Sarah Harvey. Niece: Alice Ball. Ex: Mungo Harvey. Wits: William Lawson, John Tarpley, David Galloway. W.B. 22, p. 16.

JONES, Lewis. Ap. Rec. 21 Feb. 1791.

By Chas. Hubbard, Wm. Hubbard & Thos. Haydon. W.B. 22, p. 146.

KEENE, Elizabeth. Appr. Rec. 10 Dec. 1736.

Returned by John Waughop, gent., adm. W.B. 13, p. 22.

KELLY, Roger. 20 Aug. 1682. Rec. 10 May 1683.

Wife not named, but is Extrx. Sons: Charles, John, Roger, and Hugh. Between the last this plantation is to be divided. Daus: Blanche and Sara Kelly. Wits: John Kelly, John Morris, John Coane. W.B. 5, p. 84.

KELLY, John. Inv. 2 July 2, 1691. Rec. 13 Jan. 1691.

By Uriah Angell, John Moore, John Kelly Cooper. W.B. 8, p. 31.

KELLY, John. Inv. 3 May 1703. Rec. 10 May 1703. W.B. 10, p. 128.

KELLY, Giles. Inv. 9 July 1718. Rec. 13 Aug. 1718.
Returned by Mary Kelly, adm. W.B. 10, p. 271.

KELLY, Wm. Inv. Rec. 12 Nov. 1718.
Proved by oath of Ann Fox, adm. W.B. 10, p. 278.

KELLY, Charles. Rec. 8 Mar. 1726.
Geo. Lite, guardian of Chas. Kelly, orphan of Charles Kelly.
W.B. 10, p. 534.

KELLY, Letitia. Inv. Rec. 8 Feb. 1726.
Hugh Kelley and John Wale, adm. W.B. 10, p. 515.

KELLEY, Letitia. Inv. Rec. 14 June 1727.
Returned by John Wale & Hugh Kelley. W.B. 12, p. 7.

KELLY, Thomas. Ap. Rec. 9 Mar. 1749.
Returned by James Gordon, Gent., adm. W.B. 14, p. 274.

KELLY, Martha. Inv. Rec. 9 Nov. 1750.
Returned by Chas. Flimming. W.B. 14, p. 318.

KELLEY, Wm. Inv. 27 May 1753. Rec. 15 June 1753.
Returned by Jno. Bailey & Jno. Rogers. W.B. 15, p. 134.

KELLEY, John. 26 Feb. 1757. Rec. 15 Apr. 1757.
Edward Cox. Dau: Sarah Kelley. Exors: Friends, John Fleet &
Edward Cox. Wits: Thomas Oharrow. W.B. 15, p. 286.

KELLY, Hugh. 16 Dec. 17 Mar. 1758.
Sons: Roger, William and Hugh Kelley. Daus: Frances Kelly,
Betty Snelling. Son: Winterbottom Kelley. Exors: Friend Mr.
Nicholas Martin and Thomas Hunton. Wits: Thos. Hunton,
Bartlet James, William Kelley. W.B. 16, p. 2.

KELLY, Benjamin. Appraisement. 5 Nov. 1773. Rec. 18 Nov. 1773.
By Nicholas Currell, Eppa Lawson & James Currell. W.B. 20,
p. 67.

KELLY, Hugh. Nuncupative. Sunday, Feb. 15, 1778. Rec. 19 Mar.
1778.
Daus: Joanna Anderson, Elizabeth Williams, Margaret Aires,
Mary Ashburn. Sons: Jesse Kelly and Hugh Kelly. Wits: Gil-
bert Currell & Henry Currell. Sworn to by Henry Currell 16
Feb. 1778 and proved by oath of Henry Currell and his son
Gilbert Currell. W.B. 20, p. 120.

KELLY, William. Appraisal. Mar. 1785. Rec. 22 July 1785.

By William Gibson, William Kirk, William Doggett, Jr. & George W. Yerby. W.B. 22, p. 95.

KEM, Joseph. 25 July 1790. Rec. Feb. 1791.

Wife: Amy. Son: Burgess Kirk Kem (not 21) Daus: Susanna Kem (not 20) & Molly Thompson. Son-in-law: Richard Davis. Dau-in-law: Judith Davis. Sister: Sukey Kem. Exors: John Degges, James Carter, John Doggett. Wits: James Gordon, John Gundy, Andrew Chilton. W.B. 22, p. 294.

KEMB's, (Kem) Henry orphans. Rec. 18 Feb. 1765.

Thomas Kemb bound to Thos. Stott until 21 Joseph Kemb bound to Thomas George until age of 21 to learn trade of ship carpenter. W.B. 17, p. 100.

John Kemb bound to Wm. Stott. Wm. Brumley appointed guardian of Susanna Kemb, orphan of Henry Kemb. Henry Kemb, orphan of Henry K. bound to Wm. Sydnor. 18 Mar. 1765. W.B. 17, p. 100.

KEMP, Robert. 22 Mar. 1663. Rec. 8 Feb. 1664.

Wife: Elizabeth Kemp. Extrx. Wits: Wm. Copland, Francis Broughton, Daniel Long, Joseph Smith. W.B. Loose Wills.

KENNER, Brereton. Appraisement. 18 June 1772. Rec. 18 June 1772.

Legatee: Thos. Rouand. Edwin Conway, guardian. Met at the house of Capt. Hugh Brent. W.B. 20, p. 43.

KENT, James. Appraisement. 10 Mar. 1765. Rec. 15 Apr. 1765.

By Richard Mitchell, Wm. Stott, Thos. George. W.B. 18, p. 34.

KENT, Edwin. Appraisal. Feb. 1786. Rec. Mar. 16, 1786.

By Stephen Chilton, Robert Walker, Benjamin George. W.B. 22, p. 116.

KEY, James. Inv. Rec. 14 July 1725.

Returned by Wm. Rankin, adm. W.B. 10, p. 463.

KIBBLE, George. Nuncupative will. 10 Oct. 1665. Rec. 11 July 1666.

Deposition of John Shapley age 45 yrs. Wife Mary and her children. John Blakes and John Humphreys. Wife, Extrx. George Mummes age 20 yrs. makes same deposition.

KILGORE, Peter. 23 Sept. 1706. Rec. 8 Mar. 1709.

Sons: Peter, plantation I now live on; and John. Daus: Ann

and Margaret. Wits: Jno. Laughne, Will Hight and Isaac Robison. W.B. 10, p. 7.

KING, Henry. Appraisement. 10 Jan. 1675. Rec. 1 Feb. 1675. W.B. 2, p. 13.

KING, William, of Parish of Christ Church. 25 Jan. 1715-16. Rec. 11 Apr. 1716.

Son: Edward, plantation and all my land in a valley called Long Valley which said land was laid out for my son William in his lifetime and to his heirs. Son, John, land on both sides of Mill Swamp which land was formerly laid out for my son Edward. Daus: Tabitha Gibson & Eleshe Mash. Wife: Name not given. Exors: Son Edward and wife. Overseers: Mr. Thos. Lee & Edw. Conway. Wits: Thos. Lee, Wm. Brent, Francis Hathaway. W.B. 10, p. 109.

KING, John. 2 Mar. 1752. Rec. 19 June 1752.

Wife: Judith. Sons: John (not 21 and William King. Dau: Mary King. Exors: Wife and John Kent, Sr., & Thos. Brent. Wits: John Shelton, Thos. Brent. W.B. 15, p. 100

KING, John. Division of estate. 17 Feb. 1758. Rec. 19 May 1758.

William Brent in right of his wife, widow of sd deceased. Coleman Doggett in right of Mary his wife, orphan of deceased. William King and John King, orphans of John King. W.B. 16, p. 12.

KING, John. Division. Rec. 15 Oct. 1764.

William Brent guardian of John King, orphan of John King, Dec. W.B. 18, p. 38.

KING, John, dec. Rec. 15 Oct. 1764.

Hugh Brent appointed guardian of John King, orphan of John King, dec. W.B. 17, p. 71.

KING, William. Appraisement. 17 June 1773. Rec. 15 July 1773.

By Henry Carter, Richard Lock, John Nicholas. W.B. 20, p. 61.

KING, William. 10 Dec. 1781. Rec. 17 Oct. 1782.

Capt. Isaac Degge and Mr. Wm. Sydnor, guardians of John, Elizabeth, Mary & Caty King, orphans of Wm. King, dec. By Edwin Conway, Benj. George, Charles Lee. W.B. 20, p. 246.

KING, William. Division of estate. Dec. 1784. Rec. 16 Feb. 1786.

Isaac Degge & William Sydnor, guardians of Mary, Katherine

and John King. Lawson Hathaway husband of Elizabeth King. By Henry Lawson, William Merridith, William Lawson. W.B. 22, p. 114.

KIRK, James. Est. Rec. 10 Jan. 1721.

John Kirk, Ex., guardian of James Kirk, orphan of James Kirk, dec. W.B. 10, p. 344.

KIRK, James, of White Chappell. 22 Oct. 1717. Rec. 12 Feb. 1718.

Wife's name not given. Son: James. Dau: Katherine. Debts due Mr. John Heale, Richard Davis and Thomas Marshall. Exors: Thomas Carter and David Jones. Wits: John Fairman, Elizabeth Fairman, John Brown. W.B. 10, p. 250.

KIRK, Christopher. 21 Mar. 1722. Rec. 10 Oct. 1722.

Sons: Christopher, my land; Thomas, John; 20 Acres of land; William all rest of land. Daus: Alice and Rebecca Kirk. Wife: Ann and her heirs except my gr.children whose father received several things of me in their life time. Exors: Son William and Wife Ann. Wits: Thos. Hubbard, Thos. Pinson, John Hubbard. W.B. 10, p. 405.

KIRK, William. 10 July 1725. Rec. 8 Sept. 1725.

Wife: Margaret. Son: Christopher. Dau: Hannah Kirk. Couzin: Thos. Kirk. Mother: Ann Kirk. Exors: Wife and Geo. Brent. Wits: Jas. Pollard, Thos Hubbard, Gabriel Thatcher. W.B. 10, p. 464.

Inv. returned by Geo. Brent, Ex. 8 June 1726. W.B. 10, p. 489.

KIRK, Thos. 12 May 1727. Rec. 12 July 1727.

Wife: Sarah. Sons, Thos. and Jno. Extrx: Wife. Wits: Thos. and Ann Haydon and Clement Lattimore. W.B. 12, p. 10.

KIRK, Robt., of Christ Church Parish. 3 Mar. 1727. Rec. 9 Aug. 1727.

Wife: Margaret. Children, Geo., Sarah, Jeremiah, Hezekiah, Charity and Jas. the youngest. Extrx: Wife. Wits: Geo. Kirk and Thos. Wells. W.B. 12, p. 31.

KIRK, William. Ext. Rec. 14 June 1727.

Peter Riveer, guardian of Chris. Kirk, orphan of Wm. Kirk. W.B. 12, p. 10.

KIRK, Chris. 5 Nov. 1733. Rec. May 1736.

Wife: Elizabeth. Sons: Jas and Anthony. Exors: Wife two sons and Jno. Stepto. Wits: Wm. Hutchings, Wm. Stepto. W.B. 13, p. 9.

KIRK, Hezekiah. Inv. & Appr. Rec. 12 June 1741.

Returned by Sarah Kirk, admx. W.B. 13, p. 229.

KIRK, Hezzekiah. Division of estate. 16 Sept. 1757. Rec. 16 Dec. 1757.

Benj. Williams possessed with his wife Elizabeth's part of estate. W.B. 15, p. 312.

KIRK, Anthony. 30 Dec. 1763. Rec. 20 Jan. 1764.

Sons: James Kirk, Thomas Kirk, Land bought of James Tendle. Wife: Sarah Kirk. Exors: Wife Sarah and brother James Kirk and Mr. Hugh Hugh Brent. Wits: James Kirk, Wm. Stamps. W.B. 17, p. 29.

KIRK, Anthony. Appraisement. 20 Jan. 1764. Rec. 16 Mar. 1764.

By James Kirk, Hugh Brent, Sarah Kirk. W.B. 18, p. 6.

July 21, 1768. Estate divided between his widow, Mrs. Sarah Kirk and 3 children, James Kirk, Judy Grigs and Thomas Kirk. Thomas Grigs intermarried with Judith the dau. of Anthony Kirk. Capt. Hugh Brent guardian of Thomas. W.B. 18, p. 6.

KIRK, James, of Parish of Christ Church. 10 Feb. 1776. Rec. 20 Mar. 1777.

Wife: Mary Kirk. Son: William Kirk, all my land. Daus: Sarah Gibson, Judith Hathaway & Elizabeth Hathaway. Gr.children: James Gibson, Elizabeth Hathaway and James Hathaway. Exors: Friends, Wm. Yerby, Wm. Kirk, Wm. Gibson, Lawson Hathaway & Thomas Hathaway. Wits: Wm. Yerby, Robert Cornelius, John Hutchings, Wm. Yerby, John Yerby, Jr. W.B. 20, p. 102.

KIRK, Sarah, of Christ Church Parish. 25 Feb. 1778. Rec. 19 Mar. 1778.

Son: Thomas Kirk. Gr.children: Anthony, Mary and Catharine Kirk and Sarah Griggs. Exors: Friends: John Yearby & Elias Edmonds. Wits: George Brent, Andrew Robertson, Elizabeth Mott. W.B. 20, p. 119.

15 Oct. 1779. Appraisal. By George Norris, Wm. Edwards, Thos. Robb, James Gordon. W.B. 20, p. 149.

KIRK, Thomas, of Christ Church Parish. 22 Feb. 1778. Rec. 19 March 1778.

Mother (name not given). Brother: James Kirk and his children. Wits: Elias Edmonds, Elizabeth Mott. W.B. 20, p. 119.

KIRK, Sarah. 20 Oct. 1778. Rec. 19 Nov. 1778.

Thomas Griggs, guardian to his dau, Sarah Griggs for her part of estate of Mrs. Sarah Kirk, dec. and Elias Edwards and John Yerby, Exors. W.B. 20, p. 152.

KIRK, James. Rec. 1 Sept. 1781.

Edward Carter, guardian of James and Thomas Kirk, orphans of James Kirk, Negroes, etc. mentions grandmother Mrs. Sarah Kirk. W.B. 20, p. 210.

KIRK, James. Orphan's estate. Oct. 1786. Rec. 17 Sept. 1787.

Anthony, Mary & Catherine Kirk, orphans of James Kirk. William Kirk, Gent., their guardian. Catherine Carter former guardian. By William Gibson, John Yerby & Elias Edmonds. W.B. 22, p. 156.

15 June 1789. Division.

Heirs: William Kirk, guardian. Wm. Degges with wife's part. Katherine Kirk & Anthony Kirk. By Henry Lawson, John Yerby, James pinckard, John Miller. W.B. 22, p. 211.

KIRK, Anthony. Inv. Rec. 20 Jan. 1794.

By John Degges, William Edwards & Elias Edmonds. W.B. 22, p. 406.

KIRKLAND, Richard. Nuncupative will. Presented in court by Thos. Thornton & Mathew Machan. Rec. 13 Jan. 1724. Ellinor Boot said that Dr. Thornton asked Kirkland whether he had settled his affairs and he answered "not in Virginia." Said he had a sister's son in Scotland who would be at Mr. Payne's or Mr. Mitchell's. This is all he said. Ellinor Boot. W.B. 10, p. 455.

KIRKUP, Geo. Nuncupative. Rec. 11 Mar. 1701/2.

Deposition of Jos. Kelly, age about 20 yrs. that on the 2d day of Mar. 1701/2, being at the home of Mr. Jno. Kelley, Geo. Kirkup being on his death bed, gave all he had to Jno. Kelly. Randolph Mackdanoll, age 30 yrs. and Catherine Kelly, aged 22 yrs., make same deposition. W.B. 8, p. 108.

KITT, Wm. 13 Nov. 1678. Rec. 20 Nov. 1678.

Inv. returned by Thom. Martyn. W.B. 2, p. 51.

LADNER, Hugh.   8 Oct. 1708.   Rec. 12 Jan. 1708.

Wife: Shusanna.   Dau: Elizabeth.   Other legatees: William and Ann Payne, children which wife had by former husband; William Fox, Mrs. Ann Fox, wife of Mr. William Fox; William Payne, my son-in-law.   Exors: Son-in-law, Wm. Payne.   Wits: William Fox, Joseph Carter and George Chowning.   W.B. 10, pp. 1-2.

LAKE, Richard.   Rec. 16 Oct. 1654.

Administration granted Geo. Kibble.   W.B. 1, p. 162.

LATHER, Nicholas.   Inv.   Rec. 8 Nov. 1684.

Presented by Mary Curtis, relict.   W.B. 5, p. 98.

LATTIMORE, Clement.   31 Mar. 1755.   Rec. 2 May, 1756.

Dau: Sinai Lattimore, plantation I now live on.   Gr.dau: Ann George Lattimore.   Dau: Joanne Lattimore ½ the land whereon my grandfather Clement Latimore, deceased, formerly lived.   Ex. Brother: David Lattimore.   W.B. 15, p. 246.

LAUGHLER, Jeames.   Inv.   8 Feb. 1750.   Rec. 14 June 1751.

Returned by Thos. Edwards, Jr., adm.   W.B. 15, p. 43.

LAWRENCE, Thos., merchant.   1 Apr. 1678.   Rec. 12 Jan. 1680.

Heirs: Azrikam Parker, son of Azrikam Parker, of Northumberland Co., 1500 lbs of tobacco; Ann Doggett, daughter of Benjamin Doggett, minister of Lancaster Co., personalty.   Wife Dorothy Lawrence and her son Wm. Lyster.   Wits.: Francis Emanuel, Wm. Brown.   W.B. 5, p. 109.

LAWRENCE, William.   Inv.   8 Dec. 1698.   Rec. 14 July 1698.

Presented by Mary Lawrence.   W.B. 8, p. 87.

LAWRENCE, William Est.   Inv.   Rec. 11 Oct. 1721.

Mary Lawrence granted adm. bond with Robert Gibson and John Wale.   W.B. 10, p. 333.

LAWRY, James.   17 Oct. 1713.

Wife: Jane.   Sons: James, land I now live on; and Will.   Dau: Alison.   Sister's children, John Vangover, Mary and Alison Vangover.   Exors: Wife and Wm. Fox, James Ball, Jno. Vangover. Wits: Noah Rogers, Arthur Clark, James Camell.   W.B. 10, p. 115. 13 Jan. 1713.   Est. Ap.   W.B. 10, p. 117.

LAWRY, James. 13 Sept. 1727. Rec. 13 Sept. 1727.

James Camell Apointed guardian of Wm. Lawry, orphan of James Lawry. W.B. 12, p. 35.

LAWRY, Mary. Inv. 18 Oct. 1770. Rec. 17 Jan. 1771.

Presented by Gavin Lawry. By Merryman Payne, Geo. Carter, Henry Carter, Dale Carter. W.B. 20, p. 9.

LAWRY, Gavin. 14 Aug. 1790. Rec. 20 Sept. 1790.

Nephew: Stokley Lawry, deceased. Niece: Mary Lawry. John Lawry, son of Stokley and Fanney Lawry, dau. of Stokley Lawry. Gavin Garner. Exors: James Gordon, John Chowning, William Biscoe, Joseph Carter. Wits: L. Lunsford, James Gordon, Ellen Carter. W.B. 22, p. 281.

LAWSON, Epaphroditus. 31 Mar. 1652. Rec. 12 Jan. 1652.

Wife: name not mentioned, her accustomed thirds. Child unborn. Administrators: Mr. Richard Bond, Merchant, Mr. John Carter. Wits: Eliz. Loes, Joan Lee, Wm. Harper. W.B. 1, p. 34.

LAWSON, Epa. Inv. 5 June 1655. Rec. 12 June 1655. W.B. 2, p. 15.

LAWSON, Rowland. 24 Mar. 1704/5. Rec. 11 Sept. 1706.

Wife: Ilein (?). Sons: Henry and Rowland. Wits: Jno. Turberville, Jno. Robertson, Jno. Inman. Es: Son, Rowland Lawson. W.B. 8, p. 137.

LAWSON, Rowland, of Psh of Christ Church. 23 Nov. 1716. Rec. 9 Jan. 1716.

Wife: Jane. Sons: Rowland, all his land etc; John, Anthony and Thomas. Daus: Sarah, Joanna and Elizabeth. Rowland L. son of Hannah Lawson. Exors: Wife, son Rowland and my brother Chas. Barber. Wits: Jno. Tuberville, Epa. Lawson and Wm. Sydnor. W.B. 10, p. 189.

LAWSON, Rowland. Inv. Rec. 10 Oct. 1718.

Presented by Charles Barber & Jane Lawson, Exors. W.B. 10, p. 275.

LAWSON, Epa. 2 Nov. 1721. Rec. 12 Dec. 1722.

Wife's name not given. Sons and one dau. names not given. Brother: Jno. Lawson. Fortunatus Sydnor. Sister: Catherine Lawson. Exor: Fortunatus Sydnor. Wits: Jos. Cooper and Hugh Kelley. W.B. 10, p. 408.

LAWSON, Catherine. 25 Jan. 1721. Rec. 9 Jan 1722.

Legatee: Brother, John Lawson. Nephew, Epa Lawson's youngest son, Niece, Judith Lawson, daughter of Epa Lawson and Elizabeth Lawson, Dau. of Brother, John Lawson. Rest of Estate divided between the daughters of Epa and John Lawson. Exors: Brothers Epa and John Lawson. Wits: John Tuberville and Fortunatus Sydnor. W.B. 10, p. 415.

LAWSON, Nicholas. Orphans' estate. Rec. 13 Oct. 1736.

Returned by Nicholas Martin, gent., guardian. W.B. 13, p. 18.

LAWSON, Jane. 20 Sept. 1735. Rec. 8 Sept. 1738.

Gr.son: John Stepto. Dau: Joanna Stepto. Son: Thomas Lawson. John Biscoe, son of Robert Biscoe. Exor: Thomas Lawson. Wits: Robert Biscoe and Chr Collins. W.B. 13, p. 111.

LAWSON, Epaphroditus. 25 Mar. 1745. Rec. 12 Apr. 1745.

Wife: Sons: Eppa and John (not of age). Daus: Elizabeth, Anna Stepto. (not of age). Ex: James Haynes, Sr., John Stepto, James Haynes, Jr. Wm. Dymer. Wits: Jas. Kirk, Uriah Angell. W.B. 14, p. 128.

12 Apr. 1745. Inv. returned by John Stepto, his executor. W.B. 14, p. 75.

Eppaphroditus Lawson, son of Eppaphroditus Lawson, dec., lately of Co. of Lancaster of his free will and with the consent of his mother Anna Lawson has put himself apprentice to David Galloway & George Ker & Co. of Northumberland, merchants. 11 Mar. 1747. W.B. 14, p. 179.

LAWSON, Anna. Rec. 17 Jan. 1752.

Anna Lawson allotted her part of her husband's negroes. W.B. 15, p. 88.

15 June 1753. Mrs. Anna Lawson. Inv. Returned by George Ker, adm. W.B. 15, p. 133.

LAWSON, Thomas. 14 July 1747. Rec. 14 Aug. 1747.

Son: Thomas (not 21). Wife: Margaret. Nephew: John Steptoe, Jr. Exors: Wife, Mr. Samuel Blackwel, Mr. Jas. Steptoe, Capt. Peter Conway. Wits: Jno. Steptoe, Anna Lawson, Cath. James. W.B. 14, p. 147.

LAWSON, James. Inv. Rec. 14 Apr. 1749.

Returned by Thos. Edwards, adm. W.B. 14, p. 233.

LAWSON, Nicholas. 6 Feb. 1749/50. Rec. 13 Apr. 1750.

Wife: Sarah. Daus: Catherine, Betty, Judith & Sarah Lawson. Ex: David Currie, William Dymer, Sarah Lawson, John Yerby. Wits: Wm. Gibson, Jona. Willder, Uriah Angell, John Griggs. W.B. 14, p. 277.

LAWSON, Nicholas, estate, division. Rec. 16 May 1751.

Widow, now wife of John Schon. W.B. 15, p. 41.

LAWSON, Henry. 21 Nov. 1751. Rec. 19 June 1752.

Wife: Winifred. Children: not named. Exors.: Wife, Winifred, Wm. Hathaway, Nicholas Currell. Wits: Nicholas Currell, Henry Lawson, Jr., John Biscoe. W.B. 15, p. 96.

LAWSON, Harry. Inv. & Ap. 19 June 1752. Rec. 17 July 1752.

Returned by Winifred Lawson, Extrx. W.B. 15, p. 103.

LAWSON, Nicholas estate, division. 20 Jan. 1758.

Benjamin George, Jr. Married Katherine one of the orphans of Nicholas Lawson and guardian of Judith and Sarah, orphans of deceased. W.B. 15, p. 319.

LAWSON, Anne. 23 Oct. 1760. Rec. 20 Nov. 1761.

Winford Lawson and her dau. Mary Lawson. James Hathaway, Elizabeth Hathaway, Mary Lawson, William Hataway, Sr. Saarh Biscoe, John Biscoe, Henry Lawson. Ex. Em. Hathaway, Sr. Wits: Geo. Currell, James Currell. W.B. 16, p. 176.

LAWSON, Capt. Thomas, guardian to Margaret Reid. 16 Aug. 1771. Rec. 19 Sept. 1771.

Orphan of Nocholas Reid, certain negroes due her from the estate of Capt. Wm. Dymer her late Guardian, dec. W.B. 20, p. 26, 44.

Thomas Lawson, part of his father's estate delivered to him May 8, 1760. Recorded Aug. 21, 1760. of Mr. Nicholas Currell. Wits: Henry Lawson, Richard Bland. Rec. 16 July 1772. W.B. 20, p. 44.

LAWSON, Epa. Deposition. 7 Feb. 1778. Rec. 7 Feb. 1778.

Age about 44 yrs. States that he heard Mr. Thomas Lee say that Charles Lee should not pay any of the debts due from his Brother Richard Lee, deceased. W.B. 20, pp. 127, 133.

Will of Epa Lawson. Dated 16 Jan 1778. Rec. 18 June 1778. Wife Mary Lawson. Dau: Elizabeth Hunt. Son: Epaphroditus

Lawson. "All my children." Extrx: Wife Mary Lawson. Wits: Richard E. Lee, Henry Lawson, Lawson Hathaway. W.B. 20, p. 133.

LAWSON, Elizabeth, of Parish of Christ Church. 2 May 1774. Rec. 19 Feb. 1778.

Brother: William Lawson. Sister: Ann Lawson, Niece: Ann Reveer. Wits: Robert Clark, John Flowers, Ann Lawson. W.B. 20, p. 117.

LAWSON, Epaphroditus, Jr. Appraisal. Nov. 1786. Rec. 18 Jan 1787.

By Henry Lawson, Martin Shearman & James Currell. W.B. 22, p. 140.

LAWSON, William of Christ Church Parish. 5 Mar. 1789. Rec. 19 Apr. 1790.

Wife: Betty. Son: Anthony Lawson. Daus: Elizabeth Sydnor Lawson & Ann Lawson. Unborn child. Rowland Lawson. Exors: Brother, Henry Lawson & Lawson Hathaway. Mentions brother & sister's children. Wits: John Sydnor & Henry C. Lawson. W.B. 22, p. 258.

19 July 1790. Appraisal. W.B. 22, p. 278.

LAWSON, Eppa. Division of estate. 16 Feb. 1790. Rec. 21 June 1790.

Allotted to widow, Nancy Lawson. By Martin Shearman & Robert Fergusson. W.B. 22, p. 269.

LAWSON, Eppaphroditus. Settlement. Rec. 17 Jan. 1791.

James Brent, adm. By Henry Dawson & Martin Shearman. W.B. 22, p. 285.

LAWSON, John. Appraisal. 16 Feb. 1795. Rec. 20 July 1795.

By William Gibson, George W. Yerby, Thomas Pitman. W.B. 22, p. 460.

LEATHEAD, John. 20 June 1749. Rec. 11 Aug. 1749.

Wife: Mary. Daus: Mary, Elizabeth & Ann. Brother's children in Scotland. Ex. Wife, Mary, Dale Carter, Wm. Dymer, Thomas Dudley. Wits: Wm. Griggs, Jonathan Morris. W.B. 14, p. 255.

LEDFORD, John. 10 May 1751. Rec. 15 Nov. 1754.

Wife: Elizabeth. Son: James (not 20). Dau: Elizabeth Ledford. Ex. Wife, Elizabeth. Trustees: Thos. Gaskins and Thos. Edwards. Wits: Harry Currell, Thos. Cottrell, Thos. Winter. W.B. 15, p. 190.

LEE, Henry. Inv. 7 Mar. 1652. Rec. 10 Aug. 1653.

Taken by Edward Grimes & Wm. Neesham. W.B. 1, p. 126.

LEE, Thomas. 16 June 1733. Rec. 11 June 1735.

Name of wife not given. Sons: William, Thomas, Richard and Charles to whom is given "the land I now live on." Child unborn. Son: John. Exors: Wife, brother Charles Lee and Nicholas Martin. Wits: Ezekiel Gilbert, Isaac Currell. W.B. 12, p. 342. Inv. returned by Elizabeth Lee his Extrx. W.B. 12, p. 243.

LEE, Thomas. Division of estate. Rec. 12 Nov. 1742.

James Scrosby & Eliza. his wife, Exors. Estate divided between Elizabeth & her children Leanna, Elizabeth, Thomas, Richard, John, Charles, & Lucy Lee. W.B. 13, p. 303.

LEE, Richard, orphan of Thomas Lee, Gent. Ezekiel Gilbert his guardian. 12 Aug. 1743. Rec. 12 Aug. 1743. W.B. 13, p. 341.

LEE, Lucy, one of the daus. of Thos. Lee, dec. Rec. 2 Dec. 1746.

Division of estate. Legatees: John Lee, Thomas Lee, Leana Fearn, Betty Lee, Richard Lee, Charles Lee, John Lee. W.B. 14, p. 147.

24 Mar. 1745. John Lee and Lucy Lee, orphans of Thomas Lee. W.B. 14, p. 104.

LEE, Richard, of Parish of Christ Church. 12 June 1758. Rec. 15 Dec. 1758.

Died without making a will in writing but desired his brother, Charles Lee, of Fleets Island, marriner, might have certain negroes. Thomas Lee his brother complies with this request. Wits: Spencer Currell, Epa Lawson, Constantine Rock. W.B. 16, p. 47.

LEE, Thomas. 1 Dec. 1758. Rec. 16 Mar. 1759.

Dau: Mary Lee. Brother: John Lee, Richard Lee, died. Son George Lee. Wife: Lucy Lee. Brother: Charles Lee, land I now live on. Sister, Elizabeth Dobull's eldest son. Exors: Wife, Lucy, Chas. Lee, Eppa Lawson and Geo. Currell. Wits: Benj. Kelly, James Scrosby, Jr., Charles Lee, G. Currell. W.B. 16, p. 52.

18 June 1762. Rev. Mr. John Leland appointed guardian of Mary Lee, orphan of Thos. Lee and sd Leland possessed with ⅓ part of estate in right of his wife as also her part of her deceased son, George Lee's estate. W.B. 16, p. 52.

LEE, Thomas. Rec. 19 Aug. 1763.

John Leland guardian of Mary Lee, orphan of Thomas Lee. W.B. 17, p. 15.

LEE, Chas. 15 April 1765. Rec. 15 April 1765.

Chas. Lee, son of Peter Lee of Christ Church Parish, apprentices himself to Wm. Lawson. Susanna Lee, mother of sd. Charles Lee agrees to this. W.B. 18, p. 35.

LELAND's account of LEE's estate. Rec. 18 Aug. 1766.

Mary Lee orphan of Thomas Lee. W.B. 18, pp. 66, 85.

LEE, Thomas. Settlement. 21 Apr. 1774. Rec. 16 June 1774.

Rev. John Leland former guardian for Mary Lee, orphan of Thomas Lee. Mr. Richard Hall Possessed with his wife's part of her father's estate. By Nicholas Currell, Thomas Lawson, Epp. Lawson, Henry Lawson. W.B. 20, p. 72.

LEE, Susannah. Appraisement. 19 May 1774. Rec. 16 June 1774.

By Richard Hutchings, Wm. Davis, John Hill. W.B. 20, p. 73.

LEE, Charles. Appraisement. Rec. 18 Apr. 1777.

By Henry Carter, John Carter, Wm. Saunders, Wm. Broun. W.B. 20, p. 110.

LEE, Charles. Est. Aug. 1782. Rec. 19 Sept. 1782.

John Doggett, administrator. W.B. 20, p. 243.

LEE, Charles, of Christ Church Parish. 1791. Rec. 19 Mar. 1792.

Wife: Joannah all my land. Sons: Thomas and Richard Lee. Dau: Elizabeth Beale and at her death to be divided between her children Charles and John Beale. Daus: Sarah and Ann Lee. Mentions negroes which his wife Joannah Lee holds under the last will of Wm. Morgan, dec. which are to be divided between Thomas & Richard Lee & Elizabeth Beale, Sarah & Ann Lee. Exors: Wife and sons Thomas & Richard. Wits: Wm. G. Doggett, Thos. Currell, Jr., Elizabeth G. Shearman. W.B. 22, pp. 179, 330.

Inv. returned 7 Jan. 1794. Rec. 20 Jan. 1794. By Thos. Lee & Richard Lee. W.B. 22, p. 403.

LELAND, John. 15 Feb. 1789. Rec. 15 June 1799.

Wife: Judith Leland. Sons: John Lee Leland, Leroy Peachey Leland, & Baldwin Leland. (sons not 20). Dau: Maira Leland. Sister: Susannah Leland. Exors: Wife, Col. LeRoy Peachey &

Col. James Ball. Wits: Wm. Warren, Charles Leland & Sally Leland. W.B. 22, p. 217.

LELAND, Rev. John. Appraisal. 15 June 1789. Rec. 18 Jan. 1790. By Jas. W. Ball, Wm. Warren, Hancock Lee. W.B. 22, p. 244.

LEMUEL, William. 6 Apr. 1683. Rec. 15 Sept. 1683.
Wife: Jane. Dwelling and plantation. Dau: Christian Flint. Exors: Wife, Jane. Wits: Alex. Atkins, Sam'l Dickson, Robt. Gill, Wm. Clarke. W.B. 5, p. 88.

LEMON, Peter. Inventory. 17 Dec. 1675. Returned 1 June 1675 by Thos. Berkof. W.B. 5, p. 23.

LEWIS, Robert, of Christ Church Parish. 25 Feb. 1720. Rec. 8 Nov. 1721.
3 children: Judith, Elizabeth and Robert Lewis. Ex: Friends, Mr. Thomas Carter & Wm. Dymer. Wits: Thomas Davis, Jno. Lewis, Jno. Johnson. W.B. 10, p. 339.
Elizabeth Lewis, admtrx. presents will. W.B. 10, p. 339.

LEWIS, Jno. 29 Mar. 1729. Rec. 14 May 1729. Jno. Lewis of Christ Church Parish.
Name of wife not given. Thos. Wells. Exors: Wife and Thos. Wells. Wits: Dan'l Carter and Lettice Griggs. W.B. 12, p. 96.

LEWIS, William. 13 Dec. 1733. Rec. 9 Jan. 1733.
Legatees: Capt. Geo. Heale my farm in Great Britain containing 48 acres called Webstershall in the parish of poles Warden in the County of Harfordshire, given me by my great grandfather Charles Lewis. Exor: Capt. Geo. Heale. Wits: Jas. Wharton, Jno. Norris, Timothy Thornton. W.B. 12, p. 289.

LEWIS, William. Inv. & Ap. 17 Dec. 1743. Rec. 13 Jan. 1743.
Returned by William Ball, Gent., admr. W.B. 14, p. 4.

LEWIS, Richard. 14 July 1762. Rec. 18 Nov. 1763.
Wife: Margaret. Dau: Mary. Wits: Wm. Sanders, John Bean. W.B. 17, p. 26.

LEWIS, Dr. John, possessed with two negroes from his wife's estate agreeable to her father's will. 16 Dec. 1784. Rec. 17 Mar. 1785. By Henry Lawson & James Currell. W.B. 22, p. 72.

LEWIS, Margaret. 18 Sept. 1783. Rec. 21 July 1785.
To Mary Bean. Friend—John Bean. Wits: Stephen Lock, John Cundiff, Peter Bean. W.B. 22, p. 89.

LIGHT, George. 1 Jan. 1744. Rec. 9 Dec. 1748.

Wife: Jean. Youngest son: Joseph Light. Eldest son: George Light, Jr. Mentions 3 children. Wits: Wm. Cornelius, Moses Kelley. W.B. 14, p. 226.

LIGHT, Joseph. 26 Mar. 1751. Rec. 10 May 1751.

Wife: Mary Light. Wits: Jon. Harriss, Obediah Lowrie. W.B. 15, p. 32.

LIGHT, Joseph. Inv. 10 May 1751. Rec. 14 June 1751.

Returned by Mary Light, Extrx. W.B. 15, p. 42.

LIGHT, George, dec. Rec. 17 Nov. 1766.

Administration granted Jesse Light. W.B. 17, p. 224.

LIGHT, George. Inv. 17 Nov. 1766. Rec. 15 Dec. 1766.

Jesse Light reports this is a true inventory of all the estate of "my father George Light." W.B. 18, p. 73.

LISTER, William of Christ Church Parish. 3 May 1709. Rec. June 1709.

Godson: John Kent, son of John and Catherine Kent. Goddau: Mary Grason. Mother: Mrs. Dorothy Jackson. Exors: Father, Andrew Jackson and mother, Dorothy Jackson and Jno. Grason. Wits: Robt. Roebuck, Jos. Kelly, Geo. Brown, Thos. Brown. Codicil: Catherine, Wife of Jno. Kent. Wits: Thos. Brown, Jno Hutchings, Jos. Kelly. W.B. 8, p. 138.

LIZENBY, Thomas. Ap. 12 Apr. 1745. Rec. 10 May 1745.

Returned by Cathr. Lizenby, admx. W.B. 14, p. 69.

LIZENBY, Wm. Inv. 12 Oct. 1750.

Returned by Wm. Winter, adm. W.B. 14, p. 315.

LIZENBY, Thomas. Appraisement. 8 Mar. 1776. Rec. 19 June 1766.

By Samuel Wornum, George Webbe, Thos. Brent. W.B. 18, p. 57.

LLOYD, Edward. 27 Oct. 1690. Rec. 13 Mar. 1691.

No wife. Sister: Ann. Mrs. Hannah Fox, Wm. and Sam'l Fox, Thos. Cooper, Edwd. White, David Fox. Exor: Wm. Fox. Wits: Thos Cooper, Nathaniel Phipps. W.B. 8, p. 10.

LOE, Thomas. 18 July 1713.

Wife: Margaret. Son: Thomas, my plantation. Judith Collens. Exors: Wife, Mathias Rose and Judith Collen. Wits: Edwd. Harris, Noah Rogers, John Brown. W.B. 10, p. 183.

LOE, Thomas. 8 Dec. 1750. Rec. 8 Feb. 1750.

Sons: William Loe (to have plantation) Thomas Loe. Wife: Mary Loe. Daus: Sarah and Margaret Loe. Exors: Wm. Shel ton, Jr., John Rogers. Wits: Merriman Payne, James Smith. (Mentions next oldest son—but gives no name.) W.B. 15, p. 1.

LONGWORTH, Robert. Inv. 12 Dec. 1690. Rec. 13 Jan. 1691.

Presented by Mary Longworth. W.B. 8, p. 13.

LOUTHER, Jon. Inv. Rec. 9 Aug. 1710.

Presented by Relict. W.B. 10, p. 48.

LOWRY, Elias. 3 Dec. 1743. Rec. 13 Jan. 1743.

Wife: (name not given). Sons: Elias, John, William, Henry. Dau: Judith. Darius Thomas. Ex.: John Simmons & Edny Tapscott. Wits: Chas. Hammonds, Janus Waugh. W.B. 14, p. 4.

LOWRY, Obediah. Inv. Rev. 27 May 1751. (See Lawry.)

Returned by Gavin Lowry, adm. W.B. 15, p. 44.

LOWRY, Stokely. Inv. & Apprais. 19 May 1774. Rec. Jan. 25, 1776.

Inv. presented by Gavin Lowry. Appraised by Henry Carter, George Carter, John Harris. W.B. 20, p. 77.

LUCKHAM, Isaac. Inv. & Ap. 9 Mar. 1719. Rec. 13 Apr. 1720.

Proved by oath of James Roberson, adm. W.B. 10, p. 302.

LUCKHAM, William. 9 Jan. 1751/2. Rec. 8 Feb. 1751.

Son: James Luckham. Wife: not named. "All my children." Test: John Tomblin, John Carpenter, Stephen Stott, James Bush, James Luckham. W.B. 15, p. 4.

LUNSFORD, Mrs. Lettice, dec'd. Aug. 1778. Rec. 15 Jan. 1784.

Division of estate. Formerly wife of Joseph Carter, dec'd. To sd Carter's children, John Lunceford in right of his wife Sarah, Mrs. Ann Pines Haynie, widow, Mathew Syars, Exec of Joseph Carter. Appraisors: James Gordon, Henry Towles, Chas. Rogers. W.B. 22, p. 9.

LUNSFORD, Rodham. 11 Apr. 1791. Rec. 15 Aug. 1791.

Sons: John, Rodham & Lenton Lunsford (not 21). Daus: Judith Carter and her children. Exors: Sons John & Rodham Lunsford. Wits: James Gordon, James Hill. W.B. 22, p. 312.

Appraisal. W.B. 22, p. 317.

LYELL, John. Est. Rec. 8 Mar. 1726.

By Jonathan Lyell, adm. W.B. 10, p. 525.

LYNE, Thomas (of parish of St. Mary's white Chappel). 23 Oct. 1716. Rec. 8 May 1717.

Legatees: Wife, Elizabeth; son, Thomas; dau., Susanna; other children (not named). Extrs.: Wife and Henry Towles. Wits.: Wm. Lawrence, Jno. Reeves, Jno. Barlowe, Noah Rogers. W.B. 10, p. 214.

MADESTARD, Thomas. Inv. 10 Nov. 1675. Rec. 1 Dec. 1675.

Returned by Robert Griggs. W.B. 5, p. 12.

McCALL, George. Inv. Rec. 8 Mar. 1751.

Returned by Samuel McCall, adm. W.B. 15, p. 18.

McCARROLL, Wm. Inv. Rec. 8 June 1744.

Returned by Robert Mitchell. W.B. 14, p. 22.

McCARTY, Col. Thaddeus. 25 Oct. 1787. Rec. 17 Dec. 1787.

Sons: James Ball McCarty & Frederick McCarty (not 19). Daus: Mildred Smith McCarty, Sally McCarty, Nancy McCarty, Elizabeth McCarty, Mary Chinn McCarty, Fanny McCarty. (To James, Mildred & Sally 6 pounds each in full satisfaction of the estate they got by their mother). Exors: James Ball, Jr., James Gordon, Wm. Sydnor. Wits: Robert Fergusson, Ozwald Newby, Wm. Mitchell, Wm. Hunt. W.B. 22, p. 159.

Appraisal. W.B. 22, p. 170.

McCARTY, Col. Thaddeus. Division of estate. Rec. 10 Feb. 1788.

To Frederick McCarty, Mrs. A. Lawson, Cap. James Craine, Miss Fanny McCarty, Miss Molly McCarty. By Jas. Newby, Ozwald Newvy, Rawl. Davenport. W.B. 22, p. 325.

McCARTY, Frederick, orphan of Col. Thaddeus McCarty. Rec. 18 Feb. 1792.

Rawleigh W. Downman, administrator. Account of estate from will of Thadd. McCarty. By Jos. Chinn, Wm. Carpenter, Philip Warrick, Jno. Carpenter. W.B. 22, p. 343.

Division of estate. 18 June 1792. To Misses Elizabeth, Nancy, Mary, Sally, Mildred S., Fanny McCarty and James McCarty. W.B. 22, p. 344.

McDANIEL, Edward. Adm. bond. Rec. 12 Oct. 1727.

Hugh Brent, adm. W.B. 12, p. 40.

McDANIEL, Roger. 28 July 1774. Rec. 15 Sept. 1774.

Wife: Catherine McDaniel. Extrx: Wife. Wits: William Mountague, Thomas X. Marsh. W.B. 20, p. 75.

MACGAE, John, not dated. Rec. —— 1713.

Son: Joseph. Daus: Ann, Mary, Margaret & Catherine, John Flannagan & Ellin his wife have tuition of daus, Mary & Catherine until 18 yrs. of age. Mr. Will Bertrand & Susanna his wife have tuition of dau. Margaret until 18 yrs. of age. Jos. Brasier to have tuition of son Joseph until 20 Yrs. of age. W.B. 10 p. 180.

McGRAW, Daniel. Inv. Rec. 8 March 1749.

Returned by Jos. Chinn, gent., adm. W.B. 14, p. 274.

McGOUREN, Margaret. Ap. 18 May 1753. Rec. 15 June 1753.

Returned by Wm. Taite, adm. W.B. 15, p. 129.

McTIRE, Robert. 27 Jan. 1775. Rec. 20 Apr. 1775.

Wife: Elizabeth McTire. Sons: William, Frizel, Robert and his children, & John McTire and his children. Daus: Frances Yerby, Hannah Dilliard, Catherine Davis. Son-in-laws: Wm. Yerby, John Dilliard, dec, and John Davis. Gr.sons: Robert Yerby and Robert McTire son of my son John. Ex: Son-in-law, Wm. Yerby and friend Wm. Montague. Wits: William Montague, Richard Ball. W.B. 20, p. 83.

McTYRE, Robert. Division of estate. Feb. 1791. Rec. 18 Apr. 1791.

By James Ball, Rawl. W. Downman, James W. Ball. Heirs: Representatives of Hannah Yerby, dec., delivered to Frances Yerby, Extrx. of Wm. Yerby, dec., who was Exor. of Robt. McTire. Catherine Davis, John McTyre, Robert McTire, Jr. dec. his representatives. William McTire, Frizzell McTire, Hannah Harley's representatives. W.B. 22, p. 303.

McTYRE, Mary M. Division of estate. 4 Feb. 1792. Rec. 20 Feb. 1792.

Agreeable to the will of Coleman Doggett, dec. is allotted to Wm. Doggett his part of sd dower. By John Degges, James Carter, Moses George. W.B. 22, p. 326.

19 Jan. 1795. Rec. 16 June 1795. Division of estate. To Priscilla and Dennis Doggett. By James Pollard, James Carter, Peter Tankersley. W.B. 22, p. 459.

McTYRE, Elizabeth. Appraisal. Rec. 28 Feb. 1792.

By James Ball, Henry Hinton, William Newby. W.B. 22, p. 329.

MACHAN, Matthew. Rec. 12 Mar. 1734.

Son: James. Wife: Name not given. Children. Ex. John Mott. Wits: Thomas Williams, Ralph Rutherford, Sarah Rutherford. W.B. 12, p. 331.

MACHAN, Mathew. Inv. Rec. Mar. 26, 1735.

Returned by John Mott, Ex. W.B. 12 p. 337.

MACCRONY, Patrick. Inv. Rec. 9 Feb. 1725.

Returned by Col. Wm. Ball, adm. W.B. 10, p. 470.

MAHON, Patrick. Inv. Rec. 8 Nov. 1721.

Returned by Frances Mahon, admtrx. W.B. 10, p. 340.

MAIZEY, David. Rec. 13 Jan. 1713.

Son: James Maizey to friend Isaak Basey until sd son comes to age of 19 yrs. Dau: Frances Maizey to friend Wm. Nash until she comes to age of 18. Dau: Rebeccah Maizey to friend Wm. Lawrence until she comes to age of 18. Appoints friends Wm. Nash and Wm. Lawrance, Exors. Wits: Wm. King, Wm. King, Jr., Tabitha King. Marked "not fully proved." W.B. Loose Wills.

MAPLES, George. 5 Dec. 1684. Rec. 16 Mar. 1685.

All left to wife and children. No names given. Extrx: Wife and eldest dau. Wits: Wm. Ball, Wm. Therriot & Wm. Day. W.B. 5, p. 99.

Presented in court, 9 Sept. 1685, by Hannah Maples, relict of George Maples. W.B. 5, p. 101.

MARSH, Francis. 9 Dec. 1651. Rec. 10 Apr. 1753.

Wife: Lucy, 200 acres of land lying at Nyemcock adjoining the upper side of Rich'd Loes' land. Extrx. Wife. Wits: More Fantleroy, John Edcombe. W.B. 2, p. 9.

MARKS, Patrick. Est. Rec. 8 Mar. 1726.

Wm. Bertrand, adm. W.B. 10, p. 532.

MASCALL, Robert. 27 Sept. 1653. Rec. 10 Nov. 1653.

To Wm. Newsom, John Pine, Epaphroditus Lawson, Mary Tomson, the younger. Robert Newsom, son of Wm. Newsom. Richard Coleman, Thos. Hanks, Robert Towson. Wits: Thomas Hanks, Robert Pare. W.B. 2, p. 10.

MARSHALL, William. Inv. 5 Aug. 1676. Rec. 18 Sept. 1676.

Presented by Stephen Tomlyn. W.B. 5, p. 26.

MARSHALL, Thos. 25 June 1686. Rec. 13 Mar. 1690.

Wife: Agnes. Son: Thomas (eldest) land I now live on, Scarborough, John and Sackville. Daus: two but not named. Extrx. Wife. Overseer, Jno. Sharpe. Wits: Edward Dale, Alex. English. W.B. 8, p. 10.

MARSHALL, Thomas. Inv. 21 Apr. 1691. Rec. 10 June 1691.

Presented by Agnes Marshall. W.B. 8, p. 13.

MARSHALL, Sackfield. Inv. Rec. 11 May 1710.

Presented in Court by Thom. Marshall and Robert Marshall. W.B. 10, p. 29.

MARSHALL, John, of St. Mary's White Chappel, ship carpenter. 30 Jan. 1736/7. Rec. ——.

Sons: Thomas and John a gold ring. Dau: Kathrine Marshall. Rachel English "my housekeeper." Lucretia English, daughter of Rachel English. Not probated or signed. Loose Wills.

MARSHALL, John. Est. Rec. 8 Mar. 1726.

Jos. Carter, Adm. W.B. 10, p. 533.

MARSHALL, Thomas. Est. 12 June 1728.

Robert Marshall, adm. W.B. 12, p. 59.

MARTIN, Thomas. Inv. 12 Apr. 1684. Rec. 9 July 1684.

Presented by Robetta Martin, relict. W.B. 5, p. 96.

MARTIN, Thomas. Inv. 9 Jan. 1687. Rec. 12 Apr. 1688.

Presented by Rebecca Corroll, relict of Thomas Martin. W.B. 5, p. 119.

MARTIN, Thomas. Rec. 13 May 1692.

Wife: Hagar. Catherine Soaper, dau. of Elizabeth Soaper, to be under the care of Thos. Barker & Richard Flint. Richard Flint, Jr., William Barker, son of Thos. Barker. Exors: Richard Flint and Thos. Barker, Sr. Wits: Josiah ——, Wm. Fox, Hen. Pullen. W.B. 8, p. 36.

MARTIN, Tho: Inv. 10 May 1710. Rec. 14 Jan 1710.

Presented in Court by Susan Martin, relict. W.B. 10, p. 28.

MARTIN, Thomas. 19 Feb. 1711.

Wife: Elizabeth. Son: Thomas "all lands and plantation whereon he now lives." Daus: Anne Martin & Margaret Martin. Sept-daus: Thomasin —— & Catherine Dare, wife of Mr. Will

Dare, daus of my now wife. Exors: Wife & Maj. Wm. Ball. Wits: Nicholas George, Ellinor George, Geo. Wale. W.B. 10, p. 130.

Estate appraised 8 Apr. 1713. W.B. 10, p. 134.

MARTIN, Thos., of Parish of St. Mary's White Chappel. 5 Apr. 1727. Rec. 14 June 1727.

Wife: Katherine. Daus: Elizabeth and Katherine M. Cousin: Thos. Wale & Thos Martin. Extrx: Wife. Wits: Jno. Withersow, Thos. Dare, Catherine Horne. W.B. 10, p. 549.

MARTIN, Thomas. Inv. 11 July 1727. Rec. 12 July 1727.

Taken by his wife, Katherine Martin, Extrx. W.B. 12, p. 16.

MARTIN, William. 1 May 1739. Rec. 8 June 1739.

Brothers Isaac and James Currell. Nephews Wm. Martin; Thos. Martin and Wm. Currell.Niece Rebeckah Basey; brothers Nich. Martin and Abraham Currell. Godson Benony Angell; Nephews Rebehah George, Abraham Currell, son of Isaac Currell; Elizabeth Kelley; Elinor Perkins; Wm. Cook, Jas. Brent; Spencer Currell. Extrs: Three Brothers, Nicholas Martin, Isaac and Abraham Currell. Wits: Hugh Kelley, Jas. Fleming and Wm. Angell. W.B. 13, p. 135.

MARTIN, Nicholas. 26 Jan. 1756. Rec. 19 June 1761.

Daus: Elizabeth Hill, Rebecca Baisie, Catherine Pope. Sons: Thomas Martin, William Martin, all my land. Gr.son: Leroy Pope. Wife: Elizabeth. Exors: Three sons-in-law: William Baisey, Jon Pope, John Hill, and wife, Elizabeth Martin. Wits: Daniel Carter, Jr., Harry Currell, John Carter, Geo. Currell. W.B. 16, p. 150.

MARTIN, William. Appraisal. Rec. 20 July 1786.

By Lawson Hathaway, Isaac Degge, William Lawson. W.B. 22, p. 123.

Appraisement of estate in Richmond Co. By Thos. Clarke, Andrew Morgan, Griffin Garland. Certified by Wm. Miskell. W.5. 22, p. 131.

Division. 18 Jan. 1787. Hannah Martin, widow. By Thos. Carter, Lawson Hathaway, William Lawson. W.B. 22, p. 141. 16 June 1794. Hannah Martin, widow. By Henry Lawson, Lawson Hathaway, James Pollard. W.B. 22, p. 431.

MASON, Jno. 29 Dec. 1737. Rec. 10 Mar. 1738.

Wife: Mary & children. Exors: Jas. Donnellon. Wits: Frances Walker and Jas. Donnellon. W.B. 13, p. 77.

MASON, Thomas. Inv. 19 Sept. 1753. Rec. 17 Oct. 1755.

Returned by Wm. Mason & Thomas Mason, admors. W.B. 15, p. 225.

MASON, Wm. Nuncupative will. 13 Sept. 1765. Rec. 16 Sept. 1765.

Nuncupative will made before John Dye & Sarah Davis. Wife, Sarah, all his estate and to bring up the children. W.B. 18, p. 52.

MASON's, Wm. account of Davis' estate. Rec. 19 Aug. 1765.

George Davis orphan of Ambrose Davis. W.B. 18, p. 45.

MASON, Thomas. 26 Mar. 1761. Rec. 16 Nov. 1769.

Wife: Judith Mason. Son: William Mason (to be under care of friend Wm. Dymer). Ex: Wife, Judith. Wits: William Mason, John Schon. W.B. 18, p. 154.

MASON, John. 11 July 1781. Rec. 16 May 1772.

Wife: Pegga Mason. As wife is with child and if this child is a son that he may have my whole lands whereon I now live but if a dau. she only an equal part with my other daus. Exors: Wife and James Bush. Wits: John Hazard, Jr., Thomas Mason, Margaret X. Bush. W.B. 20, p. 238.

MASON, Joseph, of Parish of White Chappel. 18 Dec. 1776. Rec. 15 May 1777.

Son: George Mason one shilling. Wife: Winny Mason. Children: Betty, Peter & Caty. Exors: Friends John Bailie & Rawleigh Davenport. Wits: Moses Chilton, John Mason, Rawleigh Davenport. W.B. 20, p. 111.

MASON, John. Inv. & Ap. 18 Nov. 1777. Rec. 16 July 1778.

By Wm. Dogget & John Nichols. W.B. 20, p. 137.

MASON, Sarah, of Parish of Christ Church. 30 Sept. 1783. Rec. 15 Jan. 1784.

Son: John Mason dec'd. Children: William Mason & Thomas Mason. Dau: Caty Dunaway. Ex: William Mason, Thomas Mason. Wit: Jesse Robinson Jr.; Leannah Cornelius. W.B. 22, pp. 7, 8.

Ext. appraised. Jan. 15, 1784. W.B. 22, p. 13.

MASON, Sarah, dec'd. 19 Feb. 1784. Rec. Jan. 18, 1784.

Estate appraised & Division. Thomas Mason, William Mason & Caty Dunaway. W.B. 22, p. 13.

MASON, William. Estate. 17 Mar. 1785. Rec. 21 Apr. 1785.

By Henry Lawson, Isaac Degge, Thos. Carter, Jesse George. W.B. 22, p. 75.

MASON, Sarah and Lucy—John Edwards Guardian. Mar. 1785. Rec. 17 June 1785.

Report of Elijah Percifull of estate of Sarah Mason. John Mason adm. of sd Lucy. By Edwin Conway, John Yerby, Jas. Gordon. W.B. 22, p. 77.

MATTHEWS, Wm. Inv. & Ap. Rec. 14 June 1727.

Presented by Elinor Matthews, admx., and Sam. S. Brumley. W.B. 12, p. 9.

Additional inv. Presented by Elinor Reason. 12 Feb. 1728. W.B. 12, p. 90.

MATHEWS, Samuel. 4 Mar. 1745/6. Rec. 9 May 1746.

Wife: name not mentioned. Ex: Wm. Stott. Wits: Wm. Luckam, Henry Newby. W.B. 14, p. 107.

MATTHEWS, William. 15 Jan. 1755. Rec. 21 Nov. 1755.

Son: John Matthews. "If my son dies before he comes of age, estate to return to St. Peters Parish in Tolberd's Co., Md. on the Eastern Shore. John Pollard of Princess Ann Co. being in his debt. Likewise, John Caminon of Fredericksburg Town, also Richard Brent of Lancaster, also Wm. Morris of Gloucester Co. Debts to be paid Mr. Mord. Booth. Ex: Wm. Dymer. Wits: John Sampson, Statford Lightburne, Dorcas Jankeesey. W.B. 15, p. 230.

MATHEW, Wm. Inv. & Ap. & Div. Rec. 19 Mar. 1756.

William Dymer possessed with ⅓ part for widow of sd. Mathew. W.B. 15, p. 238.

MAVER, Alex. 8 Mar. 1753. Rec. 17 Mar. 1753.

Mary Maver allotted her dower in estate of her husband Alex. Maver, dec. W.B. 15, 122.

Inv. & ap. 15 May 1753. W.B. 15, p. 93.

MAYES, Henry. 24 Mar. 1775. Rec. 15 June 1775.

Wife, Sinah Mayes; children: John; Judith; Sarah; Thomas;

Frances; Gemima; Ann; Henry; Elizabeth and M. Mayes. Extr. Johnson Riveer. Wits: Jesse Robinson Jr., Johnson Riveer and Thos. Norris. W.B. 20, p. 85.

MAYES, Henry. Appraisement. 15 June 1775. Rec. 17 Dec. 1775. By James Norris, Jesse Robinson, Jr., Rich'd. Goodridge. W.B. 20, p. 86.

MEAD, Thomas. 5 Mar. 1654. Rec. 12 June 1655.

Wife not given. Dau: Mary, the plantation I now live on and all land this side of the creek. Sons: Thomas and John all lands on the western side of the creek. Daus: Margaret, Joyce and Anne. Wits: Rawleigh Travers, John Richardson, Edward "—" Bradshaw. W.B. 2, p. 12.   his mark

MECCONICO, Enis. 28 Aug. 1683. Rec. 8 Jan. 1687.

Wife: Agnes, who was also Extrx; and to whom is given all his estate. Wits: Henry Pullee, Edward Johnson. W.B. 5, p. 112.

MERCER, Isaac. 26 Aug. 1779. Rec. 16 Nov. 1780.

Wife: ——. Daus: Molly, Nancy & Ellen Mercer. Nephew: John Mercer, son of my brother James. Brother; James Mercer. Exors: Friends: Edward Blackmore, Wm. Chowning, Jesse Shelton. Wits: Overton Cosby, Lawrence Meachum, William Graham. Will Presented by Mary Mercer, the widow of dec. W.B. 20, p. 183.

17 May, 1781. Martin Norris who Married Nancy Mercer, the dau. of Isaac Mercer, possessed with his part of sd. Mercer's estate. W.B. 20, p. 191.

MEREDITH, John. Inv. & Ap. Rec. 20 Jan. 1758.

Returned by John Meredith & Judith Gibson, admx.

MEREDITH, John, of Christ Church Parish. 27 Mar. 1784. Rec. 20 May 1784.

Wife: Ann. Sons: William, eldest, James John. Daus: Sarah Edwards wife of Charles Edward. Elizabeth Yearby wife of George. Mary George & Judith. Ex: Wm. Yerby, W. Merrideth, John Yerby. Wits: Wm. Yerby, John Hill. W.B. 22, p. 26.

MEREDITH, John. Appraisal & Inv. May 1784. Rec. 18 Aug. 1785.

Returned by William Merridith. By William Yerby, Elias Edmonds, John Yerby. W.B. 22, pp. 98-99.

Division of estate. Heirs: James Merridith, William Merridith,

Charles Edwards (for wife), John Merridith, Jesse George (for wife), Judith Robb, George Yerby (for wife), Mrs. Merridith (widow). W.B. 22, p. 100.

MERRIMAN, John. Inv. 3 Dec. 1674. Rec. 13 Jan. 1674. W.B. 2, p. 6.

MERRIMAN, Richard. 8 Apr. 1696. Rec. 13 Oct. 1696.

Dau: Susanna Payne and her husband William Payne. Gr.sons: William Payne, Jr. and Richard Payne. Exor: son Wm. Payne. Wits: —— Christian, Jno. Farmer, Alex English. W.B. 8, p. 60.

MERRIMAN, Thos. 19 July 1718. Rec. 12 Nov. 1718.

Wife: Ellinor. Sons: John, Adam and Benjamin. Brother: Wm. Merriman. Exors: wife and Henry Towles. Wits: Chris Stevens, Jas. Gayler, Thos. Sharp. W.B. 10, p. 275.

MERRYMAN, John. Est. Rec. 8 Mar. 1726.

Mary Merryman, adm. W.B. 10, p. 530.

MERRYMAN, John. Inv. 20 June 1727. Rec. 12 July 1727.

Presented by Mary Merryman, admx. W.B. 12, p. 11.

MERRYMAN, Wm. 27 Apr. 1740. Rec. 13 June 1740.

Godson: Daniel Burn. Grandau. Eliz. Newsom & her father & mother, Sam'l Newsom and Anne his wife. Wits: Robt. Newsom, Geo. Light, Jr. W.B. 13, p. 163.

MERRYMAN, John. 15 Mar. 1775. Rec. 17 Aug. 1775.

Gr.son: John Mercer (not 21). Dau: Judith Mercer. Son: John Merryman. Ex: Son, John Merryman. Wits: Matt. Myars, James Flemming. W.B. 20, p. 86.

MERRYMAN, John. Appraisal. 15 June 1786. Rec. 15 June 1787.

By William Chowning, Wm. Bristoe, Wm. Biscoe. W.B. 22, p. 213.

MERRITT, Thomas. Rec. 8 Dec. 1716.

Wife: Ann Merritt. Child: Easter Merritt. Exors: Wife Ann, and Mr. Wm. Fox. Wits: Thomas ——, Wm. Goodridge. W.B. 10, p. 230.

MILLER, Peter. 12 Feb. 1717. Rec. 12 Feb. 1717.

Wife's name not given. Son: eldest, Peter all my lands; Stephen and George. Exors: Wife and her father, Wm. Mitchell. Wits: Thos. Chattin, Wm. Keith, Wm. Barber. Proved by oaths of Mary Miller and Wm. Mitchell, Exors. W.B. 10, p. 249.

MILLER, John. Administration granted Margaret Miller, widow. 12 June, 1717. Rec. 14 Aug. 1717. W.B. 10, p. 238.

MILLER, Will. 20 Dec. 1718. Rec. 13 May 1719.

Wife's name not given, estate left by her father. Sons: Eldest, William, John. Dau: Frances Miller. Exor: His father whose name is not given. Wits: Rich. Ball, Wm. Mitchell, Therriat Taylor. W.B. 10, p. 286.

MILLER, William. Inv. Rec. 8 July 1719.

Proved in Court by oath of Randolph Miller, Ex. W.B. 10, p. 296.

MILLER, Randolph. 31 Jan. 1720. Rec. 10 Jan. 1721.

Wife: Katherine. Sons: John and William (both dead) Grandsons: John Miller, son of William Miller; Henry and William Miller, sons of John Miller; Peter, Stephen and George Miller, sons of Peter Miller; Randolph Mott, son of dau. Katherine Mott. Grandaughters: Katherine and Mary Miller, daus of John Miller, and their sister Sarah Miller; Anne Miller. Daus: Katherine Mott and Margaret Chattin. Dau-in-law: Margaret Miller and her dau. Joan and son John Miller. Exors: Wife and sons-in-law Jno. Mott and Thos. Chattin. Wits: Geo. Murdock, Jno. Hogan, Eliz. Jones. W.B. 10, p. 347.

MILLER, William. Rec. 8 Feb. 1726.

Thomas Wharton appointed guardian of William. Miller, orphan of Wm. Miller, dec. W.B. 10, p. 516.

MILLER, John. 28 Nov. 1726. Rec. 8 Feb. 1727.

Mother: Margaret Miller. Brother: Henry Miller. Extrx: Mother. Wits: J. Carter, Catherine Carter Miller, Edwin Con way. W.B. 10, p. 509.

MILLER, Margaret. 12 Nov. 1732. Rec. 14 March 1732.

Sons: William and Henry. Daus: Ann, Mary, Catherine & Sarah. Gr.dau: Elizabeth Rogers. Friend Edwin Conway tutor to son Henry until he comes to age of 21. Exor: Son Henry Miller. Wits: Robert Edmunds, Thos. Battony, Edwin Conway. W.B. 12, p. —.

MILLER, John. Apprais. 9 Dec. 1737. Rec. 14 Apr. 1738.

Returned by William Miller, adm. W.B. 13, p. 89.

MILLER, Stephen, of Parish of Christ Church. 8 Jan. 1743. Rec. 11 May 1744.

Godson: Stephen Miller, son of brother George. Bros: Peter Miller & George Miller. Ex. Peter Miller, Geo. Miller. Wits: John Mitchell, Mary Mott, Dale Carter. W.B. 14, p. 17.

MILLER, George. Division. 11 June 1767. Rec. 18 June 1767.

Geo. Yerby, Guardian of William Miller, orphan of Geo. Miller. W.B. 18, p. 81.

MILLER, Peter. Appraisement & Inv. Rec. 17 Dec. 1772.

Presented by Judith Miller, widow. Appraised by Dale Carter, John Yerby & James Hill. W.B. 20, pp. 48, 80.

Division of estate: Mrs. Miller, John Miller, Thomas Miller, Wm. Mitchell, Josiah Harris, Betty Miller, John Bean, George Miller, Ann Miller, Sarah Miller. Rec. 16 Mar. 1775. W.B. 20, p. 80.

MILLER, Martha, widow "being old." 22 Apr. 1774. Rec. 21 Mar. 1776.

Nephew: John Taylor, son of my Brother Thomas Taylor. Cousin: Martha Ball, dau of Capt. Geo. Ball, Frankie Carter, dau of Dale Carter. Nephew: Thomas Ball. Sarah Ball, dau of Capt. Geo. Ball, Elizabeth Portes Ball, dau of my nephew Thomas Ball. Sister: Anna Ball. Newphew: David Ball. Cousins: Sarah Ball & Martha Taylor. Overseer: Benj. Willis. "To old Jenny her bed" and 1 cow. "To my nephew John Taylor my blind Boy Adam and the Care of old Patrick as a Freeman." Nephew: David Ball, Jr. Exors: David Ball, Jr. & John Taylor. Wits: Joseph Williams, Margaret Ball, Sarah Jones. W.B. 20, p. 94.

MILLER, Martha, dec'd. 21 Mar. 1776. Rec. 19 Aug. 1784.

Inventory. Wm. Montague, Richard Ball, Edwin Conway. W.B. 22, p. 38.

MINSON, Monor. App. 9 May 1659. Rec. 20 May 1659. W.B. 2, p. 128.

MITCHELL, Robt. 16 Nov. 1702. Rec. 13 Jan. 1706.

Sons: John, Robert and George. Dau: Sarah. Overseers: Thos. Parfitt and Jno. Wills. Wits: Robt. Pollard, Jas. Smith, Jno. Wells. W.B. 8, p. 123.

MITCHELL, John. Inv. Rec. 4 Feb. 1710. W.B. 10, p. 68.

MITCHELL, Robt. Rec. 1709.

Robert Mitchell Married Mary, late wife of Jon. Sharp. W.B. 10, p. 36.

MITCHELL, George, of St. Mary's White Chappel. 11 Dec. 1716. Rec. 10 Apr. 1717.

Wife: Hannah. Dau: Sarah. Cousin: Wm. Mitchell. Extrx: Wife. Wits: Jas. Ball, Geo. Lovatt. W.B. 10, p. 192.

MITCHELL, James. Apprais. 13 Aug. 1718. Rec. 10 Sept. 1718. Alice Mitchell, adm. W.B. 10, p. 274.

MITCHELL, Wm., of Parish of St. Marie's White Chappel. 28 Jan. 1726. Rec. 10 Dec. 1729.

Wife: Margaret. Sons: William, my now dwelling place and plantation, and John. Daus: Mary, wife of Jno. Mott; Ann; Grace, wife of Mathias Machen; Sarah; Margaret, wife of Peter James Baily. Extrx: Wife. Wits: Chas Burgess, Wm. Smith, Martin Shearman, Jr. Codicil. Nov. 10, 1729. W.B. 12, p. 125.

MITCHELL, Wm., of St. Mary's White Chappel. 6 Apr. 1737. Rec. 14 Apr. 1738.

Wife: Ann. Sons: Wm. Wyatt and Thos. Daus: four; not named. Extrx: Wife & brother John Mitchell. Wit: Jesse Ball. W.B. 13, p. 79.

MITCHELL, William. Apprais. 9 May 1738. Rec. 12 May 1738. Returned by Ann Mitchell, Extrx. W.B. 13, p. 87.

MITCHELL, Robert. 12 July 1748. Rec. 9 Sept. 1748.

Sons: Robert, land where he now lives in Richmond Co. that I bought of Mrs. Belfield; John; Richard plantation where I now live & land in R'd. & Northumberland Co. Daus: Eliza, wife of Moore Fauntleroy, Judith Mitchell, Sarah, wife of Thomas Chinn, Frances Mitchell. Gr.children: Robert, Thomas, Rawleigh and Mary Chinn, children of dau. Sarah. Sister: Sarah Pitman. Wife: mentioned but name not given. (Page 236—Susannah, wife of Robert Mitchell, dec, renounces legacy.) Exors: Sons, Dr. John Mitchell, Robert and Richard Mitchell. W.B. 14, p. 212.

MITCHELL, John. 7 Feb. 1758. Rec. 20 Apr. 1759.

Son: Richard, "land formerly belonging to my father, William Mitchell, dec., which I bought of my nephew, Thomas Mitchell, adjoining the plantation where my brother William Mitchell, dec., did live." Son: James Mitchell, George Mitchell, William Mitchell. Dau: Frances Welch and her children. Exors: Wife Charity, Col. James Ball, Joseph Chinn and two sons, Wm. &

George. Wits: Thomas Coleman, Hannah Coleman, Robert X. Brooke. W.B. 16, p. 56.

Division of estate. Frances Welch is given as wife of David Welch. W.B. 16, p. 68.

MITCHELL, Susan. Rec. 19 Feb. 1762.

Division of estate. John Pope & Elizabeth Davenport's part Thomas Chinn. Robert Mitchell's children. Moore Fauntleroy, Richard Mitchell, John Sydnor, Geo. Glascock. Jas. Ball, M. Shearman, Thos. Stott. W.B. 16, p. 184.

MITCHELL, John. Rec. 18 Feb. 1765.

John Mitchell died without making a will. Betty Mitchell, widow, granted certificate of administration. W.B. 17, p. 98.

MITCHELL, John. Appraisement. 18 Feb. 1765. Rec. 15 July 1765.

By William Taylor, William Sanders, Dale Carter. Returned by Betty Mitchell. W.B. 18, p. 39.

MITCHELL, Jno. Division of estate. 15 June 1767. Rec. 18 June 1767.

Wife's dower. Wm. Mitchell John Mitchell, Ruth, Eliza, Grizzel & Hannah Mitchell. W.B. 18, p. 81.

MITCHELL, Richard. 14 Feb. 1779. Rec. 20 Sept. 1781.

Nephews: Richard Mitchell, Robert Mitchell, land in Richmond and Northumberland Co. Sarah Chinn, dau of "my nephew" Robert Chinn. Nephews, Robert & Richard Mitchell to have remainder of negroes provided they will deliver up all the negroes they had from their Father's estate to their two sisters Susanna Glascock & Hannah Mitchell. Dec'd. sister, Sarah Chinn's children. Sisters: Frances Sydnor, Elizabeth Fauntleroy, Judith Glascock. Exors: Nephews, Robert & Richard Mitchell. No witnesses. Ann Mitchell, widow of sd deceased, renounced by Deed proved in Court all her right in her deceased Husband's will. 20 Sept. 1781. W.B. 20, p. 207.

Mrs. Ann Mitchell allotted ½ of personal estate of her late husband, Mr. Richard Mitchell, dec. W.B. 20' p. 213.

MITCHELL, Thomas & Sarah, Orph William Mitchell. Sept Court. Rec. 16 Sept. 1784.

Thomas Flint dec'd former guardian. Thomas Mitchell guardian to Sarah. W.B. 22, p. 51.

MOHON, Patrick. Rec. 12 July 1732.

Wm. Mohon & Patrick Mohon, orphans of Patrick Mohon, by

John Wale their guardian. Absalom Mohon, orphan of Patrick Mohon, by John Angell his guardian. W.B. 12, p. 222.

MOHON, Absalom. 17 Dec. 1772. Rec. 15 Apr. 1773.

Division of estate among widow and children. John Fleet guardian to George, Mathias & Elizabeth Mohon. Susanna Mohon, Sr., James Mohon, John Mohon, Susanna Mohon, Jr. W.B. 20, p. 57.

MONOHAN, John. Inv. and Apprais. 17 Feb. 1764. By Hugh Brent, Geo. Wale, Jno. Yerby. W.B. 14, p. 10.

MONTAGUE, Peter. 27 Mar. 1659. Rec. 1 July 1659.

Wife: Cicely. Sons: Peter and Will all land lying in Rapp. river. Daus: Ellen, wife of Will Thompson, Margaret, and Elizabeth Montague. The child of Anne late wife of John Jadwyn. Exors: Wife and son Peter. Wits: Geo. Marsh, Thos. James. W.B. 2, p. 62.

Cicely Montague, widow and Peter Montague her son-in-law, Exors of last will of Peter Montague, dec. O.B. 3, p. 123.

MONTAGUE, William. Feb. 1784. Rec. 21 Oct. 1784.

Wife: Lucy. Sons: Thomas, Dragon Quarter plantation; William, John. Daus: Hannah Montague, Frances Montague. Daus-in-law: Judith Leland and Mildred Smith sisters of son William Montague. Godson: Baldwin Mathews Leland. Ex: Dr. William Ball, John Montague, Thomas Montague. Wits: John Leland. W.B. 22, pp. 51, 52.

Oct. 1784. Apprais. by John Leland, Edwin Conway, Jas. Tapscott. W.B. 22, pp. 58-61.

17 Feb. 1785. Land in Essex appraised by Richard Street, John Sadler, Josiah McTyre.

MOONE, Abraham. Inv. 23 Feb. 1655. Rec. 15 Apr. 1656.

By Thomas Carter, William Leech, Cuthbert Potter, Dennys Conner. W.B. 2, p. 29.

MOON, Abraham. Rec. 6 Feb. 1655.

Administration granted John Curtys. W.B. 1, p. 255.

MOORE, Frances. 7 June 1700. Rec. 11 Mar. 1701/2.

Devisees: Mottrom Wright, Jr., and Frances, dau. of Mr. Mottrom Wright, Sr. Nephew: Nicholas Atkins. Sisters: Mary, —— Knight & —— Atkins. Exors: Mottrom Wright, Sr. Wits: Eliz. Dox, Thos. Walters. W.B. 8, p. 108.

MOOR, John, of Christ Church Parish. 28 Feb. 1712-/13.

Wife: Elizabeth. Son: Gowin. Daus: Sarah, Isabel, Margaret, Ellinor. Winifred, Elizabeth and Mary. Exor: Son Gowin. Wits: Leonard Knight, Raw. Cornelus, Walter Heard. W.B. 10, p. 178.

MOORE, Joseph. Appraisement. Oct. 1773. Rec. 18 Nov. 1773.

By Bailie George, Jonathan Wilder, Micael Wilder. W.B. 20, p. 66.

MORE, William, of Great Wiccomoco in the Co. of Northumberland. Wife: Hannah. Sons: William (eldest), Jonathan "my plantation I now live on," Robert and Joseph More. Daus: Elizabeth (eldest), Martha. Exor: Son Jonathan. Wits: Thos. and Sarah Pitman & Jos. Edser. Ages of 3 youngest children should be put down: Son Robert More was born 26 day of Oct. 1719. Son Joseph More was born 17 day of Apr. 1721. Dau. Martha More was born 17 day of Apr. 1713. Thos. Pitman & Isaac Basye to divide estate. W.B. 12, p. 57.

MORGAN, John. 26 Feb. 1681/. Rec. 12 May 1682.

Dau: Elizabeth Keene. Wife: Mary Morgan. Nurse child I had from Robert Botos named Elenor Botos. Exrx. Wife Mary. Wits: Edward Walder, Ambros Pamer, Mikall Cartarig. W.B. 5, p. 78.

MORRIS, Wm. 19 Mar. 1727. Rec. 14 Mar. 1727.

Sons: Wm., Thos., Benj., & John M. Daus: Elizabeth and Mary. Henry Curtis. Exors: Dau. Mary and Her husband. Wits: Jno. Wale, Jno. Bond, 'Jas. Oshaldestone. W.B. 12, p. 50.

MORRIS, John. 5 June 1745. Rec. 13 Sept. 1745.

Son: John. Daus: Eliza Hazard, Margaret Mathews, Ellen Stott. Son-in-law: Wm. Stott. Wife: Mary. Ex. Wm. Stott. Wits: John Stott, Jr., Wm. Bush. W.B. 14, p. 96.

MORRIS, John. Inv. 14 Feb. 1745. Rec. 11 Apr. 1746.

Returned by Winifred Morris, adm. W.B. 14, p. 103.

MOTT, John. 6 Feb. 1698. Rec. 2 July 1698.

Son: John, all land I now live on and elsewhere. Daus: Ann, Mary, and Winifred Alcock. Dau-in-law: Ann. Gr.dau. Sarah Wells. Exor: John Mott. Wits: Jno. Chattin, Geo. Carpender. W.B. 8, p. 88.

MOTT, John. 4 Mar. 1754. Rec. 21 June 1754.

Wife: Ann Mott and her grdau, Ann Boatman, dau of Henry

Boatman. Dau: Ann Smither and her children; Mary Hanks and her children; Catteran Shelton and her children. George Smither. Ex: Wife, Ann. Wits: Charles Betts, Jr., Thomas Cotrell. W.B. 15, p. 172.

MOTT, Joseph. Appraisement. 16 Nov. 1775. Rec. 21 Dec. 1775. By James Pinckard, Jr., Thomas Robb, James Kirke. W.B. 20, p. 90.

MOTT, John, of Parish St. Mary's White Chappell. 2 Feb. 1732. Rec. 4 Mar. 1732.
Wife: not referred to. Sons: Eldest Son John, Jr. plantation where I now live; Joseph, Randolph, William Mosely & Thomas Mott. Daus: Katherine and Mary Ann Mott. Exors: John, Joseph, Randolph and Katherine Mott. Wits: Elenor Carpenter, George Warrick, Robert Bygrave. W.B. 12, p. 247.

MOUGHON, Absalom. Inv. & Ap. 19 Oct. 1759.
Returned by Susannah Moughon. W.B. —, p. 73.

MOUGHAN, Patrick. 27 Dec. 1762. Rec. 18 Feb. 1763.
Wife: Sarah. Son: John Fogg. Friends: John Boggess & Thomas Toleson Ex. Wits: Jno. Yerby, Geo. Yerby, Jr., Robert Horton. W.B. 16, p. 253.

MOUGHON, James. 12 Dec. 1774. Rec. 16 Feb. 1775.
Mother: Susanna Moughon. Brothers: John, George and Matthias Moughon. My . . . . Elizabeth Moughon. Ex: Friend Vailie George. Wits: Thomas Shearman, Lancelot Moore, Matthias Moughon. W.B. 20, p. 78.

MOUGHON, Susanna. 1 Aug. 1778. Rec. 16 July 1778.
Memo. of distribution of goods by her own desire. Sons: Matthias, George, John. Daus: Betty & Susanna. Wits: Bailie George. W.B. 20, p. 140.

MAUGHON, James. Rec. 15 July 1779.
Bailie George, Executor. W.B. 20, p. 167.

MOHOUGHN, Christopher. 10 Nov. 1768. Rec. 21 Apr. 1769.
Administration granted John Roggers. W.B. 18, p. 142.

MULLIS, Stephen. 25 Oct. 1760. Rec. 20 Feb. 1761.
Wife: Dorothy. To John Cundiff, son of John Cundiff all my land. Rawleigh Shilton. Exors: Wife, Dorothy Mullis, Andrew

Davis & Moses Davis. Wits: Thomas James. Rawleigh Shilton, Sarah X. Wilder. W.B. 16, p. 122.

MOULD, Margaret. 2 June 1722. Rec. 8 Aug. 1723.

Legatees: mother, not named. Sisters: Sarah and Charity. Cousin: Jane Heard. Exor: Cousin, Henry Heard. Wits: Thos. Lee and Robt. Kirk. W.B. 10, p. 401.

MURPHY, Simon. 27 Aug. 1673. Rec. Sept. 1673.

Heirs: John Davenport, Jr., George Davenport, George ——. Wits: Robert Sadge, George ——: Bundle of Loose Papers 1653-79.

MUSE, Thomas. 20 Oct. 1755. Rec. 16 May 1775.

Wife: Sarah Muse. Two little sons: Richard and Thomas Sanford Muse. Ex.: Wife, John Hill and John Hill, Jr. Wits: Nathanl. Carpenter, James Robinson, Sarah Martain. W.B. 15, p. 204.

MUSE, John. Inv. & Apprais. Rec. 17 Apr. 1761.

Returned by Frances Muse, admx. W.B. 16, p. 131.

MYERS, Thomas, Sr. 7 May 1794. Rec. 20 July 1795.

Division of estate. Grandson: Thomas Myers, Jr. Mrs. Jane Arms' children: Elizabeth, George, Molly Norris, Sally Arms (now Myers), William Arms, George Arms. Mrs. Behethaland Claughton's children: William Claughton, Elizabeth L. Cannon now Pullen, Mary Cralle, Jane Claughton, Pemberton Claughton. Henry Towles, Joseph Carter, Jr., Thos. Hathaway. W.B. 22, p. 462.

MYLES, David. 22 Dec. 1674. Rec. 3 Jan. 1674.

Wife: Martha, who is also Extrx. Dau: Elizabeth. Wits: Wm. Pitcher, Richd. Shurley, John Cooper. W.B. 5, pp. 5, 6.

NASH, Thomas. Inv. 12 July 1676. Rec. 1 Aug. 1676.

Returned by William Nash. W.B. 5, p. 25.

NASH, William. Inv. 5 Nov. 1697. Rec. 4 Oct. 1698.

Presented by Amey Nash, relict. W.B. 8, p. 80.

NASH, Amey. 21 May 1708. Rec. 14 Mar. 1710.

Daus: Rebecca and Elizabeth Nash. Son: William Nash. Exors: Elias Edmonds and Chris Kirk. Wits: Edward Eidson and John Wirght. W.B. 10, p. 80.

NASH, William. 4 Feb. 1718. Rec. 8 Aprl 1719.

Wife: Anne. Son: William. Godson: William Basye. Overseers: Mr. Elias Edmonds, Mr. John Kirk and Charles Craven. Extrx: Wife. Wits: John Norrish and Thomas Flint. W.B. 10, p. 283.

NASH, Jno. 16 Jan. 1734. Rec. 12 Mar. 1734.

Wife: Elizabeth. Daus, Betty, other children but not named. Exors, Chas. Craven And John Kent. Wits: Wm. Boroman, Edwin Conway. W.B. 12, p. 333.

NASH, John. Appraisement. 12 Mar. 1735. Rec. 14 May 1735.

Returned by John Kent, Jr. W.B. 12, p. 335.

NEAL, John. Appraisement. 19 Jan. 1769. Rec. 16 Mar. 1769.

By Jos. Carter, Geo. Carter, Henry Carter. W.B. 18, p. 140.

NEALE, Arthur. Inv. 9 Mar. 1743. Rec. 11 May 1744.

Returned by Eliza Neale, his admx. W.B. 14, p. 18.

NEALE, Presley. Died Jan. 31, 1792. Oral Will. 31 Jan. 1792. Rec. 20 Feb. 1792.

Wife: Elizabeth. Nephew: John Chitwood. Two children (names not given). Ex.: Relative William Biscoe. Wits.: William Warwick, William Smith, George Warwick, John Rice. W.B. 22, p. 326.

NEESHUM, Anthony. Inv. Rec. 10 Apr. 1654.

Returned by Henry Dedman. W.B. 2, p. 85.

NEASUM, Robert. Rec. 9 Mar. 1743.

Sons: Parr, Benjamin, John, Jeremiah, Robert, William, Samuel .Neasum. Daus: Frances, Anne and Margaret Neasum. Exors: Sons Robert & Samuel. Wits: Sto. Towles, John Wright. W.B. 14, p. 9.

Inv. of Robert Neasum returned by Behthelan Neasum, his administrator. 10 May, 1745. W.B. 14, p. 74.

12 Aug. 1748. Ann Neasum orphan of Robt. Neasum. Stokely Towles her guardian. W.B. 14, p. 205.

NEASOM, Samuel, died without making a will. Rec. 18 Oct. 1765.

John Carpenter & Thos. Stott Appointed administrators. W.B. 17, p. —.

NEASOM, Samuel. Appraisement. 19 May 1766. Rec. 18 June 1766.

By Richard Mitchell, Ozwald Newby & Aaron Robinson. W.B. 18, pp. 61, 81, 71.

Division: To William Neasom,, Eliza Neasom for a legacy left her by her grandfather William Merryman. To John Hazzard guardian of Rachel Neasom. To Wm. Stott guardian of George Neasom. To Jno. Carpenter, guardian of Easter Neasom. Dated 17 Sept. 1766. Rec. 17 Nov. 1766. W.B. 18, p. 71.

NEASOM, George. Appraisement. 12 Apr. 1780. Rec. 20 Apr. 1780. Wm. Stott, guardian, & Spencer Brown, adm. W.B. 20, p. 178.

NORSUM, Robert, being bound for England. 20 Dec. 1693. Rec. 10 Oct. 1695.

Sons: William and Robert Norsum. Dau: Elizabeth. Wife: name not given. Wits: Edward Carter, William Lowre. W.B. 8, p. 53.

NEWSOM, William. 26 Apr. 1700. Rec. 10, 8 Br, 1700.

Sons: William & Robert Newsom. Wife: name not given. Wits: Robert Baldicke, Mathias Giles, Robert Neasom, Samuel Papp, Walter Armes, Wm. Cornelius. W.B. 8, p. 95.

Inventory presented in court by Margt. Newsom, relict. W.B. 8, p. 101.

NEASOM, Rachel, now wife of Spencer Brown. 16 Jan. 1777. Rec. 17 Apr. 1777.

Her guardian pays to Spencer Brown her husband the sum of 14 poinds, 13 shillings and 3 pence half penny. W.B. 20, p. 108.

NEWSOM, George, dec'd. 20 Nov. 1783. Rec. 15 Jan. 1784.

Land divided between his two sisters: Rachel wife of Spencer Brown and Easter Newsom. James Ball, James W. Ball, Ozwald Newby. W.B. 22, p. 8.

NELMS, William. Inv. & Ap. 10 Apr. 1741. Rec. 8 May 1741.

Returned by Jno. Steptoe, Jr., adm. W.B. 13, p. 223.

NEWBY, Henry. 14 Oct. 1741. Rec. 12 Mar. 1741.

Wife: Mary. Sons: Henry, Ozwald, Whaley, James, William (youngest, not 15). Daus: Sarah & Hannah. Exors: Wife and son Henry. Wits: John Alexander & Robt. Mitchell, Jr. W.B. 13, p. 265.

NEWBY, Mary. 10 Apr. 1761. Rec. 15 Jan. 1762.

Sons: James, Whaley, Willaim Newby. Daus: Hannah Bailey, Sarah Brumley. Son: Ozwald Newby. Exors: Sons James & Ozwald Newby. Wits: John Bailey, James Robinson. W.B. 16, p. 181.

Memo. Mary Newby reports a case & 9 bottles which she kept out of her husbands inventory for the reason that her husband's brother gave the use of it to him during life & after his death to go to his son Wm. 10 Apr. 1761.

NEWBY, Henry died without making a will. Rec. 21 May 1764. Mary Newby widow applies for certificate of administration. W.B. 17, p. 32.

NEWBY, Henry. Appraisement. 21 May 1764. Rec. 10 June 1764. By Wm. Sydnor, Sam'l Brumley, Thad. McCarty. W.B. 18, p. 13.

NEWBY, Robert. Nuncupative. 12 Feb. 1772. Rec. 16 Apr. 1772. Grandmother: Margaret Davis. Sisters: Sarahann Newby, Mary Newby & Easther Newby. Mother: Sarahann Newby. Father: Ozwald Newby. All his brothers and sisters. Wits: Ozwald Newby & Sarahann Newby. "This was put into writing the 15th Instant Feb. (being the second day after his death). W.B. 20, p. 40.

NEWBY, Ozwald. 1784. Rec. 17 Jan. 1791. Wife: Sarahann. Sons: Pritchett, Edward, Ozwald & William Newby. Daus: Mary Newby, Peggy Newby, Siller Newby (not 12 yrs. old), Esther Ficklen, Margarett Davis the grandmother of daughter Sarahann Newby. Exor: Ozwald Newby. Wits: James Newby & James Newby, Jr. Codicil 9 Apr. 1786. 16 July 1792. Division. By Larkin Pemberton and Edward Newby. Heirs: Widow, William Newby, Eza Newby, Peggy Newby, Easther Fechlen, Sarah A. Norris, Precilla Newby, Mary Pemberton, Pritchd. Newby, Edward Newby. W.B. 22, p. 284.

NEWBY, James. 26 Apr. 1791. Rec. 18 July 1791. Wife: Jane Newby. Sons: John, Cyrus, James & Dennis Newby. (If Dennis does not return home within 7 yrs. after my death.) (Cyrus forbidden to marry any dau. of Abner Palmer.) Daus: Ann & Junny Newby. Exors: Col. James Ball & Capt. John Chowning. Wits: James Ball, And. Robertson, William Bryan. W.B. 22, p. 308.

NEWBY, John. Appraisal. 16 Dec. 1793. Rec. 21 Apr. 1795. By George Campbell, Rawl. Davenport, Abner Palmer, Charles Dotson. W.B. 22, p. 448.

NICHOLAS, Jno. Rec. 14 Dec. 1726. Thomas Flint appointed guardian of John Nicholas, orphan of

Jno. Nicholas, dec. David Alex. Flint appointed guardian of Mary Nicholas, orphan of John Nicholas. W.B. 10, p. 508.

NICHOLS, John. 26 9ber, 1669. Rec. 6 Jan. 1669.

Sarah Lunsford, dau. of Ann Lunsford. Charles Carpenter, Jr., John Edwards', my son-in-law's two orphans and my son Nicholas his daughter, & my son John his dau. Exors: Stephen Chilton & John Berry. Wits: Thomas Shirley, John Flower. W.B. Loose Wills.

NICHOLS, John. 23 Oct. 1778. Rec. 18 Feb. 1779.

Brother: Thomas Bell. Godson: Benjamin Goerge, son of Benj. George and Catherine George his wife. Brother: Valentine Bell. Wife: Mary Nichols. After her death to be divided among my brothers Thomas Bell and Valentine Bell's children. Exors: Friends: Edwin Conway, Benj. George, Thomas Bell, Jr. Wits: Maryan Doggett, Milly S. Fendley. W.B. 20, pp. 156, 180.

Articles produced for appraisement by Mary Sullivant, late the widow of sd John Nichols, now wife of John Sullivant. 15 June 1780. W.B. 20, p. 180.

18 Feb. 1779. Mary Nichols, widow of John Nichols, dec., allotted her dower. 20 Jan. 1780. W.B. 20, p. 174.

NICKENS, Edward, of Parish of Christ Church. 21 Sept. 1735. Rec. 12 Nov. 1735.

Wife: Mary. Sons: Tun, John, Robert, Edward, Richard, James. Daus: Sarah and Aner. Exors: Wife & John Yerby. Wits: Rich. & Elizabeth Weaver, Simon Shewcraft. W.B. 12, p. 355.

NORRIS, John. Inv. 9 Mar. 1719. Rec. 11 May 1720.

Presented by Mary Norris, adm. W.B. 10, p. 305.

NORRIS, William, of White Chappel. 3 Dec. 1732. Rec.14 Mar. 1733.

Wife: Susanna. Sons: Joseph "my plantation where I now live"; William. Daus: Susanna "the plantation I formerly lived at being given or intended to have been given her by Richard Cotten, dec.," Elizabeth. Thos. Pitman of Northumberland Co. to have care of children until they come of age. Extrx: Wife. Wits: Thos. Thornton & Reuben Young. W.B. 12, p. 238.

NORRIS, Mary. Apprais. Rec. 8 Sept. 1738.

Returned by John Norris, adm. W.B. 13, p. 118.

NORRIS, John. 16 June 1773. Rec. 19 Feb. 1778.

Wife: Judith Norris. Sons: George and William Norris. Dau:

Judith Edwards. Gr.dau: Mary Pollard. Son-in-law' Thomas
Pollard, money paid for him and sent him by his wife Mary Ann
Pollard, to remain in his hands provided his brother James
Pollard never troubles my Executors nor any part of my estate
for the sum of 26 pounds 1 shilling and two pence which I was
security for the sd Thomas Pollard to his sd brother James Pol-
lard. To John Davis & Col. James Gordon. Gr.children: Robert
& Judith Pollard. Exors: Wife Judith Norris and 2 sons George
and Wm. Norris. Wits: John Miller, Jos. McAdam, Jr., Edwin
Conway. W.B. 20, p. 117.

NORRIS, Thomas & Peter, dec. Inv. Rec. 15 Oct. 1778.
Belonging to the estate is a horse, saddle & bridle, etc. which
remains in the estate of Joseph Norris, dec. N.B. "The Court
Siting for Lancaster May 21, 1778, *Permited* me to *admistor* on
the above Estate and appointed *apprasers* to appraise same but
whereas the aforesaid Joseph Norris did part with the sd Horse
being left in his care and there appearing nothing to be appraised
I thus make my report to the Court. Charles Norris. 15 Oct.
1778." W.B. 20, p. 150.

NORRIS, Joseph. 2 Sept. 1783. Rec. 19 Aug. 1784.
Wife: Sarah. Sons: Septamus, Thaddeus, "all my children."
Ex: James Newby, Sr., Septamus Norris, Thaddeus Norris. Wits:
George Scurlock, Daniel Scurlock, John Hazard. W.B. 22, p. 46.
Appraisal & Division of estate: To Sally, Eppa, Richard, Molly,
Thaddeus, William, Septamus, Sarah Norris & Sarah Norris,
widow. By James Newby, James Norris & Jesse Robinson, Jr.
W.B. 22, pp. 79-84.
21 Jan 1788. Second Division. To: Eppy Norris, Richard Norris,
William Norris, Septamus Norris, Sarah Norris, Mary Norris,
Thaddeus Norris. By James Newby, Ozwald Newby, James
Norris. W.B. 22, p. 166.

NORRIS, Sarah, wdw. Joseph Norris. 22 June 1784. Rec. 15 July
1784.
Renounces benefits of will of husband. Wits: Iac Ball, Jesse
Robinson, Jr., Lucy Rogers. W.B. 22, p. 37.

NORRISS, John. 20 Mar. 1782. Rec. 19 Oct. 1789.
Sons: James, William, Martin & John Norriss. Daus: Agnes
Robinson, Elizabeth Noriss & Judith Norriss. John Stonum's
children. Exors: Martin Norris & William Stonum. Wits: ohn
Norriss, Wm. Stonum, Wm. Stonum, Jr. W.B. 22, p. 225.

20 Sept. 1790. Rec. 17 Jan 1791. Division of estate. To John Norris & his heirs, Agnes Robinson, Elizabeth Norris, Judith Norris, John Stoneham's children. By Jas. Newby, Ozwald Newby & Richard Goodridge. W.B. 22, p. 283.

Norriss, William. 7 Nov. 1788. Rec. 21 Dec. 1789.

Wife: Judith Horton Norriss. Sons: George H. Norriss, Wm. Norriss, Richard Norriss. Dau: Charlotte Norriss. Mentions Elaner Horton, grandmother of George H Norriss. Ex: James Brent, Wm. Gibson, Wm. Kirk. Wits: James Gibson, James Pierce, Wm. Kirk. W.B. 22, p. 228.

Norris, William. Appraisal. Rec. 19 Apr. 1790.

By James Brent, Wm. Gibson, Newton Brent. W.B. 22, p. 259.

Norton, Wm. Inv. 1 Oct. 1675. Rec. 10 Nov. 1675. W.B. 5, p. 15.

Nutt, James. 16 Nov. 1693. Rec. 20 Jan. 1794.

Wife: Nancy. Sons: Joseph, James & Mosley Nutt. Daus: Ruthy, Winny & Sally Nutt. Exors: Wife & Thomas Plamer. Wits: Thomas Haydon, Henry Hudson, Joseph West. W.B. 22, p. 404.

Obert, Bartram. 30 Nov. 1659. Rec. 25 Jan. 1659. Prob. 1 Mar. 1659.

Eldest son: Bartram Obert land called Brad Neck adjoining Richard Lewis. Son: Chichester Obert. Dau: Lettice Obert land called Long Neck. Dau: Agatha Obert land called Cherrys Neck. Unborn child. Wife: Anne. Wits: Thomas Roots, Thomas Willis. W.B. 2, p. 72.

O'Harrow, Thomas. Appraisement. 16 Apr. 1764. Rec. 18 June, 1764.

By John Fleet, Nicholas Currell, Sam'l Hunton. Estate divided between widow and 10 children. W.B. 18, pp. 12, 13.

Oldham, William. Appraisement. 15 May 1777. Rec. 21 Aug. 1777.

By Nicholas George, John Bailey, Wm. Weblin, Thomas Howard, James Alderson. Mentions land in Richmond Co. W.B. 20, p. 114.

Oliver, William. Inv. Rec. 14 May 1742.

Returned by Martha Oliver, admx. W.B. 13, p. 270.

Olliver, William. 22 Oct. 1750. Rec. 8 Feb. 1750.

Wife: Ellison. Son: John. Other children. Exors: Wife, Ellison, Isaac White, Martin Shearman. Wits: Ann, Shearman, Hannah Tomblin. W.B. 12, p. 323.

OLIVER, Martha. Inv. 9 May 1750. Rec. 11 May, 1750. Returned by Geo. Currell, adm. W.B. 14, p. 283.

OLIVER, Wm. 18 Dec. 1767. Rec. 21 Jan. 1768.
Wife: Elizabeth. Sister: Elizabeth Brumly. Son: William Oliver (not 15). Brother: Lowery Oliver. Exors: Friend Wm. Davenport & Wm. Davenport, Jr. Wits: Wm. Davenport, Sr., Bailie George, Daniel Brumley. W.B. 18, p. 99.

OLIVER, William, appraisement. Rec. 16 June 1768.
By James Currell, Henry Lawson and Thos. Hunton. W.B. 18, p. 115.

OLIVER, Ellison. Appraisement. 17 Dec. 1772. Rec. 18 Mar. 1773.
By William Stott, William Brumley, Stephen Stott. W.B. 20, p. 55.

OLLARD, James. Appraisement. 20 May 1773. Rec. 15 July 1773.
By Wm. Gibson, Wm. Kelly, Maurice Brent. W.B. 20, p. 62.

OPIE, Lindsey. 14 June 1763. Rec. 15 July 1763.
Deed between Lindsey Opie of Northumberland Co. and Elizabeth his wife and Andrew Robertson of Lancaster Co., physician, for 105 lbs. current money land in Lancaster containing 103½ acres being part of a tract devised by last will and testament of George Heale, gent., of Lancaster Co. bearing date 13 Dec. 1697, to son Joseph, remainder to his son John, both of whom died without issue. The 1st sd tract descended to Elizabeth, Sarah, Anne & Catharine, daughters & coheirs of George, eldest son of sd Geo. Heale, in Fee simple but being equally divided the above mentioned part descended to Lindsey Opie heir at law of sd Sarah except ⅓ part which Mrs. Hannah Crump holds as her dower during her natural life. W.B. 17, p. 11.

OVERSTREET, Richard. 25 Oct. 1774. Rec. 20 Apr. 1775.
Sons: Henry, William and Richard Overstreet (not of age) Dau: Mary Dogget. Exors: Friends, Burges Ball, Matthew Myars and son Henry Overstreet. Wits: Henry Towles, Nicho. George, John Payne. W.B. 20, pp. 84, 106.
Division 19 Oct. 1776. To Henry and William Overstreet and Jeremiah Doggett. Rec. 17 Apr. 1777. W.B. 20, p. 106.

OWEN, Humphrey, & Oliver Segar. Inv. 11 Nov. 1663. Rec. 20 Nov. 1663.

Returned by Eleanor Owen. W.B. 2, p. 271.

Eleanor Owen deed of gift for love and affection to her children Oliver Segar, Randolph Segar & Ellinor Owen. 30 Oct. 1663. W.B. 2, p. 270.

PAINE, William (of parish of White Chapell). 24 Sept. 1696. Rec. 12 Nov. 1700.

Legatees: Wife (name not given); sons, William and Richard (two eldest) to whom their grandfather (Rich. Merriman) gave land; John and George, the youngest; daus., Susanna and Margaret; Wits: Rich. Flacknell, Ann Palmer, Alex. English. W.B. 8, p. 99.

PAINE, Will. Inv. Rec. 9th, 8br. 1700.

Presented to court by Susan Paine, widow and relict. W.B. 8, p. 95.

PAINE, Richard. 4 Apr. 1709. Rec. 9 Aug. 1709.

Brothers: Will, George and Jon. Paine. Mother: Susanna Ladner. Sisters: Susannah, Margaret and Katherine Paine. Exor: William, brother. Wits: Thomas Barker, and Thomas Cattlett. W.B. 10, p. 54.

PARFITT, Thomas, of Parish of St. Mary's White Chappell. 7 Jan. 1709. Rec. 8 Mar. 1709.

Wife's name not given. Daus: Frances Miller and Elizabeth Parfitt, "and I now possess." Grandau: Mary Dukeshall. EXtrx.: Daughter Elizabeth Parfitt. Wits: Thos. Taylor, Will Mitchell, Rich'd Dutten. W.B. 10, p. 8.

PARFIT, Thomas. Inv. Rec. 14 May 1710.

Presented by Mary Parfitt. W.B. 10, p. 19.

PARKER, Joseph. Inv. & Ap. Rec. 9 Jan. 1733.

Returned by Elizabeth Parker, admx. W.B. 12, p. 286.

PARTOR, Shadrack. 10 June 1742. Rec. 8 July 1743.

Difference between Shadrack Partor & Thos. Purcifull & Letitia his wife, late widow of Wm. Partor. Thos. Percifull & Letitia his wife to have ⅓ estate and Shadrack and his brother Meshack to have the other ⅔. W.B. 13, p. 338.

PARTER, Mesheck. Inv. Rec. 11 May, 1750.

Returned by Thos. Percifull, adm. W.B. 14, p. 285.

PARRISH, Ann. 20 Nov. 1755. Rec. 19 Dec. 1755.

Son: Josias Parrish. Gr.dau: Jean Williams. Daus: Judith Williams, Margaret Bailey, Averilla Parrish. To John Hanks. Exors: Son Josias Parrish and son-in-law, Joseph Bailey. Wits: Jno. Bailey, Wm. Reaves, Mary Cheatom. W.B. 15, p. 231.

PARROT, William. 28 July 1744. Rec. 12 Oct. 1744.

Wife: Betty. Dau: Sarah Parrot. Ex. Wife. Wits: John Bailey, Jesse Ball, Wm. Sydnor, Jesse Ball, Sr. W.B. 14, p. 30.

PASQUET, Charles. Inv. Rec. 10 June 1724.

Returned by Ann Pasquet, adm. W.B. 10, p. 452.

PASQUET, Jerome. 24 Oct. 1728. Rec. 12 Feb. 1728.

Name of wife not given. Legatee, son-in-law Jno. King. Extrx, Wife. Wits: Robt. Gibson, Benj. George. Edwin Conway. W.B. 12, p. 83.

12 Mar. 1728. Inv. returned by Elisia Pasquet, Extrx. W.B. 12, p. 47.

PASQUET, Walter. 6 Dec. 1726. Rec. 11 June 1729.

Wife: Ann. Sons: Jno. Other children not named. In event of wife's death or remarriage then Rich. and Jno. Boatman become Executors. Wits: Edwin Conway. W.B. 12, p. 97.

PASQUET, Elizabeth, of Parish of Wiccomoco. 6 June 1729. Rec. 11 Feb. 1729.

Sons: Wm. Pasquet (land I now live on), John, Henry, Walter (deceased), Damason. Daus: Mitchell Rosson, Eliz. George. Gr.dau: Mitchell Pasquet, dau of son Chas., dec. Gr.son: John Pasquet, eldest son of Walter, dec. Exor: Son Wm. Pasquet. Wits: Robt. & Elizabeth Edwards, Edwin Conway. W.B. 12, p. 139.

12 Aug. 1730. Inv. returned by Wm. Pasquet. W.B. 12, p. 176.

PASQUETT, William, of Parish of Wiccomoco. 16 Nov. 1775. Rec. 15 Feb. 1776.

Niece: Leannah Haydon, dau. of Thomas Haydon and Mishael his wife. Ex: Brother-in-law, Thomas Haydon. Wits: Jesse Dameron, John Haydon, Ezekiel Haydon. W.B. 20, p. 91.

PASQUET, John. 4 Jan. 1742. Rec. 10 Aug. 1750.

Sons: Edney and John Pasquet. Wife: Prudence. Ex: Brother William Pasquet & Wm. Hayden. Wits: Frances Timberlake, Benj. George, Jr. W.B. 14, p. 297.

PASQUET, William. 26 Aug. 1749. Rec. 21 Oct. 1763.

Nephew: William Pasquet, son "of my Brother" John Pasquet; John Pasquet, son "of my Brother" John Pasquet; Jerome Pasquet, son "of my brother" Henry Pasquet; Edney Pasquet, son "of my Brother" John Pasquet. Neices: Frances Pasquet, dau. "of my brother" John Pasquet; Tabitha Pasquet, dau. "of my brother" John Pasquet; Lucy Pasquet, dau. "of my brother" John Pasquet. William George, son of Abijah George. Sister-in-law: Elizabeth Pasquet. Frances, Tabitha, Lucy, Elizabeth, Mishall, Judy, Edney and John Pasquet, children "of my brother" John Pasquet. Ex.: George Ball, Wits: Prudence Pasquet, Tabitha X. Pasquet. W.B. 17, p. 23.

PASQUET, Wm. Additional Inv. Rec. Apr. 16, 1764.

Returned by Geo. Webb. administrator. W.B. 18, p. 10.

PASQUET, Jno. Inv. 16 Dec. 1767. Rec. 17 Dec. 1767.

By John Pasquet. W.B. 18, p. 94.

PASQUET, John. Division, Oct. 1782. Rec. 21 Nov. 1782.

To Margaret Pasquet, Wm. Chilton. By Eliza Edmonds, John Miller, Edwin Rent. W.B. 20, p. 243.

PASQUET, Margt. 24 Nov. 1784. Rec. 22 Apr. 1788.

Son-in law: William Chilton land which was given me by my father. Brother: John Hill. Sister: Judith George. Exors: Wm. Chilton & John Hill. Wits: James Gordon, Jeduthan James, James Hill. W.B. 22, p. 171.

Appraisal. W.B. 22, p. 185.

PATEY, Herbert. 15 Mar. 1686. Rec. 8 Jan. 1687.

Wife: Faith. Son: Thomas, should he die without issue then his part to go to Rich. Welch son of Walter Welch. Wits: Wm. Grymes, Ann Cambell, Ann Bush, Olive Grymes. W.B. 5, p. 113.

PAYNE, William, of Parish of St. Mary's White Chappell. 27 Aug. 1726. Rec. 14 Sept. 1726.

Wife: Judith. Sons: Merryman and William Payne. Daus: Susanna and Judith Payne. Dau.-in-law: Katherine, wife of Mark Bannerman. Brothers: John and George Payne. Brother: Robert Mitchell. Friend: Charles Burgess. Mother: Susanna Laidner. Exors: Wife and brother, Robert Mitchell; son-in-law Mark Bannerman and Charles Burgess. Wits: Jo. Chichester and John Flint. W.B. 10, p 505.

PAYNE, William. Inv. 14 Sept. 1726. Rec. 14 June 1727.

Returned by Judith Payne, Robert Mitchell & Charles Burges, three of the Exors. W.B. 12, p. 1.

PAYNE, Judith. 29 Mar. 1747. Rec. 9 Sept. 1748.

Sons: Merryman & William Payne. Dau.: Judith Ball. Gr.dau.: Judith Ball. Dau.-in-law: Catherine Payne. Extr.: Son Merryman Payne. Wits: John Taylor, Jesse Ball. W.B. 14, p. 212

PAYNE, Wm. Division of Estate. 11 Mar. 1747. Rec. 12 May 1749.

To Merryman Payne. Geo. Ball in right of his wife Judith; Wm. Payne   W.B. 14, p. 241.

PAYNE, George. 19 Sept. 1760. Rec. 15 May 1761.

Sons: William, George, John, Richard Payne. Daus: Katharine "her part of her uncle Robt. Edmond's estate; Anne, Margaret Payne, Susanna Brent, Frances Stevens. Wife: name not given. Exors: Wife, Richard Mitchell, Hugh Brent, Merryman Payne, Richard Stevens and two sons William & George Payne. Wits: Wm. Blackerby, Wm. X. Goodridge, John Towles, Mary Smith. W.B. 16, p. 138.

Invty. and Appm't. returned by Frances Payne. W.B. 16, p. 141.

PAYNE, Frances   Rec. 21 May 1767. Re

Frances Payne appointed guardian to George Payne, orphan of Wm. Payne. W.B. 17, p. 266.

PAYNE, Richard, of Christ Church Parish. Rec. 15 Sept. 1768.

Wife: Ellin Payne. Father to let wife reside with him. "I give unto my wife my mare during her widowhood and then to dispose of her to either of my brothers as she think fit." Proved by oath of Merryman Payne, James Newby, Richard Stephens and John Bailey. W B. 18, p. 127.

PAYNE, Richard. Appraisement. 4 Oct. 1768. Rec. 17 Nov. 1768.

Ellen Payne, administrator. By John Taylor, Richard Stephens, James Ewell. W.B. 18, p. 130.

PAYNE, Merryman   3 July 1773. Rec. 15 July 1773.

Sons: Merryman, John, Nicholas & Daniel Payne. Gr.son: Merryman Payne. Gr. dau: Catharine Payne. Elizabeth Payne, dau. of "my cousin," John Payne. Exors: Friends: Matthew Myars & Henry Towles and two sons Merryman and John Payne. Wits: Abraham White, Charles Rogers, Stockley Towles. W.B. 20, p. 60.

PAYNE, George. Division 16 Feb. 1775. Rec. 17 Apr. 1777.

To Geo. Payne's son, Richd. Housin Payne. James Brent, son & Heir of Susanna Payne, John Payne, William Payne's son, George Payne, Catharine Payne, Richard Payne, Frances Stephens, Moses Lunsford, Benjamin Waddy. Whereas each child's part amounts to the sum of 54 pounds, 15 shillings and six pence half penny, Current, we do direct that Richard Housin Payne, son of Geo. Payne, pay to Richard Payne the sum of 4/5½ and that James Brent, son of Susanna Payne, pay to Moses Lunsford 5.4.5 ½ and that Mr. Benj. Waddy pay to Catharine Payne the sum of 14.15.6 ½, and to Richard Payne 5.8.11 and that George Payne, son of Wm Payne pay to Frances Stephens the sum of 5.4.5 ½ and that Frances Stephens pay to Richard Payne the sum of 8.11 and that Moses Lunsford pay to Richard Payne the sum of 13.5 ½, etc. W.B. 20, p. 107.

Inv. of est. 15 June 1780. By Benj. George, Edny Tapscott & John Sullivant. (p. 181).

PAYNE, Daniel. Dated Norfolk, 20 July 1774. Rec. 16 Sept. 1779.

To brother, Nicholas Payne. Wits: William Lee Catt., Richd. Clegg. W.B. 20, p. 171.

PAYNE, Merryman, Jr. 25 Sept. 1779. Rec. 20 Apr. 1780.

Wife not named, after her decease, to John Hughlet. Brothers: Nicholas and Daniel Payne. Nephew: Merryman Payne. Wm. Glascock. Catherine Payne, dau. of "my bro., John Payne. Exors: Friends, Mathew Myers, John Hughlett and brother, Nicholas Payne. Wits: Henry Towles, John Chowning, Thos. Carter. W.B. 20, p. 177.

PAYNE, Merryman. Settlement. Rec. 17 June 1785.

Nicholas Payne, Exec. By Matt. Myers, Wm. Chowning, Jno. Chowning. W.B. 22, p. 84.

PAYNE, William. Division. Feb. 1784. Rec. 16 Mar. 1786.

Heirs: Merryman Payne. Samuel Moore ⅓ of the estate. By James Ewell, William Chowning, Joseph Stephens. W.B. 22, p. 118.

PAYNE, John. 27 June 1783. Rec. 15 Dec. 1788.

Wife: Not named. Son: Edward "my land." Daus: Catherine, Judith & Beharthalland Payne. Exors: John Chowning, Henry Towles, & brother Nicholas Payne. No witnesses. W.B. 22, p. 193.

PEARSON, John. 13 Mar. 1782. Rec. 18 Apr. 1782.

Wife: Sarah. Sons: Lewis, John Baly, Francis, Samuel and Hartswel Pearson. Daus: Sarah Pearson and Mary Bancas Pearson. Child not christened. Exors: Friend Isaac Degge and wife. Wits: Isaac Degge. W.B. 20, p. 231.

PEARSON, John. Appraisal & Division. Nov. 1785. Rec. 15 Dec. 1785.

Heirs: Lewis Pearson, John Bailey Pearson, Frances Pearson, Sarah Pearson, Samuel Pearson, Mary Lancaster Pearson, Hartswell Pearson. By John Berryman, Henry Lawson, Thomas Carter. W.B. 22, p. 110.

PEELE, John. 25 Jan. 1675. Rec. 29 Nov. 1677.

Legatees: Thos. Bonnison, Godson: Thomas Sibley; Margaret Coane, Margaret Garton, Roger Kelley, John Coane, Sr., Brother-in-law: Thophilus Ashley; Godson; John Coane, Jr. Ex.: John Coane, Sr. Wits: Wm. Batry, Wm. Garton. W.B. 5, p. 44.

PERCIFULL, Eppa A. Appraisal. Mar. 1789. Rec. 20 Apr. 1789.

By Elijah Percifull, William Brent, Thomas Garner. W.B. 22, p. 207.

PERKINS, Thomas. 26 May 1750. Rec. 13 July 1750.

Son: Thomas. Wife: name not given. Ex: Wm. Dymer & Geo. Currell. Wits: Richard Blade, Daniel Carter. W.B. 14, p. 292. Apr. 14, 1750. Returned by Elinor Perkins, Admx. W.B. 14, p. 308.

PETERSON, Edward. Ap. Rec. 14 June 1727.

Wm. Dare, adm. John Bond. W.B. 12, p. 8.

PHILIPS, John. 30 Oct. 1655. Rec. 7 Jan. 1655.

Wife: Sarah is given all. Exor: Moore Fantleroy. Wits: Vincent Stanford, James Yates. W.B. 2, p. 18.

PHILIPS, James. 30 Jan. 1689. Rec. 14 Apr. 1690.

Wife: Mary. Sons: James, my plantation in the freshes of Rapp. R., George, plantation in the freshes of Rapp. R., Samuel. Wits: Jno. Philips, Jas. Stott, Abraham Goard. The minister Andrew Jackson to take into his care his son Geo. Philips. Mr. Francis Daughty, minister, to take care of James Philips. Exors: Sons James & George Philips. W.B. 8, p. 2.

PHILLIPS, Anne. 6 June 1768. Rec. 18 Aug. 1768.

Gr.son: William Brumley, Sarah Brumley, wife of William Brumley (Wm. Brumley to pay Ellen Carpenter 150 lbs of tobacco) Grdau: Ann Phillips. Gr.son: William Phillips, Dau: Elizabeth Brumbley. Ex.: Gr.son: Wm. Brumbley. Wits: James Newby, Rawh. Stott. W.B. 18, p. 123.

PHILLIPS, Joshua. Division. 26 Mar. 1774. Rec. 21 Apr. 1774.

Heirs: Joseph Norris, for his wife's part. Ann Phillips (guardian Joseph Norris) William Phillips (guardian John Stonum). By Richard Mitchell, Thadeus McCarty, Robert Chinn. W.B. 20, p. 70.

PHIPPS, Mary, of Psh of Christ Church. 12, June 1709. Rec. 10 Aug. 1710.

Legatees: Thos. Cox's wife and son who with Will Hatherway were her Godsons. Son: John Wallace. John Bradley. Eliz. Hall. "To my beloved Friend Amy Palmer." Ellinor Hall, Richard Garret & Mary his wife; Priscilla Palmer. Ex.: Friend Richard Chichester. Wits: Jon. Cooke, Will Martin, Nicholas Martin. W.B. 10, p. 49.

PHROND, Philip. 27 Aug. 1745. Rec. 11 Oct. 1745.

Dau: Betty Phrond. Son: Benj. Frond. Wits: John Pollard, Jr., Mary Callahan. W.B. 14, p. 129.

11 Apr. 1746. Inv. of Benjamin Phrond returned by Betty Phrond. adm. W.B. 14, p. 104.

PIERCE, Thomas. Inv. Rec. 12 Feb. 1723.

Returned by Thos. Pullen, adm. W.B. 10, p. 449.

PILCHER, William. Inv. Rec. 12 July 1710. W.B. 10, p. 32.

PINCKARD, John. 24 Mar. 1689. Rec. 10 Dec. 1690.

Wife not named. Sons: John, Thomas to whom is given the land I now live on, James. Exors: The three sons. Daus. names not given. Wits: Wm. Jones, Thos. Tillet, Jno. Shelton. W.B. 8, p. 7.

PINCKARD, Capt. John. Inv. 8 Jan. 1690. Rec. 10 June 1691. W.B. 8, p. 14.

PINCKARD, Elizabeth. Inv. 14 June 1699. Rec. 2 July 1699.

Returned by Thomas Pinckard. W.B. 8, p. 175.

PINCKARD, John, of Parish of Christ Church. 10 Dec. 1733. Rec. 13 Nov. 1734.

Wife: Mary. Sons: James, William, John and Thomas. Daus: Judith (others referred to but not named). Extrx: Wife. Wits: Edward Bailey, Richard Boatman and Sarah Biddlecome. W.B. 12, p. 325.

PINCKARD, John. Inv. & Ap. 10 Mar. 1737. Rec. 14 Apr. 1738. Returned by Eliza Pinckard, admx. W.B. 13, p. 86.

PINCKARD, Thos. 29 Aug. 1740. Rec. 10 Oct. 1740.

Wife: Elizabeth. Sons: Thos., all land I now live on; John. Daus: Eliza Brent and Margaret Ball. Exors: Sons and cousin Wm. Stepto. Wits: Thos. Stepto and Thos. Bridgford. "That my daughter Margaret Ball may be maintained out of my estate as long as she behaves herself well and lives from her husband John Ball." W.B. 13, p. 183.

PINCKARD, John. Rec. 13 May 1743.

Wife: Sarah Ann. Kinsman: Charles Lee. Sisters: Elizabeth Brent and Margaret Ball. Godson: Thomas Pinckard and Archibald Campbell. Cousin: Elizabeth Lee. Bro: Thomas Pinckard. Exor: Brother, Thomas Pinckard, and friend, Collin Campbell. Wits: W. Jones, Charles Lee, Thomas Steptoe. W.B. 13, p. 322.

PINCKARD, Mary. 20 Sept. 1748. Rec. 14 Apr. 1749.

Sons: Wm. Pinckard, James Pinckard. Dau.: Judith Norris. Gr.dau.: Mary Ann Norris, dau of Judith Norris. Gr.son: James Pinckard, son of Wm. Pinckard. Exors: Sons, Wm. & James. Wits: John Carter, Dale Carter. W.B. 14, p. 236.

PINCKARD, James. 16 Apr. 1751. Rec. 10 May, 1751.

Sons: Robert, John, Charles, James, Richard (not 15). Exors: Friends: Thos. Yerby, Geo. Payne, Jno. Meredith, Jno. Norris, Dale Carter & "my brother" Wm. Pinckard. Wits: Eliza Pinckard, Eliza Mason, Judith Chilton, John Edwards, Joseph Hubbard. W.B. 15, p. 32.

PINCKARD, James division of estate. Rec. 6 Dec. 1762.

To Robert Pinckard, John Pinckard under guardianship of Robert Pinckard, James Pinckard under guardianship of John Norris, Charles Pinckard under guardianship of Robert Pinckard. W.B. 16, p. 245.

PINCKARD, William, division of estate. Rec. 15 Dec. 1762.

Spencer Pinckard, Thomas Pinckard, Jeduthan Pinckard. The above being children that are under guardians. W.B. 16, p. 247.

16 Apr. 1762. Inventory returned by Mary Pinckard, widow. W.B. 16, p. 204.

PINCKARD, William. Division of estate. Rec. 17 Dec. 1762.

To Spencer Pinckard, Thomas Pinckard, Jeduthan Pinckard. W.B. 17, p. 247.

PINCKARD, Thomas. 8 June 1768. Rec. 17 Nov. 1768.

Son: Thomas Pinckard. Wife: Elizabeth Pinckard. Daus: Judith Pinckard, Ann Pinckard. Gr.son: son of my daughter Judith. Exors: Wife and son Thomas. Wits: James Pinckard. W.B. 18, p. 129.

PINCKARD, Spencer. Estate. Inv. 20 Apr. 1769. Rec. 17 Aug. 1769.

By James Pinckard, Jr., Peter Miller, John Norris. W.B. 18, p. 152.

PINCKARD, Amos. 15 June 1769. Rec. 20 July 1769.

Administration granted Eliza Pinckard. W.B. 18, p. 144.

PINCKARD, Thomas. 23 Feb. 1779. Rec. 19 Sept. 1782.

Wife: Frances. Grson: Thomas Pinckard (not 21). Armistead Currie, Frances Hill Currie, David Currie, Ellyson Currie, being the children of my good friend, Rev. Mr. David Currie and Elizabeth his present Consort, when they arrive at age of 21 or marry. George Lee, son of my friend Mr. Kendal Lee of Northumberland Co. Kendall Lee, son of my friend Capt. Chas. Lee of Northumberland Co. Dear Friend, Rev. Samuel Smith McCroskey, and after his decease to the eldest son of sd S. S. McCroskey or eldest dau. Miss Jane Swan. Exors: Wife Frances and friend Charles Carter, Esq. of Corotoman and Rev. David Currie, Rev. Samuel Smith McCroskey, John Hill Carter, son of sd Charles Carter, William Lee, son of Mr. Kendall Lee and Ellyson Armistead, Esq. and Gr.son, Thos. Pinckard. Wits: Sam'l S. McCroskey, Jane Swan, Christ. Miller, Ellyson Armistead. W.B. 20, p. 267.

PINCKARD, Thomas. Appraisal. 14 Dec. 1784. Rec. 16 Dec. 1784.

Left negroes to his grandson Thomas Pinckard. By John Berryman, Henry Lawson, James Brent. W.B. 22, pp. 53-55.

PINCKARD, Mary. 12 Oct. 1782. Rec. 17 Feb. 1785.

Sons: Jeduthen, James, William, Thomas & John Pinckard. Dau: Amy Pitman. Gr.dau: Fanny Pinckard Lowry, dau. of Amy

Pitman. Exors: Sons John & Jeduthen. Wits: Thad. McCarty & James Pinckard. W.B. 22, p. 57.

17 Mar. 1785. Division. Heirs: Jeduthan Pinckard, Amy Pitman, Thos. Pinckard, John Pinckard. By James Pinckard, Thad. McCarty, John Yerby. W.B. 22, p. 69.

PINCKARD, Jeduthan. Division. 18 Feb. 1788. Rec. 21 Apr. 1788. Widow given her dower. By James Pinckard, John Yerby, Thomas Hubbard. W.B. 22, p. 181.

Appraisal. Mar. 1785. Rec. 17 June 1785. By Elias Edmonds, John Yerby, George Norris. W.B. 22, p. 78.

PINCKARD, James. 9 Nov. 1789. Rec. 21 June 1790.

Brothers: Robert, John & Charles Pinckard. To Cyrus Pinckard, son of Robert and Charlotte Pinckard, dau of Robt. To Charles Hubbard, friend Elias Edmonds, John Yerby, Capt. John Degge. Codicil Mar. 5, 1790. To Elizabeth Yerby, dau. of brother Robert Pinckard and wife of George Yerby. Exors: Elias Edmonds, Sr., John Yerby & John Degge. Wits: Robert Fergusson & William Edwards. W.B. 22, p. 270.

Settlement. W.B. 22, p. 276.

13 July 1793. Elias Edmonds & John Yerby (dec) exors. W.B. 22, p. 389.

PITMAN, John. 6 May 1702. Rec. 14 Sept. 1702.

Wife: Elizabeth, Extrx. Sons: Thos, the eldest, William and John. Dau: Ann. Wits: Raw. Chinn, Wm. Goodridge, M. Walters. W.B. 8, p. 113.

PITMAN, Elizabeth, of St. Mary's white Chappell. Rec. 14 June 1710.

Sons: Youngest John, Will, and Thomas Pitman. Goddau: Elizabeth Sandon, Miles Walters. Overseers: Raw. Chinn, Miles Walters. Exors: Sons, Thomas and William Pitman. Wits: Raw. Chinn, Bryan Pullen and Anne Brosier. W.B. 10, p. 17.

PITMAN, William. Inv. Rec. 13 May 1719.

Returned by Mary Pitman. W.B. 10, p. 287.

PITMAN, Benjamin. 28 Oct. 1761. Rec. 20 Aug. 1762.

Sons: Robert & Jeduthan Pitman to be "under the care of my brother William Pitman." Wife: Elizabeth Pitman. Exors: Brother William Pitman and friend Henry Edwards. Wits: Geo. Wale, Isaac Pitman, William Pitman. W.B. 16, p. 226.

PITTMAN, William, dec., Ex. of Benj. Pitman, dec. Rec. 10 Nov. 1785. Wife: Elizabeth Pittman. Thos. Potts Ex. of Robert Potts, dec'd, who was security for William Pittman, dec. Ex. of Benjamin Pittman, dec. and Robert & Jeduthan Pittman. Edwin Conway, James Tapscott. W.B. 22, p. 109.

PITMAN, Robert. Appraisal. 17 Dec. 1787. Rec.

By John Beane, Stephen Locke, Joseph Samson. W.B. 22, p. 160.

PITMAN, Thomas. Appraisal. 21 Dec. 1789. Rec. 19 July 1790.

By Isaac Basye, Richard Cundiff, Fortunatus Pitman. W.B. 22, p. 280.

PITTMAN, Benjamin. Appraisal. 16 Jan. 1792. Rec. 15 Oct. 1792.

By Richard Selden, Richard Cundiff, Thos. Taylor, Jeduthin More. W.B. 22, p. 355.

POLLARD, Robert. 23 Apr. 1709. Rec. 8 June 1709.

Wife's name not given. Sons: Robert, John, Richard, Thomas and James. Dau: Mary Newby. Wits: Robt. Miller, Jno. Grice, Abigail Robertson. W.B. 10, p. 87.

POLLARD, John, division estate. 8 Feb. 1750.

Widow not named. Aaron Carter, James Newby, Richard Pollard, James Pollard, Thomas Pollard (in hands of administrator), William Pollard (in hands of administrator), Margaret Pollard (in hands of administrator). Administrators: Jas. Ball, Jr., M. Shearman, Jno. Bailey. W.B. 15, pp. 1-2.

8 Feb. 1750. Inv. returned by Margaret Pollard, admx. W.B. 15, p. 8.

POLLARD, Thomas. 29 Mar. 1751. Rec. 18 Oct. 1751.

Sons: Thomas Pollard (not 21), James Pollard, George Pollard. Wife: name not given. Wits: Richard Pollard, Martha Carter, Antho. Kirk. W.B. 15, p. 72.

Inv. & Ap. returned by Mary Pollard, admx. W.B. 15, p. 76.

POLLARD, Thomas. Acct. of estate. Rec. 15 Sept. 1758.

James and Mary Pollard, orphans' account returned by John Carter, their guardian. W.B. 16, p. 41.

21 Sept. 1759. James & Mary Pollard, orphans of Thomas Pollard, account returned by John Carter. W.B. 16, p. 70.

POLLARD, George. 15 Mar. 1759. Rec. 20 June 1760.

Uncle: James Kirk. Brothers: Thomas Pollard and James Pollard. Sister: Mary Pollard. Exors: Uncles James Kirk & Anthony Kirk. Wits: Mary Carter, George Miller. W.B. 16, p. 96.

POLLARD, William. 1 May 1762. Rec. 18 June 1762.
Wife: Elizabeth Pollard. Nephew Williamson Newby, son of James Newby. Mother: Margaret Pollard. Brother: Thomas Pollard. Exors: James Ball, Geo. Heale, Gent. Wits: George Mitchell, James Ball. W.B. 16, p. 213.

POLLARD, Thomas. Rec. 14 Sept. 1763.
John Carter, guardian of Mary Pollard, orphan of Thomas Pollard. W.B. 17, p. 21.

POLLARD, Mary, orphan of Thomas Pollard, dec. Rec. 17 Sept. 1764.
To John Carter, her guardian. W.B. 18, p. 21.

POLLARD, Margaret, widow. 20 Nov. 1767. Rec. 21 Jan. 1768.
Son Thomas right in negroes purchased of my Son William's estate. Children: Martha Carter, John Pollard, Richard Pollard, James Pollard, Jean Newby, Thomas Pollard, Margaret Bryan. Ex: Son Thomas. Wits: James Ball. W.B. 18, p. 99.

POLLARD, Betty, deed of gift. 18 Jan 1770. Rec. 18 Jan. 1770.
For love and affection to children: Braxton Pollard, Caty Pollard and John Pollard, certain negroes. Wits: James Newby, John Newby. W.B. 18, p. 160.

POLLARD, Thomas, of upper part of Christ Church Parish. W.B. 20, pp. 3, 4, 210.
Dated, 29 Dec. 1769. Rec. 20 Sept. 1770. Dear Friend: Betty Pollard the use of my estate during her widowhood, etc. Braxton, Katy and John, Children of sd. Betty Pollard. Exors: Friends James Ball and James Newby. Wits: Jas. Ball, James Newby. 17 Aug. 1775. John Bailey, guardian of Braxton, Catherine and Thomas Pollard, orphans of Thomas Pollard, dec. Rec. 20 June 1776. The sd. guardian never having received any personal estate from James Newby acting Ex. sd Thos. Pollard. Estate now in the hands of Edwin Conway, Gent., adm. of James Kirk, dec. 20 Sept. 1781. W.B. 20, p. 210.
20 June 1776. John Bailey, guardian to Braxton, Catherine & Thomas Pollard, orphans of Thomas Pollard, dec. James Newby, acting Exor. W.B. 20, p. 97.

POOLE, John. 25 Jan. 1675. Rec. 14 Nov. 1677.
Heirs: Thomas Bonison. Godsons: Thomas Sibley, John Cone,

Jr. Margaret Cone, Margaret Garton, Roger Kelly, John Cone. Brother-in-law: Theophilus Ashley. Wm. Garton. Overseer of Will: Friend John Cone, Sr. Wits: Wm. Bally, Wm. Garton. (Bundle of Loose papers 1653-79.)

PORTER, Francis. Inv. 4 July 1680. Rec. 16 July 1680.

Presented in Court by Thom. Wells and Margaret, his wife, relict of sd. Francis Porter. W.B. 5, p. 66.

PORTER, Mesheck. Inv. Rec. 11 May 1750.

Returned by Thomas Percifull, adm. W.B. 14, p. 285.

POWELL, Thomas. 19 Jan. 1669. Rec. 9 Mar. 1669.

Sons: Rawleigh (not 18) and Thomas Powell. Cozen: John Gibson and Son Thomas Powell overseers of will. Wits: Adam Gittens, Rich. Simes. W.B. bundle of loose papers 1653-79.

POWELL, Rawley, planter. 6 Feb. 1686. Rec. 11 Mar. 1686.

Father-in-law: John Kerby, Ex. Sister: Ann Dacres. Brother: Thomas Kerby. Nathaniel Horton. God-dau: An Mason. Wits: Nathaniel Brown, Jno. Derrin, Stephen Tomlyn, Jno Hawkins. W.B. 5, p. 109.

PRETTYMAN, Thomas. Rec. 27 July 1659.

John Bonner, age 30 Years, swears that about the last of April Mr. Thos. Prettyman two or three days before his death gave to Mr. Matthew Kempe all his worldly goods. Bridget Bonner, age 20 Years, makes same deposition. Wits: Henry Fleet, Rowland Lawson. W.B. 2, p. 64.

PRICE, William. Inv. 9 May 1688. Rec. 12 May 1688.

Presented by Ann Worser, relict. W.B. 5, p. 121.

PRICE, Elinor. 9 June 1702. Rec. 9 Sept. 1702.

Devisees: Granddau: Elinor Sharpe, Mary Barlow, Elizabeth Hopkins, Phillis Flint. Sons: Rich. and David Flint. Wits: Jno. Barlow, Martha Loe, Phebe Barlow, Garson Thomas Sharpe. W.B. 8, p. 111.

PRITCHARD, Frances, wife of Robert P. 2 Oct. 1679. Rec. 12 Nov. 1680.

Grandchildren: Franciose Frizell, Margaret Frizell, Mary Frizell. Guardian for grandchildren: Mary Stone, wife of Col. John Stone. Son-in-law: George Finch and Ann his wife Rebecca Finch, their daughter; grandchild: Elizabeth Finch. Oswell

Whalley. Daughter: Ann Finch. Exors: Thomas Marshall & Mr. Thomas Barker. Wits: John Stone, John Simpson, John Tavener. John Morgan, Josn Wesford. Overseers to carry out will: Husband, Robert Pritchard and Edwin Conway. W.B. 5, p. 67.

PRITCHARD, Robert. 28 July 1696. Rec. 27 Aug. 1697.

Wife: Ann to whom is given the plantation he now lives on. Children: Elizabeth, Hannah, Martha, Ann, Mary. Son: Robert. Extrx: Wife. Wits: Hen. Jenkins, Ann Sparks, & Jno. Mecks. W.B. 8, p. 69.

PRITCHARD, Griffin. Inv. Rec. 10 Oct. 1718.

Returned by Allison Pritchard, adm. W.B. 10, p. 274.

PRITCHARD, Robert. Inv. & Ap. 11 Feb. 1736. Rec. 8 Apr. 1737.

Returned by Margaret Pritchard, adm. W.B. 13, p. 31.

PULLEN, Henry. Inv. 31 May 1698. Rec. 30 July 1698.

Presented by Mary Pullen relict. W.B. 8, p. 79.

PULLEN, Henry. Inv. 31 May 1698. Rec. 30 July 1698.

Presented by Mary Pullen relict. W.B. 8, p. 79.

PULLEN, Brian. 4 Jan. 1753. Rec. 16 Jan. 1756.

Son: Henry Pullen. Dau: Ann Stoneham. Gr.son: Brian Stoneham. Dau: Sina Pullen, Maryann Pullen. Wife: Mary. 7 children: Jesse, John, Jidudiah, Jonathan, Jeremiah, Sinah and Chloe Pullen. Exors: Wife, Mary and son Jidudiah. Wits: John Rogers, Mary Rogers, Jos. Chinn. W.B. 15, p. 236.

PULLEN, Mary. 29 Mar. 1761. Rec. 17 July 1761.

Sons: Jonathan Pullen, John, Jesse, Jedidiah, Jeremiah Pullen. Gr.son: Everitt Pullen, son of Jesse. Daus: Sinah Stott, Chloe Pullen. Ex: Son, Jonathan. Wits: Richard Mitchell, Jno. Carpenter, James X. Stott. W.B. 16, p. 162.

PULLEN, William. 6 Aug. 1767. Rec. 17 Sept. 1767.

Sons: Thomas and Moses Pullen. Daus: Betty Hammond, Ann Swain, Sarah Porter, Mary Lowry. Exors: Son Moses & Harry Carter. Wits: Thomas Everitt, Nancy Everitt. W.B. 18, p. 90.

PULLENS, Wm. Rec. 19 Nov. 1767. Est. appraised. W.B. 18, p. 94.

PULLEN, Jonathan. Appraisal. 17 Jan. 1791. Rec. 25 Feb. 1791.

By John Yerby, Elias Edmonds, Charles Hubbard. W.B. 22, p. 289.

PULMAN, Henry. 1 Mar. 1669. Prob. 14 Sept. 1670. Rec. 1 Oct. 1670.

Wife: Elizabeth plantation until son John Pulman comes of age. Daus: Millicent, Mary & Elizabeth. Wits: Thomas Naylor, George Cooper. W.B. Loose papers 1653-79.

PURCELL, Tobias. 18 May 1710. Rec. 9 Aug. 1710.

Wife: Mary. Sons: Thomas all my land in Lan. Co., Tobias, and John all my land in North'd Co. Daus: Judith, Mary. Speaks of debts to Collo. Churchill. Exors: Wife and Robt. Carter. Wits: John Hart, Luke McDaniel and Sharshall Grasty. W.B. 10, p. 40.

PURCELL, Tobias. Inv. 22 May 1711. Rec. 13 June 1711.

Presented by Mary Purcell, widow and relict. W.B. 10, p. 103.

PURCELL, Thos., of Parish of Christ Church. 11 Feb. 1732. Rec. 9 May 1733.

Wife: Elizabeth. Sons: Thos, Jno. Chas. and George Purcell. Dau: Sebra Purcell. Exors: Wife and Geo. Brent. Wits: Jno. Fendley, Alex. Poor. W.B. 12, p. 266.

PURCELL, George. Inv. 25, Feb. 1761. Rec. 17 Apr. 1761.

Returned by Geo. Flower. W.B. 16, p. 128.

PURCELL, Thomas. Appraisement. Rec. 16 Mar. 1764.

By James Kirk, John Yerby, George Yerby, Jr. W.B. 18, p. 6.

PURCEL, Leannah, dower in land her son, Wm. Thatcher, sold to Mungo Harvey. Dec. 1700. Rec. 20 Dec. 1770. W.B. 20, p. 8.

PYNES, John. 25 Apr. 1736. Rec. 12 May 1736.

Christopher Stevens sole heir. Wits: Lawrence Blade, John Stevens, Thos. Kelley. W.B. 13, p. 3.

QUIRK, James. Inv. Rec. 9 Apr. 1718.

Returned by Thos. Carter. W.B. 10, p. 260.

RADFORD, Roger. Rec. 29 Sept. 1658.

Hannah Hood, age 21 years, swears that Roger Radford on his death bed did give to Mary Cole, the daughter of the widow Cole, his land. Will Price makes same affidavit. W.B. 2, p. 56.

RAINS, John. Oct. 1783. Rec. 18 Mar. 1784.

Inventory. James Brent, William Norris, George Carter. Apps. W.B. 22, p. 23.

RAINS, John. Settlement of estate. Rec. 17 June 1785.
He was drowned in Indian Creek. Henry Lawson coroner. W.B.
22, p. 78.

RAMSEY, Thomas & Martha. Inv. Rec. 11 May 1698.
Returned by Thos. Buckley. W.B. 8, p. 78.

RAMSEY, Henry. Inv. 12 Aprl 1721. Rec. 18 May 1721.
Presented by Nicholas George, adm. W.B. 10, p. 314.

RAMSEY, John. Rec. 22 Aug. 1752.
Wife: name not given. Sons: Robert, John, Elexander, James
and William. Exors: Wife, son Robert and friend Dale Carter.
Wit: John Meredith. W.B. 15, p. 112.
Inventory returned by Jane Ramsey, Extrx. 16 Mar. 1753.
W.B. 15, p. 123.

RAMSEY, Jane, widow. Aug. 25, 1762. Rec. 17 June 1765.
Five sons: Robert, Alexander, John, James & William "and if
my son John shall not return back to these parts to receive his
share" then his part to be divided among the other four. Wits:
John Mitchel, Henry Hinton, Dale Carter. W.B. 16, p. 38.

RAMSEY, Jane, dec. Inv. Rec. 17 June 1765.
Presented by Robert Ramsey & Alex. Ramsey. W.B. 17, p. 126.

RAMSEY, Alexander. 5 Aug. 1767. Rec. 18 Feb. 1768.
Brothers: Robert, all my land, John Ramsey & James Ramsey.
Friend: Dale Carter. Exors: Dale Carter & Samuel Yap. Wits:
William Brent, Edward Carter. W.B. 18, p. 100.

RANGER, Charles. 14 Nov. 1677. Rec. 15 Nov. 1677.
Inv. returned by Elizabeth Parker, relict. W.B. 2, p. 43.

REASON, Michael. Apprais. 14 May 1735. Rec. 13 Aug. 1735.
Returned by Samuel Brumley, adm. W.B. 12, p. 248.

REDE, Alexander. 22 Feb. 1669. Rec. 9 May 1669.
Dau: Ann Rede land adjoining Chas. Hill (not 16 yrs of age).
Wife: Liddie & her son Thos. Yant. Servants: John Shaw &
John Hester. Youngest dau: Elizabeth 1 shilling to be paid her
by her mother or by John Ball. Wits: Henry Parker, Thos
Young. Bundle of loose papers 1653-79.

READE, Alex. Inv. Rec. 14 Oct. 1685.
Presented by Ralph Briggs. W.B. 5, p. 102.

READ, Nicholas. 12 Dec. 1716. Rec. 8 May 1717.

Wife Anne. Sons: John & James. Exors: Jno. Hendly and Geo. Chilton. Wits: Jno. Gibson, Jno. Bond, Daniel Carter. W.B. 10, p. 213.

READ, Jno. Account of estate. Rec. 7 May 1741.

John Cox & Mary his wife against Geo. Flowers, Ex. of John Reade, dec. Said Mary her dower of ½ part of sd estate. W.B. 13, p. 224.

REASON, Michael. Inv. Rec. 13 Aug. 1735.

Returned by Samuel Brumley. W.B. 12, p. 348.

REID, Nicholas. Appraisement. 22 Feb. 1769. Rec. 16 Mar. 1769.

By Thomas Lawson, Thomas Hunton, George Yerby. W.B. 18, p. 136.

DYMER, Capt. Wm., guardian to Margaret Reid, orphan of Nicholas Reid, dec. Rec. 15 May 1770. W.B. 18, p. 168.

REID, Nicholas. Division. 17 Jan. 1772. Rec. 20 Feb. 1772.

John Hathaway, guardian of James Reid, orphan of Nicholas Reid, 1/5 part. Eppa Timberlake, administrator. By Anthony Sydnor, Benj. George. W.B. 20, pp. 34, 66.

Josiah Gaskins in right of his wife, one of the orphans of dec. 21 Oct. 1773. W.B. 20, p. 66.

19 Feb. 1778. Nicholas Read. Division of estate. Epaphroditus Timberlake, adm. Heirs: Daniel George who intermarried with Elizabeth Read ⅓ part. Nicholas George, attorney for sd Daniel. Given under our hands in Fauquier Co. 19 Nov. 1777. Chas. Ball, W. Edmonds, Martin Pickett. W.B. 20, p. 126.

REEVES, John. 10 Apr. 1731. Rec. 12 May 1731.

Wife: Phebee. Sons: William, Eaton, James. Daus: Elizabeth Flint, Wife of Richard Flint. Servant: James Munro. Exor: Son, James Reeves. Wits: Joseph Carter, James Monroe, Esther Johnson. W.B. 12, p. 199.

REEVES, Phebe. 29 June 1732. Rec. 9 May 1733.

Granddaus: Phebe Harris, Mary Reeves dau. of Jas. Reeves. Grsons: Jno. Harris. Exor: Son-in-law, Jas. Reeves. Wits: Jos. Carter, Jas Monro. W.B. 12, p. 266.

REAVES, Mary. Inv. & Ap. Rec. 14 June 1751.

Returned by John Harris, adm. W.B. 15, p. 40.

REAVES, John. July 1790. Rec. 17 June 1793.

Benjamin Garton possessed with estate in the hands of James Reaves, adm. By Martin Shearman, Lawson Hathaway, Robert Currell. W.B. 22, p. 381.

21 June 1790. Appraisal. By Martin Shearman, Isaac Degge, Spencer Currell. W.B. 22, p. 267.

REDFORD, John. 13 June 1740. Rec. 12 Aug. 1740.

Legatees: James Clark, schoolmaster at Mrs. Whitings in Gloucester, Mrs. Elizabeth Chichester. Ex: Merryman Payne. Wits: Gawin Lowry, Ellen Downman. W.B. 14, p. 209.

REDWAY, John. Inv. 6 May 1675. Rec. 12 May 1675. W.B. 4, p. 219.

REVEER, Peter. Inv. & Ap. 9 Sept. 1737. Rec. 14 Oct. 1737.

Returned by George Brent, adm. W.B. 13, p. 69.

RICE, Augustine. 5 May 1776. Rec. 18 July 1776.

Wife not named. Son: John P. Rice. Exors: Friends Nicholas George & Matthew Myars. Wits: Matt. Myars, Charles Edwards, Wm. Chilton, John Harris. W.B. 20, p. 98.

RICH, Daniel. Appraisal. 20 Nov. 1792. Rec. 21 Jan. 1793.

By Jno. Miller, William Edwards, James Carter, Jno. Doggett. W.B. 22, p. 363.

RICHARDSON, Nathaniel. Inv. 12 July 1677. Rec. 17 July 1677. W.B. 2, p. 42.

RICHESON, Wm. Inv. 31 July 1703.

Appraised by Thos. Catlett, Thos. Barker, Jr., Sam Parr, John Taitman. W.B. 10, p. 265.

RIE, Henrie. 20 Feb. 1650. Rec. 30 Mar. 1659.

Son: William Rogers to be given Thos. Phillips. Wits: Tho. Bunbury, Lucy Forde. Loose wills.

RIGBY, Peter. Inv. 11 July 1660. Rec. 1 Aug. 1660. W. B. 2, p. 129.

RIGHT, James. 20 Dec. 1753. Rec. 18 Nov. 1757.

Richard Hinton, William Hinton. Wife: Sarah. Four children: James, Spencer, Betty, & Kendal Right. Samuel Hinton "the rest of estate that Mrs. Rebekah Banton gave me."Ex. Friend, Samuel Hinton. Wits: John Crowther, Mary Foster. W.B. 15, p. 311.

RIVEER, Elizabeth. Inv. & Ap. 13 Feb. 1776. Rec. 16 May 1776.

By Henry Lawson, Thomas Carter, Thomas Shearman. W.B. 20, p. 96.

RIVEER, Richard. Inv. 23 Nov. 1778. Rec. 17 Dec. 1778.
By Jesse Robinson, Jr., Richard Goodridge, Peter Riveer. W.B. 20, p. 152.

RIVEER, Bushrod. Inv. & Appraisement. 17 May 1781. Rec. 16 May 1782.
By Johnson Riveer, Richard Goodridge, Jesse Robinson, Jr. W.B. 20, p. 237.

RIVEER, John, Sr. of Christ Church Parish. 24 Jan. 1775. Rec. 18 June 1787.
Wife: Joannah. Sons: Peter, Wyatt, Richard, Bushrod & John Riveer. Daus: Amy, Agge Riveer, Hannah Webb, Sarah Brown. Gr.dau: Milly Brown. Exors: Wife, brother Johnson Riveer and son Richard Riveer. Wits: Dale Carter, John Carter & Thomas Davis. W.B. 22, p. 151.
18 Jan 1790. Appraisal & Division. Heirs: John Riveer (son), Meredith Nelms, John Webb, Rawleigh Brown, John Wilks & Wiatt Riveer, orphans of Bushrod Riveer, dec. their part left in the hands of Peter Riveer. W.B. 22, p. 243.

RIVEER, Bushrod. Settlement of acct. 31 July 1794. Rec. 15 Sept. 1794.
John Wilka Riveer & Wiat Riveer, orphans. Peter Riveer, adm. By Richard Goodridge, James Tapscott, Henry Hinton. W.B. 22, p. 440.

ROACH, John. Inv. Rec. 11 Feb. 1718. W.B. 10, p. 281.

ROACH, Will. Inv. 13 Apr. 1744. Rec. 8 June 1744.
Returned by Judith Roach, admx. W.B. 14, p. 23.
11 May 1744. Rec. 8 June 1744. William Roach, son of Wm. Roach. John Roach his guardian possessed with his estate. W.B. 14, p. 23.

ROACH, Solomon. Inv. 5 Jan. 1744. Rec. 5 Mar. 1744.
Returned by Judith Roach. W.B. 14, p. 52.

ROACH, Wm., estate, division. 8 Mar. 1750. Rec. 12 Mar. 1751.
Solomon Roach & Geo. Roach, dec., orphans of William Roach, dec., and Judith Mason, admx. and Wm. Roach orphan of sd William. Thomas Mason, Jr., husband of Judith pays to Jno. Roach, guardian of sd orphan, William. W.B. 15, p. 23.

ROB, James. Ap. Rec. 13 Nov. 1747.
Returned by Frances Rob, admx. W.B. 14, p. 110.

ROBB, Agatha. Appraisement. 21 Sept. 1775. Rec. 21 Dec. 1775. By Dale Carter, James Kirk, Jr., Elias Edmonds. W.B. 20, pp. 90, 95.

Division: Mrs. Robb, Elias Edmonds, Job Carter, Thomas Robb. 21 Mar. 1776. W.B. 20, p. 95.

ROB, Marget. 10 June 1777. Rec. 21 Aug. 1777.

Niece: Margaret Carter dau. of "my sister" Sarah Carter. Sister Sarah Carter. Ex.: Brothr-in-law, Job Carter. Wits: Edwin Conway, John Miller. W.B. 20, p. 115.

ROBB, Thomas. Appraisement. 17 Jan. 1782. Rec. 17 Jan. 1782. By James Pinckard, John Yerby, Wm. Edwards, John Seldon. W.B. 20, p. 219.

ROBB, Thomas. Appraisal & Division. 20 Jan 1795. Rec. 16 Feb. 1795.

Heirs: Frances Robb, James Robb, Thomas, Elizabeth & John M. Robb (minors) By Wm. Kirk, John Miller, James Carter. W.B. 22, p. 448.

ROBERSON, Alexander, of Christ Church Parish. 10 Sept. 1710. Rec. 13 Sept. 1710.

Wife's name not given. Daus: Ellinor, Nelly and Mary. Sons: Charles, John, Wm. Right and Charles Chrisley. Exors: Chris Kirk, John Hutchins and William Right. Wits: Peter Kilgore and Thomas Alex (Ellis). W.B. 10, p. 62.

ROBBERSON, Giles. 12 Mar. 1755. Rec. 19 Sept. 1755.

Mother: Agness Robberson. Sisters: Agness Robberson, land given me by my father, dec., Maryann Robberson. Exors: Mother and Sisters. Wits: George Payne, Frances Payne, Elizabeth Flint. W.B. 15, p. 221.

ROBINSON, Giles, Dec. Rec. 18 Oct. 1765.

Estate appraised by Wm. Robinson, Richard Ball, Johnson Riveer and Thos. Flint. W.B. 17, p. 181.

ROBINSON, Giles, of Christ Church Parish. 20 Apr. 1761. Rec. 19 May 1766.

Sons: Aaron, Eleazer, Winfield, Elijah & Elisha. Dau: Mary Pullen. Wife: Mary Robertson. Ex: Wife, Mary. Wits: Richard Mitchell, Johnson Riveer, Jas. Cammell, Jr. W.B. 18, p. 55.

190   ABSTRACTS LANCASTER COUNTY, VIRGINIA, WILLS—1653-1800

ROBERTSON, Giles, of St. Mary's Christ Church Parish. 26 Dec. 1784.
Rec. 20 Jan. 1785.

Brother: Moses Robertson. Ex: Moses Robertson. Wits: Ozwald
Newby, Robert Clark. W.B. 22, p. 56.

ROBERTS, Eleanor. Verbal will. Rec. 13 May 1730.

Proved by oath of Charles Russell and Mary Pinckard. Estate
Left to Wm. Cone and his mother for taking care of her during
her sickness. W.B. 12, p. 169.

10 June 1730. Appraisement by Wm. Cone, adm. W.B. 12,
p. 177.

ROBERTS, John. Appraisal. 18 June 1792. Rec. 15 July 1793.

By William Kirk, Wm. Eustace, Wm. Meredith. W.B. 22, p. 387.

ROBERTSON, Ann, widow. 15 June 1795. Rec. 15 June 1795.

Renounces benefits of will of Dr. Andrew Robertson her late
husband, dated 22 Feb. 1795. W.B. 22, p. 458.

ROBINSON, Wm. 8 Jan. 1724. Rec. 10 Jan. 1724.

Wife's name given. Sons: Giles, William my now plantation;
Moses R. Dau: Martha. Exors: Giles and Wm. Robinson. Wits:
Chas. Burges, Robt. Mitchell, Thos. Chattin. W.B. 10, p. 454.

ROBINSON, Isaac, of Psh, White Chappell. 20 Sept. 1713.

Sons: Isaac and George. Daus: Anne and Elizabeth. Brother:
Giles R. who is also Exor. Wits: Geo. Finch, Penelope Lucham,
Theophilus Morgan. W.B. 10, p. 186.

ROBINSON, Giles, of St. Mary's White Chappell. 17 Oct. 1734. Rec.
8 Oct. 1735.

Wife: Agnes. Sons: Jesse, Giles and James. Daus: Margaret,
Agnes, Gemimia and Mary Ann. Exors: Wife and son Jesse.
Wits: Robt. and Sarah Mitchell, Mary Darby. W.B. 12, p. 351.

ROBINSON, Archibald. Verbal will. 3 Aug. 1729. Rec. 10 Sept. 1729.

Name of wife not given. Son: Joseph. Dau: Sarah. Wits: Wm.
Roach, Robt. Alexander, Wm. Badger. W.B. 12, p. 122.

ROBINSON, John. Inv. 29 July 1735. Rec. 13 Aug. 1735.

Returned by Edwin Conway, Gent., his adm. W.B. 12, p. 347.

ROBINSON, Jane. Inv. & Ap. 13 Dec. 1736. Rec. 13 May 1737.

Returned by Thomas Hubbard, adm. W.B. 13, p. 41.

ROBINSON, James, of Christ Church Parish. 12 Jan. 1761. Rec. 20 Aug. 1764.

Sons: James and Jesse Robinson. Dau: Winny wife of Eleazer Robinson. Wife: Elizabeth Robinson. Daus: Ann, Sarah and Betty Robinson. Exors: Wife Elizabeth and son Jesse and Mr. Jos. Chinn. Wits: Lazarus Webb, Judith Stoneham, M. Shearman. W.B. 18, p. 19.

ROBINSON, James. Rec. 20 Aug. 1764.

Presented by Elizabeth Robinson and Jesse Robinson, executors, and proved by oath of Martin Shearman one of the witnesses. W.B. 17, p. 62.

ROBINSON, William, of St. Mary's & Christ Church Parish. 27 Aug. 1767. Rec. 15 Oct. 1767.

To: Rebecca Riveer, Swan Lunsford, Wm. Robinson, Aaron Robinson's two sons, Wm. & Moses R. Exors: Aaron Robinson & Swan Lunsford. Wits: Henry X. Davis. W.B. 18, p. 93.

ROBINSON, William, division of estate. 15 Oct. 1767. Rec. 19 May 1768.

To William Robinson, Rebecka Riveer, Moses Robinson. Exec.: Richard Ball, Johnson Riveer, Thomas Flint, Joseph Wilkinson. W.B. 18, p. 111.

ROBINSON, Aaron, of St. Mary's Parish. 3 Jan. 1768. Rec. 19 May 1768.

Sons: Giles, Aaron Robinson. Wife: Rebecka Robinson. Ex.: Wife. Wits.: Richard Ball, Joseph Wilkinson, John Hazard, Jr. W.B. 18, p. 113.

ROBINSON, James. Division. 19 Oct. 1770. Rec. 15 Nov. 1770.

To Jesse Robinson, Anne, Betty and Sarah Robinson. Betty Robinson's part delivered to James Robinson her guardian, and Sarah Robinson's part left in the hands of Jesse Robinson, Ex. of estate as sd Sarah is under age. By Richard Mitchell, Joseph Norris, John Norris, Jas. Newby. W.B. 20, p. 5.

ROBINSON, Eleazor, of Christ Church Parish. 1 May 1782. Rec. 20 Feb. 1783.

Wife: Winny Robinson. Son: Epaphroditus Robinson. Exors: Wife and son Epaphroditus. Wits: Jesse Robinson, Jr., Ann Robinson. W.B. 20, p. 250.

ROBINSON, Jesse. 22 June 1787. Rec. 16 Feb. 1789.

Wife: Juanna. Son: Jesse Robinson. Daus: Juanna Kem & Fanny Robinson. Son-in-law: Robert Clark. Exors: Wife & Edward Newby. Wits: Ozwald Newby, Edward Newby, & Epaphroditus Robinson. W.B. 22, p. 205.

ROBINSON, Jesse. Appraisal. Rec. 20 July 1789.

By Ozwald Newby, Johnson Riveer, Epaphroditus Robinson. W.B. 22, p. 220.

ROCK, Constantine. Appraisal. 16 Mar. 1786. Rec. 20 Apr. 1786.

By Wm. Sydnor, James Newby, John Christopher. W.B. 22, p. 120.

ROCK, Francis. Appraisal. Rec. 17 Feb. 1794.

By Rawleigh Davenport, Abner Palmer, James Clemmons, Peter Mason. W.B. 22, p. 409.

ROGERS, Noah. Inv. Rec. 10 July 1717. W.B. 10, p. 236.

ROGERS, Thomas. Inv. 11 June 1718. Rec. 10 Oct. 1718.

Returned by Geo. Light, adm. W.B. 10, p. 268.

ROGERS, Wm., of St. Mary's White Chappell Parish. 29 Apr. 1728. Rec. 14 June 1728.

Wife: Elizabeth. Sons: Jno., Wm., Rich'd. Daus: Elizabeth and Anne. Exors: Wife and brother, Geo. Rogers. Wits: Jno. Rogers, Bryan Pullen and Chas. Sanford. W.B. 12, p. 54.

Inv. returned by Eliza Rogers & George Rogers, Exors. 10 July 1725. W.B. 12, p. 65.

ROGERS, Eliz. widow of Wm. R. of White Chappell. 17 Sept. 1728. Rec. 13 Nov. 1728.

Sons: Wm. Dodson. Dau: Ann Rogers. Others, Thos, Robt, and Reuben Young, Chas. Dodson. Exor: son Thos. Young. Wits: Abraham Dale, Jos. Rogers and Jno. Roach. W.B. 12, p. 76.

ROGERS, Mary, of St. Mary's White Chappell. 10 Apr. 1727. Rec. 8 Sept. 1731.

Sons: Thos, Jno., Wm. and Brian Pullen. Dau: Frances Blackobe. Gr.dau: Mary Eatchinson. Exor: Son Brian Pullen. Wits: Jno. Stott, Jr. and Brian Stott. W.B. 12, p. 206.

ROGERS, William. Estate. Rec. 11 Aug. 1738.

George Rogers, guardian of Richard Rogers, orphan of Wm. Rogers, Dec. W.B. 13, p. 111.

George Rogers, guardian of Richard, orphan of Wm. Rogers, dec. 10 Oct. 1740. W.B. 13, p. 187.

ROGERS, John. 13 Feb. 1750/1. Rec. 19 June 1752.

Son: John land purchased of John Aldridge in Northumberland. Wife: Jane. Daus: Eunice Bailey, Ellen Rogers & Hannah Rogers. Son: Charles. Exors: John Bailey & son Charles Rogers. Wit: James Ball, Jr. W.B. 15, p. 96.

ROGERS, Jane. 31 June 1760. Rec. 10 June 1760.

Son: Charles Rogers. Daus: Eunice Bailey, Ellen Carter, Hannah Chowning. Ex.: Son Charles. Wits: James Ball. W.B. 16, p. 92.

ROGERS, John. 11 Mar. 1760. Rec. 18 Apr. 1760.

Mother: Jane Rogers. Brother: Charles Rogers. Sisters: Names not given. Ellen Bailey. Cousin: John Bailey. Ex. Brother, Charles Rogers. Wits: William Stamps, Sam'l Murphy. W.B. 16, p. 84.

ROGERS, John. 13 Jan. 1765. Rec. 18 Mar. 1765.

"The following was Exprest in presence of the subscribers by Mr. John Rogers on Sunday the 13th day of Jan. 1765, being the day before his death and sat down in writing on Wednesday the 16th of the month, Vizt: 'I desire that all my estate be kept together till my son Richard comes to the age of 14 years and then to be equally divided among all my children. Only I desire that my Daughter Margaret should have fifty pounds less that the rest of my children she having already received that sum and at my wife's death I desire that my land may be equally divided between my two eldest sons and their heirs." Richd. Mitchel., Richd. Rogers, Jonathan Pullen, Thomas Dunaway. W.B. 18, p. 31

Division of estate: To William Rogers, To William Mitchell for Elizabeth Rogers part. To William Rogers for Richard Rogers part; William Mitchells part in right of his wife. 27 June 1766. W.B. 18, p. 64.

ROGERS, John. Rec. 18 Mar. 1765.

Presented by Richard Mitchell and Jonathan Pullen. Mary Rogers, widow renounces all benefits from will. W.B. 17, p. 114.

ROGERS, Wm., of Christ Church Parish. 10 Jan. 1768. Rec. 21 Jan. 1768.

Bros: Richard Rogers, John Rogers. Sisters: Betty Rogers and Margaret Mitchel. Exors: Mr. Richard Mitchell & Mr. John

Chinn. Wits: Richard X. Rogers, Thomas Brannum, Lowary Oliver. W.B. 18, p. 99.

ROGERS, Richard. Division. 12 Apr. 1771. Rec. 16 May 1771.

Joseph Norris, administrator. James Blackerley who intermarried with Ann one of the daus. of sd Richard. Susanna Stonum, another of sd. daus, and to Hannah Rogers, Katy and Lucy Rogers and Susanna Norris. By Richard Mitchell, Thadd. McCarty, Thos. Stott. W.B. 20, p. 13.

ROGERS, William. Rec. 21 Jan. 1773.

Mungo Harvey, administrator of estate. W.B. 20, p. 53.

ROGERS, John. 29 Nov. 1787. Rec. 15 Sept. 1788.

Wife: Ann. Son: John, also other children. Exors: William Carpenter, John Carpenter & Edward Blackmore. Wits: Lucy Rogers, Ann Stonum, John Bailey, William Wilson. W.B. 22, p. 186.

15 June 1789. Appraisal. By Philip Warwick, John Dunaway, Henry Pullen. W.B. 22, p. 212.

ROGERS, Charles. 4 Apr. 1793. Rec. 17 Sept. 1793.

Wife: Ann, money from the estate of her father Henry Tapscott, Gent. Sons: Chas., John (land in Albemarle Co.), William Henry (not 21). Dau: Jane Rogers (not 18), estate I got by her mother or since the death of her mother. The four children of Ann Rogers, Peggy, Hannah, Nancy & William Henry Rogers. Exors: Wife, Charles Rogers, James Tapscott, Joseph Carter. Wits: James Gordon & William Biscoe. W.B. 22, p. 393.

ROOTS, Thos. 25 Jan. 1660. Rec. 1 Apr. 1660.

Legatees: Thos. Marshal, Thos. Roten, god-son; Sam'l Cusher, Sister Roten, Eliz. Robinson's two children, Elizabeth & Robt. Dudley. Sister, Anne White. God-son: Thos. Edwards, son to Jno. Edwards, Chirurgeon. Wits: Jno. Flower, Nich. George. Exor: Jno. Edwards, Chirurgeon. W.B. 2, p. 387.

ROSSE, Robert. 10 Mar. 1666. Rec. 10 May 1667.

Legatees: Henry Kinsman, Mathew Mashoyd. Son: James Rosse not of age. Wits: James Phillips, Henry Kinsman, Edward Royly. Loose wills.

ROSSON, William. 5 Apr. 1762. Rec. 15 July 1763.

Son: William Rossen. Wife: Mary. Mentions children by his

first wife: William, Joseph, Mary Ann, Nancy and Amy Rosson, children by last wife. Exors: Wife Mary and friend Anthony Kirk and son William. Wits: Dale Carter, Antho. Kirk, John Norris. W.B. 17, p. 14.

ROWDEN, Isaac. Nuncupative. 2 Sept. 1715. Rec. 9 Aug. 1727. Wife: Sarah. Friend: Thomas Pinson. Ex: Elias Edmonds. Wits: John Kirk, Lawle Welch, John Lahower. W.B. 12, p. 32.

ROWLEY, Rowland. 24 May 1679. Rec. 25 Sept. 1679. Prob. 10 Sept. 1679.
Wife: Susanna all my Plantation. Son: William (not 21). Daus: Elizabeth & Ann Rowley. Extrx. wife and after her death dau. Ann. Overseers: Friends Capt. David Fox, Capt. Wm. Ball, Mr. Edward Parton & Wm. Arkes. Wits: John Herbert, Thos. Sarroll. W.B. 5, p. 59.

RUDDERFORD, Ralph. 7 Mar. 1732. Rec. 8 Sept. 1738.
Wife: Sabrah. Sons: Wm. Exors: Wife and Jas. Straton. Wits: Thos. Williams, Thos. Murphey and Eliz. Sampson. W.B. 13, p. 112.
Ap. returned by Sabrah Camell, his Extrx, 13 Oct. 1738. W.B. 13, p. 122.

RYE, Henry. 20 Feb. 1658. Rec. 1 Apr. 1659.
Son: Will Rogers, to be raised by Tho. Philips, Peter Kinght. Wits: Tho. Bumbury, Ed: Lunsford. W.B. 2, p. 59.

SALLARD, Simon. 9 July 1679. Rec. 10 July 1679.
Inv. returned by Eliz. Berkit, relict. W.B. 2, p. 56.

SALLARD, Simon. 2 Nov. 1747. Rec. 11 Mar. 1747.
Wife: Blanch, plantation in Richmond Co. Sons: Simon, John, Wm. & Charles. Daus: Eliza Sallard, Mary Sallard, & Ann Sallard. Exors: Wife and 2 sons Charles & Simon. Wits: John Lethed, Mary Letthead. W.B. 14, p. 181.

SAMPSON, Thomas. 12 Jna. 1708. Rec. 8 June 1709.
Presented by Grace Sampson, widow and relict. W.B. 10, p. 4.

SANDERS, Duke, of White Chappell. 1 Jan 1713.
Wife: Margaret & child unborn. Son: John. Daus: Elizabeth, Anne. Extrx: Wife. Overseer of will, Thos. Pitman. Wits; Darby Calahan, John Macgae, Jos. Ball. W.B. 10, p. 181.

SANDERS, Capt. Edwd. Rec. 13 July 1739.

Capt. Edwd. Sanders by his last will divided his land equally between his 4 daughters: Sarah Porter, Eliza Reeves, Joshen Frame & Hannah Owen. John Frame & Hannah Owen give bond to Wm. Eustace of Northumberland Co. W.B. 13, p. 138.

SANDERS, John. Inv. & Ap. 13 Mar. 1740. Rec. 8 May 1741.

Returned by Mary Sanders, admx. W.B. 13, p. 219.

SANDERS, William. 26 June 1779. Rec. 20 Apr. 1730.

Wife: Betty Sanders. Sons: William & James Sanders (not 21); Thomas and Jesse Sanders. "Children of my dau: Winny Ellett, dec." Dau: Franky's part be divided among her children she had by Mr. Abraham White, dec. Children of son Edward Sanders, dec. Following children: Mary, Presly, Joseph, Ephraim, William, And James Sanders. Exors: Wife, Betty and Col. Edwin Conway and son Thomas Sanders. Wits: Joseph Taylor, John Bean, Thos. Garner. W.B. 20, p. 176.

SANDERS, William. Appraisal. Rec. 18 Jan 1790.

Negro woman and child part of estate of Thomas Hubbard, dec., found on the plantation of Wm. Sanders, dec., and left by sd Hubbard to be equally divided between all the living children of Betty Sanders, dec. W.B. 22, p. 247.

SANDS, Anthony. 10 July 1685. Rec. 10 Sept. 1685.

Inv. returned by John Baley. W.B. 2, p. 100.

SAUNDERS, Philip. 29 Mar. 1697. Rec. 2 July 1697.

Wife: Ann. Sons: Thomas, the eldest, John, Duke, to whom is given the land he now lives on; Robert, the youngest. Dau: Margaret. Exor: John Ingoe. Wits; Jno. Ingoe, Jas. Mortimore. W.B. 8, p. 68.

SAX, Thomas. 18 Apr. 1654. Rec. 10 June 1654.

Legatees: Dorothy Downman, widow, Richard Dudley, 2nd son of Edwd. Dudley; Mary Thomson, dau. of Robt. Tomson, Mary Tomson, wife of Robt. Tomson; Virginia, wife of Mr. Lumpkin. Rich. Hugh, Servant to Wm. Neasham. Wits: Howell Powell, Edwd. Dudley. Exors: Wm. Neasham & John Pine. W.B. 2, p. 11.

SCHOFIELD, Robert. 7 July 1696. Rec. 16 Sept. 1698.

Wife: Elinor. Son: Robert. Daus: Elizabeth, Sarah, Elinor.

Exors: Wife and Robert. Wits: Jos. Tayloe, Barbary Tayloe, Geo. Flowers. W.B. 8, p. 92.

SCHOFIELD, Robert. Ap. Rec. 14 Aug. 1747.
Returned by Wm. Schofield, adm. W.B. 14, p. 148.

SCHOFIELD, Thomas. Appraisement. Sept. 17, 1778. Rec. 19 Nov. 1778.
By Ephraim Edmunds; Jonathan Pullen; Jas. Fendla. W.B. 20, p. 150.

SCHOFIELD, William. Appraisal. Dec. 1784. Rec. 17 Feb. 1785.
By William Gibson, Eliza Edmonds, John Yerby, William Dogget. W.B. 22, p. 66.

SCHOFIELD, Thomas. Division of estate. Feb. 1789. Rec. 15 June 1789.
Heirs: Henry Schofield, John Schofield, John Yerby for Betsy Schofield, Joseph Dobbs for his wife's part. By John Miller, James Carter, John Doggett. W.B. 22, p. 215.

SCOT, Wm. Nuncupative. 24 Sept. 1681. Rec. 1 Oct. 1691.
Henry Segar aged about 29 yrs being at the house of Mr. Robert Pritchard when Wm. Scot was dying he said he gave what he had to said Pritchard. Wm. Chappell aged 22 yrs makes same affidavit. W.B. 2, p. 78.

SEBASTIAN, Joseph. Appraisement. 17 Jan. 1771. Rec. 21 Mar. 1771.
By James Yerby; Wm. Yerby and Jas. Kirk, Jr. W.B. 20, p. 10.

SEAGER, Oliver. 21 Jan. 1658. Rec. 30 Mar. 1659.
Eldest son: Oliver Seager. Wife: Eleanor Seager. Children: Oliver, Elizabeth, & Randall Seager. Exors: Friend Richard Lee & Nicholas Cock. Wits: Ann Tharkwell, Jane Carter, Nich. Cock. W.B. 2, p. 60.
20 Nov. 1663. W.B. 2, p. 271.

SELDEN, John, of Elizabeth City Co., Gent. Rec. 21 Aug. 1752.
Apprenticed son John Selden "age 13 years the 4th day of October last" to Thos. Edwards, Jr., Clerk of Lancaster Co. Court, to learn the science or trade which he now useth. Wits: Richard Selden, Wm. Mountague. W.B. 15, p. 107.

SELDEN, Elizabeth, of Christ Church Parish. 28 Jan. 1766. Rec. 19 May 1766.
Brothers: William and John Selden. Godson: son of my brother

Joseph Selden, Uncle Robert Brass and his daus, and Agatha Probey. Brother Richard Selden. Ex: Brother William Selden. Wits: Richard Selden, James Selden, William Hunt. Brother: Wm. lot of land in Hampton Town. W.B. 18, p. 56.

SELDEN, Elizabeth. Rec. 19 May 1766.

Will proved by oath of Richard Selden, Gent. And James Selden. W.B. 17, p. 180.

SELDEN, Richard. 27 Jan. 1769. Rec. 17 Jan. 1771.

Wife: Mary Selden. Son: James. "If he should die before his present wife, then executors to sell so much of estate of sd son James as will comply with a contract of marriage between Col. James Ball and myself in behalf of our children." Sons: John & Richard, 1000 acres of land in Fauquier Co. left him by his grandfather, Maj. James Ball. Exors: Wife and 3 sons, James, John & Richard. Wits: Thos. Brent, Mils Ball, John Taylor. W.B. 20, p. 8.

SELDEN, Maj. James, order 19 Dec. 1776. Rec. 19 Aug. 1784.

Inventory, /1482. William Montague, William Boatman, Peter Conway. Apprs. W.B. 22, pp. 42-3-4-5-6.

SELDEN, John. Appraisal. 25 Sept. 1784. Rec. 18 June 1787.

James Ewell & Richard Selden, adm. By Wm. Warren, Jas. W. Ball, John Wormely. W.B. 22, p. 149.

SELDEN, Mildred (of Richmond Co.) 29 Mar. 1793. Rec. 16 Sept. 1793.

Sisters: Sinah Beale, Judith Fauntleroy, Ann Ball, Sarah Fauntleroy, Frances Lee. Nieces: Ann Ball, dau. of brother Col. Jesse Ball & Louisa Fauntleroy. Brother: Col. James Ball. Nephews: William Ball, son of Col. Jesse Ball, James Ball McCarty, Wm. Henry Fauntleroy. Ex: James Ball. Wits: Fanny Ball, Fanny McCarty, Mary W. Ball. W.B. 22, p. 394.

SEPHTON, John. Inv. 8 Apr. 1702.

Returned by Wm. Fox and recorded. W.B. 10, p. 220.

SHAMLOTT, Randall. 15 Jan. 1655. Rec. 30 Mar. 1659.

Legatees: Child of Mary Bennett, Daniell Johnson. Godson: Randall Seager. George Marsh. Ann Thatchwell Extrx., plantation of 100 acres. Wits: Geo. Marsh, John West, Wm. Richards. Probated by Ann Thatchwell & George Marsh. W.B. Loose wills.

SHARPE, John, of White Chappell parish. 5 Apr. 1709. Rec. 12 July 1710.
Wife: Mary. Brother: Thos. Sharpe "my Plantation whereon I now live." Extrx.: Wife. Wits: Wm. Barker, Richd. Watts, Scarbrough Marshall. (Robert Mitchell who married Mary the Extrx of sd John Sharpe.) W.B. 10, p. 35.
Deposition of Wm. Paine, age about 24 yrs. That Wm. Barker & the above sd Wm. Paine being together at the house of ye above sd Barker discoursed concerning the will he had written for John Sharpe and what Capt. Wm. Fox intended to do in behalf of Thos. Sharpe, brother of Jon. Sharpe, dec. Said that if he could see Capt. Wm. Fox he would persuad him to let it alone and not to go to law for he said he really thought it was ye man's will that his wife should have both the negroes and all that he had except that plantation where Robert Hopkins lived, etc. W.B. 10, p. 35.

SHARP, Thos. 26 May 1726. Rec. 13 July 1726.
Wife: Elizabeth. Son: Thos. S. Daus: Mary, Elinor, Elizabeth. Exors: Wife and Chas. Burgess. Wits: Jno. Vangover, Martin Shearman, Jr., and Geo. Finch. W.B. 10, p. 490.

SHARP, Thomas. 3 Mar. 1750/1. Rec. 16 Aug. 1751.
Wife: Sarah. Son: Elias Edmonds Sharp. "land whereon my mother, Elizabeth Horne, now dwelleth." Children: Elizabeth, Tomzo, Sarah, Elias Edmonds & Anne. Exors; Wife and friends, Col. Jas. Ball, Jur. & Mr. Dale Carter. Wits: John Davis, George Coal. W.B. 15, p. 52.

SHARPE, Thomas. Division of negroes. 17 Sept. 1764. Rec. 15 Oct. 1764.
To: Elizabeth, Thomazin, Sarah, Anne, Elias Edmonds. Due from Mrs. Sarah Bond for their part of their Father's estate. W.B. 18, p. 24.

SHARP, Elias Edmonds. Appr. & division. 16 July 1772. Rec. 17 Dec. 1772.
Fortunatus Sydnor ¼; William Chowning ¼; Rawleigh Carter ¼; William Lewis ¼. By Richard Carter, Thaddeus McCarty. W.B. 20, p. 50.

SHAW, Jno. 11 Mar. 1705. Rec. 10 July 1706.
Son: John Asher Shaw. Wits: Jno. Lahore, Peter Kilgore, Zach. Vichow. W.B. 8, p. 137.

Shearman, Martin. Appraisement. 20 June 1771. Rec. 19 Sept. 1771. W.B. 20, p. 27.

Dated. 15 Dec. 1769. Proved 20 June 1771. Will of Martin Shearman of Parish of Christ Church. Wife: Ann. Sons: Raw-leigh & Martin, Joseph "my plantation," & Thomas Shearman. Daus: Mary Tapscott, Ann Christian, Sarah Haynes, Elizabeth Shearman & Alice Shearman. Exors: Wife and Friends Col. Jas. Ball & Mr. Richard Mitchell. W.B. 20, p. 15.

Shearman, Ann, widow of Martin Shearman. 28 June 1793. Rec. 21 Oct. 1793.

Sons: Rawleigh, Martin & Joseph Shearman; Thomas Shearman's (dec.) children. Daus: Mary Tapscott, Ann Christian, Sarah Haynie wife of Bridgar Haynie, Elizabeth Shearman, Alice Payne. R. W. Downman, Co.l James Ball, Joseph Chinn, Joseph Shearman. Wits: George Cammell, Philip Warwick, James Ball. W.B. 22, p. 399.

Shearman, Thomas. 4 July 1777. Rec. 15 July 1779.

Sons: Thomas Shearman and Samuel Martin Shearman. Daus: Ann, Winifred and Alice Chinn Shearman. Exors: Wife, Ann, and friend Capt. Wm. Downing. Wits: Raw. Shearman, Eliza-beth Shearman. W.B. 20, p. 162.

Shearman, Thomas. Appraisal & devision. 20 Dec. 1790. Rec. 16 Apr. 1792.

Heirs: Thomas Shearman, Ann Shearman, Winifd. Shearman, Sam Shearman. By Thomas Robertson, Thos. Edwards, Thomas Harcum. W.B. 22, p. 333.

Shelton, Nich. 11 Oct. 1737. Rec. 11 Aug. 1738.

Wife: Rebecca, sole legatee and Estrx. Wits: Wm. Boman and Jos. Sulevan. W.B. 13, p. 107.

Shelton, Benjamin. 23 Apr. 1748.

God-daughter Mary Shelton all my land. Sister Winifred Shel-ton ½ my stock. Mr. Thos. Everit, son of John Everit a negro boy. Sister-in-law: Rhoda Craven. John Everit and Craven Everit children of my sister-in-law certain negroes and "my share of the personal estate at my mother-in-law's death." Thos. Crowder, Mary Whaley. "To be buried by my wife." Brother, Wm. Shelton and his son John Shelton. Maj. Peter Conway. Mother-in-law Rebeccah Craven and brother Wm. Shelton, Exors. Wits: Mary Whaley, Thos. Crowder. W.B. 15, p. 164.

SHELTON, John. Appraisement. 16 Jan. 1772. Rec. 19 Mar. 1772. W.B. 20, p. 46.

SIDNOR, Fortunatus. 12 Mar. 1683. Rec. 15 Mar. 1683.
Inv. returned by Joanna Lawrence, relict. W.B. 2, p. 93.

SIMMONS, John. Inv. Rec. 8 June 1750.
Returned by Elizabeth Simmons. W.B. 14, p. 287.

SIMMONS, John. Division of estate. 20 Sept. 1751. Rec. 18 Oct. 1751. Geo. Brent given his part. W.B. 15, p. 71.

SIMMONS, John, division of estate. 14 Mar. 1758. Rec. 17 Mar. 1758.
John Yerby (who married Sarah, orphan of Mr. John Simmons) Eliza Simmons. Adms: Wm. Waugh, Edna Tapscott, Dale Carter. W.B. 16, p. 1.

SIMMONS, John. Appraisement. 19 Nov. 1767. Rec. 17 Dec. 1767. W.B. 18, p. 96.

SIMMONS, John. 29 June 1771. Rec. 16 Jan. 1772.
Jesse George allotted ⅓ part of estate, having married the widow. W.B. 20, p. 30.

SIMMONS, John. 15 Apr. 1776. Rec. 16 May 1776.
Sally Simmons, orphan of John Simmons. Jesse George her late guardian, Henry Lawson her present guardian. W.B. 20, p. 97.

SIMMONS, James, administrator of John Simmons. 29 June 1771. Rec. 16 Jan. 1772.
Debts due from the estate: James Simmons, Bridger Haynie, Humphry Simmons, Elizabeth Hill, John Lock, William Lawson, John Mason, Funeral charges. Brandy. Thomas Reid. W.B. 20, p. 30.

SIMMONS, Elizabeth, of parish of Wicoco. 28 Jan. ——. Rec. 19 May 1774.
Gr.daus: dau. of my son John Simmons, dec., Sarah Ann Simmons. Daus: Mary Yopp, wife of Samuel Yopp, and her children; Elizabeth Hill, widow of James Hill, dec.; Margaret Brent and her children. Son: James Simmons. Exors: Son, James Simmons and Samuel Yopp. Wits: John Clayton, George Brent, George X. Edwards. W.B. 20, p. 72.

SIMMONS, Sarah Ann, wife of George Brent. Rec. 16 July 1784.
Settlement by Capt. Henry Lawson, guardian. By Ja. Ball, James Tapscott, Edwin Conway. July 15, 1784. Received of Capt.

Henry Lawson for George Brent a loan office certificate for $400 being money due the loan office by the sd Lawson for a negro fellow that belonged to Sarah Ann Simmons, wife of sd Brent, that was condemned and executed for Felony in the County of Lancaster. W.B. 22, p. 33.

SIMMONDS, Elizabeth. Division of estate. Dec. 1768. Rec. 17 Sept. 1787.

Heirs: James Simmonds, John Yerby, George Brent for his wife, Samuel Yopp. By Benjamin George, William Brent, Jonathan Wilder. W.B. 22, p. 157.

SIMMONDS, James. Devision of estate. Jan. 1788. Rec. 18 July 1791.

Thos. Haydon, guardian of John Simmonds. Heirs: John, Charles, James & William Simmonds. James Hammond, guardian to Charles & Wm. Simmonds. By James Brent, William Kirk, William Meredith, William Gibson. W.B. 22, p. 310.
21 Oct. 1788. Appraisal and sale of estate. By William Norriss, Thomas Hayden, Benj. George. W.B. 22, pp. 190-192.

SIMPSON, John. 27 Sept. 1684. Rec. 19 Jan. 1684.

Gr.child: George Phillips, son of James Phillips 100 acres of land. Son-in-law: James Phillips my now dwelling plantation with my wife Ann Simpson during her life. Dau: Jane Calahan. Darby Callahan to enjoy land whereon he now lives. Gr.children: James & George Philips & John Callahan. Extrx.: Wife Ann, with James Phillips. Wits: Bryan Stott, Jno. Phillips, Thos. Owen. W.B. 5, p. 99.

SIMPSON, Ann, of Parish of White Chappell. 24 Aug. 1685. Rec. 13 June, 1690.

To: George Phillips son of James Phillips. Gr.son: James Phillips. Jane Callahan, wife of Darbe Callahan. Son-in-law: James Phillips, John Phillips, Darbe Callahan. Gr.dau: Elizabeth Brian at age of 21 to have a mare. Exors: Darbe Callahan and Jane his wife. Wits: Nath. Brown, John Wells. W.B. 8, p. 5.

SIMPSON, Ann, of Parish of White Chappell. 24 Aug. 1688. Rec. 13 June 1690.

Devisees: Geo. Philips, son of James Philips. Gr.son: James Philips. Sons-in-law: James Phillips, John Phillips & Darbe Callahan. Gr.dau: Elizabeth Brian. Jane Callahan, wife of Darbe Callahan. Ex.: D. Callahan and Jane his wife. Wits: Nathaniel Brown, Jno. Wells. W.B. 8, p. 5.

SIMPSON, Percival. 7 Oct. 1702. Rec. no date.

Wife, Mary, what she had from her former husband. Daus: Elizabeth and Jane. Sons: two not named. Exors: Wife, Wm. King and Edwd. Carter. Wits: Wm. King and Chris Kirk. W.B. 8, p. 125.

SMALL, John. Inv. Rec. 8 July 1719.

Returned by John Hughes, adm. W.B. 10, p. 292.

SMITH, Thomas. 23 Nov. 1662. Prob. 20 Jan. 1662.

Brother: Nathaniel Hedgeman all my wearing clothes. Wm. Frissell to be brother's guardian until he is of age. John Hanson, Master Wiat. Donesom Bohonon & his wife. John Richards, Master. Wits: Richard Clark, William Hood, Donesom Bohonon. W.B. Loose wills.

SMITH, Joseph. Nuncupative will.

Doctor Walter Andrews, age 30 yrs, Makes deposition. Thomas Hutton, aged 30 yrs. same deposition. Inv. of Joseph Smith. Dec. 12, 1664, presented by John Vause, Robert Chowning, Henry Nicolas, Richard Hull. Will Dated 23 July 1660. Rec. 14 Sept. 1664. To friend Elizabeth Kempe & my children. W.B. Loose wills.

SMITH, Margaret, adm. of Wm. Smith. 8 Sept. 1679. Rec. 10 Mar. 1679. W.B. 4, p. 349.

SMITH, Sam'l. 2 Feb. 1687/8. Rec. 11 Apr. 1688.

Wife: Susan. Dau: Susan Davis. Gr.child: Sam'l Davis. Devisee, Brian Grone. Exors: none. Wits: Nicholas Dymer, Edwd. Gibson, Garrold Kith Garrold. W.B. 5, p. 117.

SMITH, Rev. Charles. Inv. 3 June 1734. Rec. 12 June 1734.

Returned by Mrs. Elizabeth Smith, widow. (Estate which does not descend to the residuary legatees of Geo. Chelton.) W.B. 12, p. 299.

SMITH, Elizabeth. 8 Apr. 1735. Rec. 14 May 1735.

Gr.son: Charles Purcell. Gr.daus: Judith and Margaret Dameron. Gr.dau: Judith and her husband Edney Tapscott, Exors. "All my grandchildren." Wits: Charles Craven, Henry Tapscott. W.B. 12, p. 335.

SMITH, Baldwin Matthews. Division of negroes. Rec. 20 Jan. 1764.

To: Mrs. Lucy Smith, widow. Col. John Lee for Mary & Frances part. Mrs. Smith for Judith & Mildred's part. Mr. Geo. Heale for Burgess part. Mr. John Smith for Phillip Smith's part. W.B. 17, p. 33.

SMITH, Baldwin. Division of negroes. 16 Nov. 1775. Rec. 21 Dec. 1775.

To Rev. John Leland, Jr., Clerk, in right of his wife & Mildred Smith, orphan of Baldwin Smith. By Thomas B. Griffin, Richard Ball, Jas. W. Ball. W.B. 20, p. 91.

SMITH, John. 14 June 1765. Rec. 21 Oct. 1765.

Wife: Ann Smith. Four children: Robert, Frankie, John and Thomas Smith, also child wife now goes with. Exors: Wife Ann and friend Mr. Edward Blackmore. Wits: Dale Carter. W.B. 18, p. 53.

SMITH, John. Rec. 21 Oct. 1765.

Will presented by widow proved by oath of Dale Carter. W.B. 17, p. 166.

SMITH, Col. Burges. Est. 16 Mar. 1775. Rec. 15 Feb. 1776. W.B. 20, p. 92.

Alice Smith, allotted dower of her deceased husband, Col. Burges Smith. 16 Jan. 1783. W.B. 20, p. 246.

SMITH, Burges. Est. Rec. 17 Apr. 1792.

Colo. Burgess Ball, adm. LeRoy Peachy, atty. Accounts examined by Jas. W. Ball and James Tapscott. W.B. 22, p. 339.

SMITHER, George. 8 Nov. 1755. Rec. 19 Mar. 1756.

Wife: Ann Smither. Sons: John, Thomas, Gabriel and William Smither. Exors: Wife, Mr. George Payne and Maj. Richard Selden. Wits: Wm. Stoneham, John Muse. W.B. 15, p. 240.

SMITHER, George. Division of estate. 23 Apr. 1764. Rec. 19 July 1764.

Peter Miller guardian of orphans. Allotted to Gabriel Smither 1 negro, paying the other two children 4/2:7. By Richard Selden, John Yerby, Dale Carter. W.B. 18, p. 17.

SMITHER, Thomas. Inv. Aug. 1782. Rec. 19 Sept. 1782.

By John Clayton, Wm. Doggett, Wm. Doggett, Jr. W.B. 20, p. 242.

SMITHER, Thomas. Estate. 16 Mar. 1786. 20 Apr. 1786.

Edward Kent & Samuel Kent, Adm. By Vincent Brent, Elias Edmonds, John Doggett. W.B. 22, p. 119.

SNELLINGS, John. Inv. 11 Aug. 1703. W.B. 10, p. 259.

SNALE, Elizabeth Weathers. Apprais. 21 Jan. 1763. Rec. 18 Feb. 1763.

By Raw. Shearman, Wm. Hathaway, James Kirk. W.B. 17, p. 253.

SPARKS, Margaret. Rec. 17 June 1765.

Left no will. Administration granted to Henry Tapscott. W.B. 17, p. 124.

SPENCER, Geo. 13 Nov. 1690. Rec. 13 June 1691.

Wife: Elizabeth. Devisees: Capt. Rich. Newsom, Wm. Downman, son-in-law, Thos. Martin, Jno. Chyn, Jno. Chyn, Jr., Alice Chyn; sons-in-law, Raw. and Giles (Chyn), Jno. Jones, Nathaniel Cale, Chris. Cale, Elizabeth Carter, Mrs. Downman, Jno. Bertrand, minister. If wife, who is a widow, die or remarry estate to go to Millison Downman. Bequests, 1—Twenty Pounds to buy Communion Plate for St. Mary's White Chappell Church. 2—A cirplis for St. Mary's White Chappell Church. 3—That I be buried in St. Mary's White Chappell Lan. Co. Va. under the southside of the Communion Table. Wits: Alex. Dane, John Mathew, Alex. King. Ex.: Friend Capt. Richard Newsom. W.B. 8, p. 11.

STAMPS, Timothy. Inv. Rec. 12 Nov. 1698.

Presented in court by Margt. Stamps, relict. A large pair of andirons given to his dau. Margaret Stamps. W.B. 8, p. 84.

STAMPS, Wm. Rec. 12 Aug. 1748.

Chattin Chowning, guardian of Wm. Stamps orphan of Wm. Stamps, dec. W.B. 14, p. 206.

15 Mar. 1745/6. Rec. 9 May 1746. Wm. Stamps. Inv. returned by Chattin Chowning, adm. W.B. 14, p. 105.

STAMPS, Wm. Division of estate. 9 Dec. 1752. Rec. 15 Dec. 1752.

Chattin Chowning, former adm. Wm. Stamps now in possession. Wm. Tayloe, Gent., guardian of Mary Stamps. Margaret Stamps. W.B. 15, p. 110.

STANFORD, Vincent. 16 Nov. 1658. Rec. 28 Nov. 1658.

Wife: Mary. Niece: Lydia, wife of Antho. Tibbor, Mary, dau of Edwd. Dale patent of 200 acres lying upon Lawson's creek. Exors: Edwd. Dale and wife Mary. Wits: Robert Pollard, Elyas Wilson. Probated 20 Mar. 1659. W.B. 2, p. 57.

(Order Book 3, p. 88. Robert Pollard married the widow of Vincent Stanford.)

STEEL, Sam'l, Nun-cupative will. Rec. 8 Jan. 1706/7.
Son: Sam. Girl, Betty, and his wife, who is not named. 2 children by first wife. Delivered by Denny Cameron. W.B. 8, p. 135.

STEPHENS, Thomas, died intestate. 6 Aug. 1654. Rec. 17 Nov. 1654.
Elizabeth, relict wishes commission of administration. W.B. 2, p. 5.

STEPHENS, Anthony. 15 Sept. 1662. Rec. 15 7ber, 1663.
Friends: Wm. Ball, Wm. Noosum. Mrs. Phebe Smith, widow; kinswoman Mary Brackett ye only surviving daughter of Wm. & Mary Brackett of ye parish of White Chappell, London. Wits: Richard Merryman. Loose wills.

STEPHENS, Wm. Inv. Rec. 27 Feb. 1679. W.B. 5, p. 64.

STEPHENS, Hannah. 24 May 1731. Rec. 10 Apr. 1741.
Legatees, son Dan'l and his wife. Grdau.: Eliz. Jasper. Exor: Son Dan'l. Wits: Chas. Burgess, Jeremy Yeap and Chas. Ewell. W.B. 13, p. 209.

STEPHENS, Joseph, dec. Division of negroes. 11 Dec. 1747. Rec. 6 Jan. 1747.
Division of negroes, in the possession of Daniel Stephens, into 3 parts. Edward Blackmore is given ⅓ part of them. W.B. 14, p. 168.

STEPHENS, Christopher. Inv. Rec. 10 Mar. 1748.
Returned by John Stephens, adm. W.B. 14, p. 230.

STEPHENS, William. Inv. Rec. 10 July, 1749.
Returned by Richard Stephens, adm. W.B. 14, p. 249.

STEPHENS, Joseph. Orphans estate. 18 Oct. 1751. Rec. 15 May 1752.
Richard Stephens, orphan of Joseph Stephens. Settlement between Merryman Payne, Gent. & Edmund Blackmore late guardian of sd. orphan. W.B. 15, p. 95.

STEPHEN, Daniel. Inv. Rec. 20 July 1753.
Returned by Wm. George, adm. W.B. 15, p. 138.

STEPHENS, Richard. 19 Nov. 1761. Rec. 21 May 1762.
Wife: Ann Stephens. Children not named. Exors: Wife and friend Thos. Carter & Dale Carter. Wits: Betty Hunton, Ann Hunton, Dale Carter. W.B. 16, p. 211.

STEPHENS, Richard. 8 Mar. 1772. Rec. 20 May 1773.

Wife: not named, all estate. Sons: Joseph & George Stephens to be bound to such trades as Exors. shall think proper. Exors: Friends, Richard Mitchell, Edward Blackmore and Richard Payne with wife. Wits: Catharine Payne, Richard Payne. W.B. 20, p. 58.

Division. Fortunatus Sydnor ⅓ part and the balance divided among William Stephens, Joseph Stephens, Susanna Stephens, Judith Stephens and George Stephens. 17 Apr. 1777. W.B. 20, p. 106.

STEPHENS, William. Est. 16 Sept. 1779. Rec. 21 Oct. 1779.

Richard Mitchell, administrator. W.B. 20, p. 172.

STEPHENS, Division. Sept. 1784. Rec. 10 Oct. 1785.

Heirs: Jedithan James, John Connolly & James Hill. W.B. 22, p. 67.

10 Feb. 1785. Division. By James Gordon, James Tapscott, John Yerby. W.B. 22, p. 68.

19 Apr. 1790. Joseph & George Stephens, orphans of Richard Stephens, due orphans from Richard Mitchell's, dec., est. By James Ball & James Newby. W.B. 22, p. 260.

STEPTO, Thomas. Inv. & Ap. 12 Oct. 1744. Rec. 9 Nov. 1744.

Returned by Will Stepto, Gent., adm. W.B. 14, p. 33.

STEPTO, Capt. John. Estate Div. 22 Aug. 1752. Rec. 16 June 1753.

William, Thomas & Lucy Stepto, children, of brother Thomas Stepto, dec., Elizabeth Stepto, relict, of John Stepto, Est. of Wm. Stepto, dec., to est. of Mr. Thomas Stepto, dec., brothers of Capt. John Stepto. W.B. 15, p. 137.

STEPTO, John. 9 Aug. 1753. Rec. 16 Apr. 1755.

Wife: not named. Son: William (not married) Dau: Nancy. Exors: Friend, Nicholas Currell, Thos. Edwards, Jr. and John Ledford. Wits: Nicholas Currell, John Hinton. W.B. 15, p. 202.

STEPTOE, John. Division. 18 Aug. 1768. Rec. 17 Nov. 1768.

Administration granted Jno. Stepto. To Mrs. Joannah Stepto, Jno. Stepto, Will Powell. W.B. —, p. 129.

STEPTOE, William. 4 Apr. 1782. Rec. 20 June 1782.

Wife: Joanna. 4 Daus: Hannah Housin, Eliza Washington, Ann & Sarah Hill. Son: John. Exors: Mr. James Brent, Wm. Brown,

Newton Brent. Wits: Wm. Brown, Elmour Doggett, John X. Masden. W.B. 20, p. 240.

STEVENS, Rich'd, of St. Mary's White Chappell Parish. Wife: Hannah. Sons: William and his wife Margaret; Daniel, and Joseph. Gr.son: Rich'd Stevens. Daus: Ellinor and Hannah. Exors: Wife and son Dan'l. Wits: Wm. Owen, Jas. Barton, Rich. Plunkett. W.B. 12, p. 81.

STEWARD, John. Adm. Bond. Rec. 13 Sept. 1727.
John Parish & Anne his wife, adms. of estate of John Steward. W.B. 22, p. 34.

STILL, Henry. 6 Feb. 1748/9. Rec. 15 Apr. 1749.
Brother: Wm. Still, Jas. Ball, Jr., Jeduthan Ball. Ex.: Jas. Ball, Jr. Wits: Jas. Ball, Jr. W.B. 14, p. 237.

STONEHAM, Henry, Sr., 15 Oct. 1705.
Sons: John Stoneham & Joan his wife 114 a. of land; Henry Stoneham & Sarah his wife, 125 a. of land consisting of plantation on which I now live; William Stoneham. Son-in-law: Darby Dunaway and his wife Mary, my daughter; Sam Dunaway and Ann his wife, my daughter. Ex.: Son Henry. Wits: Geo. Finch, Sr., & Eliz. Finch. W.B. 10, p. 184.

STONUM, John, Sr. 28 Sept. 1716. Rec. 9 Oct. 1717.
Wife: Jane. Children but not named. Exors: Brothers, George Davenport and William Stonum. Wits: Dennis Cameron, Darby Dunaway. W.B. 10, p. 244.

STONEHAM, Henry, of Parish of St. Mary's White Chappell. 11 Sept. 1730. Rec. 11 Aug. 1738.
Wife: Sarah. Son: William; other children but not named. Exors: Wife and son William Stoneham. Wits: William Norris, Thos. Young and Chas. Burgess. W.B. 13, p. 108.

STONEHAM, William. 23 Feb. 1749/50. Rec. 8 Mar. 1750.
Sons-in-law: Homer Webb, Lazarus Webb. Dau: Judith Stoneham. Wife: Mary. Exors: Wife and son-in-law, Homer Webb. Wits: Joseph Norris, Henry Stoneham. W.B. 15, p. 14.

STONEHAM, John. Rec. 17 Feb. 1764.
Left no will. Administration granted Wm. Pitman. W.B. 17, p. 1.

STONEHAM, John. Appraisement. 17 Feb. 1764. Rec. 16 Apr. 1764.
By Hugh Brent, Geo. Wale, John Yerby. W.B. 18, p. 10.

21 July, 1766. George Yerby guardian of Margaret Stoneham, orphan of John Stoneham. W.B. 18, p. 63.

STONEHAM, Henry. Appraisement. 18 Oct. 1770. Rec. 15 Nov. 1770. W.B. 20, p. 6.

Division of estate, among widow and seven children: Widow's part, Homer Webb, Henry Stoneham's children, Bryan Stoneham, James Stoneham, Rachel Stoneham, Bryan Stoneham guardian of Richard Stoneham, Thos. Branan. George Stoneham, son and heir of Henry Stoneham, refused to take any part and desired that the whole estate should be divided between his mother & brothers & sisters. 18 May 1772. Rec. 21 May 1772. W.B. 20, p. 42.

STONEHAM, John. Appraisement. Mar. 1782. Rec. 20 June 1782. By James Newby; Wm. Carpenter; Richard Stott. W.B. 20, p. 239.

STOTT, William. 14 Sept. 1681. Rec. 9 Oct. 1681.

Nuncupative. Legatee: Robert Pritchard. Proved by oath of Henry Segar, aged 29 yrs. and Robert Chapell aged 22 yrs. W.B. 5, p. 78.

STOTT, Thomas. 28 Apr. 1670. Rec. 15 Mar. 1695.

Son-in-law: Thomas ——. Dau-in-law: Elizabeth. John Raney's dau, Ann. Bro's dau: Elizabeth. Exors: John Raney & Nathaniel Brown. Wits: Thomas Goodson, John Raney. W.B. 8, p. 55.

STOTT, Brian. Rec. 14 Mar. 1704/5.

Sons: James. Brian and John Stott. Gr.son: Nathaniel, son of John Stott. Daus: Mary Pullen and Ann Potts. Son-in-law: John Potts. dau-in-law: Mary Stott. Ex. Son John. Wits: Jno. Wilcox, Brian Philips, Dan'l Bryan. W.B. 8, p. 119.

STOTT, James. Inv. Rec. 13 Sept. 1710.

Presented in court by Richard Wooding. Frances Stott, widow, of St. Mary's White Chappell to pay Dr. Hen. Rose, Chirurgeon, 275 pounds of tobacco. 27th day of Oct. 1707. W.B. 10, p. 59.

STOTT, John. Est. Rec. 10 Jan. 1721.

Bryan Pullen, guardian of John Stott, orphan of John Stott. W.B. 10, p. 249.

STOTT, Benjamin. Inv. Rec. 15 Mar. 1729.

Returned by James Stott. W.B. 12, p. 150.

STOTT, Luke. 1 June 1734. Rec. 12 June 1734.

Sister: Elizabeth and her sons, John and James Phillips, and John Phillips, Sr. Exor: John Callahan. Wits: John Rogers, Isaac White, Martin Shearman. W.B. 12, p. 308.

STOTT, Thos. 13 Sept. 1747. Rec. 11 Dec. 1747.

Son: Thomas Stott. Wife: Grace "plantation whereon Jas. Bush now lives." Dau: Frances Stott. Richard Machen "the son of my wife." Brother: Bryan Stott. Deceased brother John Stott. Ex. Brother Bryan Stott. Wits: Robert Mitchell, Samuel Brook, Mary Stott. W.B. 14, p. 164.

8 Jan. 1747. Division of estate. Grace Stott, Frances Stott, Thos. Stott, Richard Stott? W.B. 14, p. 169.

STOTT, Henry. Inv. Rec. 12 May 1749.

Returned by Jas. Ball, Jr., Exor. W.B. 14, p. 239.

STOTT, John. 8 Oct. 1761. Rec. 15 Jan. 1762.

Gr.sons: James Tapscott, John Tapscott. Gr.dau: Ann Tapscott in the hands of her father, Mr. Henry Tapscott. Wife: Elizabeth Stott. Gr.sons: Henry Tapscott, William Tapscott. Easter Newby, dau. of Ozwald Newby, a years schooling. Exors: Son-in-law Henry Tapscott and friend Richard Mitchell. Wits: Samuel Brumley, William Sydnor, Martin Shearman, Jr. W.B. 16, p. 182.

STOTT, Wm. Jr. Rec. 20 May 1763.

Nuncupative. Wife: Sarah all his estate. Proved by Jonathan Pullen, Chloe Pullen, and Susannah Rogers. W.B. 17, p. 1.

STOTT, William. 14 Apr. 1781. Rec. 20 Sept. 1781.

Two grandsons: William & John Carpenter. Dau: Lucy Stott. Gr.son: William Stott. Niece: Winnifred Hughlet. Three grandchildren: Samuel Brumley Stott, Wm. Stott & Elizabeth Phillips Stott. Exors: Friend, Mr. Wm. Sydnor, Capt. Robert Chinn and Mr. Richard Mitchell. Wits: Jas. Ewell, Thos. Glascock, Wm. Stonum, Sarah Chinn. Codicil to will dated 28 June 1781. W.B. 20, p. 207.

STOTT, Thomas. 13 May 1786. Rec. 21 Sept. 1786.

Wife: Betty Stott. Dau: Ann Stott (not 18) Nephew: Thomas Stott son of Richard Stott, his land. Exors: Wife, William Sydnor & James Newby, Sr. Wits: Septimus Norris, Henry Pullen Judith Pullen. W.B. 22, p. 135.

Appraisal. By John Carpenter, William Carpenter, Richard Mitchell. 19 Oct. 1786. W.B. 22, p. 136.

19 Feb. 1787. Estate of Thomas Stott, deceased, to the estate of John Stonum, dec. To each of the children of John Stoneham (viz) Jenny, John, John, Nancy, Peggey, Betty, & Mary, their portion of a bed in the hands of Newman Miskell. 31 Oct. 1786. Jas. Ball, Rayleigh Tapscott. W.B. 22, p. 141.

21 Jan. 1788. Division of estate. To Philip Warwick in right of his wife, dau. of Thomas Stott, dec. By James Ball, Jr. & J. B. Downman. W.B. 22, p. 163.

15 Sept. 1788. George Cammel married the widow Stott. W.B. 22, p. 186.

STOTT, Richard. Appraisal. Rec. 15 Dec. 1788.
By William Carpenter, Phillip Warwick, John Dunaway. W.B. 22, p. 196.

STOTT, Mrs. Elizabeth. Appraisal. 21 Feb. 1791. Rec. 19 Sept. 1791. By James Ball, Raw. W. Downman, John Carpenter. W.B. 22, p. 315.

STOTT, Wm. Est. settled. Rec. 16 Apr. 1792.
Wm. Sydnor, Ex. Paid Rawleigh Stott his wife Lucy's part of her father's estate. By William & John Carpenter & Winifred Hughlett. W.B. 22, p. 331.

STOTT, Stephen. Division. 19 Dec. 1791. Rec. 17 Apr. 1792.
Samuel B. Stott representative of Wm. Stott Benj. Doggett in right of Eliza P. Stott his wife. By J. B. Downman, Raw. W. Downman. Wm. Hunt, Rawleigh Tapscott. Estate of Wm. Stott, dec., divided between Wm. Stott, grandson of deceased, & Benj. Doggett who intermarried with Elizabeth P. Stott, grandau. of aforesaid deceased. W.B. 22, p. 241.

STOTT, Eliza. Est. 18 Sept. 1792. Rec. 15 Apr. 1793.
George Hunt, Exor. Divided among six children. W.B. 22, p. 374.

STRATCHAN, James. 15 Jan. 1709/10. Rec. 10 May 1710.
Wife: Elizabeth. Son: James, my plantation where I now live; and John. Dau: Margaret. Wits: Jos. Heale, Sam'l Davis, Peter James Baley. W.B. 10, p. 25.

STRACHEN, James. Inv. 1 June 1710. Rec. 14 June 1710.
Presented in Court by Elizabeth Strachen. W.B. 10, p. 21.

212   ABSTRACTS LANCASTER COUNTY, VIRGINIA, WILLS—1653-1800

STRATON, Jas. 1 Oct. 1739. Rec. 14 Mar. 1739.
Wife: Eliz. Son: James. Dau: Eliz. Stott and six others whose names are not given but unmarried. Extrx: Wife and William George. Wits: Dale Carter and Robt. McTire. W.B. 13, p. 150.

STRATON, James. Orphans' estate. Rec. 13 June 1740.
Wm. Stott, guardian of Sarah Straton, orphan of James Straton. W.B. 13, p. 166.

STRETCHLEY, John. 6 Dec. 1698. Rec. 14 Dec. 1698.
Wife: Alice. Daus-in-law: Catherine Chinn, Anne Chinn. Son-in-law: Raw. Chinn. Cousin: Edwd. Audley. Sister: Sarah Bambridge. Extrx: Wife. Wits: Wm. Ball, Rich. Ball, Geo. Haile. W.B. 8, p. 87.

STRETCHLEY, Alice, wife of Jno. Stretchley of St. Mary's White Chappell. 29 Aug. 1701. Rec. 8 Oct. 1701. Daus: Anne Fox the portion bequeathed her by Jno. Chinn, her father, and by Jno. Stretchley, her father-in-law); Catherine Heale. Sisters: Dorothy Durham and Tomassin Marshall. Son-in-law: Capt. Wm. Fox. Son: Rawleigh Chinn "all money in the hands of Mr. Jno. Pemberton, Mercht. of Liverpool." Cousin: Mary Dodson. Exor: Son, Rawleigh Chinn. Wits: Jas. Taylor, Lewis Pugh, David Smith. W.B. 8, p. 106.

STUART, Charles. Inv. Rec. 21 Feb. 1752.
Returned by John Mitchell, adm. W.B. 15, p. 85.

SULLIVANT, Dennis. Inv. Rec. 10 Apr. 1747.
Returned by Daniel Sullivant, adm. W.B. 14, p. 143.

SULLIVANT, Jos. 25 Jan. 1782. Rec. 21 Mar. 1782.
By Henry Carter; Stephen Locks; Jno. Bean. W.B. 20, p. 228. Vincent Brent, Admr. W.B. 20, p. 236.

SULLIVANT, Joseph, dec'd. Jan. 1785. Rec. 28 Mar. 1785.
Accounts of Vincent Brent, adm. of Joseph Sullivant. Judith Sullivant guardian of orphans of sd Joseph. John Clayton, John Cundiff, Stephen Lock. W.B. 22, p. 74.

SULLIVANT, Joseph. Jan. 1785. Rec. 21 Apr. 1785.
Vincent Brent, adm. W.B. 22, p. 74.
21 July 1785. Joseph Sullivan, dec., adm. of estate of Thomas West, dec., orphans estate in the hands of Vincent Brent, adm. of Jos. Sullivan. Stephen Lock possessed with estate as guardian of orphans of Thos. West, dec. W.B. 22, p. 94.

SULLARD, Simon. Inv. 6 June 1679. Rec. 10 July 1679. W.B. 5, p. 56.

SWAN, Alexander. 12 Mar. 1709. Rec. 10 May 1710.

Wife: Mary. Son: John, all lands in Lan. and Rich'd Cos. Daus: Margaret Pinckard and Judith Jones. Exors: Wife, son, John and Brother Robt. Carter. Wits: Thos. Pinckard, Katherine and Hugh Brent and Martha Anderson. W.B. 10, p. 11.

SWAN, John. Inv. Rec. Oct. 1721.

Sarah Swan and John Ingram, adms. W.B. 10, p. 335.

SWAN, John. Inv. Rec. 11 Apr. 1722.

Returned by Sarah Swan. W.B. 10, p. 375.

SWAN, Mary. 20 Jan. 1721. Rec. 14 Feb. 1721.

Leaves to management of her brother Mr. Robert Carter, Esq. Legatees: Lucie Carter and her eldest son, Landon; Mary Carter, Judith Steptoe, Nanny Carter, George Carter, her two sons (not named). Exors: Her brother and Ann Carter. Affidavits of John Bell, Isabel Clements, and George Carter, her three cousins. W.B. 10, p. 363.

SWAN, Mrs. Mary. Inv. Rec. 8 Aug. 1722.

Returned by Robt. Carter, adm. W.B. 10, p. 398.

SWAN, John. Gent. Division of land. 21 Feb. 1737/8. Rec. 13 Apr. 1744.

Thomas Edwards & Sarah his wife as her full dower of all lands, etc. belonging to sd John Swan. Griffin Fauntleroy land in Richmond Co. John Edwards land in King George Co. Judith Fauntleroy, wife of Griffin Fauntleroy and Ann Edwards, widow & relict of John Edwards. The said John Swan was in his lifetime husband of sd Sarah and father of sd \Judith & Ann. W.B. 14, p. 20.

SWEATHAM, Joshua. 26 Feb. 1703/4. Rec. no date.

All left to his two children Joshua and Mary. Wits: Wm. Anderson, Jno. Barker, Sam Baker. Ex.: Son, Joshua. W.B. 8, p. 127.

SWENIE, John. Inv. Rec. 15 Aug. 1690.

Presented by Mary Swenie, Relict. W.B. 8, p. 6.

SYDNOR, Fortunatus. Inv. 25 Sept. 1683. Rec. 15 Mar. 1683.

Presented by Joanna Lawrence, relict. W.B. 5, p. 93.

SYDNOR, Fortunatus. 6 Nov. 1723. Rec. 10 Apr. 1723.
Wife: Ruth. Sons: William, Fortunatus, Anthony. Daus: Judith, Joanna. Exors: Wife and sons Wm. and Fortunatus. Wits: Jno. Stepto, Hugh Brent. W.B. 10, p. 427.

SYDNOR, Ruth. 22 Nov. 1736. Rec. 10 Oct. 1740.
Legatees: Sons, Wm. and Fortunatus S. Grsons: Robt. Sydnor and Elias Edmonds, Wm. Edmonds. Gr.daus: Franke and Johannah Edmonds. Wits: Jno. Stepto and Ellinor Campbell. Son: Anthony Sydnor. Exor. W.B. 13, p. 186.

SYDNOR, William, of St. Mary's White Chappell. 22 Jan. 1750. Rec. 19 July 1751.
Wife: Catharine. Son: William (not 21). To: Fortunatus, son of Anthony Sydnor and Eliza his wife; John Sydnor, son of Anthony and Eliza his wife; Joseph Sydnor, son of Anthony and Elizabeth his wife. Exors: Wife, Mr. George Payne and Mr. Richard Mitchell. Wits: Susanna Mitchell, M. Shearman. W.B. 15, p. 48.

SYDNOR, Anthony. Division of estate. Rec. 18 Feb. 1788.
Heirs: Robert Currell & wife, Mar. Catherine King. By James Brent & Martin Shearman. W.B. 22, p. 188.

SYDNOR, William, of Christ Church Parish. 12 Jan. 1794. Rec. 16 June 1794.
Wife: Ellen. Sons: Wm. Fauntleroy Sydnor ½ land Frederick Co. George Sydnor, Moore Sydnor "land left me by Capt. Moore Fauntleroy; Samuel Griffin land in Frederick Co.; James, Fauntleroy. Daus: Caty, Fanny. Ex.: Wm. Fauntleroy Sydnor, Moore Sydnor. Wits: Jas. Ball, Raw. N. Downman, T. Tarpley, Wm. Hunt, Judith Pullen. W.B. 22, p. 428.

TAPSCOTT, Henry. Inv. Rec. 12 Apr. 1727.
Christopher Kirk, adm. W.B. 10, p. 546.

TAPSCOTT, Henry. Rec. 12 Apr. 1727.
Chris. Kirk, late administrator, but upon the court having this day discharged the sd. Chris. from the sd administration and committed the same to Benja. George, Jr., and Ann his wife late widow of sd deceased. W.B. 10, p. 553.

TAPSCOTT, Henry. Adm. 14 June 1727. Rec. 14 June 1727.
Benj. George, Jr. & Ann his wife, admx. of Henry Tapscott. W.B. 12, p. 7.

TAPSCOTT, James. 16 Dec. 1773. Rec. 16 Dec. 1773.

John Clayton, guardian of Ann Tapscott, orphan of James Tapscott, dec. By Thomas Rowand, John Maxwell. W.B. 20, p. 69.

TAPSCOTT, Katty. 20 Jan. 1774. Rec. 21 Sept. 1775.

John Clayton Possessed with her estate. W.B. 20, p. 87.

TAPSCOTT, Henry, of Parish of Christ Church. 29 Dec. 1777. Rec. 19 Apr. 1781.

Wife: Mary. Sons: Henry, Rawleigh, William (land in Northumberland), Martin (land in Richmond Co.), Chichester, Richard, Joseph and Samuel Tapscott. Daus: Sarah, Betsy and Polly Tapscott, Ann Rogers, Alice Tapscott. Child unborn. Exors: Wife and friends Richard Mitchell and sons Joseph and Rawleigh Tapscott. Wits: John Chinn, Richard Mitchell, Jos. Shearman. W.B. 20, p. 190.

TAPSCOTT, Henry. Sale of estate. 21 Sept. 1789, Rec. W.B. 22, p. 238.

15 Feb. 1790. Division of estate. Heirs: Mrs. Mary Tapscott (widow), Henry, William, Sally, Rawleigh, Martin, Chichester, Richard, Joseph, Betsy, Polly, John Tapscott. By James Ball, Rawl. W. Downman, William Sydnor. W.B. 22, p. 251.

TAPSCOTT, Mary, of Wicocomico Parish. 16 Dec. 1790. Rec. 17 Jan. 1791.

Daus: Mrs. George and her dau Ellen; Mrs. Mason and her dau Judith; Mrs. James and her son Bartlett. Gr.children: Betsy Baisey Waters George, Molly Mason, Solomon Mason, Judith Mason. Son-in-law: Ezekiel Tapscott. Ex.: Elias Edmonds, Jr., Anthony Sydnor. Wits: William Lee, Charles Hammonds. W.B. 22, p. 286.

TAPSCOTT, Mary. Appraisal. Feb. 1791. Rec. 16 Jan. 1792.

By Benjamin George, Nicholas L. George, Thomas Haydon. W.B. 12, p. 324.

TAPSCOTT, Edney. 7 Jan. 1782. Rec. 17 Jan. 1782.

Wife: Mary. Sons: Henry, Ezekiel and John Tapscott. Daus: Elizabeth Clayton, Sukey, Danno and Catharine Tapscott. Gr.-son: Charles Hammonds. Exors: Sons, Henry, Ezekiel and John Tapscott and friend, Col. Edwin Conway. Wits: Wm. Mason, John Sydnor, Edwin Conway. W.B. 20, p. 220.

TARPLEY, Elizabeth. 7 Mar. 1788. Rec. 19 Jan. 1789.
Sisters: Alice Smith and her daughter Ann Griffin Smith. ——
Montague. Nephew: John Smith. Wits: Helen Gilmour, Reuben Sanders. W.B. 22, p. 198.

TATNALL, Thos. Inv. 8 July 1691. Rec. 10 July 1691.
Returned by Elizabeth Tatnall. W.B. 8, p. 40.

TAYLOE, Ann. Inv. 10 Oct. 1716. Rec. 14 Nov. 1716.
Presented in Court by Edwin Conway, adm. W.B. 10, p. 193.

TAYLOE, Joseph. 23 Aug. 1716. Rec. 14 Nov. 1716.
Legatees: Wife and two children mentioned, but not named; Anne Burn; Thomas Thornton. Extrs: Wife and children. Proved by oath of Barbary Tayloe. W.B. 10, p. 188.

TAYLOE, Joseph, Gent. Inv. 14 Nov. 1716. Rec. 11 Dec. 1716.
Proved by oath of Barbara Tayloe, one of the Exors: W.B. 10, p. 197.

TAYLOE, William. 5 Feb. 1767. Rec. 17 May 1770.
Land containing about 800 acres to Mr. Wm. Diggs who intermarried with my granddaughter, Elizabeth Wormley. Dau: Ann Wormley, wife of Mr. John Wormley. Exors: Nephew, John Tayloe, esq. and my grandson, Mr. Wm. Diggs. Wits: Apphiax Boatman, Elizabeth Davis, Dale Carter, Elizabeth McDaniell, Wm. Rains. W.B. 18, p. 169.

TAYLOE, Co. Wm., Gent. Appraisement. Rec. 20 July 1770.
By James Selden, Edwin Conway, Richard Ball, John Wormley. W.B. 20, p. 2.

TAYLOR, John. Administration granted Eliza, relict. Rec. 10 Jan. 1652. W.B. 1, p. 24.

TAYLOR's, John, estate. 29 July 1657. Rec. 1 Aug. 1657.
Record of not paid by Tobias Horton. W.B. 2, p. 54.
Inv. 2nd Oct. 1645. Presented to court by Tobey Horton and Elizabeth his wife. Recorded 10 Oct. 1654. W.B. 2, p. 54.

TAYLOR, Robert. Oct. 23, 1662. Rec. 28 Jan. 1662. Prob. 20 Jan. 1662.
Daniel Welch my son-in-law. Wife: Margarett, Extrx. Unborn child. Friend: Richard Parrott overseer. Wits: Rich. Parrott, James Blackmore. Servant: Jason Taylor. W.B. Loose wills.

TAYLOR, John, of St. Mary's white Chappell. 20 Mar. 1721. Rec. 13 June 1722.

Legatees: Wife, Catherine; son, Joseph Taylor, Jr., "my plantation where I now live"; dau., Anne and a youngest not yet christened; bros., Moses, Benjamin and James Taylor. Extr: Wife, Catherine. Wits: Robt. Mitchell and Wm. Cotes. W.B. 10, p. 386.

TAYLOR, Capt. Richard. Inv. 29 May 1683. Rec. 19 July 1683. W.B. 5, p. 85.

TAYLOR, Thomas. Inv. Rec. 11 Aug. 1703.

Returned by Mary Taylor, relict. W.B. 10, p. 249.

TAYLOR, Thomas. 7 Feb. 1718. Rec. 11 June 1718.

Wife's name not given. Sons: Thomas, plantation in Wiccocomoco Psh, and Theriatt Taylor. Daus: Martha, Elizabeth, Ann and Sarah. Wits: Rich. Cundiff Jr. and Rich. Ball. W.B. 10, p. 265.

TAYLOR, John, of St. Mary's White Chappell. 20 Mar. 1721. Rec. 13 June 1722.

Wife: Catherine. Son: Joseph Taylor, Jr. my plantation where I now live. Dau: Anne and a youngest not yet christened. Bros: Joses T., Benj. T. and James Taylor. Extrx: Wife Catherine. W.B. 10, p. 386.

TAYLOR, Barbara. 10 Dec. 1726. Rec. 8 Feb. 1727.

Legatees: Ann Mott, eldest dau. Jno. Mott, the younger;. son Joseph, dead. Daus: Elizabeth, her issue begotten by another not of Jno. Thornbury. William son of Wm. Baker, Richmond Co. To John Mott, one suit of my dec'd son Joseph's Clothes. Extrs: Jno. Mott Jr. and Dau: Elizabeth. Wits: Jno. Selden and Margaret Miller. W.B. 10, p. 509.

TAYLOR, John. Est. Rec. 11 Sept. 1728.

Catherine Taylor, admx. W.B. 12, p. 73.

TAYLOR, John. Inv. 10 July 1737. Rec. 10 July 1737.

Returned by Wm. Sydnor, adm. Division. Joseph Taylor ¼ part of his father's estate. Anthony Sydnor & Eliza his wife, the sd Eliza's part of her father's estate. 8 July 1737. Differnce between Anthony Sydnor & Eliza his wife and Wm. Sydnor and Catherine his wife Extrs. of John Taylor. W.B. 13, p. 55.

TAYLOR, Theriat. Apprais. 12 May 1738. Rec. 9 June 1738. Returned by Thomas Taylor, adm. W.B. 13, p. 92.

TAYLOR, Thomas. Inv. 11 Jan. 1744/5. Rec. 8 Mar. 1744. Returned by Eve Taylor, admx. W.B. 14, p. 53.

TAYLOR, John. Inv. 14 Mar. 1745/6. Rec. 11 Apr. 1746. Returned by Simon Sallard, adm. W.B. 14, p. 103.

TAYLOR, Moses. 29 Apr. 1748. Rec. 8 July 1748.

Wife: Mary Taylor. Sons: Thomas, Isaac and John Taylor. Dau: Sarah Pope. Gr.dau: Mary Pope. Exors: Wife and son Thomas. Wits: Geo. Conway, John Everitt, Tho. Brent. W.B. 14, p. 204.

Inv. returned by Thos. Taylor one of the Esors. 2 Aug. 1748. W.B. 4, p. 208.

TAYLOR, John. 3 Feb. 1749/50. Rec. 9 Feb. 1749.

Legatees: Mr. John Graham, Stockly Towles, John Graham, Jr., land in Northumberland Co.; Elizabeth Towles, Wm. Payne, Jr. Exors: John Gresham & Stokley Towles. Wits: Sto. Towles, Samuel Neasum. W.B. 14, p. 271.

TAYLOR, John. 10 May 1751. Rec. 10 May 1751.

Stokely Toles the writer of John Taylor's will deposeth and saith that the sd John intended to give the land mentioned in the sd will to John Graham, Jr. W.B. 15, p. 34.

TAYLOR, Thomas. 23 May 1751. Rec. 14 June 1751.

Brother: Isaac Taylor, land my father gave me. Sister: Sarah Pope. God-son: Thomas Pope, Joseph Pope. Brother: John Taylor. Exors: Brothers Isaac & John Taylor. Wits: Charles Fallin, Jr., Joseph Pope, John Pope. W.B. 15, p. 39.

21 Nov. 1753. Estate divided between Mr. Solomon Ewell in right of Eve his wife late widow of Thomas Taylor and John Taylor, son and heir of sd. Thomas. Rec. 16 Jan. 1756. W.B. 15, p. 237.

TAYLOR, Thomas. Inv. 29 Jan. 1751. Rec. 19 July 1751. Returned by Isaac Taylor, Ex. W.B. 15, p. 49.

TAYLOR, Elizabeth. 20 Oct. 1746. Rec. 18 Oct. 1751.

John Taylor, son of my son Thomas Taylor, dec'd. Thomas Ball, son of my dau. Anna Ball, wife of Mr. Geo. Ball. Son-in-law: George Ball Guardian to gr.son John Taylor. Dau: Martha

Miller. Gr.son: Joseph Damaron. Gr.dau: Elizabeth Ball. Dau: Eliz Flowers. Exors: Son-in-law Geo. Ball and dau. Martha Miller. Wits: Robert Boatman, Wm. Miller, Dale Carter. Codicil Sept. 2, 1751. W.B. 15, p. 64.

TAYLOR, Eliza. Inv. & Ap. Rec. 15 Nov. 1751.

Returned by Geo. Ball, Ex. W.B. 15, p. 74.

TAYLOR, Edward. 26 Jan. 1758. Rec. 21 Apr. 1758.

Friends: Daniel Plummer, Mr. Richard Chichester, Rawley Downman, Jr., William Ball, Jr. Ex.: Mr. Wm. Downman. Wits: Wm. Ball, Wm. Downman, Richard Payne. W.B. 16, p. 6.

TAYLOR, Isaac. 5 Apr. 1764. Rec. 17 Sept. 1764.

Wife: Ann Taylor. Son: Thomas, Youngest son: Isaac. "All my children." Exors: Wife and friends Mr. David Boyd and Mr. Charles Coppedge. Wits: John Leland, Henry Leland. W.B. 18, p. 20.

TAYLOR, Isaac. Rec. 15 Oct. 1764.

Will presented by John Leland & Henry Leland. W.B. 17, p. 65. Ann Taylor, Executrix. W.B. 17, p. 69.

TAYLOR, Richard, of Parish of Wiccomico. 15 May 1774. Rec. 17 Nov. 1774.

Wife: Judith, a negro wench now living in Fauquier Co. Sons: John Young Taylor and Richard Taylor, land in Fauquier Co. Cousin: Nancy Taylor, 1000 lbs of tobacco, "for intending on me in my sickness." Daus: Nancy & Betsy. Exors: Friends, Mr. Wm. Edmonds, my brother Joseph Taylor of Fauquier Co., Isaac Basye & John Gibbons of Northumberland Co. Wits: Charles Coppedge, James Wallace, Ann Taylor, Elizabeth Wallis. W.B. 20, p. 76.

TAYLOR, Richard, dec'd. 17 Nov. 1774. Rec. 19 Feb. 1784.

Inventory & Ap. Elias Edmonds, Sr., John Coppedge, John James. Apprs. W.B. 22, p. 11.

TAYLOR, Richard. Sale of estate. Rec. 17 Nov. 1785.

John Gibbins & Isaac Basye, Exors. W.B. 22, pp. 104, 106.

21 Dec. 1789. Appraisal & Division. By Wm. Edmonds, Edward Diggs, Thomas Diggs. Heirs: Mrs. Taylor, Elizabeth Taylor, John Young Taylor, Richard Taylor, Richard Baisey. W.B. 22, p. 236.

TAYLOR, John, Col., dec. Division of estate. Dec. 1786. Rec. 16 Apr. 1787.

Heirs: Thomas Taylor and his brother & sister Ann Taylor (widow). By James Ball, Jr., Jas. W. Ball, James Tapscott. W.B. 22, p. 148.

19 Jan. 1789. Settlement Admx. account, Ann Taylor, admx. Children: Fanny, Patty, John, Betsey, (James Ball Taylor, Nancy, Maryann & Salley Henner Taylor. By Edwin Conway, James Tapscott, William Warren. W.B. 22, p. 197.

18 Sept. 1792. Ann Taylor, admx. W.B. 22, p. 352.

THACKER, Wm. 27 Oct. 1694. Rec. 30 July 1698. Prob. 3 July 1698.

Son: Gabriel (not 21) land. Wife: Alise Thacker Extrx. Children: Catharine & Susana. Wits: Chris. Kirk, Robt. Robinson, Clamence Savilie. W.B. Loose wills.

THARKELSON, Nicholas. 27 May 1746. Rec. 8 Sept. 1749.

Wife: Grace. Sons: Nicholas, John and Joseph. Dau: Mary Ann. Ex.: Wife Grace. Wits: Thos. Pinckard, Dale Carter. W.B. 14, p. 256.

THARKLESON, Joseph. 28 Jan. 1792. Rec. 17 Sept. 1792.

Wife: Judith. Sons: William & Tharkle. Dau: Betty Tharkleson. Wits: Geo. P. Olliver & John Tarkelson. W.B. 22, p. 351.

THATCHER, Gabriel. 26 June 1744. Rec. 9 Nov. 1744.

Sons: John and Gabriel. Daus: Mary Robinson and Judith Thatcher. Wife: Judith. Exors: Wife and son Gabriel. Wits: Geo. Brent, Moses Robinson. W.B. 14, p. 34.

THATCHER, James. 11 Feb. 1745/6. Rec. 16 Feb. 1755.

Judith Thatcher. Sister: Mary Robinson. William Robinson. Brother: Gabriel Thatcher. Wits: Wm. Robinson, Gabriel Thatcher. W.B. 15, p. 119.

THATCHER, Judith. 8 Oct. 1754. Rec. 20 June 1755.

Sons: Wm. Schophill, Henry Schophill. Gr.daus: Betty Schophill, dau of son Henry; Sarah Schophill, dau of son Henry; Sarah Walker. James Walker, son of John Walker. Gr.son: Francis Walker. Gr.dau: Judith Walker wife of John Walker. Wits: Henry Commons, Moses Whealer, Betty Commons. W.B. 15, p. 208.

THATCHER, Gabriel. 3 Apr. 1757. Rec. 15 July 1757.

Son: William Thatcher, all my land. Wife and children. Exors:

Wife, George Glowers & James Kirk. Wits: Anthony Kirk, Ephraim Hubbard, James Kirk. W.B. 15, p. 296.

THATCHWELL, Will, estate. Jan. 20, 1659. W.B. 2, p. 76.

THERIOTT, Domnie. Rec, 10 Jan. 1652.
Domnie Theriott married relict of Hen. Lee, granted administration on his estate. W.B. 1, p. 23.
Her name was Joan. W.B. 1, p. 26.

THERRIOTT, Dominie. Inv. 10 Mar. 1675. Rec. 1 Apr. 1675.
Returned by Wm. Therriott. W.B. 5, p. 16.

THERRIOT, William. Inv. 10 Nov. 1690. Rec. 9 Sept. 1691.
Presented by Ann Therriot. W.B. 8, p. 29.

THOMAS, William. 5 Aug. 1666. Rec. ——. Prob. 13 Nov. 1667.
Wife: name not given. Dau: Elizabeth Thomas. Sons: Roboart & Thomas Thomas. John Raney Overseer. Wits: Thos. Haward. W.B. Loose wills.

THOMAS, Tarpley. Appraisal. 17 Jan. 1791. Rec. 19 Apr. 1791.
By John Christopher, Jos. Shearman, Rawl. Coats. W.B. 22, p. 304.

THOMPSON, Tho. Nuncupative. 14 Nov. 1694. Rec. 17 Nov. 1694.
Devisees: Nicholas George, Sr., John Mullis, John Sharpe, Benj. Dogget, Betty Dogget, Richard Flint's son that is my godson, Stephen Chilton, Sr. Wits: Geo. Chilton and John Chilton. W.B. 8, p. 47.

THOMPSON, Thos. 14 Feb. 1721. Ellinor Thompson, Admx. W.B. 10, p. 362.

THOMPSON, Thomas. Appraisement. 14 Feb. 1721. Wm. Martin, John Cooke, Henry Lawson, Wm. Brent, Apprs. W.B. 10, p. 375.

THORNTON, Thomas. 9 Oct. 1737. Rec. 10 Apr. 1741.
Wife: Agatha. Sons: Thomas; (lands in Prince William Co.) Timothy, John. Daus: Agatha, Elizabeth and Ann Thornton. Exors: Wife and sons, Timothy and Thomas. Wits: John Candree, Benjamin Neale and Robert Bygrave. W.B. 13, p. 198.

THORNTON, Thomas. Division of estate. 9 Oct. 1741. Rec. 10 Sept. 1742.
To: Widow's part, Timothy Thornton, Agatha Chinn, Elizabeth Thornton, Thomas Thornton, Ann Thornton. W.B. 13, p. 286.

THORP, Elizabeth (formerly Web), of Parish of Wiccocomoco, widow. Rec. 20 Apr. 1758.

Deed to Thomas Yerby of Northumberland Co. dower rights in 50 acres of land formerly belonging to her husband, Moses Web. lying partly in Lancaster and partly in Northumberland Co. W.B. 16, p. 2.

THRUSH, Clement. Rec. 6 Oct. 1652.

Clement Thrush Petitions court for administration of estate of Robert Vivian, dec. W.B. 1, p. 16.

TIGNOR, Wm. Inv. 1 Apr. 1657. Rec. 16 Apr. 1657.

Presented by Mabell ye relict of sd Tignor and now wife of Wm. Luck. W.B. 2, p. 121.

TIMBERLAKE, Francis. Rec. 17 June 1765.

Mr. Nicholas Read settle matter of dispute between George Ball and Richard Timberlake Ex. of Francis Timberlake. W.B. 18, p. 36.

TOMLIN, Stephen. 27 June 1704. Rec. 8 Aug. 1704.

Devisees: Edward Tomlin, Marriner in London, and Edward Tomlin's sons, Stephen and John. Gr.sons: Stephen Wilkinson, Nathaniel Stott son of John Stott, Samuel Bromley, Stephen Tomlin. Daus: Mary wife of Wm. Robinson, Jane wife of John Stott. Son: Edward Tomlin. Gr.son: Stephen Tomlin, son of Edeard Tomlin. Ann Kirk, Mr. John Foster, Capt. Sam'l Fox, Margaret Sanders, Chas. James. Exors: Sam'l Fox and Edwd. Tomlin in trust for gr.son Stephen Tomlin. Son: Edward Tomlin, sole Ex. Wits: Thomas Earth, William Samon, Charity Atkinson, Jonathan Cary. W.B. 8, p. 119.

TOMLIN, Edward. Inv. 16 Jan. 1722. Rec. 13 Feb. 1722.

Returned by Mary Tomlin, adm. W.B. 10, p. 424.

TOMLIN, Stephen. 22 Sept. 1733. Rec. 14 Nov. 1733.

Wife not mentioned. Sons: John Tomlin. Daus: Mary, Ann and Betty. Wits: Jos. Robertson, William and Sarah Roach. W.B. 12, p. 281.

TOMLIN, Mary. 19 Feb. 1742. Rec. 11 Mar. 1742.

Granddaus: Mary Newby and Ann Tomlin. Gr.son: Jno. Tomlin. Margaret Hambleton and Stephen Stott. Exor: Henry Newby. Wits: Wm. and Catherine Sydnor. W.B. 13, p. 321.

TOMLIN, Mary. Inv. Rec. 8 Apr. 1743.

Returned by Henry Newby, Ex. W.B. 13, p. 318.

TOMBLIN, Stephen.

Martha, widow of Stephen Tomblin married George Steal. Ann Stephen Tomblin, dau. of Stephen Tomblin married John Blackmore of parish of Hamilton in co of Prince William before 27 Oct. 1750. W.B. 15, p. 3¹7.

THOMPSON, Thomas. Inv. Prob. 14 Feb. 1721. Rec. 11 Apr. 1722.

Ellinor Thompson, admtrx. W.B. 10, pp. 362, 376.

TOWLES, Henry. Rec. 12 June 1734.

Wife not named. Son: Stokely Towles. Daus: Judith, Ann and Elizabeth. Exor: son Stokely and Robt. Mitchell. Not any wits. W.B. 12, p. 309.

TOWLES, Ann. 15 Dec. 1735. Rec. 11 Feb. 1736.

Sisters: Judith Neasum, Elizabeth Towles, Ann Neasum Sr., Margaret Neasum, dau. of Robert Neasum, Jr. to be deducted out of Judith Neasum's share. Brothers: Stokeley Towles and Robert Neasum, Jr. Wits: Robert Neasum, Alexander Matson. W.B. 13, p. 23.

TOWLES, Ann. Inv. & Ap. 11 Feb. 1736. Rec. 13 May 1737.

Returned by Sto. Towles, Ex. W.B. 13, p. 40.

TOWLES, Henry. Inv. & Ap. Rec. 13 May 1737.

Returned by Stokely Towles, Ex. W.B. 13, p. 41.

TOWLES, Stockly (deed of gift). 20 Oct. 1763. Rec. 21 Oct. 1763.

To Mrs. Ellinor Stamps of Bedford Co., negroes in the possession of Capt. Wm. Stamps and to her two daughters, Catherine and Mary Stamps. W.B. 17, p. 22.

TOWLES, Stockly. 8ber 12, 1763. Rec. 17 June 1765.

Wife: Elizabeth Towles. Two youngest sons, Thomas and Stockly "Land I bought of Renne Lefore which Land is in Goochland County." Five children. Exors: Friends, Mr. Richard Mitchell, Mr. Edward Carter & Mr. Chattin Chowning. W.B. 18, p. 37. Division of estate 28 Nov. 1768. Rec. 16 Mar. 1769. To: Stockly Towles, Thomas Towles, Henry Towles, Elizabeth Towles, Nancy Towles, Wife's part. W.B. 18, p. 139.

TOWLES, Elizabeth, widow and relict of Stokely Towles. 18 Jan. 1771. Rec. 21 Mar. 1771.

Her dower in the lands of Henry Towles, son and heir of sd Stokely. W.B. 20, p. 10.

TRAVERS, John. Inv. & Apprais. 12 June 1717. Rec. 10 July 1717. Presented by Susanna Ladnor, admx. W.B. 10, p. 233.

TRAVISS, John. 18 Dec. 1716. Rec. 12 June 1717.

Legatees: Wm. Paine, Susanna Ladnor. Wits: Jno. Barlowe, Geo. Payne. W.B. 10, p. 220.

TURBEVILE, John, Gent. Est. Rec. 9 Oct. 1728.

George Turbevile of Westmoreland Co., adm. W.B. 12, p. 74.

VANGOVER, Jno. Rec. 8 Feb. 1726.

Wife's name not given. Children referred to but not named. Exors: Wife and Chas. Burgess. Wits: Wm. Jones, Wm. George, Wm. Smith. W.B. 10, p. 512.

Inv. presented by Margt. Vangover & Chas. Burgess—8 Mar. 1726. W.B. 10, p. 521.

VELDEN, Francis. Inv. & Ap. 30 Nov. 1733. Rec. 9 Jan. 1733.

Returned by Mary Brewer, his admx. W.B. 12, p. 286.

VELDEN, Francis. 12 Mar. 1734. Rec. 11 June 1735.

Administrators report no estate. Nothing to deliver to Henry Horn and Ye orphan of sd Francis Velden. W.B. 12, p. 34.

VESEY, George. 25 Feb. 1665. Rec. 14 Mar. 1665.

Wife: Jone. Son: Thomas Vesey all my land. "My other children." Exors: Wife Jone and friends Nathaniel Brown & Stephen Tomlin. Wits: John Curtis, Nathaniel Browne, Stephen Tomlyn, George Gillum. W.B. Loose wills.

VINCE, John. 9 Mar. 1687. Rec. 12 May 1688.

Devisees: Francis Nash,, dau. Wm. N. Geo. Page, who are also Exors. Wits: Geo. Mallett, Hen Boatman, John Wright. W.B. 5, p. 120.

VIVION, Robert, died intestate. 10 die 10br, 1652. Rec. 12 Jan. 1652. Administration granted Clemt. Thrush. W.B. 1, p. 35.

WADE, John. 2 Mar. 1687/8. Rec. 13 Oct. 1688.

Wife: Mary. Children provided for but not named. Devissees: Philip Hummings. Wits: Ralph Whiting, Jas. Barton, Edwd. Jones. Exors: Wife and Philip Humming. W.B. 5, p. 126.

WADDEY, Hannah. Division of estate. 20 Feb. 1772. Rec. 19 Mar. 1772.

Thomas Edwards, William Edwards. Edwin Conway, guardian of John Edwards; George Yerby, guardian of Charles Edwards; Richard Ball, guardian of Sarah Edwards; William Edwards, guardian of Milly Edwards. W.B. 20, p. 38.

WAKEFIELD, John. 25 Aug. 1659. Rec. 20 May 1660.

To Rowland Haddaway, Peter Haddaway son of Rowland Haddaway. Wit: John Humphreys, Edward Bromfield. W.B. 2, p. 74.

WALDER, Edward. 6 Mar. 1693. Rec. 8 Mar. 1698.

Wife: Sowsan. Daus: Ann, the eldest, Mary the youngest. Extrx: Wife. Wits; Raw. Lawson Jr., Geo. Kirkeys, Thos. Danks. W.B. 8, p. 89.

WALE, George. Inv. 24 July 1674. Rec. 9 Sept. 1674.

Edward Wale, brother of dec. Geo. Wale made oath as to inventory. W.B. 5, p. 3.

WALE, George. Inv. Rec. 8 Aug. 1689.

Presented by Lettice Lawson, relict. W.B. 5, p. 133.

WALE, Jno. Apprais. Rec. 9 July 1701.

By Benj. Wale, Jno. Brown and Eliza. Wale, widow. W.B. 8, p. 102.

WALE, Benjamin, of Christ Church Parish. 26 Mar. 1709. Rec. 12 —— 8ber 1709.

Wife: Anne, her son John Mahallom. Cousin: Mary Wale. Godson: Robt. Edmonds. Exors: Capt. Maurice and Elias Edmonds. Wits: John Locke, William Burbridge, Peter Wood. W.B. 10, p. 10.

WALE, George. Inv. 12 Apr. 1721.

Presented by Thomazina Wale, widow and relict. W.B. 10, p. 316.

WALES, John, division of estate. 9 July 1749. Rec. 11 Aug. 1749.

Five children: Elizabeth George, Ann Hunton, Johanna Doggett, Judith Tucker, Lettishee Griggs. W.B. 14, p. 256.

WALE, George. 13 Mar. 1767. Rec. 20 Aug. 1767.

Wife: Sarah Wale. Sons: George, John (not 21), Lawson (not 21) William Wale, land in Nantapoison. Daus: Caty Wale, Maryann, Joana & Sarah Wale. Friend: Capt. Willi Dymer guardian of children. Exors: Wife & Capt. Wm. Dymer. Wits; Hugh Brent, Ann Brent. W.B. 18, p. 87.

WALE, George. Division of estate. 15 Oct. 1772. Rec. 17 Dec. 1772.

To George Wale, Joanna Wale; Sarah Wale, John Wale, Lawson Wale, Wm. Wale, Guardian. William Wale, William Brent. Joanna Wale, Wm. Grigs, guardian. W.B. 20, p. 49.

17 Oct. 1782. Azchariah Bair, appointed guardian of Lawson Wale; James Brent present guardian. W.B. 20, p. 249.

WALE, William, a soldier in the 5th Va. 28 Sept. 1776. Rec. 18 Apr. 1777.

Regiment. Brother: Lawson Wale. Godson: Richard Hudnall. Ex. Frind, James Hudnall. Wits: Edward Blakmore, Thomas West, Richard Stephens, Elmour Dogget, Jr., Isaac Currell. April 18, 1777. This last will of Wm. Wale was presented in Court and being proved to the Hand Writing of sd Wale and the Hand Writing of three of the Witnesses to the sd will, vizt. of Elmore Dogget, Jr., Thomas West & Isaac Currel, who are now in the Army at the Northard, being also proved in court held for the same County on the 7th day of April, 1777, the will of Wm. Wale, deceased, was further proved by the oath of Edward Blakemore, a witness thereto, who also proved that he saw all the other witnesses subscribe their names thereto and that all of them are deceased except Thomas West who is said to be dead. W.B. 20, p. 109.

WALE, John, dec'd. 18 Aug. 1784. Rec. 19 Aug. 1784.

Inventory goods in hands George Carter and Lawson Wale. John Berryman, Henry Lawson, William Lawson, William Norriss. Apprs. W.B. 22, p. 49.

WALE, Lawson, of Christ Church Parish. 2 May 1785. Rec. 10 Nov. 1785.

Wife: Winny Wale. Child mentioned but not named. Land owned on Fleets Bay, Henry Shelton holds Lease. Exors: Nathan Spriggs, John Flowers, William Norris. Wits: William Norris & John Brent. W.B. 22, p. 110.

16 Feb. 1786. Appraisal. By William Merridith, John Flowers, William Norris. W.B. 22, p. 114.

18 Oct. 1780. Settlement of account. Nathan Spriggs, Ex. Winney Wale, Widow. W.B. 22, p. 280.

WALLACE, James. 25 Aug. 1774. Rec. 20 June 1791.
Wife: Elizabeth. Son: William Wallace. Daus: Fanny Wallace (eldest), & Betsey Wallace. Esors: Thomas Yerby & wife Elizabeth Wallace. Wits: Hopkins Harding, Jemima Harding. Gracey Wallace appointed admx. Richard Selden, security. W.B. 22, p. 306.

WALLACE, James. Appraisal. 25 June 1791. Rec. 18 July 1791.
A sorrel mare claimed by Dicky Wallace and proved to be the property of sd Dicky Wallace by oath of James Nutt, James Mott & Elijah Purcifull to the Satisfaction of James Tapscott & Martin Shearman. Appraised by William Yerby, Lott Palmer, Elijah Percifull. W.B. 22, p. 311.

WALLIS, Francis, of county of Northumberland. 15 Feb. 1734. Rec. 12 Mar. 1734. Sole legatee, Alex. Poor. Wits: Jno. Kent, Jr.; Geo. Curtis, Jno. Kent, Sr. W.B. 12, p. 331.

WALTERS, Miles. 5 Dec. 1721. Rec. 14 Mar. 1721.
Wife: Jane. Son: John. Extrx: Wife. Wits: Robt. Mitchell, Wm. Fallin, Jane Aldridge. W.B. 10, p. 365.
Miles Walters. Invty. 11 July 1722. Jane Walters, Extrx. W.B. 10, p. 397.

WARD, William. Appraisal. Rec. 15 June 1795.
By Martin Shearman, Isaac Currell, John Haggoman. W.B. 22, p. 457.

WAUGH, William. Inv. 14 Sept. 1726. Rec. 14 Sept. 1726.
Eliza Waugh, adm. W.B. 20, p. 507.

WAUGH, Eliza. 5 Apr. 1745. Rec. 14 June 1745.
Son: James & William Waugh. Ex: Sons Wm. & James. Wits: Wm. Kelly, James Donnellan, Charles Hammonds. W.B. 14, p. 80.
14 June 1745. Rec. 8 Nov. 1745. Eliza Waugh. Inv. Returned by Wm. & Jane Waugh, Exors. W.B. 14, p. 99.

WAUGH, William. Inv. & Ap. Rec. 16 May 1760.
Returned by Mary Waugh. W.B. 16, p. 88.

WAUGH, Wm. Division. 18 June 1767. Rec. 20 Aug. 1767.
John Nicholas, John Yerby & Benj. George divide the estate of Wm. Waugh, dec., and possess Charles Hammond's wife with her part of this dec'd. Estate. W.B. 18, p. 85.

19 May, 1768. Wm. Mason possest with his wife's part of sd estate. 16 June 1768. W.B. 18, p. 115.

WAUGH, William. 31 Mar. 1771. Rec. 16 May 1771.

Bartley James possessed with his wife's part of sd. estate. W.B. 20, p. 43.

WAUGH, James. 21 May 1767. Rec. 20 Aug. 1767.

To Jno. Clayton, son of my late sister Judith Clayton. Elizabeth Waugh, dau. of my late brother Wm. Waugh. Judith Hammond, dau. of my brother Wm. Waugh. Mary Waugh, dau. of my brother Wm. Waugh. Anne Waugh, dau. of My brother Wm. Waugh. Eliza Yopp, dau. of my late sister Judith Clayton. John Clayton, son of my sister Judith Clayton. Ex. John Clayton. Wits: Thos. Pinckard, Edney Tapscott, James Simmons. W.B. 18, p. 83.

WAUGH, James. Appraisement. 8 Dec. 1767. Rec. 18 Dec. 1767. W.B. 18, p. 94.

WAY, William. Parish of White Chappel. Wife: Margaret Way. Ex: Wife. Wits: Chas. Stewart, Charles Coppedge. Frances White a servant woman to be set free after wife's decease. W.B. 14, p. 166.

WEAVER, Isaac. 30 Nov. 1777. Rec. 19 Mar. 1778.

Brother: Aron Weaver. Brother-in-law: Thomas Nicken, hogs that are now at Mr. John Longwith's & money in hands of Mr. Richard Evers Lee. W.B. 20, p. 120.

WEBB, James. Inv. 5 Mar. 1693. Rec. 17 Mar. 7693.

Presented by Margaret Webb, relict. W.B. 8, p. 44.

WEBB, John. Apprais. 11 Aug. 1738. Rec. 8 Sept. 1738.

Returned by Mary Webb, Adm. W.B. 13, p. 117.

WEBB, John. 9 Aug. 1760. Rec. 15 May 1761.

Sons: George Webb, John Webb, Moses Webb. Daus: Sarah Pitman, Mary Webb. Exors: Sons, George, James & Moses Webb. Wits: James Wallais, Thos. Brent, Thos. Everitt. W.B. 16, p. 145.

WEBB, Moses. Rec. 14 Sept. 1763.

James Webb to Richard Webb, orphan of Moses Webb. W.B. 17, p. 20.

WEBB, James. Rec. 18 Apr. 1765.

Will proved by oath of Geo. Angell and Thomas Everit. W.B. 17, p. 119.

WEBB, James. 16 Feb. 1765. Rec. 17 June 1765.

Wife: Mary. Three sons: John, Tarpley & James Webb. Exors: Wife, Mary Webb, & John Davis, Jr. Wits: Thos. Everitt, Geo. Angell. W.B. 18, p. 51.

WEBB, John. 16 June 1768.

John Webb, son of James Webb, bound by his mother to Carter until he arrives at age of 21 yrs, being 14 the 28th day of Sept. next. The said master to learn him to read and write and the trade of House Carpenter. Tarpley Webb, son of James Webb is bound to Meredith Mahanes until the age of 21 yrs, he being 12 the 1st day of Sept. next. His master to learn him to read and write and the Trade of Taylor. O.B. 18, p. 55.

WEBB, Samuel. Appraisement. 31 Dec. 1768. Rec. 16 Nov. 1769.

By Richard Selden, John Mahanes, Geo. Conway. W.B. 18, p. 156.

WEBB, George. Inv. 14 Oct. 1775. Rec. 19 Oct. 1775.

By Edwin Conway, Wm. Galloway, Elijah Percifull, Thomas Brent. W.B. 20, p. 88.

Division. To Traverse, Thomas, William, Charles, Jesse & Lucy Webb. 19 Oct. 1775. W.B. 20, p. 89.

WEBB, Rachel. July 1779. Rec. 20 Aug. 1778.

Rachel Webb, her dower in her deceased husband, Travers Webb's land. Wm. Galloway, James Wallace, Thomas Brent. W.B. 20, p. 143.

WEBB, James. 24 Feb. 1778. Rec. 16 July 1778.

Children: George, James, Mary, Anne, Judy, Sarah, Elizabeth, Joyce & Joanna one shilling. Wife: Mary. Sons: Thomas & Joseph, sons of Wilmouth my late wife when they arrive at age of 21. Dau: Martha, child of my late wife Wilmouth. Gr.dau: Nancy, child of my son James. Exors: Friends Col. Jesse Ball & Capt. James Ball. Wits: James Ball, James Ball, Jr. W.B. 20, p. 137.

WEBB, Frances, of Parish of Wiccomico. 4 Mar. 1781. Rec. 15 Feb. 1781.

Dau: Lucy. Sons: Thomas, William, Charles & Jesse Webb. Exors: Sons Thomas & William Webb. Wits: James Wallace, Sally Nutt. W.B. 20, p. 184.

WEBB, Travers. Division 18 Feb. 1794. Rec. 15 Sept. 1794.

Heirs: Widow, Hannah Webb, Jemima Webb, James Pitman. By Thos. Carter, Jr., John Carter & Charles Leland. W.B. 22, p. 439.

WELCH, Daniel. 23 Feb. 1661. Rec. 1 June 1661.

500 Acres to be divided among 4 children. Son: Daniell. Wife (name not given) Eldest daughter Elizabeth to Edm. Welch, daughter Ann to Robert Rowse. Neighbours Richard Parrott & Abraham Weeks overseers. Wits: Rich. Parrott, Robt. Taylor. W.B. Loose wills.

WELLS, John, of Parish White Chappell. 3 May 1697. Rec. 16 Sept. 1697.

Wife: Mary. Sons: Eldest, John, all my land; Thomas, Robert, William, Joseph, Benjamin, George. Dau: Ann. Wits: Judith Wenlock, Robt. Mitchell, Jas. Clayton. W.B. 8, p. 70.

WELLS, John of White Chappell. 20 Aug. 1706.

Wife: Hannah. Sons: John all lands I now live on; Daus: eldest, Sarah, youngest, Winifred Wells. Other legatees, Geo. Mitchell. Exors: Brother John Mott and cousin John Mitchell. Wits: Abraham Pauldin, Mary Voss, Miles Walters. W.B. 10, p. 107.

WELLS, Robert. 22 Apr. 1709.

Wife: Hagar. Sons: Robert and Wharton. Brother: Will Wells. Exors: Will Wells, and James Lawrie. Wits: James Lawrie, Jean Lawrie and Sarah Brown, Thos. Draper. W.B. 10, p. 109. Inv. and Apprais. presented by Hagar Wells. 10 Aug. 1709 and recorded 12 July 1710. W.B. 10, p. 55.

WELLS, William. 14 June 1709. Rec. 8 Mar. 1710.

Legatees: Cousins, Ellison Lowrie, dau of James and Jane Lawrie; cousin, Robert Wells; mother, Mary Parfitt (also Extrx.); Friend, Thos. Wharton. Extrx: Mary Parfitt. Wits: Jo. Taylor, Thos. Wharton, James Johnson. W.B. 10, p. 9.

WELLS, Robert. 21 Aprl. 1735. Rec. 11 Aug. 1736.

Names of wife and children not given. James Ball and Jess Ball,

guardian of children. Extrx: Wife (Hannah—see Order Book).*
Wits: William Abbey.

Page 17.* Appraisement 8 Sept. 1736 returned by Hannah Wells.

WEST, William. 2 Feb. 1692. Rec. 13 May 1692.

Sons: Willaim (eldest), and Thomas. Daus: Mary Porter, Elizabeth Davis, Frances & Temperance West. Wits: Wm. Ball Porter
James. W.B. 8, p. 35.

WEST, Thomas, Sr. 26 Oct. 1776. Rec. 19 Mar. 1778.

Wife: Betty. Children: Cornelius, Thomas & Joseph. Son:
William West one shilling. Exors: Joseph Sullivant and wife
Betty. Wits: Henry Martin Horne, John Sullevan. W.B. 20,
p. 120.

WEST, Thomas. Invty. and Appmt. Rec. 18 June 1778.

By William Saunders; Jno. Carter; John Bean. W.B. 20, p. 134.

WHALEY, Oswald (of parish of White Chappell). 9 Nov. 1717. Rec.
9 Apr. 1718.

Legatees: Wife's name not given; son, James; dau. Mary
Whaley; grandchildren, Oswald, Mary and Stephen Whaley.
Extrs: Son James And Richard Cooper. Wits: Jonas Orchaw,
Rich. Cooper, Charity Whaley. W.B. 10, p. 261.

WHALEY, James. Rec. 9 Jan. 1722.

Wife not mentioned. Sons: Oswald and James. Dau: Mary.
Exors: son Oswald. Overseers: Jas. Bell and Wm. Payne. Wits:
Wm. James and Matthew Stanton. W.B. 10, p. 414.

WHALEY, Stephen. 11 Jan 1726. Rec. 8 Feb. 1726.

Legatees: Henry Newby, Brother: James Whaley, Cousin: James
Newby. Wits: John Buckley, Charles A. Rossell. W.B. 10, p. 513.

WHEALEY, Oswald. 9 Jan. 1726. Rec. 8 Mar. 1726.

Wife: Susanna and child not born. Brother: James W. W.B. 10,
p. 520.

WHEALEY, Ozwell. Inv. Rec. 11 June 1727.

Presented by Susanna Whaley, adm. W.B. 10, p. 560.

WHARTON, Thos. 19 Feb. 1741. Rec. 10 Dec. 1742.

Wife: Mary. Son: Joseph. Daus: Sarah W., Ann Conners,
Ellison W. Gr.sons: Thos. W., Jno. Conner. Exors: Wife and
son Jos. Wits: Wm. and Mary Miller. W.B. 13, p. 313.

WHARTON, Sarah. 19 Oct. 1743. Rec. 13 July 1744.

Mother: Mary Wharton. Cousin: John Conner. Ex: Mother.
Wits: Lewis Conner, Mary Miller. W.B. 14, p. 24.
10 Aug. 1744. Inv. returned by Mary Wharton, Extrx. W.B.
14, p. 28.

WHARTON, Jos. 21 Oct. 1747. Rec. 12 May 1749.

Wife: Ann. Six children: Thomas, Wm., Joseph, Lindzy, Revel,
Ailec. Exor: Dale Carter & Geo. Payne. Wits: Jas. Webb, Sarah
Webb. W.B. 14, p. 238.

WHEELER, Maurice. Appraisal. Aug. 1784. Rec. 21 Oct. 1784.

By Isaac Degge, Charles Lee & Thomas Hathaway. W.B. 22,
p. 53.

WHEELER, Maurice. Apprais. Rec. 21 Apr. 1788.

By Isaac Degge, Martin Shearman, James Pollard. W.B. 22,
p. 176.

WHITE, William. 25 Jan. 1678. Rec. 14 Feb. 1678.

Wife not named. Sons: John, William, Edward. Dau: Deborah:
Dau-in-law: Mary Alford. Son John land adjoining my now
dwelling. Overseers to carry out will: Edwd. Carter, Thos.
Chowning. Wits: Edwd. Carter, Wm. White, Jr., John White.
W.B. 5, p. 53.

WHITE, William. 1 Oct. 1686. Rec. 10 June 1687.

Wife: Martha whole estate. Extrx. Wife. Wits: Thomas Wild-
gos, Wm. Clarke, John Harris. W.B. 5, p. 111.

WHITE, Thomas. 24 Aug. 1709. Rec. ——

Legatees: Wife's name not given; Sons, Richard and Isaac;
brother, William; Servant, Thomas Langley, given his freedom,
Extrx: Wife. Wits: John Crosted, John Mill, Mil Walters.
W.B. 10, p. 105.

WHITE, Thomas. 9 May 1711. Rec. 2 Nov. 1711.

Elinor White, his then wife, appointed Extrx. W.B. 10, p. 3.

WHITE, Thomas. Est. Rec. 14 Feb. 1721.

John Rogers appointed guardian of Isaac White, orphan of
Thomas White. W.B. 10, p. 361.

WHITE, Abraham. Inv. & Ap. 25 Apr. 1776. Rec. 18 July 1776.

By Jesse Ball, John Bailey, Edward Carter. W.B. 20, p. 98.

WHITE, Presley, of Christ Church Parish. 21 Feb. 1790. Rec. 19 July 1790.

Brother: Ephraim Davis. Mother: Frances Davis. Brother: Holland Davis. Exors: Uncle, Presley Saunders, William Chowning & John Chowning. Wits: John Christopher, Rawleigh Coats, Elizabeth Cornelius. W.B. 22, p. 287.

WHITTACRE, Joseph. 21 Mar. 1675/6. Rec. 10 May 1676.

Wife not named, but Extrx. Dau: Mary. Augusson Coan, dau. of Jno. Coan; Thos. Morgan son of Wm. Morgan. Wits: Rowland Lawson, Wm. Morgan. W.B. 5, p. 24.

WHYTE, Dr. William. Appraisal. Rec. 17 June 1793.

By Henry Hinton, Richard Selden, Joseph Carter, Jr. W.B. 22, p. 380.

WIBLIN, William. Inv. & Ap. Rec. 21 June 1790.

By John Christopher, Rawleigh Davenport, Abner Palmer. W.B. 22, p. 274.

WILDER, James. 26 Dec. 1786. Rec. 21 J,an. 1788.

Brother: Spencer Wilder should he ever return to Lancaster. Heirs: Francis Wilder, Molley James (not 18), daughter of Jonathan Wilder and Frances his wife. Half brothers: John, William & Vincent Wilder. Wits: Robert Yerby, Frances Yerby, Judith Schofield. Presented by Michael Wilder, adm. W.B. 22, p. 165.

16 Feb. 1789. Appraisal. W.B. 22, p. 202.

WILDER, Jonathan. 16 Jan. 1788. Rec. 21 Jan. 1788.

Sons: Spencer, William, John & Vincent Wilder. Daus: Frances & Mary James Wilder. Exors: James Brent & William Meredith. Wits: John Tapscott, William Merridith, Joshua Spilman. W.B. 22, p. 164.

Appraisal & division. J,ohn Watts, guardian of William. John Sullivant, guardian of John. James Brent, Gent., guardian to Vincent. Jesse Robinson, guardian to Frances. Michl. Wilder, guardian to Mary James Wilder. Rec. Dec. 1788. W.B. 22, pp. 195, 200.

WILDEY, Nathaniel. Rec. 10 June 1730.

Wife: Sarah dau. of Wm. Phillips. Sons: Hopkins, William, Michael, and J,ob. Daus: Sarah Catherine and Darkis. Exors: Wife and son Hopkins. Wits: Geo. Lite, Jr., Jno. Pines. W.B. 12, p. 173.

WILDY, Nathaniel. 9 July 1729. Rec. 9 July 1729.

Deposition of Nathaniel Wildy, age 62 yrs, that Mich. Wildy now in full life is ye son of this Depont, lawfully begotten on ye body of Sarah his late wife only dau of Wm. Phillips. Had heard his wife sd Sarah say there was a parcel of land of 150 acres in Elizabeth City Co. near Hampton, lately in the possession of one Curle which legally descended to her and to which the sd Michael is the only surviving heir. W.B. 12, p. 114.

WILDEY, Michael. 1 June 1746. Rec. 13 Feb. 1746.

Wife: Susannah. Daus: Lydia Wildey, Elizabeth Davis, Sydweall Nash, Sarah Wildey, Susannah Wildey, Mary Wildey. Sons: Jonathan Wildey, Michael, Nathaniel. Dau Lydia to be under son Jonathan. Wits: Wm. Gibson. W.B. 14, p. 139.

WILDER, George. Inv. 7 Dec. 1792. Rec. 21 Jan. 1793.

Returned by Wm. Chowning. W.B. 22, p. 211.

WILDER, Nathanile. Inv. 21 Oct. 1793. Rec. 20 Jan. 1794.

Appraised by Peter Tankersly, Wm. Kirk, Wm. Gibson. W.B. 22, p. 250.

WILKINSON, Isaac. Inv. 19 Oct. 1685. Rec. 14 Nov. 1685.

Presented by Mary Mason, relict. W.B. 5, p. 103.

WILKINSON, Thomas. Inv. Rec. 8 Apr. 1719.

Returned by John Hogan. W.B. 10, p. 286.

WILKS, Thos. Inv. 4 July 1686. Rec. 16 July 1686.

Presented by Eliza Wilks. W.B. 5, p. 104.

WILLCOX, John. Inv. Rec. 14 June 1727.

Presented by Wm. Bailey & Elizabeth his wife, late Elizabeth Wilcox, admx. of estate of John Willcox, dec. W.B. 12, p. 7.

WILLIAMS, James. Rec. 8 Dec. 1656.

Administration granted Mr. Wm. Underwood on behalf of orphans. W.B. 1, p. 308.

WILLIAMS, Roger. 14 Feb. 1701. Rec. 8 Apr. 1702.

Wife: Ann, also Ex. Dau: Elizabeth Emberson. Gr.dau: Mary Haines. Wits: Sam Wright, Mary Flowers. Dau: Elizabeth Haines. W.B. 8, p. 110.

WILLIAMS, Thos. Inv. Rec. 15 May 1752.

Returned by Henry Tapscott. W.B. 15, p. 94.

WILLSON, William, appraisement. 14 Nov. 1772. Rec. 15 Apr. 1773. By Wm. Brumley, Stephen Stott, Thos. Shearman. W.B. 20, p. 56.

WITHERSPOON, James. 15 Dec. 1720. Rec. 12 July 1721. Legatees: Jos. Stephens, Hannah Stephens, dau. of Rich. Stephens; Exor: Rich. Stephens. Wits: Henry Carter and Daniel Stephens. W.B. 10, p. 325.

WOOD, Richard. 2 Mar. 1720. Rec. 13 Feb. 1720. Wife: Jane, who is also Extrx. Children mentioned but not named. Wits: Jno. Pope, Jones Erwin. W.B. 10, p. 420.

WOOD, John. Inv. 11 May 1744. Rec. 13 July 1744. Returned by George Smither, adm. W.B. 14, p. 24.

WOODWARD, Wm. Inv. 20 Dec. 1704. W.B. 10, p. 268.

WORD, William. 2 Aug. 1792. Rec. 15 Oct. 1792. Wife: Caty. Dau: Betsey (not 18). Ex: Lawson Hathaway. Wits: Lawson Hathaway, James Hathaway, John King. W.B. 22, p. 355.

WORMELEY, John. 26 Sept. 1784. Rec. 16 June 1785. Wife: Frances. Nephews: Robert Wormley Carter & John Wormley. Exors: Robert Wormely Carter & Ralph Wormley, Jr. Wits: None but proved by oath of James Gordon & James Tapscott, Gent. W.B. 22, p. 76.
17 Apr. 1792. Sale of estate. LeRoy Peachy, attorney in fact. Robt. Wormley, Exor: W.B. 22, p. 337.

WORRICK, Richard. Inv. & Ap. 15 June 1757. Rec. 21 Oct. 1757. Returned by Thomas Chinn, adm. W.B. 15, p. 306.

WREN, Richard, carpenter. 20 Apr. 1676. Wife: Grace Wren. Ex: Wife. Wits: Richard Marshal, Isark Wall. Bundle of loose papers 1653-79.

WREN, Nicholas. 3 Jan. 1700. Rec. 12 Apr. 1701. Wife: Margaret to whom is given all. Sons: Nicholas and William Wren. Wits: Wm. Liggatt, Chas. Donnell, Jno. Rourk. W.B. 8, p. 101.

WREN, Will. 10 May 1709. Rec. 14 Feb. 1710. Wife: Elizabeth. Sons: John, William and Thomas (not of age). Dau: Elizabeth. Exors: Wife and brother John Steptoe. Wits:

Robt. Gibson, Will Burgin and Robt. Wright. W.B. 10, p. 67.

WREN, Wm., of Wicomico Parish, Northumberland Co. 4 Feb. 1735. Rec. 12 May 1736.

Wife: Elizabeth. Sons: Geo. and Wm. Dau: Letty. Exors: Wife and Wm. Brent, Sr. Wits: Chas. and Wm. Jones, Jr. W.B. 13, p. 7.

WRIGHT, Francis. Inv. 30 Aug. 1690. Rec. 13 Jan. 1691.

Presented by Mary Leverner. W.B. 8, p. 13.

WRIGHT, Mottrom. 8 Oct. 1700. Rec. July 1701.

Wife: Ruth. Son: Mottrom. Dau: Frances. Cousin, Jno. Wright. Overseer: Jno. Purvis. Exor: son, Mottrom. Wits: Jas. Besouth, Hannah Bradley, Thos. Quilter. W.B. 8, p. 103.

WRIGHT, Samuel. Inv. 17 Apr. 1706.

Returned by Jno. Wale and his wife. W.B. 10, p. 270.

WRIGHT, Arthur. 2 Dec. 1751. Rec. 21 Feb. 1752.

Brother: Daniel Burn. Mrs. Beheathaland Lawry. Brother: Edward Wright. Mr. Gavin Lawry. Wits: Wm. Stamps, George Edwards. W.B. 15, p. 88.

WYLEY, Robt., dec. Rec. 14 Jan. 1656.

Joanna Wiley the relict granted adminis. W.B. 1, p. 309.

WYN, Henry. 9 Sept. 1685. Rec. 11 Sept. 1685.

Inv. returned by Thos. Marshall. W.B. 2, p. 101.

YERBY, Thomas. 11 Feb. 1716. Rec. 13 Mar. 1716.

Wife: Ann. Sons: George, and Thomas all my land in Corrotoman, John. Exors: Sons Geo. Thos., and Jno. Wits: Frances Cox, Fort Sydnor and Ruth Sydnor. W.B. 10, p. 191.

YERBY, Anne. Nuncupative. 3 Feb. 1720. Rec. 8 Mar. 1720.

Son: John Yerby. Mentions "rest of my children." Wits: John Hudnall, Mary Killgore. W.B. 10, p. 306.

YERBY, John, nuncupative. 11 Dec. 1736. Rec. 8 Apr. 1737.

Sons: Wm. and Jno., other children & brothers. Ex. Wife. Wits: Geo. Yerby, Jos. George and Jno. Meredith. W.B. 13, p. 32.

Inv. returned by Katherine Yerby, Tho. Yerby & George Yearby, adm. 10 June 1737. W.B. 13, p. 54.

YERBY, John, division estate. Rec. 12 Apr. 1745.

Son: Wm, John Yerby. Daus: Eliza Yerby and Joanna Yerby. Nicholas Lawson in right of his wife one of the children of the dec. her part of the slaves which did belong to Katherine Stamps her mother. W.B. 14, p. 64.

12 Aug. 1748. Settlement of estate. Thos. Yerby guardian of Wm. Yerby, orphan of John Yerby. John Yerby, orphan of John Yerby. W.B. 14, p. 207.

YERBY, Thomas. 20 Mar. 1756. Rec. 21 May 1756.

Wife: Hannah Yerby. Son: John, Thomas. Daus: Ann Brent and her children; Betty Yerby, Hannah Edwards, Mary Hubbard. Exors: Friend, James Kirk and sons Thomas Yerby and John Yerby. Wits: George Dobson, James Kirk, John Pasquet, Dale Carter. W.B. 15, p. 252.

YERBY, Hannah. 12 Nov. 1759. Rec. 15 May 1761.

Sons: Thomas & John Yerby. Daus: Ann Brent and her dau. Judy Brent; Elizabeth's two daus., Sarah & Milly; Hannah Edwards, Mary Hubbard, Eliza. Yerby, dec., two children. Exors: Sons, Thomas & John. Wits: Dale Carter & Augustine Carter. W.B. 16, p. 145.

Division of estate. Thomas Yerby, Ann Brent, Mr. Jno. Yerby's children, Mr. Jno. Yerby, Mrs. Hannah Edwards, Mr. Joseph Hubbard's children. 19 June 1761. W.B. 16, p. 231.

YERBY, George. 14 Aug. 1764. Rec. 15 July 1765.

Wife: Elizabeth. Son: George Yerby and his children. Gr.son: Geo. Woodbridge Yerby, son of my son Jno. Yerby. Gr.dau: Amy Yerby, dau. of my dau. Judith Kirk. Daus.: Mary Yerby, and Betty Woodbridge Steptoe & her children. Son: John Yerby. Exors: Wife and my 2 cousins Wm. Yerby and his brother John Yerby. Wits: Thomazin x (her mark) Hathaway, Elmore, Dogget, Dale Carter. W.B. 18, p. 42.

YEARBY, George, dec. Rec. 15 July 1765.

Will Presented by Eliza Yerby, one of the executors and proved by oath of Dale Carter and Elmore Doggett. W.B. 17, p. 147. Geo. Phillips who intermarried with Mary Yerby orphan of Geo. Yerby, dec. W.B. 17, p. 172.

YERBY, George, appraisement. 15 July 1765. Rec. 10 Sept. 1765. W.B. 18, p. 51.

YERBY, George. Division of estate. 18 Nov. 1765. Rec. 21 July 1766. George Phillips given his wife's part. W.B. 18, p. 63.

YERBY, Elizabeth. 15 Sept. 1770. Rec. 19 Mar. 1772.

Sons: John & George Yerby land in Richmond Co. which descended to me by the death of Capt. John Woodbridge, and also lands in Fairfax, Dinwiddie & Brunswick Cos., all of which lands descended to me by the death of sd Woodbridge. Daus: Mary Phillips, Nancy Kelly, Sarah Gibson. Gr.children: Mary Kirk, Judith Kirk, Eliza Kirk & William Kirk (to be in the hands of Capt. James Kirk). Gr.sons: John Steptoe, Wm. Woodbridge Yerby, George Phillips. Gr.daus: Eliza Yerby, Eliza Woodbridge Yerby, Nancy Kent Yerby (to have equal share with her mother's children), Judith Yerby Gibson, Amy Davis. Exs: Sons: George & John Yerby, Capt. James Kirk, George Phillips, Wm. Kelly & Wm. Steptoe. Wits; Will Dymer, Francis Dymer, John Swinton, John x Angell, John Yerby, Thomas Crowder, Jesse Kelly. W.B. 20, p. 38.

YERBY, Mrs. Elizabeth. Division of est. 18 Jan. 1787. Rec. 16 Apr. 1787.

Heirs: George Yerby, John Yerby, John Steptoe, Nancy Kelly, Mary Phillips, William Kirk, Mary Kirk, Amy Davis, Elizabeth Kirk, Sarah Gibson, Judith Kirk. By Richard Glascock, Ben Smith & John Fauntleroy. W.B. 22, p. 143.

22 Apr. 1794. Heirs. Geo. Phillips & Wm. Gibson, guardian for Ann Kelley's children. Joseph Kem, Wm. Gibson, Lawson Hathaway, Wm. Kirk, John Steptoe. W.B. 22, p. 416.

YERBY, Capt. William, of Parish of Christ Church. 30 May 1785. Rec. 20 Apr. 1786.

Wife: Frances. Sons: William, Loddy & Robert Yerby. Daus: Betty Harris & Caty Meredith. Exors: Wife, cousin John Yerby and Wm. Meredith, William Kirk, Ann Kirk. Cocicil. 10 Sept. 1785. Loddy Yerby has died since will was written. Wits: William Kirk, Ann Kirk, Sally Lee Schofield. W.B. 22, p. 121. Appraisal. W.B. 22, p. 130.

YERBY, John, of Parish of Christ Church. 18 Feb. 1777. Rec. 15 May 1777.

Dau: Caty born of my wife before we were married to have equal part of estate except land. Exors: Friends: John Yerby & brother

Wm. Yerby. Wits: Wm. Brent, Wm. Schofield, Isaac Pitman. W.B. 20, p. 112.

Jan. 1782. Division of estate between widow & Charles Purcill who intermarried with Joannah dau. of sd dec., and Richard Yerby, James Yerby & Jesse Yerby, Orphans of sd Deceased. W.B. 20, p. 221.

YERBY, John. 16 Feb. 1778. Rec. 17 July 1778.

Elijah Perciful, possessed with his wife's part of her dec. father, John Yerby's estate. W.B. 20, p. 141.

YERBY, John, dec'd. Mar. 1784 Court. .Rec. 17 July 1784.

Elijah Percifull, admr. Jas. Yerby, orphan. John Hutching former guardian. Apprs.: Elias Edwards, John Miller, James Pinckard. W.B. 22, p. 32.

YERBY, Jesse (minor) Ap. 1785. Rec. 22 July 1785.

Account of Wm. Yerby former guardian of Jesse Yerby, orphan of John Yerby, dec. & possess of Richard Yerby, Present guardian. W.B. 22, p. 93.

YERBY, James. Appraisal. Rec. 21 Apr. 1788.

By James Pinckard, John Yerby, Elias Edmonds. W.B. 22, p. 182.

YOPP, William. Appraisal & Division. Apr. 1787. Rec. 21 Apr. 1788.

James Tapscott, Gent., adm. Heirs: Betty Yopp (widow), Stephen Locke guardian of William, Cloe & Charles Yopp, Mary Ann Yopp, James Nutt & Wm. Hubbard (son-in-laws), Sarah Ann Yopp, Betty Yopp. By Edwin Conway, John Yerby, John Bean. W.B. 22, p. 177.

21 Sept. 1789. Division. Heirs: Mrs. Betty Yopp (widow), James Nutt, Wm. Hubbard, Maryann Yopp, Wm. Yopp, Cloe Yopp, Charles Yopp, Betty Yopp. By Edwin Conway, John Bean, John Yerby. W.B. 22, p. 221.

YOPP, Samuel, of Parish of Christ Church. 12 Oct. 1793. Rec. 21 Oct. 1793.

Son: Samuel land and at his death to go to Seth Blumdell. Gr.-daus: Alice, Salley & Polly Yopp. Daus: Amey Yopp, Ann Hubbard & Salley Wilder. Exors: Son Samuel Yopp and friend Seth Blumdell. Wits: F. Carter, Jr., Bartley Overstreet, Sarah Brent. W.B. 22, p. 295.

21 Oct. 1793. 26 July 1794. Appraisal & division. Heirs:

Samuel & Amey Yopp. By William Kirk, William Yerby, William Gibson. W.B. 22, p. 432.

YOUNG, Chris. 9 July 1679. Rec. 10 July 1679.
Inv. returned by Alice Marmaduke, relict. W.B. 2, p. 58.

YOUNG, Robert. 10 Apr. 1705.
Youngest son: Thomas, plantation I live. Eldest son: Bryan. Ex: son Thomas. Wits: Wil. Walters, Robert Mitchell, Thomas Carpenter. W.B. 8, p. 131.

www.ingramcontent.com/pod-product-compliance
Lightning Source LLC
Chambersburg PA
CBHW070402270326
41926CB00014B/2661